Visualizing Financial Data

Visualizing Financial Data

Julie Rodriguez

Piotr Kaczmarek

Visualizing Financial Data

Published by
John Wiley & Sons, Inc.
10475 Crosspoint Boulevard
Indianapolis, IN 46256
www.wiley.com

ISBN: 978-1-118-90785-6
ISBN: 978-1-119-27751-4 (ebk)
ISBN: 978-1-118-90798-6 (ebk)

Manufactured in the United States of America

10 9 8 7 6 5 4 3 2 1

For general information on our other products and services please contact our Customer Care Department within the United States at (877) 762-2974, outside the United States at (317) 572-3993 or fax (317) 572-4002.

Wiley publishes in a variety of print and electronic formats and by print-on-demand. Some material included with standard print versions of this book may not be included in e-books or in print-on-demand. If this book refers to media such as a CD or DVD that is not included in the version you purchased, you may download this material at http://booksupport.wiley.com. For more information about Wiley products, visit www.wiley.com.

Library of Congress Control Number: 2016932285

This book is dedicated to you, the reader,
for your interest in and pursuit of bringing data to life.

—The authors

About the Authors

Julie Rodriguez is a user experience designer, researcher, and speaker on creating meaningful experiences that change the way we solve problems. As an information architect, Julie analyzes data use and needs, tests alternative solutions, and refines new solutions that deliver business value.

During her 15 years of work experience in the financial services domain she has designed for front, middle, and back office roles, restructured business processes, and solidified new business ventures with application launches. More recent ventures include designing the future state vision for institutional wealth services and defining the user experience for a new brokerage solution.

Julie holds a bachelor's degree industrial design from Carnegie Mellon University and a master's degree in digital media, Extension Studies, from Harvard University.

Piotr Kaczmarek is an information designer in the financial industry and he conceives visual tools for navigating through data collections of varied complexity. In his work, he merges roles of an information architect studying user needs and providing conceptual frameworks, and a visual designer dealing with effective delivery of the final solutions.

Though he was educated as an architect and industrial designer, Piotr's interest shifted toward visual communications, and now he has more than 20 years' experience in information design and digital media. Although financial data has been his focus these last few years, his general area of expertise is in visual explanations. Piotr's creations in this field include data visualizations for analytical software, as well as 3-D animations showing the inner workings of complex mechanisms.

Piotr studied architecture at Warsaw University of Technology and holds a master's degree in industrial design from the Academy of Fine Arts in Warsaw, Poland.

About the Technical Editors

Bob Bannon is semi-retired and living in Southern California. Most recently Mr. Bannon was the chief risk officer for Genworth Financial Wealth Management. Prior to that position, Mr. Bannon was the chief investment officer for the Wealth Management Division of Bank of the West. In previous roles Mr. Bannon served in various investment and analytical positions for Analytic Investors, IDEAglobal, and Security Pacific National Bank. Mr. Bannon earned his bachelor's degree in economics from Villanova University in 1980 and his master's degree in economics from UCLA in 1983. He holds both the Chartered Financial Analyst (CFA) designation from the CFA Institute as well as the Financial Risk Manager (FRM) designation from the Global Association of Risk Professionals.

Brandon Farr is a senior quantitative analyst at Copper Rock Capital Partners, where he is responsible for quantitative analysis, risk management, and portfolio management reporting for all the firm's investment strategies. Prior to joining Copper Rock, Brandon worked at State Street Global Advisors where he was a vice president and investment risk analyst. He also worked as an investment risk analyst at Putnam Investments for 6 years in which he collaborated directly with the investment teams on risk and performance attribution reporting for global equity portfolios. Brandon received his master's degree in mathematical finance from Boston University. He has more than 10 years of quantitative and portfolio risk management experience.

Richard Perez leads the investment effort of Aquitaine, 40 North's third-party manager platform focused on alternative investments. Prior to joining 40 North, Mr. Perez was a senior analyst on the External Manager Selection team at Soros Fund Management. Prior to Soros, Mr. Perez was a vice president in the Hedge Fund Strategies Group at Goldman Sachs, where he headed Research for Tactical Trading Strategies. Mr. Perez earned his MBA degree from the Wharton School of the University of Pennsylvania and graduated with honors from Harvard University with a bachelor's degree in applied mathematics with a focus in Economics.

Credits

PROJECT EDITOR
Tom Dinse

TECHNICAL EDITORS
Bob Bannon
Brandon Farr
Richard Perez

PRODUCTION EDITOR
Christine O'Connor

COPY EDITOR
San Dee Phillips

**MANAGER OF CONTENT
DEVELOPMENT & ASSEMBLY**
Mary Beth Wakefield

PRODUCTION MANAGER
Kathleen Wisor

MARKETING MANAGER
Carrie Sherrill

**PROFESSIONAL TECHNOLOGY &
STRATEGY DIRECTOR**
Barry Pruett

BUSINESS MANAGER
Amy Knies

EXECUTIVE EDITOR
Jim Minatel

PROJECT COORDINATOR, COVER
Brent Savage

BOOK DESIGNER AND COMPOSITOR
Maureen Forys,
Happenstance Type-O-Rama

PROOFREADER
Rebecca Rider

INDEXER
Johnna VanHoose Dinse

COVER DESIGNER
Wiley

COVER IMAGE
Piotr Kaczmarek

Acknowledgments

This book would not exist without the instigation, support, time, and interest of many individuals. First, we'd like to thank Bob Elliott for planting the seed to write the book. His interest in the topic encouraged us to pursue and sign our book contract to begin the work. Bob graciously handed us over to Tom Dinse, who has been instrumental in coordinating and guiding us through the process.

Thanks to Dave Depew for introducing us to two of our technical editors, Bob Bannon and Brandon Farr. Dave provided us with his most impressive industry and academic colleagues to closely review, challenge, and help us to structure the book contents. To that end, a special thanks to our technical editors—Bob, Brandon and Richard Perez—for their detailed reviews, comments, and questions. Collectively, they opened us up to redefine and refine our visual solutions. We appreciate the extra time our editors each took to reflect on the solutions we presented.

There are a number of others who have closely reviewed a few chapters in the book: For those, we thank Jacque Murphy, Catherine Musinsky, Matt Hull, and Michael Ledeoux, who provided spot-on feedback. Their words are embedded in the chapters they reviewed.

We also thank those that we interviewed to shape the book contents to begin with. We cannot thank each by name because we promised anonymity, but we can thank each by role. The perspective of portfolio managers, investment analysts, and controllers has proven invaluable as we discussed typical data displays, current challenges, and our visualization solutions. We could not have written this book without their perspectives as practitioners in the field.

We have immense gratitude for our families for giving us the time to write the book. Their patience and support through the months has been touching. Natalia Rodriguez's interest in knowing how close we were to finishing made our constant response of "almost done" increasingly comical. Surprise breakfasts, snacks, sandwiches, and encouraging notes from Isabela Rodriguez helped to keep our spirits and energy up. Alejandro (Julie's husband) has been her life support providing a balance of quiet time to work and fun distractions when she needed to take a break.

Contents

Foreword   *xv*

Introduction   *xvii*

PART 1: INFORMATION GAINS THROUGH DATA VISUALIZATIONS

CHAPTER 1: Paving a Path Toward Visual Communications   3

Information Delivery Needs   5

Industry Demands   6

Enabling Factors   8

Summary   11

CHAPTER 2: Benefits of Using Visual Methods   15

The Purpose of Charts   16

    Making Comparisons   17

    Establishing Connections   19

    Drawing Conclusions   22

How to Leverage Charts   25

Summary   31

PART 2: TRANSFORMING DATA FOR ACTIVE INVESTMENT DECISIONS

CHAPTER 3: Security Assessment   35

Tile Framework   36

Stocks   39

Bonds   42

Mutual Funds   44

ETFs   50

Tile Collection   55

Summary   58

CHAPTER 4: Portfolio Construction   **61**

Asset Allocation   62

Sector Analysis   67

    Sector Leadership   67

    Sectors and Alpha Factors   78

Risk Management   85

    Overlap of Holdings   87

    Stress Tests   99

Summary   106

CHAPTER 5: Trading   **109**

Ticker   110

Quote   117

Watchlist   127

Visual System: Ticker, Quote, and Watchlist   138

Summary   140

CHAPTER 6: Performance Measurement   **143**

Market Performance   144

Investment Firm Composite   151

Portfolio Gain/Loss   157

Attribution   161

    Return Attribution   161

    Risk Attribution   171

Summary   177

PART 3: SHOWCASING DATA FOR EFFECTIVE COMMUNICATIONS

CHAPTER 7: Financial Statements   **183**

Statement of Cash Flows   184

    Nonprofit Organizations   184

    For-Profit Organizations   191

Statement of Financial Activity   202

Operating Budget   206

Summary   212

CHAPTER 8: Pension Funds   **217**

Plan Members   218
   Members in Valuation   219
   Post Retirement   227
   Retirement Programs   232
Contributions versus Benefits   241
   Additions by Source   241
   Changes in Retirees & Beneficiaries   250
   History of Member Salary   253
Funding Ratio   257
Summary   264

CHAPTER 9: Mutual Funds   **267**

Core Components   268
   Allocation Profile   269
   Fees   277
   Performance   285
   Risk   293
Fund Fact Sheets   312
Mutual Fund Comparison   318
   Total Returns   319
   Ranking Against Benchmarks   324
Summary   332

CHAPTER 10: Hedge Funds   **335**

Long/Short Positions   336
Long Positions and Benchmarking   344
Fund Characteristics   349
Strategy Rank   356
   Strategy Rank and Ranges   361
Strategy Analysis   363
   All Strategy Averages   364
   Single Strategy Averages   367
   Fund Level Returns   373
Summary   378

PART 4: NEXT STEPS

CHAPTER 11: Data Visualization Principles   **383**

    Cater to Your Audience   384

    Provide Clarity   394

    Be Efficient   403

    Summary   414

CHAPTER 12: Implementing the Visuals   **417**

    Business Value Assessment   418

    Implementation Effort   422

    Available Methods   427

    Solution Score   428

    Summary   432

    Index   *435*

Foreword

As the volume and complexity of the world's data increases, so too does our requirement to find meaning and insight in the information we amass. For businesses, simply collecting and storing data is of little use. The real power lies in unlocking more informed decision-making that can drive substantial user impact, revenue growth, and process innovation.

Much of the traditional business effort around data has been focused on how best to aggregate and organize an enterprise's unstructured information into data sets for analysis. This has proven to be a massive exercise in both scale and futility. As data sets continue to grow from the proliferation of new information sources, they are simultaneously stretching and testing the boundaries of our legacy modes of analysis and making it challenging for financial services professionals to uncover relevant business insights.

Data visualization seeks to remove this complexity by presenting information in consumable, graphical ways. Good visual communications do much more than simply replace words and numbers with imagery—they reveal data patterns, themes, and changes at a quick glance to help individuals make informed decisions effectively and efficiently. In time, it is likely that machine learning and artificial intelligence will further intervene to unlock even greater insights from our visual communications.

In this book, two of Sapient Global Markets' creative directors known for running highly successful engagements with our largest clients, Julie Rodriguez and Piotr Kaczmarek, explore the power inherent in improving the visualization of financial data.

They share original solutions to push the visualization of financial data to the next level, unlocking new meaning and supporting more robust, informed decision making. These ideas are accelerators you can use to start your process to display and interact with data. I encourage you to review their work and leverage their designs to make your displays more insightful.

Chip Register
CEO, Sapient Consulting

Introduction

Financial data presentations are often riddled with incomplete, misleading, excessive, or raw data, compromising their ability to tell a full story and leading to inaccurate conclusions. As an industry, we need to improve our ability to see major issues, discover hidden details, make connections, and compare top investment ideas. Given ever increasing amounts of data, we need to work ever more diligently to ensure our decisions are based on a clear understanding of the data. This requires that we first undertake a close examination of the data, then explore data visualization solutions, making incremental refinements and continual critical assessments along the way. The chapters in this book provide a variety of data visualizations designed to improve your understanding of data and your ability to convey that understanding to your audience.

Our Approach

This book provides visualization methods that will help you navigate today's cluttered landscape of financial markets. It starts with a review of current, commonly used methods for communicating financial data and then offers methods to refine or enhance them, or create new types of visualizations that are easy to use, elegant, and that facilitate better decision-making. Many break with today's common practices for communicating data, but improve efficiency and clarity.

Core chapters (Chapters 3–10) examine current typical approaches to communicating data and contrast those against our revised visualization methods. These chapters provide industry examples organized by common portfolio management activities and by typical financial statements for pension funds, mutual funds, and hedge funds. We analyze existing, representative data sets, and keeping in mind their intended purpose, we propose alternative visualizations to improve their clarity and drive home the most important information they contain.

As information designers, we combine analytics and cognitive aesthetics to create data visualizations. We start by interviewing practitioners in the field to understand their goals; next we evaluate and interrogate the data itself for the various questions it might answer. Finally we craft design concepts that will reveal these answers most effectively. Our work is constantly evolving as we invent better ways to communicate data. The visualizations we present inform, inspire, and aspire to light the way to intelligent decision-making.

Intended Audience

This book is designed for those who work within financial services, especially within investment management firms such as foundations, endowments, estate and wealth management companies, pensions, hedge funds, mutual funds, registered investment advisories, 401k plan sponsors, third-party providers, banks, or at brokerages, in addition to those responsible for disclosing the financial status of a for-profit or non-profit firm.

Investment managers who actively manage investments, research analysts, and associates who provide insights and information to those that make investment decisions will find this a valuable resource when it comes to transforming data into active management decisions. Marketing analysts who provide sales and presentation materials and accounting and financial analysts will find visualization solutions to showcase their data.

Systems analysts, business analysts, and user experience designers who design, implement, and support systems for investment management firms can find security, portfolio, trade, performance, and risk management solutions they can adapt to their own uses. Some firms have business intelligence analysts tasked with creating specific reports to reflect departmental or firmwide conditions. These BI analysts may find they can reuse or repurpose many of the data visualizations in these pages.

Chapter Structure

This book has four parts and twelve chapters. Part 1 introduces the many uses of data visualizations and explains their many levels of importance. Part 2 provides data visualization solutions for active investing decisions across different phases of managing a portfolio. Part 3 provides ideas for how best to present data for accounting, marketing, sales, and communications needs. Finally, Part 4 enumerates key principles and provides some next steps for implementing visualizations.

Firms need to monitor, report, and identify needs on the basis of financial data. To monitor status, to answer the question, *How are we doing?* they need to consult a myriad of accounting, performance, risk, market, and transactional data. Reporting requires regulatory compliance. Various regulatory demands push standards and create rules for greater transparency. Well-documented audit trails allow firms to track accountability and answer the question, *Are we compliant?* Good decisions require clear understanding of status and strategies. Dots must connect in order to know *What should we do differently?* or *How should we adjust in order to succeed?* More than 250 charts and graphs in this book help furnish such questions with the tools to find clear and actionable solutions. From start to finish, we identify needs and design visualizations that reflect those needs. What follows is a short synopsis of what to expect from each chapter.

Part 1: Information Gains Through Data Visualizations

In his book *Exploratory Data Analysis* (Pearson, 1977), renowned mathematician John Tukey wrote, "The greatest value of a picture is when it forces us to notice what we never expected to see." In that book he encouraged translating text and numbers into visual methods like charts to explore data sets with the goal of reaching a more complete understanding of the data. The chapters in Part 1 introduce the uses of data visualizations and the value they provide.

Chapter 1: Paving a Path Toward Visual Communications

Today, we are challenged by both the size and complexity of data. Advancements in technology enable us to access, store, and share more data than ever, but have also created higher standards for onscreen displays. We expect screen presentations to be increasingly immediate, simple, and telling, not to mention aesthetically pleasing. This chapter aims to answer, *How should we best represent the data?*

Chapter 2: Benefits of Using Visual Methods

Why do we use charts and graphs? What are their benefits? How should we take advantage of these methods? If you know what something is good for, then you'll know how to apply it. Part of the puzzle is to allow the connection between data and charts and maximize the utility of both. This chapter reviews the various benefits of data visualizations to make better use of the chart and graphing ideas that follow.

Part 2: Transforming Data for Active Investment Decisions

Part 2 focuses on the art of investment management as it applies to the management of separate client accounts, either individual or institutional. Investment Managers tend to make all the investment decisions for a client's separate portfolio across multiple asset classes. You can find individuals in these roles at foundations, endowments, family offices, wealth management companies, registered investment advisories, or at brokerages. Because the investment approach, style, and process will vary from firm to firm or even individual to individual, we do not focus on process. Rather we showcase visualization techniques based on common investment activities used in the industry. The investment activities within Part 2 are organized by the major investment management phases. Each chapter provides visualizations for each phase of the Investment Process: Security Assessment, Portfolio Construction, Trading, and Performance Measurement.

At every phase of the Investment Process, members of the Investment Management firm are seeking to "add value" for the client. This term can have many different meanings. The client might define adding value as outperforming a benchmark, outperforming other peer Investment Management firms in the industry, or simply striving to achieve positive investment results most of the time (outperforming "zero" or a benchmark of cash, as it is often called).

The most important goal of the Investment Process is to gain value over some alternative. The most important function of our visualizations, therefore, is to help the Investment Management staff either find ways to add value to the Investment Process or to communicate to clients their level of success in that pursuit.

Chapter 3: Security Assessment

Each investment option has its own set of characteristics to watch and track: This may include the short-term growth of a stock, or the stability of a bond to pay coupons, the longer-term returns of a mutual fund, or the diversification of an ETF. Despite, or because of, these variations, each investment option presents data points that make it harder to review. Data inconsistency presents a difficult comparison problem: *How do we normalize this data? How do we ensure we are not missing out on the relative characteristics for each vehicle?* In this chapter we introduce how to review a mix of stocks, bonds, mutual funds, and ETFs, and how to present a rich view of each while keeping them within a consistent framework.

Chapter 4: Portfolio Construction

During the Portfolio Construction phase of an Investment, investment professionals confer to create a portfolio best suited to the client by looking at data views designed for evaluation and reaction to change. This key chapter covers asset allocation, sector analysis, and risk management and monitoring. It provides visualizations that can be tailored to unique decision-making rationales.

Chapter 5: Trading

In this chapter, we rethink how to use the data in tickers, quotes, and watchlists to provide you with better up-to-the-minute information on the current state of a security or index. This chapter explains how to create, use, and reuse a visual system to reduce the time required to learn new, additional visual markers. We provide visualizations to not only increase awareness of the data but also to improve the elegance and efficiency of the display.

Chapter 6: Performance Measurement

Market fluctuations impart volatility to the values of the instruments held in a portfolio. Tracking and analyzing the overall performance of the portfolio—in absolute terms and also relative to the fluctuations of the broader markets—is an important part of the Investment Process. Lessons can be learned by members of the investment firm from a thorough analysis of market and portfolio performance, and through a feedback loop, those lessons can be used for improvement. This chapter discusses performance at the market, firm, and portfolio level and reviews both risk and return attribution.

Part 3: Showcasing Data for Effective Communications

Effective visual communications can improve your sales, marketing, and client presentations to help you connect more clearly with your audience. Part 3 walks through key chart designs for non-profit and for-profit organizations' annual reports to showcase demographic, tributary, and funding ratio data for a pension fund. New visual techniques demonstrate how to display fund factsheet data and how to analyze the top 100 hedge funds.

Chapter 7: Financial Statements

Financial accounting is a large topic encompassing many different types of financial statements. This chapter reviews a few standard financial statements required of all public firms and which analysts are required to compile, review, and report, such as the Statement of Cash Flows, Statement of Financial Activity, and Operating Budget. These statements report fundamental data points that are not typically visualized. We suggest visualizations that observe standard accounting practices while making the data more transparent with supporting details.

Chapter 8: Pension Funds

This chapter focuses on one of the largest pension funds in the world and reviews how its annual report documents its status. We hone in on three main areas, including 1) demographics of plan members and their profiles, 2) contributions versus benefits, and 3) fund position as revealed by the funding ratio. This chapter transforms table data, then combines them into both individual and consolidated charts.

Chapter 9: Mutual Funds

Following fund profile, allocations, performance, and fees are key aspects of reviewing and marketing a mutual fund. In this chapter, we design some commonly displayed charts that represent these key components and incorporate the charts into a revised fund factsheet. The chapter ends with a few concise methods for comparing a list of mutual funds.

Chapter 10: Hedge Funds

This chapter uses pattern recognition and interactive displays to present temporal data of the top 100 performing hedge funds. We examine two important sets of hedge fund data: individual funds and overall industry analyses. We compare both hedge fund strategies and the funds within a strategy to analyze a firm's growth in AUM.

Part 4: Next Steps

To continue with the visualization ideas presented in this book, you need a way to implement and weave visualizations into your day-to-day analyses and communications. The chapters in this section provide some design principles to keep in mind, as well as a framework to help you decide your next steps.

Chapter 11: Data Visualization Principles

Chapter 11 raises key questions about the visualizations presented in the book. *How can visualizations be introduced to create a concise understanding of data? How do we ensure that those visualizations are shown within a relative perspective to provide greater context? How do we reveal underlying issues and remove the risk of masking critical information? Or, vice versa, how can we pull ourselves away from the details to see and understand the big picture?* We discovered three overarching principles that apply to all of our visualization methods. This chapter provides a detailed definition about each guiding principle and illustrates each one's practical applications.

—

Chapter 12: Implementing the Visuals

The technologies used to create data visualizations constantly evolve, as do recommendations for their implementation. This chapter suggests a framework for deciding how to design appropriate visualizations, and closes the book with a list of criteria for next steps in visualizations. We provide a set of criteria for refining and narrowing your choices based on your immediate needs.

How To Read This Book

There is an intentional flow to this book in which Part 1 introduces the need and value for data visualizations, Parts 2 and 3 show current data visualization examples, and Part 4 provides lessons learned and next steps to implement. Although core chapters (Chapters 3–10) within Parts 2 and 3 can be read in any order, we do recommend that you read Parts 2 and 3 before Part 4, and that you read each chapter in a linear fashion.

Reading the book in sequential order will provide an easier learning experience when it comes to understanding references from prior chapters. In particular, Chapter 11, "Data Visualization Principles," refers to visualizations from core Chapters 3–10 to show how a design principle is applied in practice. Reading the core chapters first prepares you to better understand the principles and points within Chapter 11. Chapter 12, "Implementing the Visuals," similarly references visualization examples from prior chapters but does not require you to be as familiar with them.

Disclosures

Disclosure 1: Selected Examples Are Based on Variety

There are countless data sets and their visualizations we could have selected as examples on which to base our work. Ultimately, we narrowed down the candidates to ones that provide variation and frequent use, and that typically result in efficiency, transparency, or usability issues that could use some alternative solutions. We wanted to represent various aspects of financial services, from the active investment phases of security assessment, portfolio construction, trading, and performance measurements, to marketing and communications, to compliance and reporting requirements.

Our choice of a starting example does not reflect any endorsement or opinion about the investment process. The industry has debated many investment processes, has standardized some, and has made others proprietary. Our starting example simply represents our search for the most familiar and representative data sets of the industry.

Disclosure 2: Visualization Solutions Are Not Firm-Specific

Creating proprietary software solutions often means customizing each solution for specific firm or client needs. In fact, most of what we do in our line of work is firm/client-specific and tailored. This book is not. The scenarios explored are commonly seen and our solutions are therefore neither proprietary nor based upon individual firm or client opinions or directions. Instead, we suggest unique solutions based on our explorations of the data sets, interviews with financial managers, and critiques from our technical editors.

Disclosure 3: Visualization Solutions Are Reusable

Consider our data visualizations as flexible and reusable. Although we have organized the chapters by investment management phases and subjects, you may find that many of the visualizations they contain can be applied to other situations. Visuals can be mixed, matched, and reused to solve problems you encounter in your own work. As you read through the book, view our examples as design patterns that can be customized to fit your own needs.

Disclosure 4: Data Reflects a Representative Sample Set

Unless otherwise noted, the source data sets are not specific to a firm or organization. Each firm's data set will vary in the size of the individual value amounts and ranges, number of values in each list, and detail data types. The data visualizations are based largely upon representative sample data, with a focus on transforming similar data ranges into visual communications. Your redesign of data visualizations may likely need to adjust to accommodate your data.

Disclosure 5: All Visualizations Can Be Designed for Interactions

Although some of the visualizations are based on printed publications or static reports, all the ideas can be applied to interactive displays. Interactive digital displays of the data sets can provide the flexibility your audience needs and enable them to get more answers from the data. A few chapters are entirely designed for interactive displays (Chapters 3 and 5) and the information they provide relates directly to screen use.

Disclosure 6: Visualization Solutions Are Technology-Agnostic

We decided to write this book to share our ideas with a larger audience. We offer ideas that focus on providing business value unconstrained by specific client needs or target technologies. With implementation technology requirements aside, we put aside interaction design details as well. The ideas we present are strictly conceptual and can be recombined with other ideas, integrated into an existing solution, and tailored to a firm's specific needs. They make no presumptions about implementation and so address the largest possible audience. Each solution can be tailored on a case-by-case basis using the technology of your choosing.

Disclosure 7: Visualization Solutions Represent New Innovations

This book provides innovative methods for visualizing data. In many regards, traditional methods no longer work. The data to which we have access tends to be more varied and complex than before, and so we need to update our visualization methods. This book will expand your vocabulary of data visualization solutions to accommodate a whole new universe of how to display and interact with data.

We hope this collection of visualizations help you to select and implement solutions that best address your needs. Because some of the visualizations are new to your audience, you may need to explain how to read them. The more a new chart is used, the more familiar it will become. As the charts become familiar, your audience will require fewer explanations.

Supplemental Information

So you can reuse and apply the examples in the book, we have provided access to the materials online. Digital assets for both data and visuals are housed on the companion website: `http://www.wiley.com/go/visualizingfinancialdata`, where you can download all the sample data sets and visualization solutions we present. You can review sample data sets, compare them to your own, and with a gap analysis, decide how to work with variations in ranges or additional data points. Vector based pdfs' layout, scale, hierarchy, color, and font treatment can all be customized to your own needs. In addition, these files give you the flexibility to scale to the size you need and adjust as required.

The online materials are small starter kits that can help you put together a presentation, new report, project proposal, or even proof of concept prototype to demo. Over time you can use the supplemental information to try out new ideas, quickly share and gain consensus, and decide how to incorporate and proceed. Use the starter kits to articulate a vision you may have for changing a current communication strategy with a concrete example.

PART 1

Information Gains Through Data Visualizations

▶ **Chapter 1:** Paving a Path Toward Visual Communications

▶ **Chapter 2:** Benefits of Using Visual Methods

1

Paving a Path Toward Visual Communications

Visual communications can alleviate problems related to your complex data deluge, extract key points from your data, and help you create a visual narrative. The sequence of events, influencing factors, and unknown truths are examples of individual data stories that can become clearer with visual communications. Visualizations tell stories with charts to address a variety of needs starting with your own needs to evaluate data, communicate to peers, convince the board, present to clients, or report regulatory compliance. This chapter evaluates the current data state and presents a paved path toward a future with hardware and software advancements that you can use to create your own visual narrative.

Over the years we (a design research team) have partnered to create improved data displays that solve information challenges for our clients. In 2010, for instance, we worked on a risk platform—a proprietary technology software solution—for one of the world's largest bank holding companies. The platform, focused on structured products, was geared to provide research analysts with standard risk scenarios for fixed income securities.

The most informative feedback we received about the platform came from an analyst named Dave (not his real name), whose job it was to sort through the data to identify the major themes and highlights and publish weekly market perspectives for the firm. As part of his work, Dave reviewed information on market data rates, detail holdings, historical prepays, current prepayment models, rates of return, and color commentary across a set of securities. In addition, he read 12 daily news feeds, including them in his reports as needed. His reports were used all across the organization to make key decisions about fixed-income securities. In other words, his work was company-critical information.

As such, Dave needed to be in a position to access and analyze enormous amounts of data and distill it into a few key points to tell a clear story. In our conversation with Dave, he said that to maintain his position as a thought leader, he needed to remain "in constant discovery mode...." The value he provided lay in his ability to separate the signals from the noise and offer relevant insights. To deliver on that, Dave needed to improve his data displays. With that in mind he revealed that his main complaint was needing even more data display space despite using four separate computer screens, and he often found himself scrolling across vast spreadsheets to access that data. Here is what Dave told us he needed:

- ▶ He wanted to review Bloomberg market data on Treasuries, Swaps, LIBOR, and other indexes to compare them against portfolios by placing the two data sets side by side on one screen.

- ▶ He wanted to analyze multiple securities at one time, and he wanted to see a portfolio summary view within the context of other related portfolios.

- ▶ He wanted this text- and numbers-based information in a more graphical form to help him better interpret the data.

Having worked as a research analyst for 15 years, Dave knew what he needed from his data displays, and it had everything to do with improving his digital experience. During our interview he even held up his smartphone, pointing to its tiny screen and then back to the four large monitors. According to Dave, despite their limited screen size, the apps were more efficient than the monitors.

Information Delivery Needs

Dave is far from alone in wanting and needing a paved path toward better visual communication. The proliferation of apps on phones and tablets has created a new generation of users with higher expectations for all their digital experiences. Mobile apps created for play are pushing people to expect more from the applications in their work environment. Today's market demands immediacy, simplicity, and aesthetic appeal from mobile and desktop applications.

Tens of thousands of people just like Dave are out there in the world. Research analysts and others in finance and many related fields study complex data sets. They deliver weekly reports that are largely qualitative but with quantitative supporting details. An ever-expanding universe of data, plus regulatory requirements and greater global reach all contribute to the world's data complexity.

Bloomberg's market data, for example, is a huge and complex data source. The popular Bloomberg terminals provide data-driven insight into 52,000 companies, with more than 1,000,000 individuals consuming the 5,000 news stories published every day. Each terminal employs more than 30,000 command functions to navigate through the information. Analysts like Dave spend a significant portion of their time in Bloomberg.

As shown in Figure 1.1, other data sources, among the thousands that exist, include news and economic commentary as well as transactional, fund, portfolio, custodian, and accounting data to be presented within the context of investor client data. And the list goes on and on. Data sources continue to increase in type and size.

The number of additional elements that compound the complexity of data is astounding: risk and compliance rules set by firms, corporate actions set by the market, and investor mandates set as client guidelines for engagement, to name just a few.

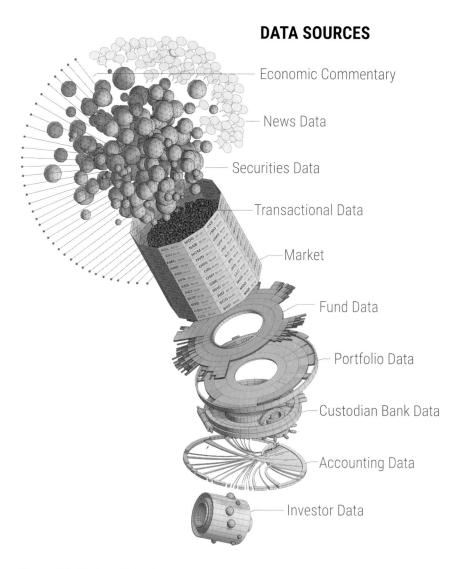

DATA SOURCES

- Economic Commentary
- News Data
- Securities Data
- Transactional Data
- Market
- Fund Data
- Portfolio Data
- Custodian Bank Data
- Accounting Data
- Investor Data

Figure 1.1 **Various Data Sources**

Industry Demands

Regulatory pressures in the industry are another necessary but complicating factor. They impact the type, format, frequency, and volume of reports issued. For example, firms must configure reports for their clients that meet regulatory requirements and disclosures set by the Dodd-Frank Act. Varying additional jurisdictional boundaries create added requirements to comply with regulations by state bureaus and local foreign regulators. Outside of the United States, MiFID II regulates how trillions of euros worth of stocks, bonds, derivatives, and commodities are traded, settled, and reported. Influences of globalization layer still more factors of complexity into available financial data.

Likewise, clients from various regions of the world, each with their own language, currency, and culture, have differing expectations of how data should be presented (see Figure 1.2). They may expect data to be grouped, subgrouped, filtered, tallied, and organized into grids, pivot tables, or charts.

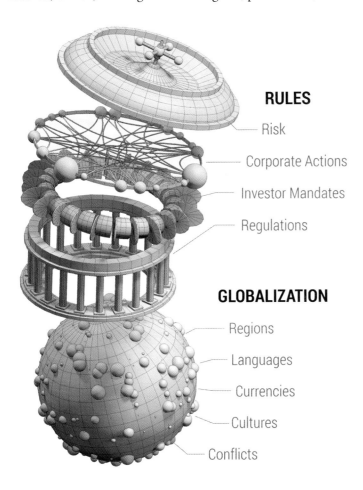

RULES

Risk

Corporate Actions

Investor Mandates

Regulations

GLOBALIZATION

Regions

Languages

Currencies

Cultures

Conflicts

Figure 1.2 **Globalization and Rule Demands**

Enabling Factors

On the one hand, these factors increase the amount and complexity of the data. On the other hand, advancements in technology enable us to *handle* these increasing amounts of data more readily and present them in numerous different ways (see Figure 1.3). Improved processing power combined with cheaper data storage, faster transfer, and mobility are what make more data readily available. The upside is that this increased availability enables us to dig deeper and learn more. Technological advancements for gathering, storing, and sharing larger data sets increase our capabilities with interactive data visualizations. However, we must be careful to create visual communications that are accurate and insightful.

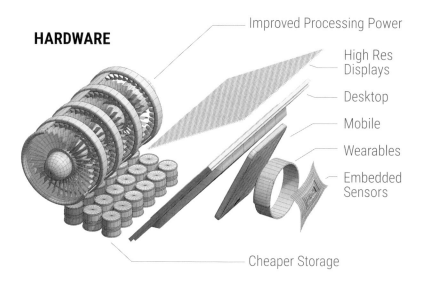

Figure 1.3 Hardware Capabilities

The world's ability to store digital information has roughly doubled every 40 months since the 1980s (see the following note). Major improvements in graphics cards and high-resolution displays have enabled the software side of the industry to create more sophisticated visuals without overburdening the computer systems, such as Business Intelligence (BI) and data visualization software (see Figure 1.4) now considered standard tools. In addition, we have powerful programming languages, open source charting libraries, technical computing packages, online visualization tools, and visualization research labs.

This statistic comes from an article in *Science* written by Martin Hilbert and Priscila López, "The World's Technological Capacity to Store, Communicate, and Compute Information" (*Science* 332 (6025): 60–65.doi:10.1126/science.1200970. PMID 21310967).

NOTE

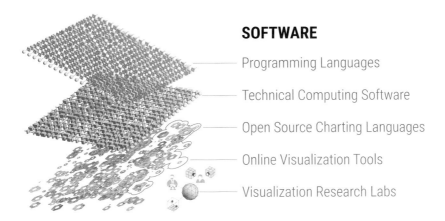

SOFTWARE

Programming Languages

Technical Computing Software

Open Source Charting Languages

Online Visualization Tools

Visualization Research Labs

Figure 1.4 Software Capabilities

We are at a point in which hardware and software can be used to present data, but we need to consider how best to represent it. Today, we can spend less time gathering and aggregating data and more time visually organizing data accurately. Although technology has enabled us to do more with our charting capabilities, demands in the marketplace push us to achieve higher standards. Because of technology, we can now move far beyond the traditional bar, line, and pie chart to create more sophisticated versions or introduce completely new visual concepts.

As the standard for a sophisticated and accurate digital experience increases, the bar for communicating financial data to more diverse audiences is set ever higher. Firms often ask us, "What can we do to improve our investment communications?" Soon thereafter, individuals at those firms often come back to us and ask, "How do I best present this data to my peers at a meeting I have next week? And by the way, the following week, I need to present this data to the review board and audit committee."

The presentation of data needs to encourage relevant conversations across audiences. Each audience group will require a slightly different set of questions and therefore needs a different perspective of the data (see Figure 1.5).

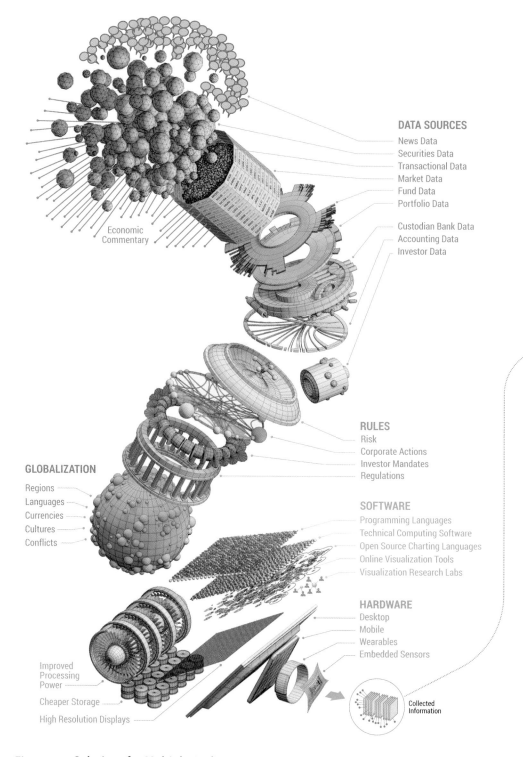

DATA SOURCES
News Data
Securities Data
Transactional Data
Market Data
Fund Data
Portfolio Data

Custodian Bank Data
Accounting Data
Investor Data

Economic
Commentary

RULES
Risk
Corporate Actions
Investor Mandates
Regulations

GLOBALIZATION
Regions
Languages
Currencies
Cultures
Conflicts

SOFTWARE
Programming Languages
Technical Computing Software
Open Source Charting Languages
Online Visualization Tools
Visualization Research Labs

HARDWARE
Desktop
Mobile
Wearables
Embedded Sensors

Improved
Processing
Power

Cheaper Storage

High Resolution Displays

Collected
Information

Figure 1.5 **Solutions for Multiple Audiences**

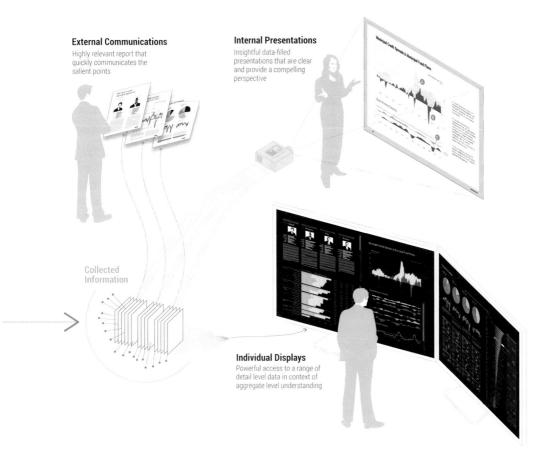

External Communications
Highly relevant report that quickly communicates the salient points

Internal Presentations
Insightful data-filled presentations that are clear and provide a compelling perspective

Collected Information

Individual Displays
Powerful access to a range of detail level data in context of aggregate level understanding

A relationship manager, for example, may want to know which of the portfolios she covers are at risk for redemption, whereas senior management would like to know the firm-wide view of accounts at risk, trends, and coverage for those accounts. From an individual presentation to a firm-wide risk perspective, the narrative needs to adjust and tilt to meet the needs of the audiences.

Summary

Dave struggled with the amount of data on his screens as well as the presentation of the data in his reports. As a result, a well-designed visual narrative was missing from the key points Dave presented, and he found it difficult to neatly connect each influencing factor back to the supporting data in his reports. His story, and others like it, has informed our work. Since then, there continues to be an increase in data, globalization, rules/regulations, and hardware and software capabilities. These increases influence the need and ability to create visual explanations of the data. As a result, we have focused our efforts on providing a much broader range of visualization solutions. Our analysis of current information needs across different audiences has effectively paved a path toward visual communications.

Visually interacting with data can provide multiple perspectives and serve multiple audiences. We have moved away from a visual narrative that provides a single perspective and shifted toward those that provide many viewpoints from the lowest level of details to the highest level of aggregation. We have more choices in how we display our data, and it is our job to present the clearest chart and most informative graph. We need to optimize how we visualize data to maximize our comprehension. In the following chapters we present a number of effective and innovative ways to chart complex data, leveraging technology, and addressing the needs of a variety of audiences.

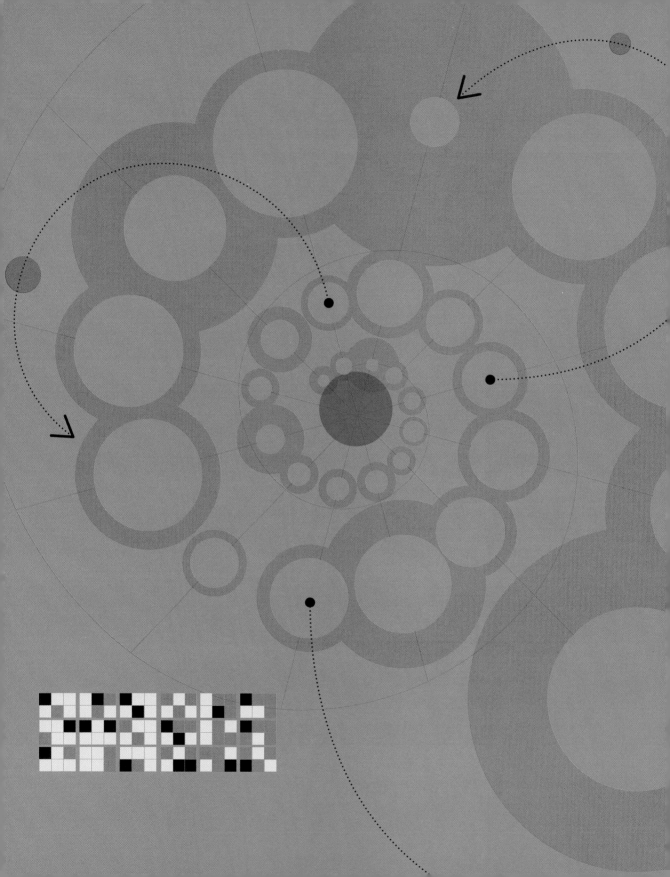

2

Benefits of Using Visual Methods

Communicating with data visualizations is not just about being more effective by replacing text and numbers. A thoughtfully crafted visualization increases our understanding of the data. It reveals patterns, quantities, changes over time, or recurring themes at a glance. It makes data so much easier to comprehend that it can elicit "aha" moments, instant epiphanies, from your audience. Fellow theoretical physicist John Wheeler attributed to Albert Einstein the statement, "If I can't picture it, I can't understand it." Einstein's quote advocates for the use of visual aids to create understanding. He understood the power of a visual and used drawings and charts throughout his notebooks to explain his observations and formulas.

What types of challenges can data visualizations of charts and graphs address? What are the inherent qualities of a chart and how can we leverage them? This chapter covers these questions as we address the overall benefits of data visualizations.

The Purpose of Charts

You can rely on data visualizations to see outliers, trends, correlations, and patterns. First, consider the case of outliers in the data. An exception report identifies instances in which some threshold was breached. Let's say these data points or outliers are the focus of interest. Maybe they show errors in a system to highlight specific work to be corrected. Maybe you want to assign levels of priority to such work on the basis of the number of outliers. *But what else could you do with the outlier data?* You could track associations between the exceptions and the data to see if the exceptions are increasing or decreasing. *Are they above or below your yearly averages? Is there a pattern in the outliers that may help identify their root cause? Does their timing correlate to other patterns in the data? Do they, for example, map to market volume, season, or something else?*

This inquiry leads you to realize that reviewing this one exception report is not enough. You need to look at the data from different angles. Every question leads to another.

In the exception report example just mentioned, you started with an unprioritized list of exceptions or outliers. You ranked them by priority for course correction. You then looked for trends by comparing outliers over time. Finally, you looked into correlations in the data to see if associations in the exceptions track to time, market volume, or another variable. Patterns in the dataset help you to draw conclusions that in turn enable you to effectively predict and prevent future errors.

Data visualizations need to anticipate and address follow-up questions. Understanding why you rely on data helps you design visualizations to meet an array of questions. Each data visualization has a stated purpose but also goes beyond its immediate purpose and serves as an entry point to multiple views. Data visualizations enable you to discover things beyond the reach of their initial intention. They prime you to compare, connect, and create your own conclusions.

The images in this chapter are meant to illustrate the purpose of data visualizations. Because they're meant to show why data visualizations are used, they do not use real-world financial data nor are they examples of the charts and graphs in the chapters that follow. The data visualizations in the chapters that follow are based on actual financial data in the industry.

Making Comparisons

Data visualizations distill data. They reduce the effort required to understand comparisons, as calculations, and results are represented directly as visual content. To compare a table of numbers with 10 rows and 10 columns would require you to make roughly 4,950 calculations to understand the relationship between the 100 individual data points. Instead a simple comparison can be made by scanning the visual representation of this same data set.

The formula used to arrive at the number of calculations mentioned in the preceding paragraph is N (N-1)/2, where N = number of data points.

Types of comparisons vary widely. You can compare like values or introduce context to provide fresh perspectives of the data. Typically, comparisons reveal rank, compare attributes, or show how an event might unfold over time. Consider the following types of comparisons:

▶ **Rank**—Ranking establishes a relationship between a list of items to introduce "greater than," "less than," or "equal to" analysis. There are various ways of showing rank. Percentile rank indicates frequency of occurrences and the distribution of data across defined intervals. Both ordinal number sequence rankings and percentile rankings are useful for comparison. Ranked data enables you to quickly find the top candidates. Figure 2.1 is an example of a bar chart listing items in sequential order, ranking from the largest to smallest amount.

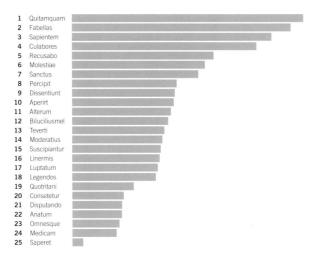

Figure 2.1 **Rank Example**

▶ **Attributes**—An attribute is a characteristic of an object. Analyzing attributes is about understanding the various characteristics of an object. For example, Figure 2.2 shows three characteristics (A, B, and C) each of which can have specific values. It charts 49 objects to visually showcase characteristics mapped to the width, height, and size of center circle.

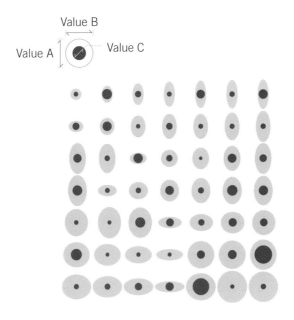

Figure 2.2 **Attributes Example**

▶ **Time**—Historical or time-based data visualizations reveal how events evolve over a period of time and are easily compared with other related time-based data sets. The ability to compare and track changes over time describes behavior and can reveal a trend. Time series charts, as shown in Figure 2.3, typically display the discrete time markers on the x-axis.

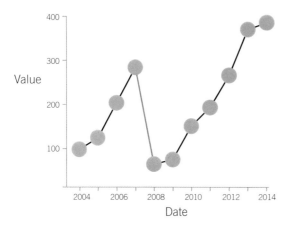

Figure 2.3 **Time Series Example**

Data visualizations that provide comparisons can help you answer questions regarding what and when. *What is the top performing fund for this year? What were the most prevalent attributes of the fund? Have those attributes changed over time, if so when?*

Establishing Connections

Relationships between data sets enable you to understand connections in the data. *Is a data set part of a subset? Does one data set impact the results of another set and how?* A visualization that connects the big picture with corresponding details enables you to inspect the data at various levels. Pointillist painting is a technique that uses small distinct dots of color and applies those dots in patterns to form a coherent picture. Individual dots in a painting are like individual data points in a visualization. Similar in effect to Pointillist painting, our individual data points, like the distinct dots in the painting, have little meaning, but when combined they form a vibrant picture. Your

eyes make those connections and allow you to see the big picture and still inspect each dot or section. Data visualizations can show connections in the data by using the techniques of drill down, networks, and correlations.

▶ **Drill down**—Drill down visualizations enable you to look into the details without compromising the larger big picture view. Seeing the details in context of a larger view provides an enhanced perspective. Figure 2.4 provides a drill down example and shows the connections between the L1, L2, and L3 columns. The highlighted blue bar in L1 is the aggregate amount of the entire L2 contents, whereas the highlighted black bar in L2 is the aggregate amount of the entire L3 contents.

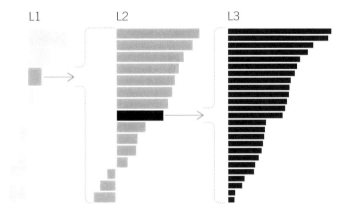

Figure 2.4 **Drill Down Example**

▶ **Networks**—Networks link individual data points or nodes together. Seeing how data points connect to each other can reveal the influence or impact of one data point to another. Figure 2.5 shows a network in which A and H are linked through G and F in tandem. It shows how certain clusters can be directly linked, indirectly linked, or not linked at all.

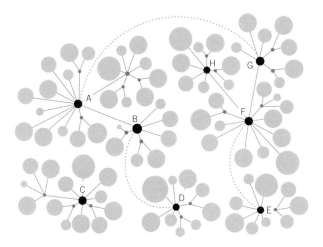

Figure 2.5 **Network Example**

▶ **Correlations**—Correlations between various data sets may reveal relationships between them that might not otherwise be apparent. Charts similar to Figure 2.6 can show how strongly related two data sets are to each other. The data sets in charts A and B have the strongest correlations to each other, whereas charts C and D have weak or non-linear correlations.

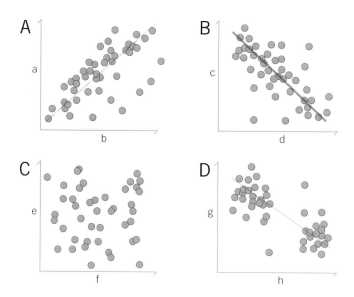

Figure 2.6 **Correlations Example**

Showing connections can answer questions as to "how and where." For example, drill down visualizations can reveal how an aggregated total is composed of underlying line items. Network visualizations can show how an event in one part of the world impacts the price of a commodity in another part of the world. The effect, influence, and means of linking datasets across locations can be shown and explained with networks. The third type of data visualizations that show connections are correlations. For example, correlations can explain if and how the size of a fund affects performance or if there exists a relationship between firm size and beta values.

Drawing Conclusions

Data visualizations enable you to draw your own conclusions and help you solve complex questions. A well-crafted visual system provides a set of answers that facilitate deeper evaluation. You can formulate theories on the basis of patterns, themes, and calculations. Visualizations that lead to conclusions can provide the mechanisms for you to advance your understanding by confirming a conclusion based on a tested hypothesis. For example, a pattern can help you to predict outcomes; groups of categories, and subcategories enable you to see themes; and complex formulas can be visualized to show you the results of a calculation.

> ▶ **Pattern recognition**—Visualizations that help you detect patterns take a step further into predicting outcomes. Discovering patterns enables you to see repeatable steps that lead into knowing what might occur next. Figure 2.7 shows a hypothetical pattern of activities and time of day with a 24-hour chart. A–L lists the activities, and the AM/PM range indicates the hour of the day. The chart then shows the pattern of which activities are completed based on time. Activities K and L are completed at night, whereas A and B are completed in the afternoon.

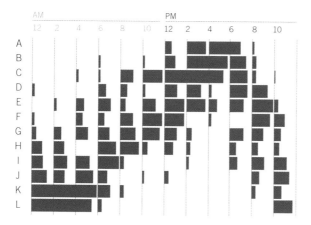

Figure 2.7 **Pattern Recognition Example**

▶ **Themes/categories**—Analysis that exposes themes in the data provides you with the ability to summarize the information and understand the important aspects of the data. Categories organically arise and can help you detect more themes. Figure 2.8 shows the data organized into four column groups that represent four themes. The black, gray, and blue represent the sentiment for each cell to buy, sell, or hold a stock. The emerging patterns show the grouping of a theme that is predominantly black cells, evenly mixed cells, gray cells, and blue cells.

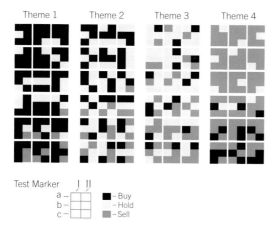

Figure 2.8 **Theme/Categories Example**

▶ **Visual calculations**—Modeling an algorithm that represents a differential equation, for example, can require the output to be as complex of an answer as the input of the formula. In contrast, visualizing calculations can show and explain the results of the calculation. Figure 2.9 shows an equation with three variables. Each variable can be displayed within the context of the chart and a sample data point can be explicitly listed with the exact numeric values.

$$z = \frac{\sin(x^2+3y^2)}{0.1+r^2} + (x^2+5y^2) \cdot \frac{\exp(1-r^2)}{2}, \quad r = \sqrt{x^2+y^2}$$

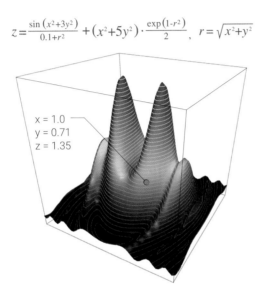

Figure 2.9 **Visual Calculations Example**

The benefit to these types of visuals is that the answer is based on the raw data, so we are able to see the results and not just ask why but also begin to understand why. *Why do small cap value funds outperform large cap core funds? Why did a financial model provide such volatile results?* These are a sample of questions that represent conclusive types of inquires that can help you understand why an event occurred.

How to Leverage Charts

We as humans have evolved robust visual processing skills to interpret our environment. Unless blindness has forced us to rely on other senses, we gather and process visual information during every waking moment. Consider a simple errand to a store across the street. Before you cross the street, you scan for the motion of cars to make sure it's safe. You read the cross-walk signal, avoid the pothole in the street, and navigate the crowd. You assess the flow of traffic and make sure a car is not turning onto the street. Within seconds you are able to cross the street untouched. This is a simple example of our visual data processing skills. Throughout the day we are able to make well-timed decisions based on seeing and assessing what is in front of us. Yet we rarely stop to think how visual data processing and analysis gets us through the day.

Imagine being limited to gathering information about your surroundings via raw numbers and text. Your ability to react and make a next move would require vast amounts of time and effort simply to consume the data. Assessing such data would require long calculations. Making sure it is safe to cross the street would turn seconds of scanning into minutes. The tasks that take you a few minutes may take hours and would lead to a higher risk of making the wrong choice. This text-and-numbers-based world seems unreasonable.

The fact is much of our work is spent in this text-and-numbers-based world. Spreadsheets of data including but not limited to cash-flow models, balance sheets, earnings valuations, investment returns, research notes, and news all consume how we navigate our work. We consume textual and numeric information, review the data, make our assessments via calculations, and decide on the appropriate next steps. However, how we communicate should reflect our visual cortex strengths and be designed around our ability to see and comprehend.

Communications should be optimized knowing the gifts of our extremely evolved powers of visual perception. Our eyes have the power of seeing visual misalignments; tracking motion, color, texture, depth; and recognizing visual patterns. Knowing our strengths and building upon these strengths can help us better navigate the world of text and numbers. The more we replace text and numbers with visual objects, the more we can set up a system that works with our own visual system of seeing. But that is not all; the characteristics of a strong visual communication are many:

▶ **Universal**—The meaning of an image can span borders and foreign languages. Much like math, images are not just relevant to one society or region. As shown in Figure 2.10, a visual communication like a chart or graph can be used across the globe to share data. Use charts to communicate more easily with colleagues and clients in other regions.

Figure 2.10 **Locations Across the Globe**

▶ **Immediate**—Consumption and comprehension of a chart can be close to instantaneous. For example, reviewing a year's performance of the NASDAQ and S&P 500 as a chart (Figure 2.11) is fast and understandable. If we contrast this chart with the text-and-numbers-based version, it would take a significant amount of time to analyze. The ability to scan the chart and understand the data is more easily achieved. Charts can be used to save time, easily interpret data, and learn and share the findings from the data.

NASDAQ Composite (^IXIC)

4,370.90 ↑ 35.93 (0.83%)

Range: 1D 5D 1M 3M 6M **1Y** 2Y 5Y

■ NASDAQ
■ S&P500

+25%
+20%
+15%
+10%
+5%
0%
-5%

SEP 13   NOV 13   JAN 14   MAR 14   MAY 14   JUL 14

Figure 2.11 **NASDAQ 1Y Chart**

▶ **Concise**—A small visual display can represent large amounts of data. Visual methods like small multiples (Tufte, 2001) display a series of individual charts with the same scale and axes to consolidate tables of numbers into concise images. Figure 2.12 displays small multiples with three datasets represented as a blue line, black line, and gray surface area within each chart. The collection of four charts shows a total of 12 data sets. What would normally require pages and pages of numeric tables can be shown in one page. Space efficiency is also introduced as an output of concise visuals; you can see more with less. You can use concise charts in small displays or when you need to display multiple data sets in one view.

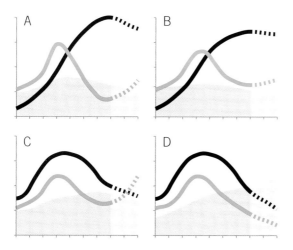

Figure 2.12 **Concise Line Charts**

▶ **Inviting**—Visualizations can be aesthetically pleasing and invite the reader to review them more closely. Appealing and engaging communications make the information more likely to be reviewed, used, and adopted. The Calendar Chart shown in Figure 2.13 is an example of such a chart that can pique your curiosity and encourage you to review the chart more closely. It lists months in chronological order and points out 3 months in the 2.5 year calendar that shares data results. Use charts to attract attention and interest your audience.

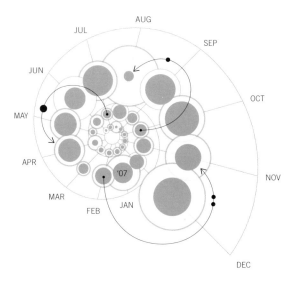

Figure 2.13 **Calendar Chart**

▶ **Memorable**—Visuals are easier to remember than text and numbers. Known as the *Pictorial Superiority Effect*, the phenomenon explains that an image is more likely to be both recalled and recognized over text and numbers. Studies show that humans can remember more than 2,000 pictures with at least 90% accuracy in recognition tests over a period of several days (Standing & Haber, 1970). Use charts to help your audience recall the data. Figure 2.14 is an illustration inspired by the children's book *The Little Prince*. The book starts with a memorable story of a drawing. The drawing is of a boa constrictor that has eaten an elephant. Chances are that if you are familiar with the book, you will recognize the illustration.

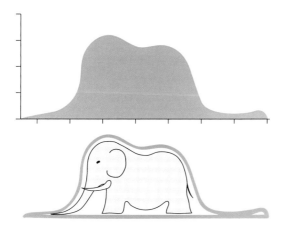

Figure 2.14 **Memorable Childhood Illustration**

▶ **Revealing**—Visualizations can reveal what otherwise may be missed or lost in translation. Discovering otherwise unnoticed information can be realized with different visualization techniques. Similar to how a photograph reveals the reality of life, charts can reveal the reality of the data. Figure 2.15 is an example of a chart that points out A, B, and C cluster groups and derives meaning from the arrangement of circles.

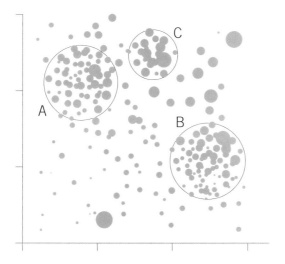

Figure 2.15 **Revealing Cluster Chart**

▶ **Reusable and versatile**—Visualizations can be reused and have a range of media applications. Charts can be reused in video, animation, and infographics, and can be designed for print, screens, or large interactive displays. You can reuse and adapt chart concepts to target your communication needs and delivery channel possibilities. Both what and how you communicate can be designed to meet specific needs. The visual communication options (Figure 2.16) to choose from increase with each delivery channel. For example, your option to show more or less data is a dynamic option in an interactive display.

Figure 2.16 **Multiple Outputs**

Data visualizations enables us to turn on the light switch and see what is available. They shine light in a way that enables you to reveal data that would otherwise stay hidden. Making data visible can provide immediate gratification to audiences around the globe. You can represent your data with concise charts and evoke an inviting or memorable display. Visualizations can also be versatile and adjust to fit different needs. You can leverage these qualities of a visualization to make the data work for you.

Summary

The ability to encode the data into a visual picture is a communication strength that enables you to understand, explain, teach, convince, and reach larger audiences. Pictures of data that carefully communicate the information needed by your audience are important and provide considerable value to compare, see connections, and make conclusions. Charts cross regional boundaries and can be used across the globe to quickly and concisely communicate large amounts of data. They can pique and keep your interest to draw you in and be remembered. You can learn, make discoveries from charts, and reuse charts across different audiences and delivery mechanisms. Data visualizations produce solutions that do much of the work for you regardless of volumes, real-time updates, or additional variations. You just need to take advantage of their capabilities.

PART 2

Transforming Data for Active Investment Decisions

▶ **Chapter 3:** Security Assessment

▶ **Chapter 4:** Portfolio Construction

▶ **Chapter 5:** Trading

▶ **Chapter 6:** Performance Measurement

Value &
Growth
Full data set

Valuation			Growth		Margins		Profitability	
18.8	9.2	1.8	9.6	22.6	13.5	9.4	17.4	53.3
Price/Earnings	Price/Book	Price/Sales	Rev Growth	Nbd. Income Growth	Operating Margin %	Net Margin %	ROA	MIE

Value & Growth
Custom weighted
aggregation

Valuation | Growth | Margins | Profitability

Capabilities
Value & Growth
reduced to one
aggregated value

Performance | Value & Growth | Risk | Ratings

3

Security Assessment

Assessing securities requires the most granular analysis of all investment processes. The approved universe of investment vehicles may differ widely across or even within firms. It may include stocks, bonds, commingled funds (for example, mutual funds or hedge funds), ETFs, money market instruments, currencies, or derivatives. Regardless of the breadth of securities in the approved universe, portfolio managers and analysts inside and outside the firm are tasked with assessing them. This chapter proposes visualization designs to those who assess securities for comparative and competitive purposes and would like to see a standardized view of those securities.

We introduce a new framework for standardizing the presentation of stocks, bonds, mutual funds, and ETFs to make each more easily compared as an investment option. A *framework* can be defined as a supporting structure to an entity, which in this case is the investment option. We extend this definition of a framework through a visualization approach that supports a range of key data points of each listed security. First we introduce and define how that framework is designed; second we apply it to the creation of profiles for stocks, bonds, mutual funds, and ETFs; and third, we present the resulting collection of profiles. Throughout this chapter we show how the framework is constructed with blueprints for each security type.

The visualizations throughout this chapter use representative sample data and are not specific to a source. In addition, the visualizations are designed as interactive displays that can be configured and navigated by an end user.

NOTE

Tile Framework

A standardized framework can be used to describe the profile of a security with a series of Tiles. *Tiles* are small visualizations of key characteristics or metrics of an entity within uniform squares that can be combined to identify the performance results of a security. Although the Tile Framework produces visual similarities between each security type, a different set of characteristics and results have to be defined for each security to make it analytically useful. This section describes the Tile Framework so that it can be used and defined for other securities.

Profile Tiles are the most fundamental. They describe the weights of a security within an asset class, market cap, sector, or region. The Profile Tiles shown in Figure 3.1 describe and summarize different security types. This figure illustrates the framework within a hypothetical security profile of a commingled fund.

Security Profile

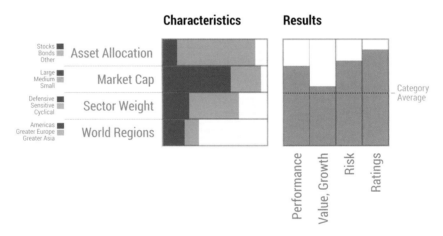

Figure 3.1 **Profile Tiles**

The Profile Tiles serve multiple purposes. They help you understand the investment's diversification and its conservative versus aggressive aspects. At the aggregate level, the profiles show you individual characteristics of a security (asset class, market cap, sector, and region), as well as corresponding results (performance, value/growth, risk, and ratings). The Characteristics Tile describes inputs used in creating the investment, while the Results Tile shows their outcomes. Asset allocations determine the degree of the risk—high or low. Based on the sector weights, performance levels are revealed to be above or below the category average.

Color bars provide a system of levels. Horizontal bars show percentage levels across sectors, and vertical bars rank levels of attributes such as risk and ratings. This two-pronged approach to the Tiles visually documents intrinsic qualities of the investment and invites you to drill deeper into the details. It encourages you to ask what lies behind each block of color. Figure 3.2 illustrates how the Characteristics Tile is composed.

Characteristics Framework

Figure 3.2 **Characteristics Framework**

To reveal the specific values that make up each Tile, additional views drill down into each band and show underlying details by redistributing the data into more refined categories (Figure 3.2). To create an understandable visual profile, the building blocks of the Characteristics Tile are arranged and colored consistently. The color sequence starts with more conservative traits shown in darker blue on the left or top and continues to more aggressive traits represented as light blue on the right or bottom. In this way, assessing color value of the whole Tile reveals if the represented security is more conservative or aggressive.

In contrast to the Characteristics Tile, the Results Tile (see Figure 3.3) aggregates values that you can influence.

Results Framework

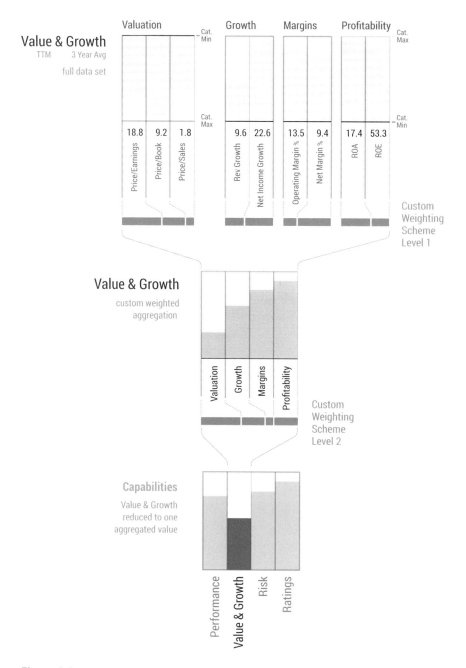

Figure 3.3 **Results Framework**

The Results Framework (Figure 3.3) acts as a funnel that captures values into an aggregated ranked level. A collection of values for each attribute travel through the first and second custom weighting scheme to accumulate the level as seen within "Value & Growth" in the Results Tile.

At each level a weighting scheme is introduced so that each individual or team responsible for security assessments can set this weighting scheme to their own needs and adjust it as needed. Such a customizable framework closely models how you might embed your own perspective into the analysis. The display becomes a combination of the investment's inherent characteristics combined with your own position.

Key Take-Aways

This section proposes a standardized Tile Framework that can be used to assess securities. The Tile Framework presents the summary or abridged level of information as an entry point to access the underlying details. Data sets are first logically grouped to compose two Profile Tiles. One Tile of data shows the characteristics of a security. Another Tile of data shows the investment results of the security. Both have the capacity to drill in to source data; however, the Results Tile enables you to apply custom weights to the security. Together, the Tile Framework produces a normalized data display designed to compare different security types.

Stocks

Asset class, market cap, sectors, and regions are stock characteristics that can be used to describe a stock. This investment type can act as our common denominator as it shares many of the same traits, such as sectors and regions, with other securities. The benefit to starting with the basic traits of a stock is that it can create the same context for comparison across other security types. The Stock Tile, shown in Figure 3.4, adopts a color band chart to identify a stock's characteristics.

Stock Profile - Characteristics

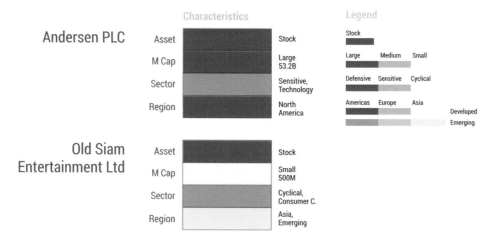

Figure 3.4 Stock Tile

Color connotes meaning and can be used to attach simple associations. The color band chart follows this lead with a set of color mappings that uses color fill to denote specific characteristics. The two stocks listed in the Stock Tile (Figure 3.4) show similarities and differences between their two profiles; the yellow overlay is one example of how to highlight such a difference. As previously stated, the characteristics provide just one aspect of the security. The next visual (Figure 3.5), shows the two Profile Tiles, Characteristics and Results, and adds a third.

Together, the three Tiles provide a suitable introduction to the stock. The first Tile shows the current stock performance. The second Tile describes the specifics of the categorical characteristics. The third Tile provides a closer analysis of the performance, valuation, risk, and ratings results and layers in the comparative peer measurement. The Stock Tiles Schematic (Figure 3.5) shows just how data-rich the display can become and exactly what is behind the color codes.

Stock Profile

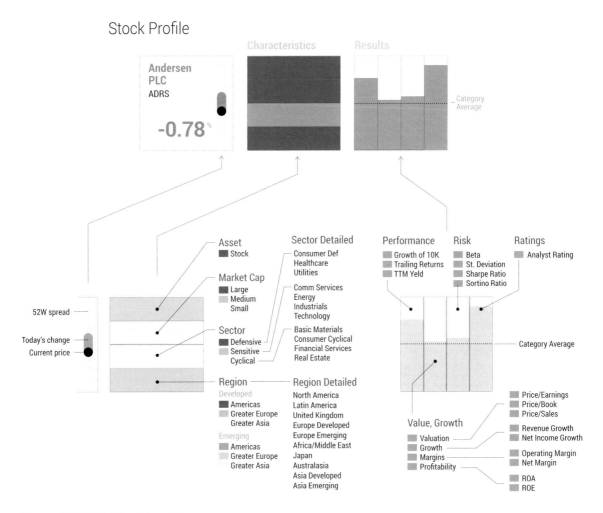

Figure 3.5 **Stock Tiles Schematic**

Key Take-Aways

The Stock Tiles display the current price, characteristics, and investment results in a framework that can be systematically applied to other stocks. The effort behind organizing the data into a visual system produces concise and informative views of the data. You can rely on the Tiles' knowing they are backed with readily available detailed schematics that explain the color bands.

Bonds

Connected to the interest rate market, bonds provide an interesting mix of both the predictability of a scheduled coupon payment and the unpredictability of interest rates. These well-known traits are exclusive to bonds and are fundamental to why investors look to bonds. Yet just as importantly, the ratings, interest rate risk, yield, and maturity are additional key characteristics of bonds to consider. These unique data points are reflected in the profile framework for bonds. The next set of Tiles, as shown in Figure 3.6, applies the profile framework and addresses the specific needs of bonds.

Bond Profile - Characteristics

Figure 3.6 **Bond Tile**

The maturity, quality, sectors, and regions can all be varied to represent different bonds (refer to Figure 3.6). The variability seen in these two examples shows how the color bands can describe and distinguish bonds. *How does the coupon rate compare to the category average? How strong is the quality rating?* The Bond Tile Schematic (Figure 3.7) addresses these questions with additional Tiles that are mapped to a schematic diagram.

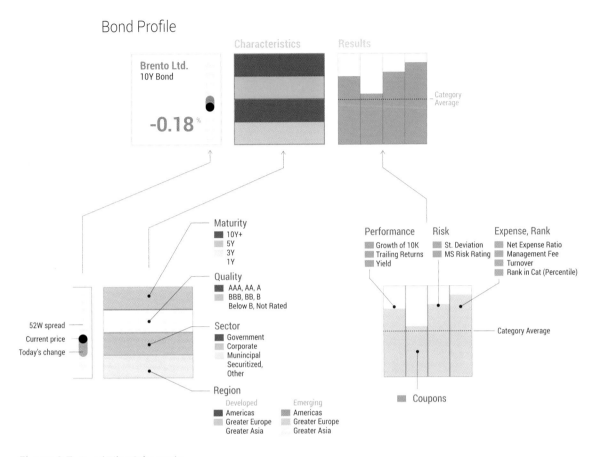

Figure 3.7 **Bond Tiles Schematic**

Simulated to show the range of possible permutations, the Bond Tiles Schematic has adapted and isolated characteristics that are unique to bonds. For example, the ability to identify a government, corporate, municipal bond, and so on is a part of the adapted sector view. The third Tile continues to show the relative comparison to the category average performance illustrated with a dashed line. With these results, you can spot bonds that perform above industry average with lower risk.

Key Take-Aways

This section illustrates how to adapt the framework to include specific bond traits like quality rating, maturity dates, and coupon rates. With the previously shown Stock Tiles and now the Bond Tiles, you can see how to incorporate the unique characteristics of each into a standardized framework. The current price, characteristics, and relative results Tiles provide an introduction, comparison, and contrast of stocks and bonds.

Mutual Funds

Although marketed as providing a good investment option of diversification for retirement accounts and beyond, mutual funds attract a range of investors. The asset class, market cap, sector, and region weights are fundamental traits of mutual funds and are well documented and commonly displayed with multiple charts. Figure 3.8 displays these traits by applying the framework of the Characteristics Tile to a stock mutual fund.

Mutual Fund - Characteristics

Large Cap Stock Mutual Fund

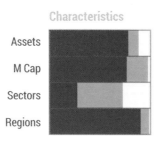
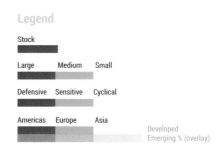

Figure 3.8 **Stock Mutual Fund Tile**

The consistency of a visual framework has both pros and cons. A quick glance of the Stock Mutual Fund Tile (refer to Figure 3.8) highlights the fund's sector diversity. However, the same quick glance may also miss the title label which tells you the investment name and and type. Consistency and standardization normalize the data for better comparison but they also require you to pay closer attention to the labels.

For this reason, explaining the visual's anatomy with labels requires a shift of attention. The Tile schematic (Figure 3.9) uses a previously shown technique that pushes the Tiles' visuals to the background to present the labels in the foreground.

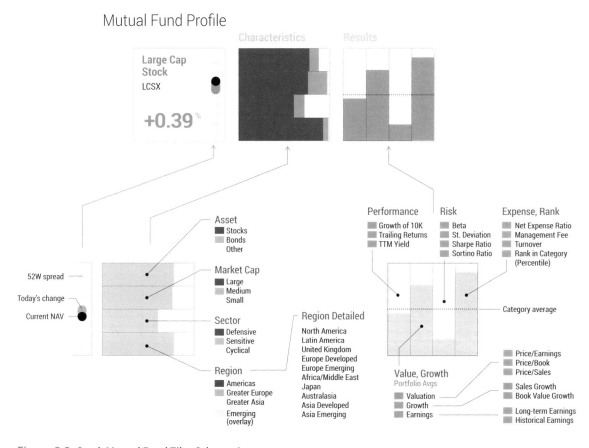

Figure 3.9 **Stock Mutual Fund Tiles Schematic**

The same schematic technique shown for bonds in Figure 3.7 and stocks in Figure 3.5 explains Tile contents by revealing differences between security type Tiles. Similar to a tool tip, data labels in the schematic provide explanations of the Tiles. In addition, each Tile has a corresponding set of drill-down displays so that you can see more details regarding the make-up of the fund. Next, Figure 3.10 illustrates a drill-down of the Characteristics Tile.

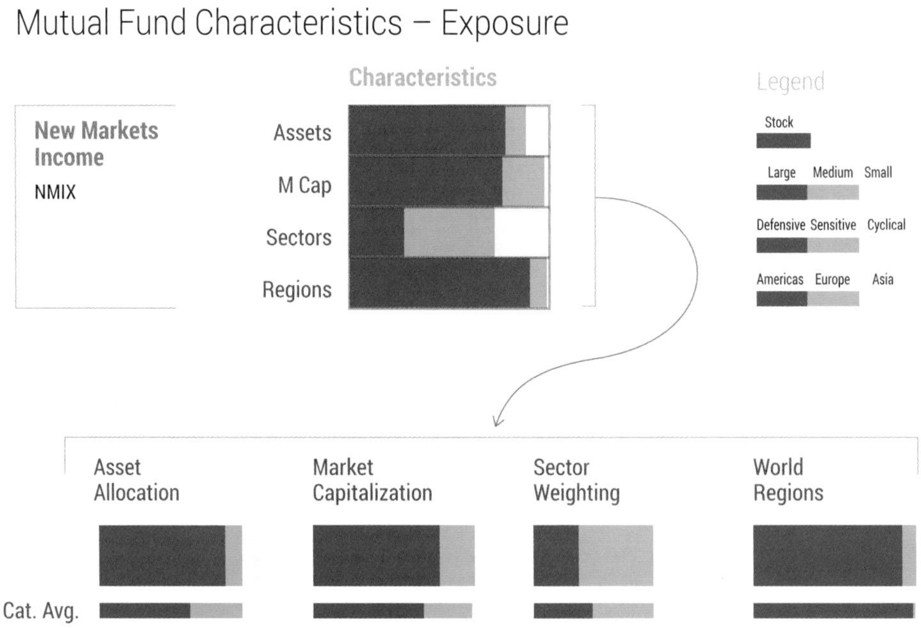

Figure 3.10 **Tile Bands**

The first level down from the Tile view compares each fund characteristic, shown as a band within the Tile, against the category average. Since the Tiles are designed for interactive use, you can next select a characteristic to see its corresponding values, as shown in Figure 3.11.

Mutual Fund Characteristics – Sector Weighting

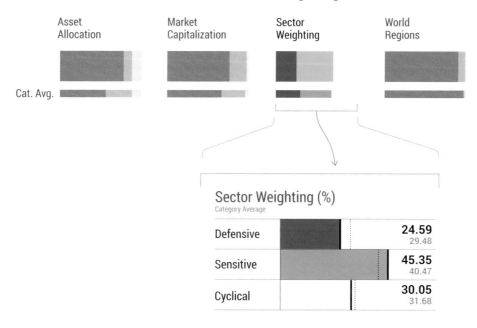

Figure 3.11 Tile Band – Level 1

Drill-down views couple graphic details with numeric forms. The bold black vertical lines and bold text mark the fund's sector weights, whereas the gray dashed lines and gray text show the category averages. Similar marks and consistent drill-down patterns throughout the framework reinforce its role as a standardized system. They help you read quickly and easily compare the fund to the category average. The next level down displays weights across the sectors, as shown in Figure 3.12.

Mutual Fund Characteristics – Sector Weighting Details

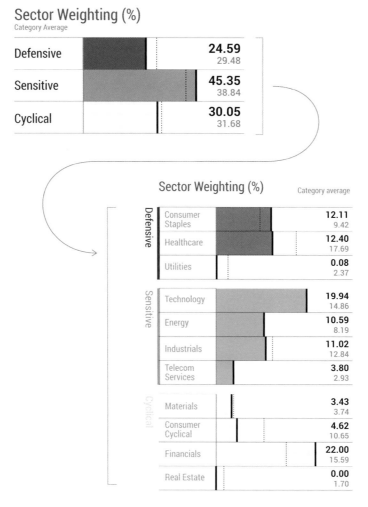

Figure 3.12 **Tile Band–Level 2**

As more data is unveiled, expanded details can be organized to emphasize different aspects. Next, Figure 3.13 illustrates two ways to design the data displays.

Mutual Fund Characteristics – Sector Weighting Details

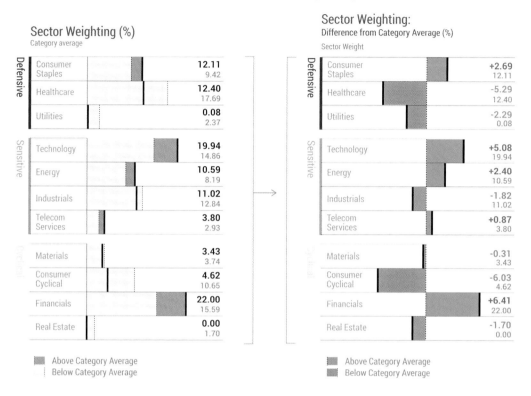

Sector Weighting (%)
Category average

Defensive	Consumer Staples	**12.11** / 9.42
	Healthcare	**12.40** / 17.69
	Utilities	**0.08** / 2.37
Sensitive	Technology	**19.94** / 14.86
	Energy	**10.59** / 8.19
	Industrials	**11.02** / 12.84
	Telecom Services	**3.80** / 2.93
Cyclical	Materials	**3.43** / 3.74
	Consumer Cyclical	**4.62** / 10.65
	Financials	**22.00** / 15.59
	Real Estate	**0.00** / 1.70

Sector Weighting:
Difference from Category Average (%)

Sector Weight

Defensive	Consumer Staples	**+2.69** / 12.11
	Healthcare	**-5.29** / 12.40
	Utilities	**-2.29** / 0.08
Sensitive	Technology	**+5.08** / 19.94
	Energy	**+2.40** / 10.59
	Industrials	**-1.82** / 11.02
	Telecom Services	**+0.87** / 3.80
Cyclical	Materials	**-0.31** / 3.43
	Consumer Cyclical	**-6.03** / 4.62
	Financials	**+6.41** / 22.00
	Real Estate	**-1.70** / 0.00

Above Category Average
Below Category Average

Above Category Average
Below Category Average

Figure 3.13 Tile Band–Level 2 Options

Figure 3.13 provides two methods to compare the fund's sector weights to the category average. In the weights representation on the left, the bars provide a dual purpose. The bar lengths indicate quantity weights and color indicates the offset from the category average and exposes either an under- or over-exposure to a sector. In the example on the right, in addition to using color to highlight offsets from the category average, alignment is a powerful technique in drawing attention to a different focus point. It is organized to pivot from the centerline of the category average, and separates the sector weights into two categories: The left side of the centerline shows under-exposed sectors and the right side shows over-exposed sectors.

Simple alignment alterations can change one's perspective on data and serve as an influential tool. With clarity comes understanding, which can ultimately lead to influence. If variation from the average is an important perspective, the left chart is ill equipped to tell that story. It requires you to calculate the variation. In contrast, the chart on the right makes the variation clear. You can elect to show one chart over another or both (Figure 3.13).

Key Take-Aways

This section applies the framework to stock mutual funds and shows how to drill down into sector weightings. The same drill-down technique can be applied to the Asset Allocation and Market Capitalization characteristics and should ideally be applied across the Tile Bands to maintain consistency.

Consistency in marks and patterns makes the framework more familiar and usable. You can include a variety of drill-down views depending on the needs of your audience. Regardless of your drill-down selections, the same set of drill-down levels should be applied across all Tiles Bands to ensure that comparison is possible.

ETFs

Tied to an index, an ETF, or exchange-traded fund, provides a holistic view of its market's economic strength, diversification, and outlook with the flexibility to purchase intra-day. As a large competitor to the mutual fund, consistent data points in the ETF provide a good comparison between the two securities. Figure 3.14 shows a case in which the ETF profile has identical characteristics to the mutual fund.

The Stock ETF Tile Schematic (Figure 3.14) is an exact replica of the previous Stock Mutual Fund Tile set. Both are based on stocks as the underlying security. For this reason, the same set of drill-downs that appear in the mutual fund (Figure 3.10–3.13) can be applied to this ETF. Similarly, certain characteristics within the Bond Tiles could apply to a Bond ETF Tile set. Figure 3.7 provides a schematic that could also be applied to a Bond ETF.

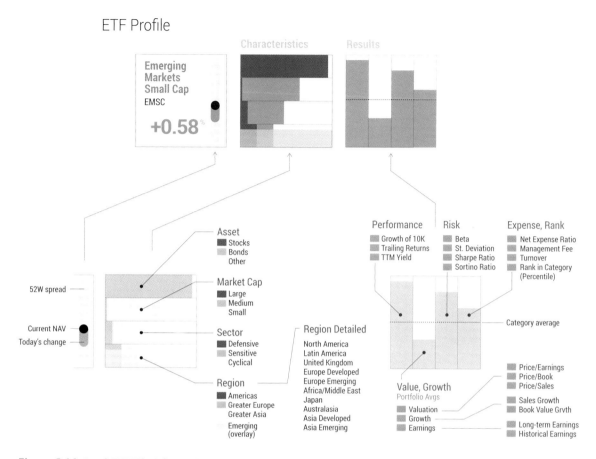

ETF Profile

Characteristics

Results

Emerging
Markets
Small Cap

EMSC

+0.58

52W spread

Current NAV

Today's change

Asset
■ Stocks
■ Bonds
  Other

Market Cap
■ Large
■ Medium
  Small

Sector
■ Defensive
■ Sensitive
  Cyclical

Region
■ Americas
■ Greater Europe
  Greater Asia
  Emerging
  (overlay)

Region Detailed
North America
Latin America
United Kingdom
Europe Developed
Europe Emerging
Africa/Middle East
Japan
Australasia
Asia Developed
Asia Emerging

Performance
■ Growth of 10K
■ Trailing Returns
■ TTM Yield

Risk
■ Beta
■ St. Deviation
■ Sharpe Ratio
■ Sortino Ratio

Expense, Rank
■ Net Expense Ratio
■ Management Fee
■ Turnover
■ Rank in Category
  (Percentile)

Category average

Value, Growth
Portfolio Avgs
■ Valuation
■ Growth
■ Earnings

■ Price/Earnings
■ Price/Book
■ Price/Sales

■ Sales Growth
■ Book Value Grvth

■ Long-term Earnings
■ Historical Earnings

Figure 3.14 **Stock ETF Tile Schematic**

In case more information is required beyond the assessment, a color band as a group can expand to show the detail data. Figure 3.15 expands one band in the Characteristics Tile to show how you can represent a detail display to understand the emerging market exposure across the regions.

ETF Characteristics - World Region

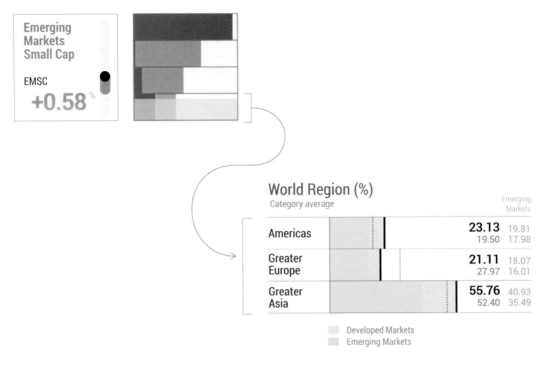

Figure 3.15 **Layered Tile Band–Level 1**

In the top Tile Band, the translucent yellow bar spans the entire row horizontally to show the percentage of the overall regional exposure within emerging markets. In the bottom bar chart, the color yellow shows you the slice of the emerging markets within each region. The vertical bold lines mark the bond fund's weights, whereas the dashed lines mark the category average weights. You may notice there is one case in which the marks slightly overlap—at the Americas category average dash line mark at 19.50 and the emerging markets yellow bar at 19.81. For these types of cases, numerical values uphold visual charts with data values. However, these specific values represent aggregated values that can be expanded upon. Next, Figure 3.16 shows the data within the region band.

ETF Characteristics - World Region Details

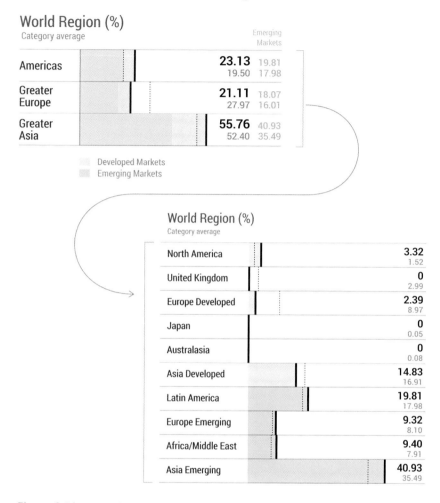

Figure 3.16 Layered Tile Band–Level 2

Layered Tile Band – Level 2 shows a more complete display of details to make the implicit explicit. The chart purposefully maintains a cross-region view. The deliberate decision to include all regions in one view rather than separate drill-down views provides the following benefits:

▶ **Context**—A view across the different regions shows the weights in context of all the regions.

- **Consistent order**—The detailed view is organized first by listing developed regions, and second by the emerging regions. This order mirrors the order of the Tile and follows the list of Americas, Greater Europe, Greater Asia, and Emerging.

- **Simple navigation**—A complete view eliminates the back and forth requirements of navigating up to drill back down again.

- **Flexibility**—You can decide which Tile views to include. For example, you are not forced to follow one sequential path but instead can bypass certain displays.

The next chart maintains the order of the regions, but changes alignment to guide an intelligent interpretation of the data. Figure 3.17 provides two displays of the data in side-by-side views.

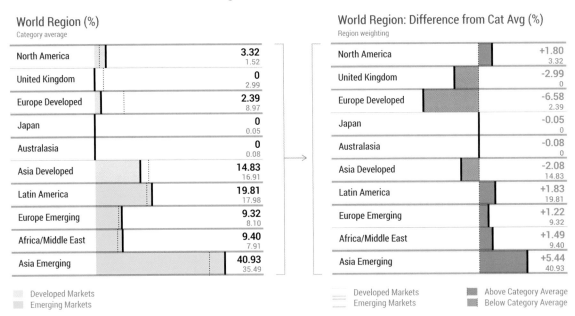

Figure 3.17 **Layered Tile Band–Level 2 Options**

Figure 3.17 shows how you can illustrate the same data, in the same order but with an altered visual structure to draw attention to a different point. The chart on the left starts the bar charts from a zero point on the left to compare region weights. The chart on the right places the starting point of the category average in the center and then assigns offsets from the category average. Under-exposure of a region is shown in orange, and over-exposure is shown in green; the yellow background highlights emerging markets.

Key Take-Aways

Seen as one of the fastest growing competitors to mutual funds, investors are flocking to ETFs, and assets managers are shifting their business structures to provide ETF selection. Similar data points and comparisons make it easy to apply the framework to both stock and bond mutual funds. The Stock ETF Tiles are an example of how to reuse the Tile schematic from one security to another. A key to reuse is to adapt the same set of drill-down displays used in other security profiles.

Tile Collection

The Tile Collection (Figure 3.18) shows the standardized Tiles and how they each apply to a few investment types. The collection displays the quote, characteristics, and resulting outcomes across stocks, bonds, stock mutual funds, and stock ETFs.

Diversity, relative rank, and conservative/aggressive profiles are all a part of the Tile communications. The push to standardize has brought with it benefits, not just for better comparison, but also for the opportunity to identify the key comparison points. You can decide to amend the framework and identify a different set of comparison points. The framework is flexible and can accommodate other aggregate values you would like to highlight.

Security Profiles

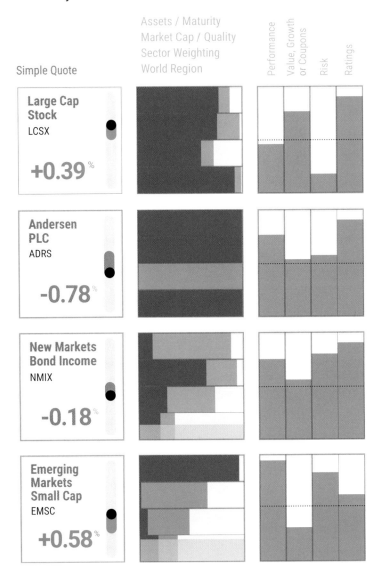

Simple Quote

Assets / Maturity
Market Cap / Quality
Sector Weighting
World Region

Performance
Value, Growth or Coupons
Risk
Ratings

Large Cap Stock
LCSX
+0.39 %

Andersen PLC
ADRS
-0.78 %

New Markets Bond Income
NMIX
-0.18 %

Emerging Markets Small Cap
EMSC
+0.58 %

Figure 3.18 **Tile Collection**

Because the top-level Tiles summarize and bring awareness to the data, additional Tiles can be displayed to represent the performance, value growth, risk, and ratings results. As an example, a variation from category average can show comparative performance results. Figure 3.19 shows how the framework can expand to include this variation with new Tile types.

Security Profiles

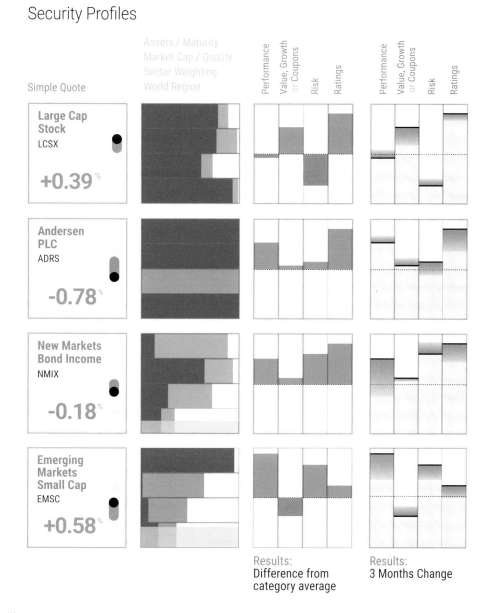

Figure 3.19 **Tile Collection with Results Tiles**

Extreme differences from the category average are a simple way to identify outliers. Both Results Tiles provide the opportunity to clearly spot those outliers (refer to Figure 3.19). Apart from the category average, you can use other types of reference points such as benchmark index, portfolio average, peer average, or a custom collection of averages. Additional Tiles can be included to show other comparative aspects of the data.

Key Take-Aways

Tiles are compact and communicate summary statements of representative data points (that is, outcomes of performance, value/growth, risk, and ratings). Each Tile is designed to summarize and surface the distinguishing traits of each security. For example, securities with unique characteristics such as stocks and other investments with emerging markets stand out from the list. The Stock Tile displays full color bands for characteristics, whereas the Stock ETF is diversified with investments in emerging markets shown with a yellow overlay. These distinctions define the security and make it easy to pick out from the collection.

As a collection, the Tiles are easy to compare and contrast. The layout enables you to review the Tiles in rows or columns. The Tile Framework enables comparison because each Tile has a consistent structure. Both the data and the presentation of the data have been normalized to make comparisons possible. For example, rows of Tiles describe the security; and each row contains the same number and order of Tiles. Meanwhile, columns of Tiles provide cross comparison of the list.

Summary

This chapter proposes a unified method to assess various securities within a single framework by using Tiles. Some visualizations require time to learn before you can immediately understand the data. The visualizations throughout this chapter do require some learning, but Tiles provide schematics to identify data points, so you don't have to memorize them. The following list includes unique visualization techniques covered in this chapter:

VISUALIZATION	DESCRIPTION	FIGURE
Tiles	A description of an entity with a set of square shapes that include current statistics and attributes of the entity.	3.1, 3.4, 3.6, 3.8
Tiles Schematic	A technique that explains and labels each data point in a Tile.	3.5, 3.7, 3.9, 3.14
Tile Collection	A list of Tiles organized in a grid to describe an entity and provide comparison across a full list of entities	3.18, 3.19

The Tile Framework is flexible and can be adapted to represent different data points. It can be extended to include more Tiles to describe a security, as shown in Figure 3.19; or it can scale to support other securities. The framework can be amended to include additional bands within the characteristics or results Tiles; or it can include different data points within each band. The framework is flexible in terms of how you drill down into subsequent detail views. You can elect which views to present when and link them together. The flexibility to adapt different data points must be paired with consistency to enable comparison: the number and type of bands, Tiles, and drill-down views must be the same throughout. Consistency makes the framework a reliable tool for assessing securities.

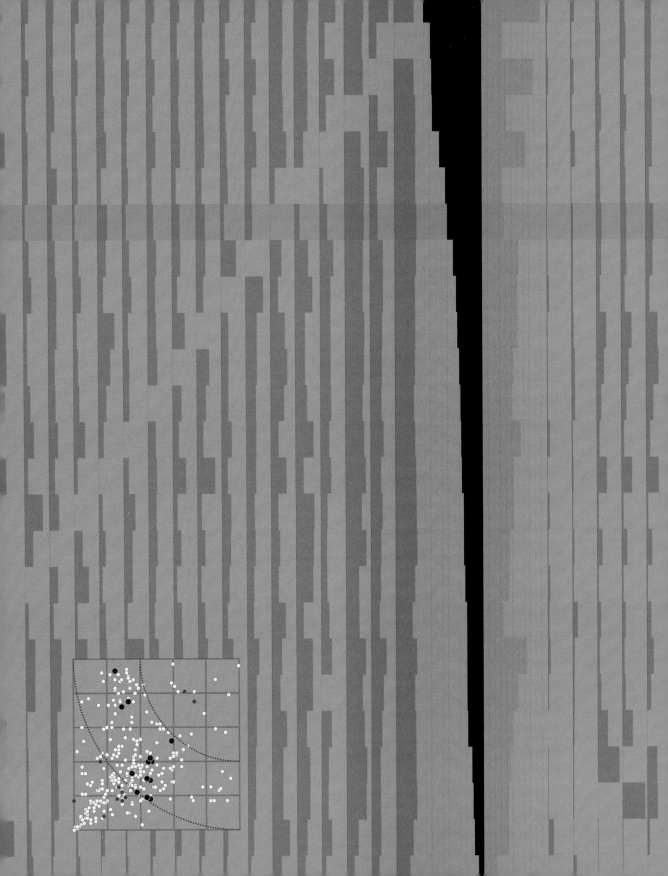

4

Portfolio Construction

Portfolio construction distinguishes itself as the phase in which all the efforts of various investment professionals come together to create the portfolio best suited for the client. In addition to the work performed in the Security Assessment phase of the Investment Process, the Portfolio Construction phase brings together three analytical tasks of a more global nature: Asset Allocation, Sector Analysis, and Risk Management.

Firms that place their primary emphasis on the Portfolio Construction phase believe there are forces at work at the market level, the asset class level, and at the sector level that are more than just the sum of the micro factors driving individual securities. Hence the focus of this chapter is on those firms that place an added priority on macro level thinking in the construct of their client portfolios.

This chapter uses macro level data sets to cover a range of Portfolio Construction activities that reflect on macro level thinking. It starts with a review of the efficient frontier to discuss the diversification space of asset allocation. Next, we review sector leadership data: One data set presents 20 years of sector performance ranking and another includes 22 alpha factors. Our last section on risk management involves multiple data visualizations: One set presents better methods to showcase the overlap of holdings and another presents stress tests across a set of portfolios.

NOTE The visualizations throughout this Chapter use representative sample data and are not specific to a source. Although the visualizations are designed as interactive displays that can be configured and navigated by an end user, they are also well suited to be incorporated into presentation materials.

Asset Allocation

The broadest, most macro-oriented level of thinking for the Portfolio Construction phase is that of Asset Allocation. This is the phase at which the organization determines the overall weights to be given in the portfolio (either at initiation or at reallocation) to major asset classes such as stocks, bonds, and cash. These weights may be expressed for some firms in absolute terms and for other firms as an over-weight or under-weight relative to some defined benchmark. The weights, when set, fluctuate with time, as discussed in Chapter 6, "Performance Measurement," and are subject to adjustment over time as the portfolio's investment results are received and interpreted.

Asset Allocation analysis can become tentative and fluctuate with the specific recommendations of the security analysts. Most Asset Allocation analysis is done through the use of asset class indexes serving as representative bogeys for the holdings of securities eventually chosen for the portfolios. This enables detailed analysis of a variety of asset mixes, and the development of useful visualizations regarding the risks and returns of those mixes, without the Portfolio Construction team having to wait on the results of the Security Assessment team. The visualizations offered here follow this accepted pattern of using broad market indexes to represent common asset classes.

As Modern Portfolio Theory (MPT) indicates, portfolio diversification leads to the "efficient frontier." The ability to show a risk and reward trade-off is often done with the context of the efficient frontier. To that end, Figures 4.1 and 4.2 use the efficient frontier as the underlying fabric to plot and compare asset allocation mixes.

Efficient Frontier/ Diversification Space

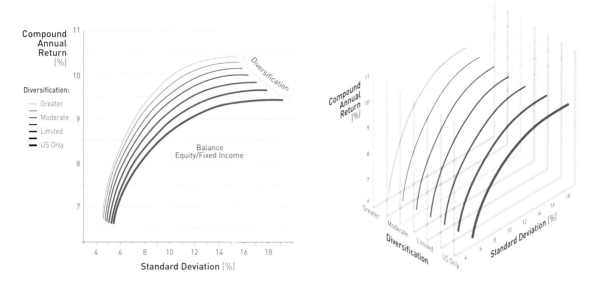

Figure 4.1 2-D to 3-D Surface

A benefit to the three-dimensional chart is that it illustrates a greater perspective of the actual shape of the object being rendered. As a contrast to a 2-D version, the 3-D version shows the true shape of the data. With the 3-D version, you can see the data as a curved plane. Because you can see the full plane, the plotted data points are also in full view.

In practice it may take a lot of computing power to identify and assess a current and proposed asset allocation mix for the wanted risk and reward levels. Depending on the firm, the universe of securities to assess and include in a portfolio can range from hundreds to tens of thousands. Because of this, binning assets (grouping by a defined interval) into the surface plot can adjust to meet what might be possible, required, and desirable from a computational performance standpoint.

Asset Allocation Coordinates

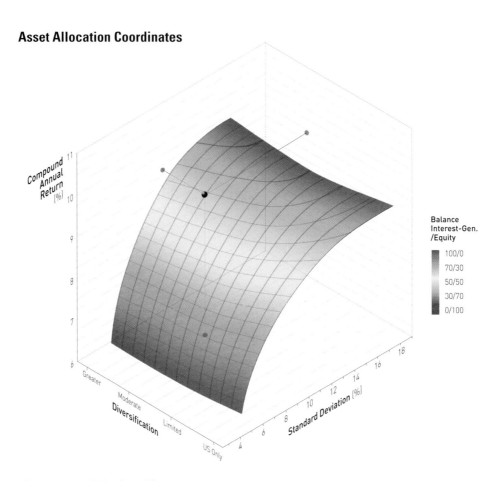

Figure 4.2 **3-D Surface Plot**

Although square binning (as illustrated on the surface of the 3-D surface plot in
Figure 4.2) is one of the simplest forms, hexagonal binning provides the best flexibility, efficiency, and data accuracy in a grid. The hexagon shape makes it more
accurate because the center point is equidistant to the vertex boarder points. It
is the shape that both creates a grid structure and has a lower perimeter to area
ratio. Figure 4.3 covers the surface plot with hexagonal binning to provide a
more flexible binning structure to mirror the universe of securities available.

Efficient Frontier: Asset Allocation Adjustments

		Current	Proposed	Adjustment
	Cmpnd. Annual Return	**8.9**	**9.6**	**+0.7**
	Simple Average Return	8.6	9.2	+0.6
	Standard Deviation	9.2	9.9	+0.7
	Sharpe Ratio	0.40	0.48	+0.08
Asset Allocation [%]	**Equity**	**43.3**	**36.2**	**-7.1**
	U.S. Stocks	34.2	21.0	-13.2
	Non-U.S. Stocks	7.1	25.2	+18.1
	Fixed Income	**48.0**	**39.6**	**-8.4**
	Short-Term Debt	27.3	22.0	-5.3
	U.S. Bonds	15.9	9.4	-6.5
	Non-U.S. Bonds	4.8	8.0	+3.2
	Alternative	**8.7**	**24.2**	**+15.5**
	Real Estate Securities	4.5	12.1	+7.6
	Commodity-Linked	4.2	12.1	+7.9

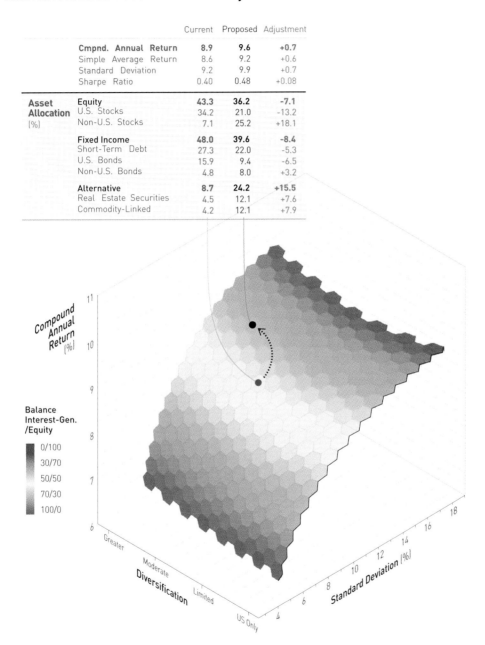

Figure 4.3 3-D Hexagonal Surface Plot

The hexagonal surface enables you to create an efficient frontier plot of your securities based on the precision you create. For example, you can control and to scale the bin sizes up or down so that large bins can target generalized asset allocation targets, whereas smaller bins can target more precise asset allocation targets.

The surface plot reveals the efficient frontier on the chart and makes the risk/ reward trade-off clear. Because the efficient frontier is based on estimates from past data and model projections, the panel is mapped to an estimated coordinate system to better optimize returns. For more specific data, the panel lists the corresponding information that maps to the identified location, current allocations based on historical data, and proposed allocations based on aggregate model projections. The data panel makes the 3-D Surface Plot more discernable.

In general, it is hard to discern a particular location or set of locations on three-dimensional charts because the perspective view loses a direct connection to the x-, y-, and z-axis. However, the data panel alleviates this challenge and pinpoints the values of the selected location. As an interactive system, the data panel can identify two locations for comparison. Therefore, the ability to identify the location on the chart with the data panel removes the general difficulties of a 3-D chart. As a means of comparing two data points across a curved plane, the 3-D version with the data panel provides a clear picture of the deltas between the two points.

Key Take-Aways

The 3-D Surface Plot (Figures 4.2 and 4.3) proves you can leverage the 3-D chart for its inherit strengths and amend its weaknesses with the introduction of data panels. As a method for comparing multiple asset allocations across a mix of asset classes, Figure 4.3 shows the location and the deltas of two specific asset balances in context of the efficient frontier. Data from the two asset balances are based on the surface locations. These locations use hexagonal binning to create the surface area of the plot. As a technique, hexagonal binning provides more flexibility and accuracy in your representation of the data. The shape creates accuracy, while the ability to scale the bin size up or down provides flexibility.

Sector Analysis

The next step down in the Portfolio Construction phase, after the Asset Allocation analysis has been performed, is to engage in Sector Analysis. The essence of Sector Analysis is that it is somewhat of a bridge between the high-level global macro factors that drive the asset classes and the most atomistic levels within those asset classes, namely the securities. Ultimately, the point of the offered visualizations will be to show how sector effects can best be visualized—the particular sector categorization scheme is less important; the offered techniques work whichever schema is chosen.

We choose to provide our visualization examples for Sector Analysis here in the Portfolio Construction chapter in keeping with the theme that there are driving factors in the market that can move either an asset class or a sector within an asset class. Studying sector returns reveals intriguing information. For example, from year to year the sector returns can vary widely between the top-performing and bottom-performing sectors. Many portfolio managers like to capitalize on these variations and are aware of their magnitude.

Sector Leadership

This section examines and compares various graphical methods for displaying sector returns. The following sector leadership charts provide a range of visual techniques that show you the advantages and disadvantages of displaying data differently. The Calendar Year Returns of the Russell 1000 equity index, as shown in Figure 4.4, shows a sector chart that is commonly used to illustrate relative ranking and absolute returns. This *sector chart*, also known and referenced in the industry as the *quilt chart* or *periodic table*, is often applied to other attributes such as asset classes, markets, and alpha factors across various timeframes.

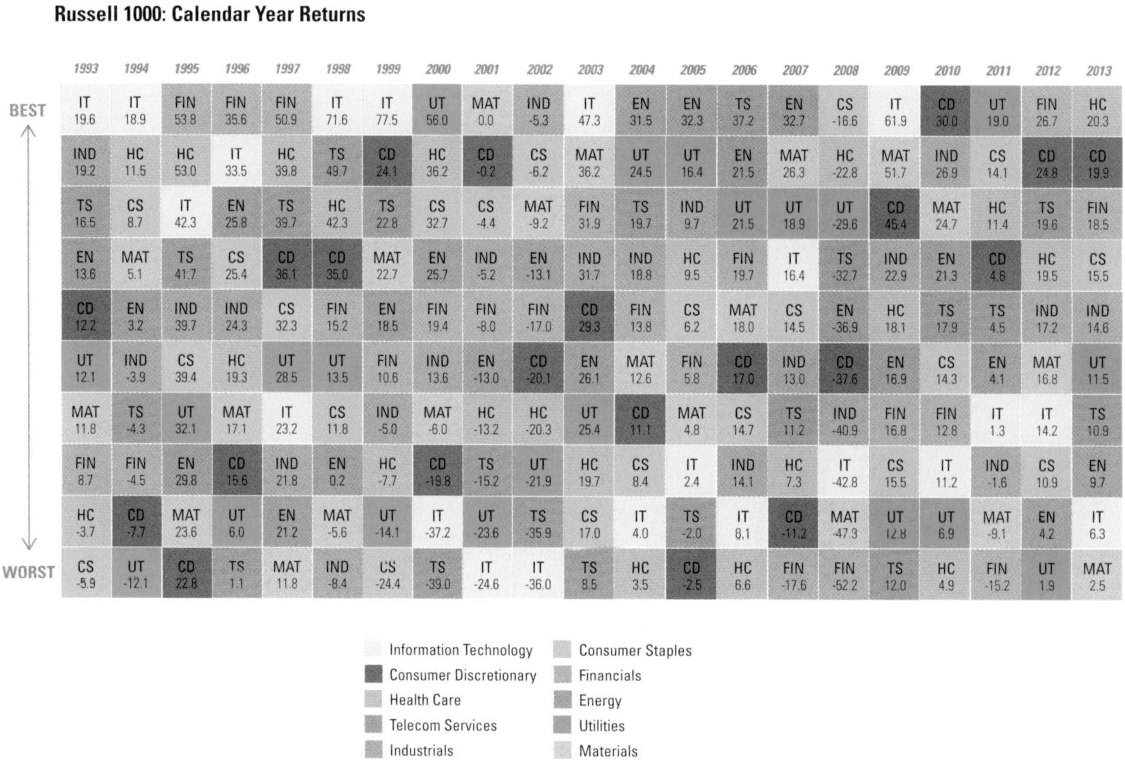

Russell 1000: Calendar Year Returns

	1993	1994	1995	1996	1997	1998	1999	2000	2001	2002	2003	2004	2005	2006	2007	2008	2009	2010	2011	2012	2013
BEST	IT 19.6	IT 18.9	FIN 53.8	FIN 35.6	FIN 50.9	IT 71.6	IT 77.5	UT 56.0	MAT 0.0	IND -5.3	IT 47.3	EN 31.5	EN 32.3	TS 37.2	EN 32.7	CS -16.6	IT 61.9	CD 30.0	UT 19.0	FIN 26.7	HC 20.3
	IND 19.2	HC 11.5	HC 53.0	IT 33.5	HC 39.8	TS 49.7	CD 24.1	HC 36.2	CD -0.2	CS -6.2	MAT 36.2	UT 24.5	UT 16.4	EN 21.5	MAT 26.3	HC -22.8	MAT 51.7	IND 26.9	CS 14.1	CD 24.8	CD 19.9
	TS 16.5	CS 8.7	IT 42.3	EN 25.8	TS 39.7	HC 42.3	TS 22.8	CS 32.7	CS -4.4	MAT -9.2	FIN 31.9	TS 19.7	IND 9.7	UT 21.5	UT 18.9	UT -29.6	CD 45.4	MAT 24.7	HC 11.4	TS 19.6	FIN 18.5
	EN 13.6	MAT 5.1	TS 41.7	CS 25.4	CD 36.1	CD 35.0	MAT 22.7	EN 25.7	IND -5.2	EN -13.1	IND 31.7	IND 18.8	HC 9.5	FIN 19.7	IT 16.4	TS -32.7	IND 22.9	EN 21.3	CD 4.6	HC 19.5	CS 15.5
	CD 12.2	EN 3.2	IND 39.7	IND 24.3	CS 32.3	FIN 15.2	EN 18.5	FIN 19.4	FIN -8.0	FIN -17.0	CD 29.3	FIN 13.8	CS 6.2	MAT 18.0	CS 14.5	EN -36.9	CS 18.1	TS 17.9	TS 4.5	IND 17.2	IND 14.6
	UT 12.1	IND -3.9	CS 39.4	HC 19.3	UT 28.5	UT 13.5	FIN 10.6	IND 13.6	EN -13.0	CD -20.1	EN 26.1	MAT 12.6	FIN 5.8	CD 17.0	IND 13.0	CD -37.6	EN 16.9	CS 14.3	EN 4.1	MAT 16.8	UT 11.5
	MAT 11.8	TS -4.3	UT 32.1	MAT 17.1	IT 23.2	CS 11.8	IND -5.0	MAT -6.0	HC -13.2	HC -20.3	UT 25.4	CD 11.1	MAT 4.8	CS 14.7	TS 11.2	IND -40.9	FIN 16.8	FIN 12.8	IT 1.3	IT 14.2	TS 10.9
	FIN 8.7	FIN -4.5	EN 29.8	CD 15.6	IND 21.8	EN 0.2	HC -7.7	CD -19.8	TS -15.2	UT -21.9	HC 19.7	CS 8.4	IT 2.4	IND 14.1	HC 7.3	IT -42.8	CS 15.5	IT 11.2	IND -1.6	CS 10.9	EN 9.7
	HC -3.7	CD -7.7	MAT 23.6	UT 6.0	EN 21.2	MAT -5.6	UT -14.1	IT -37.2	UT -23.6	TS -35.9	CS 17.0	IT 4.0	TS -2.0	IT 8.1	CD -11.2	MAT -47.3	UT 12.8	UT 6.9	MAT -9.1	EN 4.2	IT 6.3
WORST	CS -5.9	UT -12.1	CD 22.8	TS 1.1	MAT 11.8	IND -8.4	CS -24.4	TS -39.0	IT -24.6	IT -36.0	TS 8.5	HC 3.5	CD -2.5	HC 6.6	FIN -17.6	FIN -52.2	TS 12.0	HC 4.9	FIN -15.2	UT 1.9	MAT 2.5

Legend:
- Information Technology
- Consumer Discretionary
- Health Care
- Telecom Services
- Industrials
- Consumer Staples
- Financials
- Energy
- Utilities
- Materials

Figure 4.4 Quilt Chart

The Calendar Year Returns chart organizes the data into a series of small tiles that each represents a sector. The organizational principle of each column is to stack sector tiles in rank order of best to worst performance returns, whereas the horizontal sequence tracks yearly progression. Each sector is assigned a unique color, which is maintained across the horizontal sequence (i.e., over time), which when combined with the tiles creates a patchwork quilt effect.

The challenge with the Russell 1000 Calendar Year Returns chart is that it is not possible to see the actual numerical spread of sectoral investment performance within each year. The yearly spread has been visually eliminated and presented solely as numeric values—you are left to calculate the spread yourself. The Calendar Year Returns chart does not use visual cues to track spreads across the years but instead requires you to review each number and bit of text within each tile to derive the ranking, value, and name of each sector.

Next, consider an alternative approach to this same chart in which the table is organized by sector and the color scale is used to showcase the ranking. In the Calendar Year Returns: Sector Ranking version (Figure 4.5) a heatmap emphasizes sector ranking. A color gradient uses two opposite colors/hues to show a change in value.

Russell 1000: Calendar Year Returns

	1993	1994	1995	1996	1997	1998	1999	2000	2001	2002	2003	2004	2005	2006	2007	2008	2009	2010	2011	2012	2013
Energy	13.6	3.2	29.8	25.8	21.2	0.2	18.5	25.7	-13.0	-13.1	26.1	31.5	32.3	21.5	32.7	-36.9	16.9	21.3	4.1	4.2	9.7
Industrials	19.2	-3.9	39.7	24.3	21.8	-8.4	-5.0	13.6	-5.2	-5.3	31.7	18.8	9.7	14.1	13.0	-40.9	22.9	26.9	-1.6	17.2	14.6
Financials	8.7	-4.5	53.8	35.6	50.9	15.2	10.6	19.4	-8.0	-17.0	31.9	13.8	5.8	19.7	-17.6	-52.2	16.8	12.8	-15.2	26.7	18.5
Health Care	-3.7	11.5	53.0	19.3	39.8	42.3	-7.7	36.2	-13.2	-20.3	19.7	3.5	9.5	6.6	7.3	-22.8	18.1	4.9	11.4	19.5	20.3
Consumer Discretionary	12.2	-7.7	22.8	15.6	36.1	35.0	24.1	-19.8	-0.2	-20.1	29.3	11.1	-2.5	17.0	-11.2	-37.6	45.4	30.0	4.6	24.8	19.9
Information Technology	19.6	18.9	42.3	33.5	23.2	71.6	77.5	-37.2	-24.6	-36.0	47.3	4.0	2.4	8.1	16.4	-42.8	61.9	11.2	1.3	14.2	6.3
Consumer Staples	-5.9	8.7	39.4	25.4	32.3	11.8	-24.4	32.7	-4.4	-6.2	17.0	8.4	6.2	14.7	14.5	-16.6	15.5	14.3	14.1	10.9	15.5
Materials	11.8	5.1	23.6	17.1	11.8	-5.6	22.7	-6.0	0.0	-9.2	36.2	12.6	4.8	18.0	26.3	-47.3	51.7	24.7	-9.1	16.8	2.5
Telecom Services	16.5	-4.3	41.7	1.1	39.7	49.7	22.8	-39.0	-15.2	-35.9	8.5	19.7	-2.0	37.2	11.2	-32.7	12.0	17.9	4.5	19.6	10.9
Utilities	12.1	-12.1	32.1	6.0	28.5	13.5	-14.1	56.0	-23.6	-21.9	25.4	24.5	16.4	21.5	18.9	-29.6	12.8	6.9	19.0	1.9	11.5

Best of the Year ⟵----------------⟶ Worst of the Year

Figure 4.5 **Heatmap**

Figure 4.5 applies a heatmap technique to the same data and organizes the rows to track each sector performance over time. Each column contains tiles ranging from orange indicating the worst-performing sector to blue representing the best-performing sector. The years are still represented along the top to logically show the progression of time moving to the right.

Figure 4.5 illustrates incremental improvements in visual communication. Because the chart is structured with sectors listed in rows, it is easier for you to identify each sector and see how it has performed over time. The sector labels also eliminate the need to include the abbreviated sector text in each tile. The next chart takes a step further toward simplifying how to visually communicate the information. The gray scale shown in Figure 4.6 enables you to focus on a "unidirectional" system of rank.

Russell 1000: Calendar Year Returns

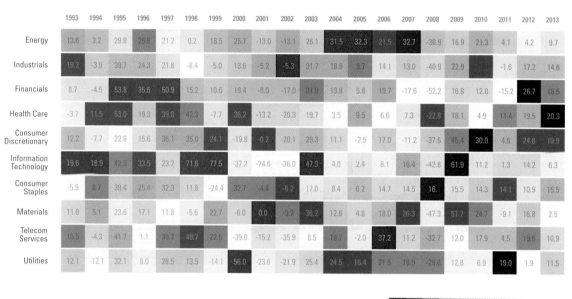

Best of the Year ←——————————→ Worst of the Year

Figure 4.6 **Grayscale Heatmap**

In contrast to a color gradient system that uses two opposite colors to represent a change in value, a unidirectional system gradually changes a single color value in one direction. The top-ranked sectors in each year are shown in black, whereas the bottom ranked sectors are shown in the lightest gray. You can quickly scan the chart and recognize the top-ranked sector as well as the bottom-ranked sector.

Though the use of gray scale can improve readability, other challenges remain. For example, the slight gradations of gray can make it difficult to distinguish between the middle-ranking sectors, fourth and fifth, or fifth and sixth sectors.

This type of chart should not be used for such granular analysis. However, Figure 4.7 shows another way to represent sector ranking that offers more precision to more directly determine relative ranking.

Calendar Year Returns: Sector Ranking

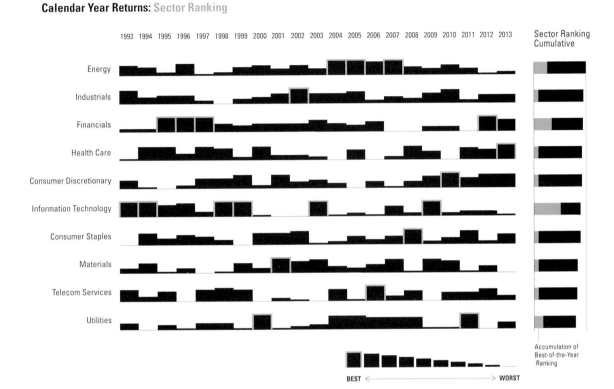

Figure 4.7 **Bar Track Chart–Row**

Much like a tapestry, Figure 4.7 shows a rich picture that tells an evolved story of the data. The height of each sector bar represents the corresponding rank as shown in the legend: The bar for the top-ranked sector in each calendar year is outlined in green and the levels to each of the bars correspond to sector ranking position. To the right of the chart, the bars under the Sector Ranking heading provide a broader contextual view of overall sector ranking. The full bar lengths represent the cumulative sector rankings across the years; Energy is listed at the top because it has the highest overall ranking, whereas Utilities listed at the bottom shows the lowest overall ranking. The green section of the bar shows how many times the sector held the top rank rating.

If you are interested in quickly seeing top-ranking sectors, you would favor a chart similar to Calendar Year Returns: Sector Ranking (Figure 4.7). The horizontal line visually attached to each sector makes it particularly easy to see how well a sector has performed over the 20 years. The green bar outline stands out and enables you to identify the top-ranked sector for each year.

The Sector Ranking Cumulative chart provides a summary view of the data to complete the data story. This cumulative data extends the chart and provides additional relative calculations in a visual easy-to-consume format. For example, as shown in Figure 4.7, the Energy sector has the highest cumulative ranking, whereas Information Technology has ranked first more often than any other sector. It is interesting to see just how close all sectors rank to each other in terms of cumulative ranking. It's likely that you would not be able to see the cumulative ranking if you had to rely solely on the yearly bar charts.

However, rank order is not the only important data point to highlight. The absolute value of returns and their variation is often essential to the overall analysis of sector performance. Figure 4.8 addresses this requirement.

The Calendar Year Returns: Sector Returns chart (refer to Figure 4.8) provides you with a sorted view based on the absolute returns of each sector. Here, individual black and red bars represent yearly intervals to indicate positive and negative return, respectively. Both sector and year average returns are also shown at the right and bottom of the chart. In this case, the averages are equally weighted by sector and calculated with losses and gains observed across the years.

The horizontal line that unites each sector enables you to read each sector as a group. The horizontal sector line serves two purposes 1) improves scanability, meaning that it provides a consistent anchor to follow a sector's performance across the years, and 2) creates space efficiency. By introducing color to represent negative or positive returns, the chart remains compact without taking up the space that would be needed to represent negative returns below the horizontal sector line. The color red is not just space-efficient but is also an easy mechanism to visually differentiate negative returns.

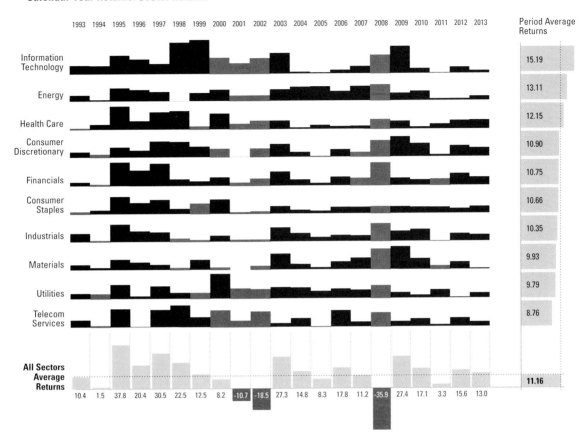

Calendar Year Returns: Sector Returns

Figure 4.8 **Bar Track Chart–Row with Pivot Summary**

The dotted line that represents the average line plus the text values enables you to compare a particular year's results to a historical average point of 11.16. For example, you can contrast Information Technology's average return of 15.19% to Telecom Services' 8.76% returns. Again, with the use of the average line, you are provided with a small but meaningful visual indicator that enables comparison across all these examples. Structuring the data in this visual format with the average line shows the deviation from the mean. You no longer have to be concerned with extracting meaning from numerical information, but instead you can extend and confirm your own knowledge with the use of the chart.

Despite these improvements to the Sector Returns chart, the relative ranking is missing. You may still question: *What was the top rank within each year?* Although the Sector Returns chart focuses on each sector, you may want to instead focus on each year. Perhaps, you would like to compare the relative returns of all the sectors within each year. Next, Figure 4.9 considers these additional points.

Calendar Year Returns: Sector Rank & Average Returns

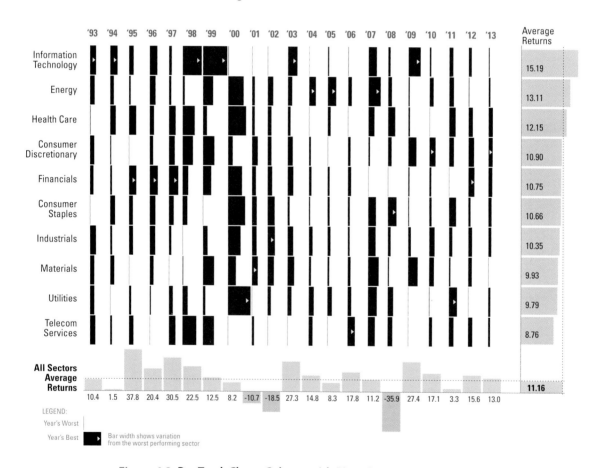

Figure 4.9 **Bar Track Chart–Column with Pivot Summaries**

Figure 4.9 focuses on sector differentiation by structuring the data to show relative sector returns. The chart introduces a yellow triangle to visually tag the best-ranking sector within each year and a thin black line to show the worst-ranking sector. In some years it might be difficult to distinguish the worst ranking sector. The width of each black bar is directly correlated to the variation from the worst-performing sector and therefore similar widths communicate small variations. The sort order and listing of the sectors is based on historical average returns. Combining the elements of rank, variation, and average returns underscores the overall relative nature of the chart:

▶ **Ranking**—In this chart (refer to Figure 4.9), iconography in the form of a yellow marker is introduced into the visualization to indicate which is the best-ranked sector. Yellow against black applies a high level of contrast that is well-suited to highlight exceptional occurrences.

▶ **Variation**—Organized by year, the relative return values are easy to detect and clearly show you the variations. The vertical alignment of the bar charts enables you to review each year and compare relative return values across sectors. For example, in 1999, Information Technology significantly over performed the worst sector, whereas Utilities only slightly over performed the worst sector. By disregarding the gain or loss aspect of performance and concentrating on sector differentiation, this view creates a clearer image of which sector performed better and by how much.

▶ **Average Returns**—As shown in the Sector Ranking chart(s), Information Technology, followed by Energy and Health Care are the top overall ranking sectors across the past 20 years. In addition, you can also put this in context with the period average returns for both the sector and year. The averages are equally weighted by sector and calculated with losses and gains observed. What is especially visible in this data representation is how relative performance spread changed from year to year, showing dramatic differences in 1999 and 2000 compared with greatly reduced sector variation in 2013.

Although Figure 4.9 provides a broad relative perspective of the data, another plausible option is part of relative performance. The Variation from all Sectors Average chart (Figure 4.10) manipulates the same data and showcases deviation from the mean.

Calendar Year Returns: Variation From All Sectors Average

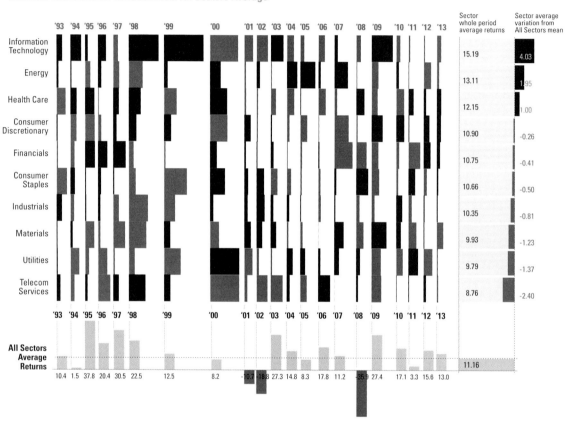

Figure 4.10 **Bar Track Chart–Column with Pivot Summaries**

The main intent of Figure 4.10 is to answer the question *With regard to sector leadership across the past 20 years, how much of a deviation from the all sectors' average (of 11.16) was observed?* This chart introduces deviation from the sectors' average with the use of color; black indicates a positive variation from the sectors' average, whereas red indicates a negative variation. The use of color in this manner introduces a concise and consistent way of displaying the Bar charts.

- ▶ **Concise Core Chart**—While maintaining a constant row height, the chart uses adjusted column widths to use horizontal space more efficiently. Without extending the width of the chart, you can understand that in 1999 Information Technology greatly over performed the 12.5% sector average for the year, whereas Consumer Staples greatly under performed.

- ▶ **Concise Average Returns**—Because the sectors are sorted by descending order, introducing color to this part of the chart enables you to quickly see the cut-off between a positive and negative deviation. To supplement, displaying the numeric value of the deviation from the mean enables you to numerically compare the averages and the deviation from the mean in the context of the visual display.

- ▶ **Consistent:** The consistent use of red and black provides a standard understanding of use. The average returns across the years are contrasted against the deviation from the mean with the use of color.

Knowing the relative nature of performance enables you to better present and analyze your own performance in a sector. At the bottom of the chart, the horizontal "All Sectors Average Returns" is shown as a reference point to review the core chart. For example, the year 2000 has the greatest under-performing deviations, as noted with Information Technology and Telecom Services, with a reference point of 8.2% as the average sector return. In contrast, in 2008, the average sector return was −35.9% and the Financials sector still had a considerable under-performing deviation from the mean. These reference points (like "All Sectors Average Returns") provide additional context to answer *"Exactly how bad is bad for this year if your money is in these sectors of the market?"*

Key Take-Aways

As shown in the Tapestry Bar Charts (Figures 4.7–4.10), different views of the same data sets can lead to better insights into sector performance. Each chart uses distinct structural and visual methods that offer a unique perspective of the data. Depending on the points you would like to make, you can select from any combination of these charts to further communicate or analyze returns. As a collection, the charts can convincingly illustrate a full spectrum of specific points you can convey to your audience.

Sectors and Alpha Factors

In Chapter 3, Security Assessment, we offer the idea of alpha factors that drive individual securities. In this chapter we offer the idea that there are sector effects separate from security factors, and we present visualization techniques for those in the preceding sections. In this section, however, we acknowledge that there is a hybrid concept—the idea that the securities within a sector might have different alpha factors—or react differently to the same alpha factors—as securities in other sectors. This information could have been offered in either chapter—we chose to offer it here.

Interactive tools that combine both sector groupings and alpha factor analysis take steps toward a powerful system that provides dynamic updates to filter, sort, and regroup the table display. The ability to select from a range of alpha factors that best align to the strategy is a key strength of a dynamic system. The ability to not only select various alpha factors but to also select date range and frequency adds flexibility to the system. You can ask the system, *Which sector performed the best in regards to alpha factor X? Which alpha factor showed the most consistent returns over the past ten years?*

The Prior Day Factor dashboard, as shown in Figure 4.11, is organized to show a spectrum of alpha factor returns across all the sectors for a specified time.

The table is constructed to show factor spreads and is organized in a range of positive to negative; green signifies positive, whereas red signifies negative. The top row, F1-FN Spread, summarizes alpha factor averages starting with the top returns of Beta and ending with the bottom returns of Long Term Momentum.

F1-FN are the factor exposures in which F1 is the first factor and FN is the subsequent list of factors. The numeric text inside each cell reinforces and reiterates the values with a corresponding color fill.

Prior Day Factor Dashboard

S&P 1500   Statistic: F1-FN Spread   Return Type: MTD Percent Change

	Beta	Vola-tility	B/P	S/P	ST Momen-tum	FY2 E/P	FY1 E/P	Liquid-ity	FCF/P	Short Interest/ Share	Lever-age	Days to Cover	14d RSI	E/P	LT Growth	90d Slope	3 Yr Sales Growth	3 Yr EPS Growth	Size	ROE	ROA	LT Momen-tum
F1-FN Spread	3.58	3.57	2.71	2.44	1.67	1.44	1.31	1.00	1.00	0.33	0.74	0.63	0.14	-0.10	-0.26	-0.41	-0.55	-1.13	-1.31	-1.83	-2.32	-4.24
Consumer Disc.	4.05	3.61	2.23	0.75	3.07	-0.87	-0.35	0.27	1.32	2.19	2.75	1.48	-0.51	-2.06	-0.70	-0.34	-0.51	-0.96	-2.17	-3.15	-3.97	-6.95
Consumer Stap.	3.84	2.52	2.66	1.98	-0.66	2.62	1.12	6.81	-1.43	4.42	-1.53	1.44	-1.05	-0.21	1.20	-1.62	2.93	1.10	-1.59	-0.17	-2.52	-3.31
Energy	3.68	-0.20	-2.69	-0.89	0.11	5.36	3.94	-0.83	5.34	-1.83	-0.95	-2.49	-0.34	2.15	5.22	4.90	-0.76	2.05	2.23	2.34	1.87	0.18
Financials	3.02	5.04	2.72	1.56	2.24	1.86	2.05	2.57	1.37	0.33	2.14	-0.30	-1.21	0.74	1.60	-0.56	-1.34	-2.39	0.54	-1.70	-0.47	-5.11
Health Care	2.06	4.37	2.38	4.27	-0.94	2.12	1.60	1.11	1.97	1.66	1.46	0.63	0.31	0.60	-0.46	-3.14	-0.92	2.14	-3.50	0.30	-1.11	-3.50
Industrials	4.18	4.21	6.33	5.54	0.70	1.60	0.64	0.19	0.66	0.00	0.34	0.29	0.45	-2.02	-0.31	-3.77	2.29	-1.12	-3.35	-4.52	-5.96	-4.94
IT	2.66	1.59	1.44	1.47	3.24	1.63	2.72	0.79	0.73	-0.18	-0.35	1.86	2.38	1.84	-3.82	1.44	1.25	-0.84	0.23	-0.44	-0.56	-2.34
Materials	7.80	9.25	6.19	7.42	1.49	2.64	1.30	4.85	-1.70	3.22	0.73	-0.26	-0.84	-0.49	2.25	2.07	-2.89	-4.45	-2.38	-4.07	-5.29	-6.59
Telecom Serv.	8.77	3.05	-5.82	2.68	8.79	-4.91	-4.91	-5.66	3.03	1.57	-3.64	5.04	3.03	-3.58	1.35	1.55	0.43	0.54	-7.74	-2.28	-3.38	-1.75
Utilities	1.33	-0.30	2.39	-0.38	0.23	0.09	-0.81	-0.10	-1.34	0.01	-0.19	-0.21	0.62	0.10	0.05	0.17	1.16	-0.44	-0.51	-1.90	-1.45	-1.36

Figure 4.11 **Heatmap–Green and Red**

Presorting and organizing data into clear groups of performance leaders and performance laggers is a useful technique many find effective. Despite this improvement of an organized table, there are a few shortcomings to the visual. The combination of the numbers and color fill is conflicting and makes a dark color and bold text fight for your attention. In addition, the list of alpha factors is shown as a flat list with no organizational constructs. This sample data shows 22 alpha factors. *How can this dashboard be designed to scale up and double or triple in size? As a dashboard display, what can be done to bubble up information into consolidated space efficient displays?*

Mixing a table of data with visual indicators is often used in spreadsheets. In theory, this overall approach is a good one because it presents both textual information and visual information. Relying solely on hue-based visual indicators can be tough for the color-blind reader to decode. Therefore, showing the text as a supplement can be the supporting attribute to the visual. Alternative methods improve the legibility of the text but enable the color to act as a supporting visual aide. To improve the legibility, first consider the step to change the cell color, as shown in Figure 4.12.

NOTE The inability to distinguish between green and red colors is by far the most common color vision deficiency and impacts 8% of the worldwide male population and 0.5% of the female population. ("Color Perception" by Michael Kalloniatis and Charles Luu. Table 1 Prevalence of congenital colour deficiencies. (http://webvision.med.utah.edu/book/part-viii-gabac-receptors/color-perception/))

Prior Day Factor Dashboard

S&P 1500   Statistic: F1-FN Spread   Return Type: MTD Percent Change

	Beta	Volatility	B/P	S/P	ST Momentum	FY2 E/P	FY1 E/P	Liquidity	FCF/P	Short Interest/Share	Leverage	Days to Cover	14d RSI	E/P	LT Growth	90u Slope	3 Yr Sales Growth	3 Yr EPS Growth	Size	ROE	ROA	LT Momentum
F1-FN Spread	3.58	3.57	2.71	2.44	1.67	1.44	1.31	1.00	1.00	0.33	0.74	0.63	0.14	-0.10	-0.26	-0.41	-0.55	-1.13	-1.31	-1.83	-2.32	-4.24
Energy	3.68	-0.20	-2.69	-0.89	0.11	5.36	3.94	-0.83	5.34	-1.83	-0.95	-2.49	-0.34	2.15	5.22	4.90	-0.76	2.05	2.23	2.34	1.87	0.18
Materials	7.80	9.25	6.19	7.42	1.49	2.64	1.30	4.85	-1.70	3.22	0.73	-0.26	-0.84	-0.49	2.25	2.07	-2.89	-4.45	-2.38	-4.07	-5.29	-6.59
Consumer Stap.	3.84	2.52	2.66	1.98	-0.66	2.62	1.12	6.81	-1.43	4.42	-1.53	1.44	-1.05	-0.21	1.20	-1.62	2.93	1.10	-1.59	-0.17	-2.52	-3.31
IT	2.66	1.59	1.44	1.47	3.24	1.63	2.72	0.79	0.73	-0.18	-0.35	1.86	2.38	1.84	-3.82	1.44	1.25	-0.84	0.23	-0.44	-0.56	-2.34
Financials	3.02	5.04	2.72	1.56	2.24	1.86	2.05	2.57	1.37	0.33	2.14	-0.30	-1.21	0.74	1.60	-0.56	-1.34	-2.39	0.54	-1.70	-0.47	-5.11
Health Care	2.06	4.37	2.38	4.27	-0.94	2.12	1.60	1.11	1.97	1.66	1.46	0.63	0.31	0.60	-0.46	-3.14	-0.92	2.14	-3.50	0.30	-1.11	-3.50
Industrials	4.18	4.21	6.33	5.54	0.70	1.60	0.64	0.19	0.66	0.00	0.34	0.29	0.45	-2.02	-0.31	-3.77	2.29	-1.12	-3.35	-4.52	-5.96	-4.94
Consumer Disc.	4.05	3.61	2.23	0.75	3.07	-0.87	-0.35	0.27	1.32	2.19	2.75	1.48	-0.51	-2.06	-0.70	-0.34	-0.51	-0.96	-2.17	-3.15	-3.97	-6.95
Utilities	1.33	-0.30	2.39	-0.38	0.23	0.09	-0.81	-0.10	-1.34	0.01	-0.19	-0.21	0.62	0.10	0.05	0.17	1.16	-0.44	-0.51	-1.90	-1.45	-1.36
Telecom Serv.	8.77	3.05	-5.82	2.68	8.79	-4.91	-4.91	-5.66	3.03	1.57	-3.64	5.04	3.03	-3.58	1.35	1.55	0.43	0.54	-7.74	-2.28	-3.38	-1.75

Figure 4.12 Heatmap–Blue and Orange

The Heatmap – Blue and Orange replaces the previous green and red colors with blue and orange; in this case, blue signifies positive performance, whereas orange signifies negative performance. The top row labeled F1-FN Spread drives the organizational structure of ordering the factors from positive returns on the left to negative returns on the right. In addition to this left-to-right organization, the sectors in the table have also been reordered by performance. Energy and Materials are both listed at the top of the list with the best overall performance, whereas Utilities and Telecom Services are listed at the bottom with the worst overall performance, which is determined by the average across the alphas.

Two modifications have been introduced in Figure 4.12. The first improves legibility to the red/green colorblind community with the use of blue and orange. The second slightly changes the organizational structure of the chart by altering the sector order by performance. These two small modifications become the foundational stepping stones that enable more improvements.

A common practice is to combine the list of alpha factors into groups to answer: *Which sector provides the best overall returns within risk or growth factors?* Figures 4.13 and 4.14 introduce the organizational construct of factor groupings.

Rather than analyzing individual factors, Heatmap Groups create categories of alpha factors for you to evaluate and see how categorical groupings either have consistent or inconsistent returns across all sectors. The dashboard display can also analyze each sector independently. For example, earnings per share of Information Technology shows positive performance both at the category level and at the individual factor level. Equipped with categorized data, you can more readily spot themes in the data.

Prior Day Factor Dashboard

S&P 1500   Statistic: F1-FN Spread   Return Type: MTD Percent Change

	Risk					Tech Trends				Value					Growth				Per Share			
	Beta	Vola-tility	Liquid-ity	Days to Cover	Lever-age	ST Momen-tum	Short Interest/ Share	14d RSI	90d Slope	S/P	B/P	FCF/P	ROE	ROA	LT Growth	3 Yr Sales Growth	3 Yr EPS Growth	LT Momen-tum	FY2 E/P	FY1 E/P	E/P	Size
Energy	3.68	-0.20	-0.83	-2.49	-0.95	0.11	-1.83	-0.34	4.90	-0.89	-2.69	5.34	2.34	1.87	5.22	-0.76	2.05	0.18	5.36	3.94	2.15	2.23
Materials	7.80	9.25	4.85	-0.26	0.73	1.49	3.22	-0.84	2.07	7.42	6.19	-1.70	-4.07	-5.29	2.25	-2.89	-4.45	-6.59	2.64	1.30	-0.49	-2.38
Consumer Stap.	3.84	2.52	6.81	1.44	-1.53	-0.66	4.42	-1.05	-1.62	1.98	2.66	-1.43	-0.17	-2.52	1.20	2.93	1.10	-3.31	2.62	1.12	-0.21	-1.59
IT	2.66	1.59	0.79	1.86	-0.35	3.24	-0.18	2.38	1.44	1.47	1.44	0.73	-0.44	-0.56	-3.82	1.25	-0.84	-2.34	1.63	2.72	1.84	0.23
Financials	3.02	5.04	2.57	-0.30	2.14	2.24	0.33	-1.21	-0.56	1.56	2.72	1.37	-1.70	-0.47	1.60	-1.34	-2.39	-5.11	1.86	2.05	0.74	0.54
Health Care	2.06	4.37	1.11	0.63	1.46	-0.94	1.66	0.31	-3.14	4.27	2.38	1.97	0.30	-1.11	-0.46	-0.92	2.14	-3.50	2.12	1.60	0.60	-3.50
Industrials	4.18	4.21	0.19	0.29	0.34	0.70	0.00	0.45	-3.77	5.54	6.33	0.66	-4.52	-5.96	-0.31	2.29	-1.12	-4.94	1.60	0.64	-2.02	-3.35
Consumer Disc.	4.05	3.61	0.27	1.48	2.75	3.07	2.19	-0.51	-0.34	0.75	2.23	1.32	-3.15	-3.97	-0.70	-0.51	-0.96	-6.95	-0.87	-0.35	-2.06	-2.17
Utilities	1.33	-0.30	-0.10	-0.21	-0.19	0.23	0.01	0.62	0.17	-0.38	2.39	-1.34	-1.90	-1.45	0.05	1.16	-0.44	-1.36	0.09	-0.81	0.10	-0.51
Telecom Serv.	8.77	3.05	-5.66	5.04	-3.64	8.79	1.57	3.03	1.55	2.68	-5.82	3.03	-2.28	-3.38	1.35	0.43	0.54	-1.75	-4.91	-4.91	-3.58	-7.74
Average	4.14	3.31	1.00	0.75	0.08	1.83	1.14	0.28	0.07	2.44	1.78	1.00	-1.56	-2.28	0.64	0.16	-0.44	-3.57	1.21	0.73	-0.29	-1.82

Figure 4.13 **Heatmap Groups**

Prior Day Factor Dashboard

Figure 4.14 Heatmap Groups–With and Without Numeric Values

Dashboard displays are often used to get an overall view of status and key performance indicators. In a relatively small amount of space, dashboards are meant to bubble up the most salient information. As an interactive display, a dashboard can be flexible to progressively display either more or less details of the data. High-level, mid-level and detail views provide the rationale for and disclosure of what is behind the numbers.

These particular types of dashboards are easy to implement with Excel's conditional cell formatting. Because of this, heatmap dashboards are commonly used to highlight individual and aggregate cell data. Yet there are specific techniques that can push the dashboard metaphor further. For example, an interactive dashboard can progressively disclose more details within the same view. Interactive systems are designed and built to display various states, each controlled by the end user. In addition, you can remove the numerical data and present only the color cells. Figure 4.15 consolidates the alpha factor groups to a single value.

Prior Day Factor Dashboard

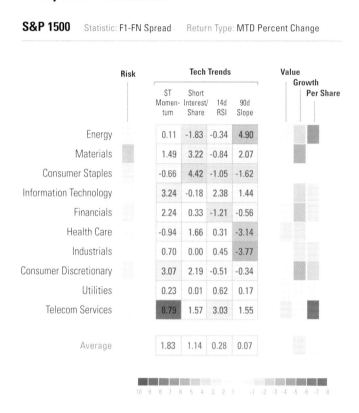

S&P 1500   Statistic: F1-FN Spread   Return Type: MTD Percent Change

	Risk	Tech Trends				Value	Growth Per Share
		ST Momen- tum	Short Interest/ Share	14d RSI	90d Slope		
Energy		0.11	-1.83	-0.34	4.90		
Materials		1.49	3.22	-0.84	2.07		
Consumer Staples		-0.66	4.42	-1.05	-1.62		
Information Technology		3.24	-0.18	2.38	1.44		
Financials		2.24	0.33	-1.21	-0.56		
Health Care		-0.94	1.66	0.31	-3.14		
Industrials		0.70	0.00	0.45	-3.77		
Consumer Discretionary		3.07	2.19	-0.51	-0.34		
Utilities		0.23	0.01	0.62	0.17		
Telecom Services		8.79	1.57	3.03	1.55		
Average		1.83	1.14	0.28	0.07		

10 9 8 7 6 5 4 3 2 1   -1 -2 -3 -4 -5 -6 -7 -8

Figure 4.15   **Heatmap Groups–Consolidated**

This display can reduce the number of columns from the original 17 (refer to Figure 4.10) to 4. This flexible approach opens the possibility for you to abstract the data, show the details, or include more group factors into the view.

In many cases, you may want to select from a range of alpha factors, inspect a few closely, and then maintain the other alpha factors in view as a point of comparison. Interactive dashboards can be flexible and enable varying levels of detail to be set by each factor group. Figure 4.16 illustrates the varying levels you can display.

Prior Day Factor Dashboard

S&P 1500

Statistic: F1-FN Spread   Return Type: MTD Percent Change

S&P 1500

Statistic: F1-FN Spread

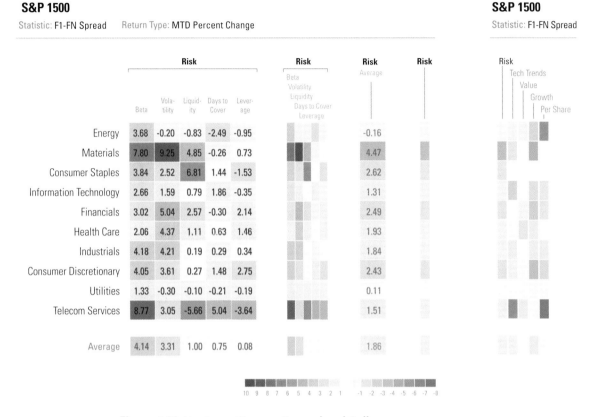

	Beta	Vola-tility	Liquid-ity	Days to Cover	Lever-age		Risk Average
Energy	3.68	-0.20	-0.83	-2.49	-0.95		-0.16
Materials	7.80	9.25	4.85	-0.26	0.73		4.47
Consumer Staples	3.84	2.52	6.81	1.44	-1.53		2.62
Information Technology	2.66	1.59	0.79	1.86	-0.35		1.31
Financials	3.02	5.04	2.57	-0.30	2.14		2.49
Health Care	2.06	4.37	1.11	0.63	1.46		1.93
Industrials	4.18	4.21	0.19	0.29	0.34		1.84
Consumer Discretionary	4.05	3.61	0.27	1.48	2.75		2.43
Utilities	1.33	-0.30	-0.10	-0.21	-0.19		0.11
Telecom Services	8.77	3.05	-5.66	5.04	-3.64		1.51
Average	4.14	3.31	1.00	0.75	0.08		1.86

10 9 8 7 6 5 4 3 2 1   -1 -2 -3 -4 -5 -6 -7 -8

Figure 4.16 Heatmap Groups–Expand and Collapse

The ability to customize and see details within aggregated data sets provides various levels of context. The benefits of a flexible system (refer to Figure 4.16) that ranges from detail to aggregate are three-fold:

▶ **Smoothly Scale**—The ability to expand and collapse heatmap groups enables you to scale. You can scale up and include more alpha factors all in the same view without compromising the results of the communication.

▶ **Track Themes**—Aggregations enable patterns and themes to emerge in the data. Secondary and tertiary levels of aggregation provide enough abstraction in the heat map views to scan the dashboard and confidently evaluate common behaviors in the data as themes. In addition, you can validate the observed theme by navigating to a more detailed view.

▶ **Focus Attention**—Fully expanded detail views of the data provide focus with color and numerical data present for close inspection. The navigation system across the levels enables you to select a set of alpha factors to closely review and still maintain a summarized view of the other factors.

Key Take-Aways

The Prior Day Dashboard is a tool that is both legible and flexible enough to reveal themes. By first converting the red/green colors to an orange/blue combination and then reordering the sectors by performance, you can improve the legibility of the dashboard. The color change also improves the legibility of the numeric values. Because the background color is subdominant, you can embed or omit the numeric values from the cell and not compromise the legibility of the color value or the numeric value. Second, flexibility is achieved through navigation. You can navigate through three levels, ranging from a detail view to an aggregate view. Combining both design principles of legibility and flexibility creates results that help you discover themes in the data.

Risk Management

Risk Management can be divided between *ex ante* Risk Management and *ex post* Risk Management. *Ex ante* Risk Management takes place during the Portfolio Construction phase of the Investment Process. The phrase *ex ante* refers to the idea of analyzing the risk in the portfolio (or even in the individual securities) prior to the portfolio being implemented. As such the analysis of risk at the pre-implementation phase of Portfolio Construction allows for, just as in the Asset Allocation phase, the consideration of many different potential combinations of asset classes, sectors, and portfolios. Whereas up to this point in the chapter the analysis of asset mixes, sector weights, and individual securities has focused on the value that each decision might add to the overall portfolio, *ex ante* Risk Management recasts those possible combinations according to what pain they might cause the portfolio if implemented. There is no free lunch, as the saying goes, and for every combination that might add value to a portfolio, there is the risk of loss and/or under-performance of a benchmark.

This section covers examples that can be used in both *ex-post* and *ex-ante* Risk Management. However, the set of three Risk Management methods provided here can be used to inform Portfolio Construction and as such have been incorporated into this section. The first method reviews the overlap of holdings and searches for high correlations in the data. The second method models various risk scenarios as a series of what-if scenarios. Stress testing provides a view into relative losses due to exogenous shocks and the absolute amount of the loss. The third example addresses multifactor risk attribution: The investigative process to identify where risk is coming from. Although the examples are shown at the firm level, you can also apply these methods to a group of funds or to an individual portfolio.

The responsibility to perform *ex ante* Risk Management may fall onto any number of individuals, depending on the investment philosophy of the investment firm. In most cases, however, *ex ante* Risk Management—especially at the Portfolio Construction level—falls to the Portfolio Management team to execute. Other parties may sometimes be involved in contributing to the *ex ante* Risk Management process as well. For example, there may be an independent risk or compliance unit in the firm that enforces the idea that there are limits and identifies what those limits should be to the *ex ante* risk that can be taken by the Portfolio Manager in the construction of the portfolio. There may also be *ex ante* risk analysis performed in the Security Assessment phase, assessing the level of individual risk inherent in a given security (such as identifying the level of beta of a stock), but by and large the true *ex ante* Risk Management task is performed by the Portfolio Manager while constructing the final portfolio. Hence the visualizations presented here focus on being of use to the Portfolio Manager in thinking about the level of *ex ante* risk suitable for the portfolio.

Overlap of Holdings

A part of managing risk is understanding exactly where investments are placed and sized and how this maps to exposure. Severe overlap of holdings among funds or client portfolios creates risk by having too much in a particular investment; it removes the efficiency gains of diversification and relies on select investments to do well for the full portfolio to do well. It should be noted that this type of risk can be both to the client—who may have holdings in many different funds that overlap and thus is not as diversified as they would like to be—and to the firm, where the repeated offerings of products for clients that are similar cause a business concentration for the firm. To understand how much is invested in a particular security, company, industry, or sector, a report that shows the overlap of holdings across funds or portfolios is often conducted. Overlap of holdings is a practical tool that illustrates both sides of the investment; how much does fund A hold of fund B as well as how much does fund B hold of fund A.

Overconcentration of a holding occurs for several reasons. First, market movements change the market value of a holding to push the overlap into a higher concentration of redundancy. Second, a specific investment style or time horizon, often set by the client, influences a similar set of underlying securities that leads to overlap. Third, because securities are selected based on a range of attributes, it is possible for the same security to be included in different funds with different investment styles. Forth, it is not uncommon for the same provider to have funds that have significant overlap in holdings.

Regardless of the overlap reasons, the first step is to be aware of the overlap by identifying high concentrations of exposure. This section showcases three alternative charts that improve how you identify these high concentrations of exposure. To take this first step to identify overlaps, review a typical overlap of holdings chart, as shown in Figure 4.17.

The Holdings Overlap chart is a common tool that often uses a tricolor coding system to identify the overlap between funds. As a representation of the frequency of occurrence in which two funds hold the same security, the holdings overlap percentages are based on market value; orange represents more than 50% market value, gray represents a 25–50% overlap, whereas blue represents less than 25%. By scanning the chart, you can identify the bands of orange that flow through the investments. You can also use the color codes to identify which funds have the largest overlap by category. Despite this ability to scan, there are a number of shortcomings to the chart that lead to misunderstanding and visual noise.

Holdings Overlap

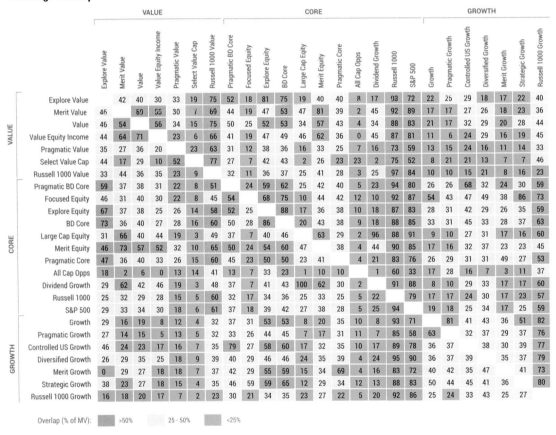

Figure 4.17 **Frequency Matrix**

The chart can easily be misunderstood. You could read the chart by first tracking the column and then the row. This interpretation would result in reading down the column label "Select Value Cap" and looking across the row label "Pragmatic Value." This order would result in an interpretation that 23% of the market value of the Select Value Cap fund consists of securities that can be found in the Pragmatic Value fund. However, this is not the right interpretation. If you read across the row labeled "Select Value Cap," and look down the column entitled "Pragmatic Value," you see the number "52." This means that 52% of the market value of the Select Value Cap fund consists of securities that can be found in the Pragmatic Value fund; this is the correct interpretation.

The second shortcoming of the chart is the visual noise attributed to the cell clutter. Each number within the cells collectively adds clutter to the visual. You do not need to be aware, nor can you simultaneously process all the numbers listed inside each cell. You can focus only on a few numbers at a time. Therefore, the additional numbers add unnecessary clutter to the chart.

Another shortcoming of the chart is how the chart tracks each number. The relationship of holdings from fund A to B and likewise fund B to A requires diligent tracking. Looking up and using the row and column headers as a coordinate system to map these two relationships are additional steps you are forced to take to compare these two numbers. Next, you are required to repeat this manual mapping for each additional set of funds, adding more complexity as multiple sets are tracked and compared.

Instead, consider an alternative that no longer requires this tracking to occur, reduces the visual noise each number creates, and reduces the instructional requirements to read the chart. The set of four visualizations shown in Figures 4.18–4.21 provides an alternative that addresses these points.

Holdings Overlap

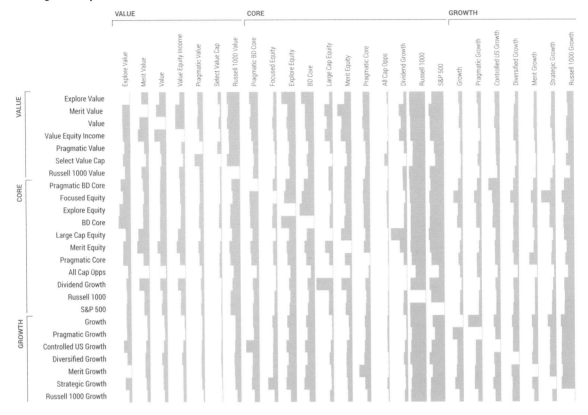

Figure 4.18 Butterfly Chart - Closed

Figure 4.18 is structured with the same row and column structure as its predecessor (refer to Figure 4.17). However, the tricolor system and numbers have been replaced with right-aligned bar graphs that represent the market value percentage overlap. The sheer size of the bar illustrates the concentration of overlap. Alignment of the market value by the column header suggests a comparison that first starts with the column header. By providing focus on the column, you start by reading the chart from top to bottom and therefore deduce the order of operations to be the funds in column header A are xx% (a certain percentage) in row header B.

Figure 4.19 shows you how to review the levels of overlap and readily see overlaps between A to B as well as B to A. The chart name, Butterfly, reflects the way the chart works, which is evident in the figure.

Holdings Overlap

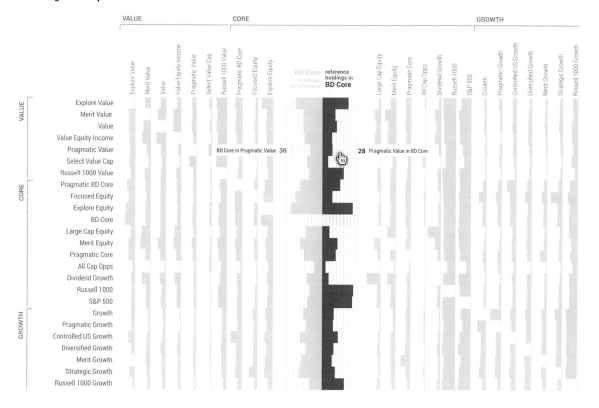

Figure 4.19 **Butterfly Chart—Opened**

The opened view displayed in Figure 4.19 shows the user controlling the chart and actively selecting a column to open and review the contents. As the column opens, the contents are revealed in a Butterfly Bar chart pattern. The column contents contain expanded bar graphs that provide more detail to the overlap between both funds. The technique of using the Butterfly Bar chart also includes light vertical lines for comparison as well as two-toned colors to delineate each percentage overlap. Within this interactive tool you can elect to open multiple funds for further comparison. The numbers that represent the percentage overlap relationship are shown within each open set of columns and map back to the column headers.

As you highlight each row, two numbers are revealed to show the overlap relationship. The yellow row highlight serves multiple functions: 1) identifies current focus location (in the case of interruption); 2) tracks each row label with the visual data; and 3) progressively reveals data details only as you inspect the chart closely. You can further organize the chart via sorting, as shown in Figures 4.20 and 4.21.

Holdings Overlap

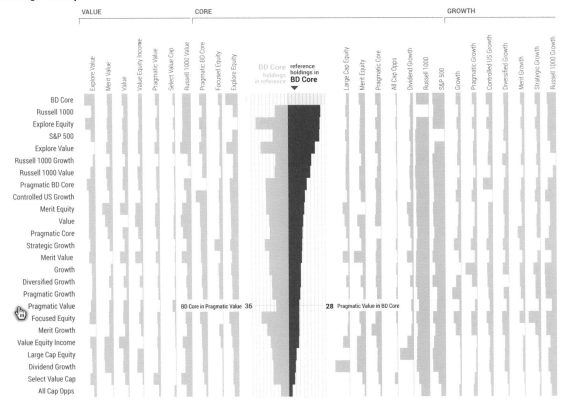

Figure 4.20 **Butterfly Chart–Opened and Sorted**

Holdings Overlap

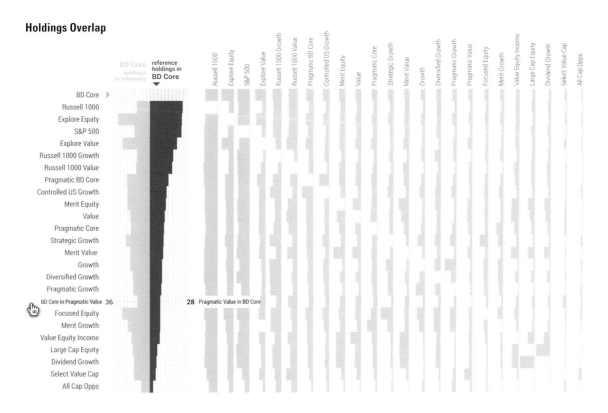

Figure 4.21 **Butterfly Chart–Opened and Sorted**

As shown in Figure 4.20, you can reorder the funds to be listed by descending order of market value % overlap. In Figure 4.21, a secondary sort organizes all funds to be sorted from left to right and top to bottom by percentage overlap. In this case, both the columns and row headers are reordered to reflect the new organization. Because the rows and columns are reordered, the group headings no longer apply and are removed from the chart. This final view resolves three major issues posed at the start:

▶ **Manual tracking**—*How can you eliminate the need to manually track each pairing?* The Butterfly bars show each set of holdings in a side-by-side view to eliminate manual tracking and the need to look up each holdings pair.

▶ **Visual noise**—*How can you reduce the visual noise each number collectively creates within each cell yet still provide this detail information?* The numbered cells are replaced with bars. Removing numbers from the majority of the chart also removes distracting visual noise that impedes your ability to focus on a set of holdings. The numbers are present on the opened set of holdings.

▶ **Instructional directions**—*How do you improve the instructional requirements and equip your audience with a clear understanding of how to read the chart?* The column headers shift so that the full labels appear only within the expanded columns. The instructions are embedded within the labels specifically tailored to each column header.

Despite these improvements, the Butterfly chart is missing the tricolor system that categorizes each band of holdings into three tiers. The next solution provides these categorical groups of holdings to reinstate the original three-tier system. Figures 4.22 and 4.23 explore this approach with the same data.

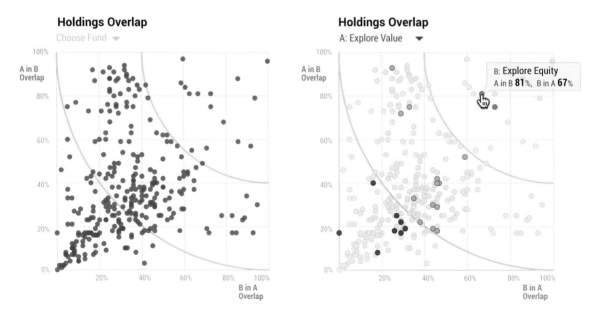

Figure 4.22 **Tiered Scatter Plot**

The Tiered Scatter Plot transfers the row/column header into an x-axis and y-axis coordinate system. The Tiered Scatter Plot is an interactive system that enables you to interact with the plot or select a fund from the drop-down list. This action highlights the fund location across the scatter plot. In addition, a mouse-over state within the scatter plot identifies the fund and displays the two percentages of A in B as well as B in A. The orange and blue arcs represent three tiers to identify each category threshold. All funds plotted within the orange arc are funds that have the highest overlap. All the funds between the blue and orange arcs are funds that have moderate overlap, whereas all funds below the blue arc represent low overlap percentages.

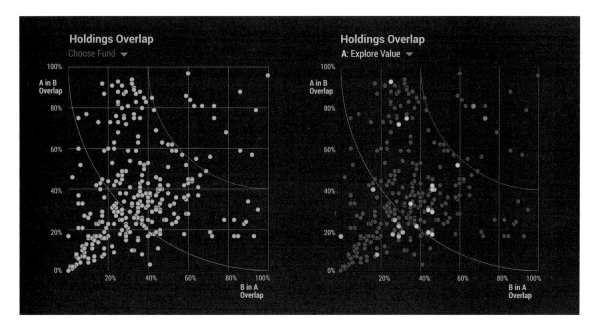

Figure 4.23 **Tiered Scatter Plot—Black**

The black background for screen use can be useful in environments in which the room lighting is dark and other applications on screen are also presented with black backgrounds. For example, if you use multiple screens and have an application like Bloomberg (or any other application that uses a black background) you will find it easier on your eyes to read the information with a black background across all your screens. The human eye can take up to 20–30 minutes to adjust from a dark environment to a bright environment (https://en.wikipedia.org/wiki/Adaptation_(eye)).

The tiered barriers, in Figures 4.22 and 4.23, are drawn as arcs to capture a nonlinear system of categorization. The categorization of the overlap is meant to give you a tool that accurately groups levels of importance into tiers. The importance and consequence of the overlap is not simply a straight categorization of overlap in holdings that are greater than 50%, as indicated in the original Holdings Overlap chart (Figure 4.17). Consider the example in which the original fund overlap is categorized within the high level of importance of > 50% overlap, whereas Figure 4.22 categorizes the same holding within the low range of importance: A fund with an A to B overlap of 60% to 5% is in the highest bracket in Figure 4.17, whereas Figure 4.22 identifies it to be in the lowest bracket. *Why?* An overlap that shows a high percentage of bidirectional overlap is more noteworthy. If the same fund instead landed an A to B overlap of 60% to 60%, then it would be placed in the highest bracket. The arc system therefore defines the tiers and categorizes the overlaps based on a bidirectional relationship instead of a one-directional relationship.

The benefit of this system is that it provides clearer focus on which funds should be closely reviewed. This solution prioritizes high concentrations of redundancies and provides a fund look-up feature. The Tiered Scatter Plot therefore provides both a mechanism to display and identify detailed data results. The display emphasizes the top bracket within the orange arc and directs you to first review these highly overlapped funds. The system also enables you to identify funds by location or by name. You can look up a fund's location in the chart with the drop-down, or you can select a location and identify the name of the fund.

The next chart, Figure 4.24, introduces yet another way to organize the data so that each fund pair is further categorized into more specific intervals.

Holdings Overlap

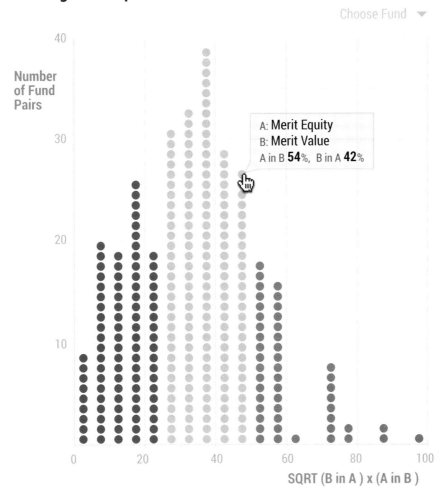

Figure 4.24 Tiered Histogram

The Tiered Histogram (Figure 4.24) bins intervals of the same data set and color codes from the previously established tiers. The x-axis lists the discrete bins to track the market value percentage overlap, whereas the y-axis counts the number of fund pairs that can be categorized in each bin. Each fund pair overlap is identified as a circle. The calculation used to categorize each pairing is based on the geometric mean such that, the square root of overlap B in A multiplied by the overlap of A in B. Consider the fund example of Merit Equity and Merit

Value pairing. The square root of (54 × 42) equals 47.6235, which means that the pairing is slotted into the 45–50 bin. The formula creates a balanced system that includes both sides of the holdings.

Similar to the Tiered Scatter Plot (refer to Figures 4.22 and 4.23), the histogram solution is interactive. As shown in Figure 4.24, the mouse-over state shows the fund pair names and the two corresponding overlap percentages for each relationship. You can also look up a fund: The Choose Fund drop-down enables you to locate a fund in the stacks of circles.

The benefit of the histogram approach is that it provides more organization to the same data set. Histograms show the distribution and categorization of data and readily show outliers across the data set. The tricolor system reinforces the categories and assigns levels of priority to the visual for you to quickly identify which fund pairs require close inspection. As a next step, you could provide an ordered list of securities and performance for each pairing to see the impact of these overlaps and further prioritize areas of focus.

Key Take-Aways

The three approaches in this section provide a suite of charts you can use depending on preferences and need. The Butterfly chart (Figures 4.18–4.21) shows the full, sortable list of funds. The Tiered Scatter Plot (Figures 4.22 and 4.23) no longer shows the full list of funds but instead uses a coordinate system to show the relative location and clustering of each fund pair overlap. Here, a bidirectional calculation is also introduced to more accurately rank the overlaps into tiers. The Tiered Histogram (Figure 4.24) capitalizes on the distribution and uses a balanced calculation to bin each fund pair with more specificity. Regardless of the chart selected to review the data, all three alternative charts provide visual solutions that remove calculation efforts, provide more accurate representations of the overlap categories, and use positive/negative space to show overlap concentrations.

Stress Tests

Because there is no certainty in risk, prudent techniques like stress tests assess risk and model reactions to various financial situations. Stress tests can cover a wide range of scenarios including tests based on one or more of the following: Historical situations, hypothetical scenarios, singular phenomenon with no indication of a repeat, multithreaded events that occur over time and concurrently, firm specific changes, and regional or global phenomenon that are wide spread. This section examines the stress test results and uses data from historical situations. You can assume the data in the test is brought to net present value and is relative to the benchmark for direct comparison of the results. Putting aside the model selection, calculation of the numbers, and data results, review the visual treatment applied to one set of results in a table. Figure 4.25 shows a table view of stress test results across a set of eight historical scenarios for five fund categories.

The Stress Test data table provides a full listing of how a categorized group of funds would react to various scenarios. Each scenario represents a significant impactful event like the Lehman Aftermath, and Long Term Capital Management (LTCM), the private hedge fund failure of 1998. The numerical data entered into each cell represents expected excess one-month (non-annualized) returns relative to the benchmark one month after the event. The color cells represent two extreme data points: Red results exceed negative 2 and blue results exceed a positive 2. The cells that are not colored maintain the middle ground range between negative 2 and 2. (any other cutoff could be set other than 2%, reflective of the user's sense of a "large market reaction.")

Stress Test

	Lehman Aftermath	LTCM	Test A	Test B	Test C	Test D	Test E	Test F
Global								
Global Growth	-0.91	-2.40	-4.13	2.46	-0.97	1.68	2.37	-4.05
Global DV Growth	2.30	0.70	2.83	2.76	-0.09	0.08	-0.52	0.98
Global Pragmatic	-0.29	-1.63	-2.38	2.03	-1.25	-0.58	-0.52	-2.95
Global Value	1.17	0.76	1.58	-0.43	1.15	0.16	0.22	1.12
Global Equity HQ	1.62	2.16	2.61	-0.52	0.56	-0.66	-1.02	1.73
Global Equity Div	0.80	1.25	1.42	-0.87	1.30	0.37	-0.72	1.57
Global Pragmatic Value	-2.70	-0.99	-3.80	-0.16	-2.46	1.98	2.99	-2.48
Global Merit Growth	1.99	0.30	2.21	4.66	-1.62	-1.57	-4.19	-0.22
Global Focus								
Scientific Equity	0.81	-4.25	-1.08	7.05	-4.21	-1.34	-3.99	-3.70
Specialized Equity	1.15	-2.18	1.07	4.06	-3.12	-2.41	-4.34	-1.18
Global Smaller Opportunities	1.85	0.37	2.07	0.54	-0.25	-0.83	-2.03	0.62
Global Inverse Equity	-2.64	-4.07	-6.11	1.03	-4.21	3.16	5.57	-4.60
Global Choice Growth	-3.04	-5.18	-6.64	3.98	-4.22	2.59	2.88	-5.92
Global Choice Outlook	2.78	1.95	2.99	0.95	1.39	-0.76	-2.23	1.14
Global Dividend Growth	4.04	3.15	8.19	-1.36	1.03	-2.00	-5.21	6.02
Global Choice Value	-0.09	0.30	-0.91	0.94	0.60	-0.15	1.47	-1.25
Global All Cap Pragmatic	-8.34	-10.29	-15.39	4.13	-7.31	6.13	10.88	-12.39
Global Growth Horizons	-2.07	-3.53	-5.54	2.39	-3.19	2.01	2.36	-4.53
International								
International Growth	-0.66	-2.18	-1.16	-0.33	-0.80	0.54	1.89	-0.60
International Diversified	-2.48	-1.25	-4.83	1.58	-1.56	1.15	2.71	-3.34
International Pragmatic	2.55	2.11	2.23	0.52	-0.04	-2.48	-3.23	0.34
International Small Cap Equity	1.48	-0.86	1.14	0.30	-0.28	-0.33	-2.16	0.07
International Inverse Value	-0.12	-1.78	-2.42	1.59	-4.05	1.84	4.13	-2.56
International Longitude	1.86	1.87	1.10	1.29	-0.01	-2.14	-3.09	0.04
Pragmatic International Growth	-0.93	-3.36	-1.65	0.11	-2.05	1.22	2.17	-1.27
Sustainable Growth	-0.03	-0.24	0.98	1.91	-0.60	0.13	-1.16	0.59
Comprehensive Value	18.56	12.69	27.28	0.06	0.34	-6.70	-12.05	12.07
International - Regional								
Europe Tactical Small Cap	0.40	-0.83	0.84	0.38	-1.24	-0.22	-1.81	0.23
Japan	0.10	0.07	0.62	0.28	-0.23	0.29	0.43	0.55
Japan Choice Conditions	-0.29	0.09	1.77	1.71	-4.14	0.91	-0.09	1.06
Japan Small Cap Equity	-0.71	-1.95	-2.60	2.74	-0.20	0.65	-1.26	-3.04
Asia Inverse Equity	-0.89	-2.12	-0.97	1.79	-3.18	0.11	1.90	-1.52
Asia ex Japan	-0.45	2.39	1.84	1.59	0.40	-1.84	-2.33	1.09
Asia Consumption Outlook	-2.07	3.31	2.28	2.15	-2.14	-3.57	-4.65	1.63
Asia Pacific Small Cap	-0.34	3.15	2.54	0.42	2.03	-1.39	-1.65	1.59
Emerging Markets Localized	0.65	0.07	-0.58	2.50	-0.23	-0.79	-1.04	-1.80
Emerging Markets Broad	-2.20	1.78	2.18	1.43	-2.58	-3.04	-4.88	1.26
Latin America	-0.08	-1.03	3.55	1.63	-2.66	-4.61	-8.65	0.93
Europe Equity Strategic	0.40	0.20	0.98	1.74	-2.49	-1.07	-2.06	-0.07
US Focus								
Choice Growth	-5.36	-7.57	-10.73	5.13	-7.07	3.77	4.91	-9.87
Choice Value Growth	-7.40	-6.74	-13.54	2.69	-1.51	4.88	7.98	-9.66
All Cap Pragmatic	-10.06	-10.55	-18.21	5.75	-8.15	6.67	10.95	-13.51
Choice Intrinsic Value	-1.90	-1.29	-1.61	0.64	-3.56	0.49	0.43	-1.05
Specialty Growth	-3.69	-2.40	-6.78	2.48	-1.85	2.28	2.81	-5.00
Convergent Equity	-0.10	-2.26	-2.10	4.04	-2.73	0.94	-0.50	-3.26
Choice Quality Equity	1.22	2.73	3.17	0.13	0.33	-0.49	-2.20	2.14
Choice Leaders	-0.28	-1.29	-0.13	-2.36	-2.06	-0.54	0.42	0.13

Figure 4.25 Data Table

Despite the color-coded cell technique used to highlight the top range and the low ranges, the table still requires you to read the numbers in each cell to understand exactly how high is the highest and how low is the lowest. A visual approach, as shown in Figure 4.26, can show the same ranges with additional data to represent the corresponding market value for each fund.

Stress Test

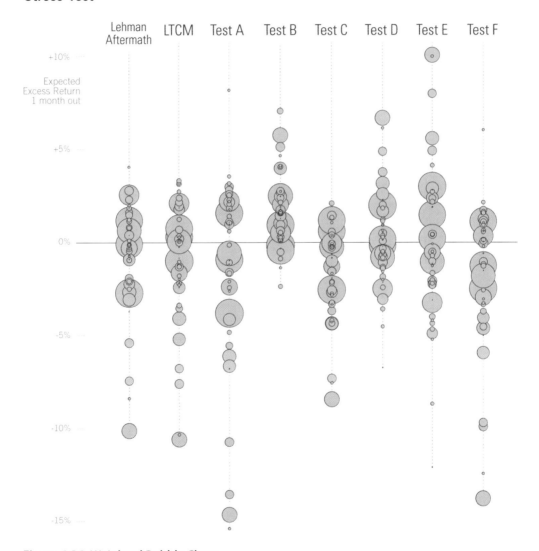

Figure 4.26 **Weighted Bubble Chart**

Figure 4.26 has the same column header structure as the original table but introduces a y-axis with the expected percentage returns. The column headers sit on dotted vertical lines to connect the collection of bubbles. Each bubble location represents a fund's excess returns relative to the benchmark 1 month after the sample event. The bubbles are layered on top of each other, sometimes overlapped based on the corresponding numeric, while the size of each bubble represents the market value to illustrate the business value at risk. Overlapping and varying sized bubbles require them to be ordered on a z-axis to ensure each fund is represented.

The Weighted Bubble Chart does not require you to review each number to understand the spread of potential results. Instead, the replacement of 376 numbers with different-sized bubbles enables you to see clusters, ranges, and estimate quantities above or below the zero mark.

Although the chart helps to quickly evaluate the results of each test, each bubble is somewhat obstructed of the full market amount. Figure 4.27 shows an unobstructed view of each fund's market value results and further rationalizes each of the test results.

Figure 4.27 builds on the same structure and benefits of the previous chart and fully displays each fund's market value. Layers are removed, and instead the open spaces to the right and left are used to place each fund results. The surface space covered by the collection of bubbles becomes the collective market value indicator. Removing the z-axis simplifies the chart and provides more information for you to see both the market value and range of returns at once.

Stress Test

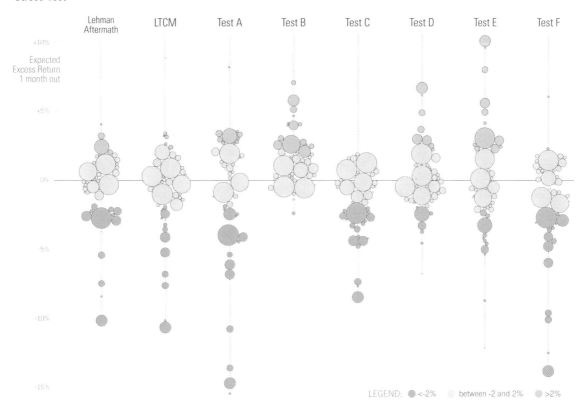

Figure 4.27 **Weighted Bubble Clusters**

In addition, color is introduced to group the results into the same three return categories identified in the original Data Table shown in Figure 4.25.

The use of color, bubble arrangement, bubble size, and coordinate system improves the chart with the following benefits:

▶ **Creates hierarchy**—Each stress test results are no longer read individually. Instead, the chart can tell the full story of range and market value impact. The tricolor system reinforces the results by creating three simple categories of performance that are clearly defined and organized.

- ▶ **Provides visual tracking**—The coordinate system, comprised of a simple y-axis, provides the framework to improve visual tracking.

- ▶ **Produces attention and focus**—Color is often used to highlight and call attention to certain areas of a table or chart. In the case of Figure 4.27, orange is used as the warning color to attract attention in the table. However, the combined strengths of color and size is more powerful and attract your attention even further.

Figure 4.28, lets you track a fund across the various stress tests. The chart is interactive with the capability to select and identify each fund's results. When you select a fund from the drop-down, the fund name displays and the return results are underscored with a bold circle alongside the numeric results.

The benefits of presenting the fund details upon request are two-fold. First, you no longer have to read 47 different fund names with the accompanying 376 numeric results. The chart enables you to study the results first. By removing the numeric results and abstracting the fund names, you are provided the big picture view of all returns. Second, obtaining the details is flexible and can be examined by selecting a bubble to reveal the fund or selecting a fund to reveal the results. The context of the big picture view in the background provides a relative understanding of a fund's results.

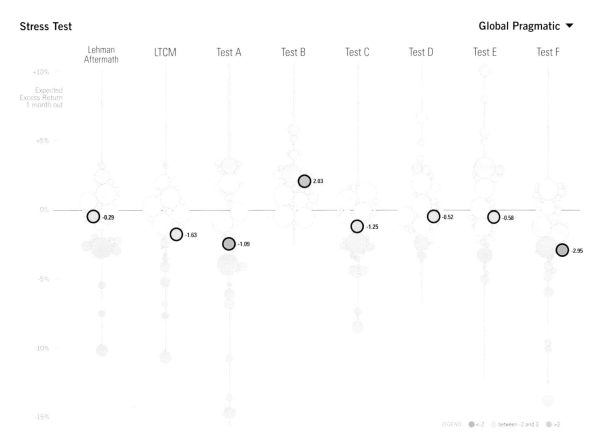

Figure 4.28 Weighted Bubble Clusters–Selected Fund

Key Take-Aways

You can take advantage of these types of stress test results for a variety of conversations and scenarios. This chart can scale and extend to a larger series of stress tests. The results can guide internal conversations within or outside of your group. As a business risk tool, the value at risk stress test results can show you the potential impact to firm revenue. Externally, these charts provide visual aides to facilitate existing or potential client conversations. You can share a portfolio's stress test results at a client meeting and provide transparency into their portfolio's potential performance.

Summary

This chapter presents a variety of Portfolio Construction data visualizations that draw from activities top-down managers employ. These activities include determining asset allocations with sector and industry weights before security selection represented with visualizations that show current and proposed asset allocations of a portfolio, sector leadership, and sector alpha factors. In addition, two common risk management techniques, overlap of holdings and stress tests, are included as indirect inputs toward Portfolio Construction activities. These types of techniques manage firm risk from a business perspective to influence Portfolio Construction decisions. They also present clients with rationale for amendments and changes in their portfolio(s).

The visualizations exhibit three types of solutions: singular, multifaceted, and varied. A singular solution represents the data with one visualization type alone. Examples of this solution include the 3-D Hexagonal Surface Plot used for asset allocations and Heatmap Groups used for sector alpha factors.

The second type of solution is multifaceted, in that the data set is represented with one visualization type that can be adjusted in multiple ways to answer multiple follow-up questions. An example of this type of visualization is the collection of Bar Track charts that can be arranged in multiple ways including row and column orientations that can include or omit corresponding pivot summaries, as shown in Figures 4.7–4.10. For example, the Bar Track charts start with a solution that shows which sector is top ranked for each year. The next shows which sector has the best returns, across multiple years.

A third type, the varied solution, represents the same date set with a variety of data visualizations. Each of the visualizations can enrich interpretations of the data by addressing various related questions. For example, the overlap of holdings data set is represented with three different data visualizations: Butterfly, Tiered Scatter Plot, and Tiered Histogram. Each data visualization addresses a distinctive aspect of the data set and can be used to make different points. The Butterfly chart can be used as a look-up tool that lists each of the holdings pairs, whereas the Tiered Histogram shows the distribution of all the pairs. These are two different aspects of the same data set that impact how you would use the data visualization as a tool.

VISUALIZATION	DESCRIPTION	FIGURE
3-D Hexagonal Surface Plot	Three variables plotted to show the relationships on a contour plane.	4.3
Bar Track Chart	A continuous set of bars connected on a horizontal or vertical line.	4.7–4.10
Heatmap Groups	A set of quantities each represented by color and each confined to a defined space.	4.13–4.16
Butterfly Chart	A set of bar charts that show increasing quantities in opposing directions	4.18–4.21
Tiered Scatter Plot	Shows the relationship between two or more points on a Cartesian coordinate system that is separated into three-color bands.	4.22–4.23
Tiered Histogram	Distribution of a range of values that are each categorized within a defined series of intervals (bins). The bins are grouped and distinguished with three colors.	4.24
Weighted Bubble Clusters	A collection of circles, each fully visible, in which the size, color, column grouping, and placement identifies relative ranking.	4.27–4.28

Different data sets can be represented with a singular, multifaceted, or varied data visualization solution. This is yet another choice you can make as you consider which approach best fits your needs and adapt the solution approach as your questions of the data evolve.

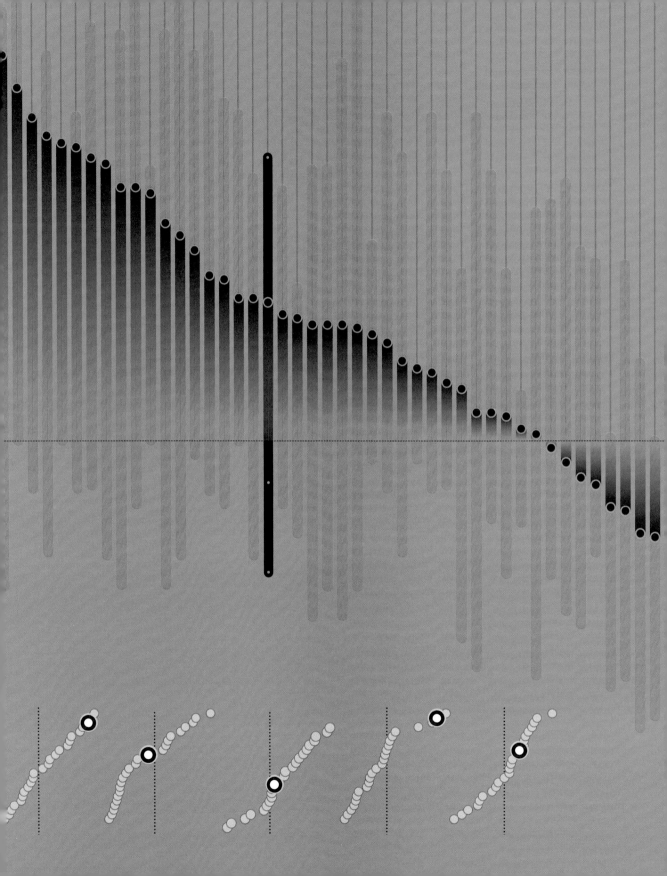

5

Trading

Tickers, quotes, and watchlists are the three standard communication tools that provide us with up-to-the-minute information on the current state of a security or index. With various global markets to keep track of, these industry displays focus on just a few data points to succinctly report market price. Staff tasked with identifying value in a security universe must have continuous access to the current price of any identified security of interest, and in most cases, continuous access to the pricing of securities compete for the analyst's attention. Tickers, quotes, and watchlists communicate fundamental information to assess the state of an investment as the markets fluctuate.

Today's displays show ticker, quote, and watchlist data in undifferentiated numeric matrices, seas of numbers with neither hierarchy nor helpful highlighting. Staff's ability to monitor and react to such data is compromised in this type of environment. In this chapter, we propose expanding the role of such displays from undifferentiated number dumps to richer, more effective tools that can increase awareness and allow staff to capitalize more rapidly on the information. As consumers of this basic data, we often need to act and act quickly.

This chapter provides out-of-the-gate solutions to improve market monitoring. We take a two-fold approach by asking *1) Which data points are important enough to showcase? 2) How can we represent these data to make them more actionable?* We provide alternative solutions to the ticker, quote, and watchlist and propose a system of information displays with consistent visual language between them. This chapter follows an iterative design approach that illustrates how to make incremental improvements to a visualization.

All the data in this chapter is hypothetical data and is representative of what is provided in the marketplace. While the data in this chapter deal exclusively with equities, it should be noted that the visualization recommendations presented here can be adapted to other market instruments such as bonds, commodities, currencies, and market indices. In addition, the visualizations are designed as interactive displays that can be configured and navigated by an end user.

Ticker

The industry has popularized the ticker and investors have become accustomed to its traditional design. It is widely and prominently displayed in public places such as New York City's Times Square, it streams across building facades and inside of building entrances, and it is affixed to the bottom of most financial news channels. While the ticker has maintained its popularity, it has also retained the same old design. Partially due to a reduced need for active engagement with the ticker, over the years the industry has become indifferent to the design of the tool. You no longer need to watch a ticker display because there are more sophisticated ways to obtain the same data using look-up tools such as quotes and watchlists. Multiple decades of using and seeing digital ticker displays stream across trade floors established a standard that now has more to do with its ornamental aspects than with delivering crucial information.

Although we recognize that the ticker is antiquated, we start with it to show how we can make a classic design more relevant in today's world. Relative to the other communication tools in this chapter, the ticker is fundamentally flawed. It requires constant monitoring and waiting for desired information to appear. Visualization techniques can do only so much to correct its constant motion and randomness. Still, the effort to improve the ticker is not pointless since the lessons learned from redesigning the ticker can be applied to the quote and watchlist. The visuals in this section explore how to simplify the data and consolidate the display to create a more useful ticker.

This section starts with a review of the Classic Ticker, as shown in Figure 5.1. Visualizations that follow show a process of design iterations on the way to its final design. We ask questions such as: *What elements can be removed? What can be replaced or added to make the ticker more efficient, readable, and useful?*

Ticker - Classic

LAPE 1.5M **61.76** ▲0.23 AAPE 15K **14.55** ▼0.05

Figure 5.1 **Ticker—Five Data Points**

The Classic Ticker displays each company's 1) symbols, 2) volume of shares traded, 3) current price, 4) increase and decrease in price, and 5) amount. These data points do not effectively enable you to compare or react to change. Instead, each display requires a quick calculation to know if the change is significant or trivial. The constant motion of the ticker introduces more complication as you are forced to read and calculate the data quickly. Another problem with the ticker design is the use of color. Although the arrow provides a supporting indicator of price change, the color choice of green and red should be adjusted for those individuals with green and red color deficiencies. (As stated in Chapter 4, studies have shown that 8% of the male population and 0.5% of the female population worldwide cannot distinguish between green and red colors.)

To simplify the ticker to the essentials and rectify the color choice we start with the following design (Figure 5.2). The streaming ticker alludes to a dynamic environment of change. As the information flashes by, the display necessitates maximum simplification. However, most tickers list a maximum of five data points for each security, overloading the brain's ability to quickly assess their meaning. Instead, identifying essential information will help ensure that key data points are effectively communicated. The ticker is meant to communicate the news on a stock: *Is the security up or down and by how much?*

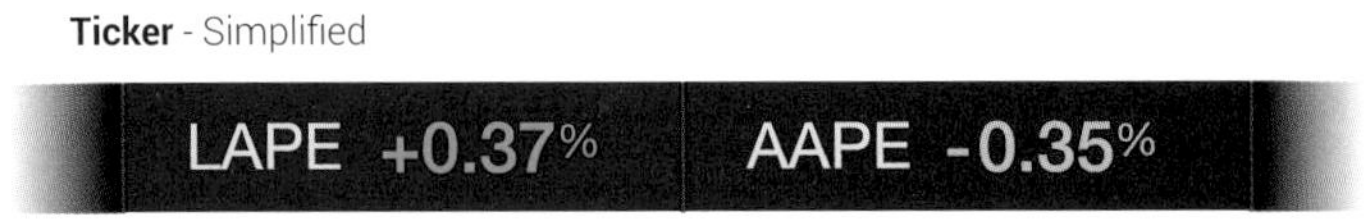

Ticker - Simplified

LAPE +0.37%   AAPE -0.35%

Figure 5.2 **Ticker—two Data Points**

The Simplified Ticker (refer to Figure 5.2) shows a considerably streamlined display with only two data points: the security symbol and the percentage change in price. As streaming data points, the information can be easily read and understood. The chosen hues solve the problem of colorblind traders. A comparison between the Classic Ticker and the Simplified Ticker is illustrated next in Figure 5.3.

Ticker - Classic

LAPE 1.5M 61.76 ▲ 0.23   AAPE 15K 14.55 ▼ 0.05

Ticker - Simplified

LAPE +0.37%   AAPE -0.35%   PAPE +0.25%

Figure 5.3 **Ticker Comparisons**

This Ticker Comparison highlights the differences between the original and modified ticker. In the same footprint, two becomes three and five becomes two: The original display of two securities can now show three securities and the five data points are reduced to two data points. Succinct and clear, the modified ticker provides more actionable information with the addition of the percentage change.

The percentage change is a key data point to highlight and expand upon within relevant contexts. For example, you can couple the percentage change in relative terms to the day's price movement. This would enable you to quickly scan across the ticker display to see which securities are at a high or low point for the day.

The ticker design shown in Figure 5.4 introduces a different way to illustrate a security's current price marker and price movement for the day.

Ticker Redesigned - Iteration 1

Figure 5.4 Ball and Hash Marks

Is the current price at the highest or lowest point of today's price? The vertical gray hash marks resemble a perforation line and serve as a scale of the day's high and low spread. The white circle marks the current price relative to the day's range of price movement. The white circle automatically connotes movement similar to a bouncing ball that changes directions and heights. As a visual data point, the ball communicates a percentage change number and reinforces the corresponding numeric value. The next iteration, as shown in Figure 5.5, incorporates more information into the current price point marker with a trailing path.

Ticker Redesigned - Iteration 2

Figure 5.5 Trailing Ball

The Trailing Ball (refer to Figure 5.5) paints a clearer picture of the day's security price. *Is the price shooting up like a rocket with nice gains or falling like a star with dust trails? Or as in the third security example PAPE, despite the day's gain, has there been a turn of events to make the price drop?* Regardless of the percentage gain/loss, the trailing price, like a vector, shows recent directional movement. The trail also uses color to show either alignment or dissonance between the day's gains and current directional movement. This small feature adds to the richness without increasing the display space.

As reflections of what has happened during the day, the price stories act as a reporting analyst would with a ten-second introduction to the stock's activity. Next, Figure 5.6 presents a variety of different price stories similar to what you might hear a news anchor deliver at the closing bell.

| Going strong, all up since Open | Volatile: Current +.37 just a fraction of todays up and down swings | Getting weaker all day, going consistently down | Still above Open but currently going down | Initially went up but now stable at the Open level |

Figure 5.6 **Trailing Story**

How volatile is the security today? How far above or below the open price has the current price swayed? The horizontal gray line marks the open price point in relation to today's price range. This one data point provides extra context to the current price.

The ticker, as shown in the Trailing Price Story, is now more interesting. You can see the day's performance story for each security—each one with a different twist. You no longer have to rely on your memory to recall previous movement during the day. The day's summarized view tracks the day's movements for you in a concise, meaningful way.

By efficiently using five data points, this version of the ticker can report a simple story of today's price movement. The ticker shows 1) security symbol, 2) percentage change, 3) current price point relative to the day's price movement, 4) directional movement of the current price, and 5) opening price relative to the day's price movement. The original ticker with five data points is redesigned replacing alphanumeric data presentation with visuals that work in unison to tell a better story of what has occurred during the day. The focus of the data explains the directional change, what's new and different, or what has not changed.

To display the current price, Figure 5.7 can incorporate the price as two options: a primary and a secondary data point. If you want to focus on the current price within the context of price swings during the day, then the top option fits your needs. If you would rather focus on the percentage change to monitor large to small movements in the market with the price as a side data point, then the second option is a more suitable candidate.

Ticker Redesigned - Iteration 3: Current Price + Day Change

Ticker Redesigned - Iteration 3: Day Change + Current Price

Figure 5.7 **Trailing Ball and Starting Mark**

A third option is also available. A trader with limit price targets for a set of securities will want to know how close the current price is to the limit price. This design suggestion is trader specific, requires configuration, and ideally integrates with a trading platform that already has the data. Figure 5.8 uses the same trailing ball visualization to fulfill this use case.

Ticker Redesigned - Iteration 3: Current Price + Limit

Going strong,
Again getting closer to my Sale limit.

Though going consistently down the price is
still far away from my Buy limit.

Aterr getting close to my Sale limit
the price started to drop.

Figure 5.8 **Trailing Ball and Goal Mark**

Is the price change moving toward the limit price or away? In Figure 5.8, the blue horizontal mark indicates the limit price and the hash marks represent the day's price change. The distance between the blue mark and the day's price range is an indication of the increasing or decreasing gap required to reach the limit price. It shows how close the price has gotten to the limit price as an indication of what is possible based on the day's activity.

Figure 5.8 applies color selection differently as well. You may have noticed that the color of the current price is the same as the color of the trailing ball color. In contrast, the trailing ball color referred to in Figure 5.7 can be different from the text color because it indicates the day's price change. Security PAPE show-cases these different color usage examples in Figures 5.6, 5.7, and 5.8.

You may ask: *Why change the color coding, and why not keep the same color coding between the two options?* Because the purpose of the trailing ball in Figure 5.8 is to track the direction and distance to the target limit price, the color choice reinforces the purpose to use the same color as the current price change. Likewise, in Figure 5.7 the color choice reinforces the purpose of the ticker option to emphasize the day's price change. The key lesson is that color selection for text and visual elements should reinforce a specific purpose. Although this variation in color use may seem like a small detail, it can impact the interpretation and overall usability of the entire ticker.

Key Take-Aways

The Classic Ticker (refer to Figure 5.1) relies on numerical information that requires a combination of memorization and quick computation to benefit from the recorded information. In contrast, the revised iterations (Figures 5.6, 5.7, and 5.8) rely on visual clues that provide the story of how the price has moved. This section suggests alternate ticker designs with the goal of removing the need to compute numbers in order to derive meaning. The final version provides a visualization that most efficiently communicates the story of the day's price movement.

Although the movement of the ticker display conveys change, the display of the data referred to in Figure 5.1 is static. The typical auto scroll movement of the ticker shows the data points in a stagnant textual way. An appeal for a continuously changing display is somewhat ingrained in our minds from decades of seeing the Classic Ticker display (refer to Figure 5.1). The display shown in the Trailing Story (refer to Figure 5.6) reinforces the idea of continuous change with visual elements that convey change. The display shows the dynamic change in price, not with the motion of the ticker, but with the trailing price point reminiscent of a bouncing ball.

Like many newly designed interfaces, the new ticker may take some time to learn. However, the learning curve is not too steep and perhaps worth the benefits of rich price stories associated with each ticker. The display provides more reasons to be drawn into a performance change with insights to take action or investigate further.

Quote

Quotes vary in the amount of data they display. Some show as few as half a dozen data points; others show dozens and are accompanied with basic line charts that track performance. To improve the effectiveness of a quote we must answer: *What can be done to clarify the quote across varying sets of data points?* Improving its display goes beyond replacing text with graphics. It is also about creating a tool that quickly yet accurately informs its audience.

This section suggests various sizes in which to package and display our quote: A small graphic can show the basic quote, a medium one adds commonly sought-after data points, and a large one provides an extended fundamental and technical listing. This section provides a step-by-step approach to redesigning the quote. Each iteration improves upon the last with a rationale provided for each design choice. To start, let's review typical data displays for a small, medium, and large quote. As shown in Figures 5.9, 5.10, and 5.11, the quote data is listed and organized in simple textual displays.

Quote - Small

Figure 5.9 **Quote—Five Data Points**

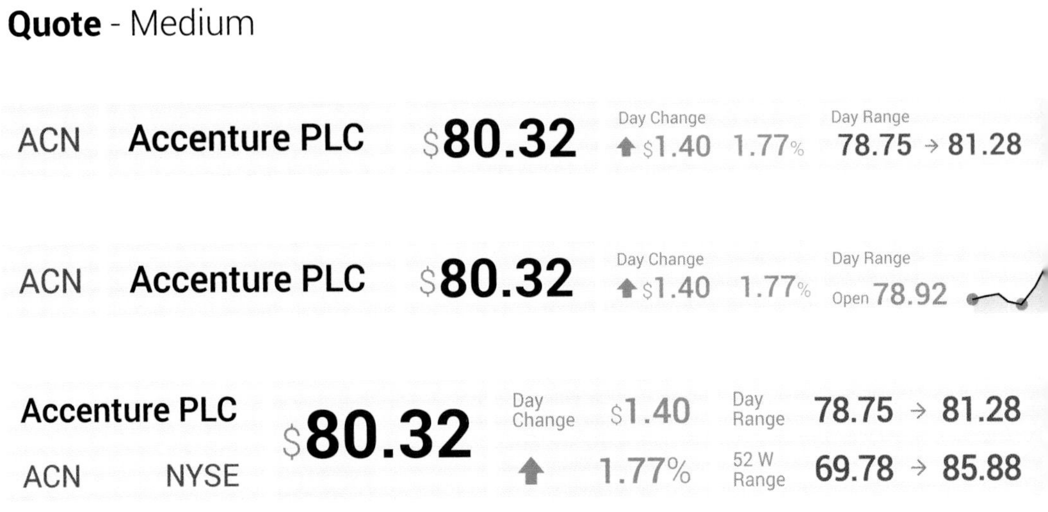

Quote - Medium

ACN	**Accenture PLC**	$**80.32**	Day Change ▲ $1.40 1.77%	Day Range 78.75 → 81.28

ACN	**Accenture PLC**	$**80.32**	Day Change ▲ $1.40 1.77%	Day Range Open 78.92

Accenture PLC	$**80.32**	Day Change	$1.40	Day Range 78.75 → 81.28
ACN NYSE		▲	1.77%	52 W Range 69.78 → 85.88

Figure 5.10 **Quote—18 Data Points**

The small quote (Figure 5.9) is akin to data within the ticker and provides the most recent pricing information. The only graphical elements are colored text and an arrow that indicates an increase or decrease in the price.

Incorporating more data points into the medium-sized quote (refer to Figure 5.10) expands the display size and creates a more complete picture with the addition of a sparkline.

NOTE

Sparklines are used to illustrate trends using small embedded line graphs that typically do not include axes, coordinates, or labels. As noted by the definition, most sparklines do not include details.

Despite the small area, details can be added to the sparkline to help you extract more information: The high and low point of the price are emphasized with a blue and red circle, respectively, the current price is emphasized with a black

52 Week Range		Volume	Market Cap	Div & Yield	P/E	
69.78 → 85.88		2.58 M	50.70 B	2.60%	15.4	

	81.28 78.75	52 Week Range 69.78 → 85.88	Volume 2.58 M	Market Cap 50.70 B	Div & Yield 2.60%

Volume	2.58 M	Market Cap	50.70 B	Price/ Earnings	15.4	Revenue Growth	9.6%
Bid/Ask Spread	6.72%	Div & Yield	2.60%	Price/ Book	9.5	Net Income Growth	22.1%

circle, and the white vertical lines mark each hour of the day. These details provide more context to the sparkline and help you see the salient data points.

The large-sized quote (Figure 5.11) is an example of how the display can grow both vertically and horizontal and continue to fit the extended data sets. The value/field pairing is repetitive and can be easily overlooked. To understand the significance of one value, it has to be reviewed in context of other values that are often not present in the quote data. In some cases, you may be very familiar with a security and will have deep knowledge of its performance, whereas in other cases you may not have the historical context of the price movements. The goal of introducing relative data points is to level the playing field and provide the knowledge of greater context. The relative data points can include the following:

▶ **The relative performance across different time periods**—*How does the current performance compare against a month or year time period? What is the significance of the price range for the year?*

Quote - Large

Basic		Changes over time		Liquidity	
Accenture PLC	$**80.32**	Open Price	**78.92**	Volume	**2,588,213**
		Day Range	**78.75 → 81.28**	Bid	**77.81** ×100
ACN NYSE	Day Change $**1.40**	Month Range	**77.56 → 82.16**	Ask	**83.21** ×100
Large Growth ⬆	**1.77%**	52 W Range	**69.78 → 85.88**	Bid/Ask Spread	**6.72%**

Basic		Changes over time	
Accenture PLC	$**80.32**	Day Range	81.2
		78.92	78.7
ACN NYSE	Day Change $**1.40**	52 Weeks	85.8
Large Growth ⬆	**1.77%**	71.09	69.7

Figure 5.11 Quote—30 Data Points

▸ **The relative performance within the time period spread**—*Is the current price a large or small change for the range of price movement? How significant is the percentage increase for the day?*

▸ **The relative comparison to the sector/industry**—*How do the fundamentals compare to the industry? How significant is a P/E ratio of 15.4 for this stock?*

Company		Value	
Market Cap	**50.70 B**	Price/ Earnings	**15.4**	Revenue Growth	**9.6%**
Div & Yield	**$2.04/2.60%**	Price/ Book	**9.5**	Net Income Growth	**22.1%**
Sector	**Technology**	Price/ Sales	**1.8**	Operating Margin	**13.4%**
Indistry	**IT Services**	Price/ Cash Flow	**18.0**	ROA	**17.4%**

Liquidity		Company		Value			
Volume	**2,588,213**	Market Cap	**50.70 B**	Price/ Earnings	**15.4**	Div & Yield	**2.60%**
Bid	**77.81** ×100	Style	**Large, Growth**	Price/ Book	**9.5**	Revenue Growth	**9.6%**
Ask	**83.21** ×100	Sector	**Technology**	Price/ Sales	**1.8**	Operating Margin	**13.4%**
Bid/Ask Spread	**6.72%**	Indistry	**IT Services**	Price/ Cash Flow	**18.0**	ROA	**17.4%**

The next set of quote designs considers relative data points of performance and comparison. Visuals that can emphasize aspects of historical change, current change, and industry-wide performance provide relative contexts for each quote. The next visualization (Figure 5.12) addresses the aspects of historical change and introduces a 1-year, 1-month, 1-day perspective into the display.

Quote Redesigned - Iteration 1

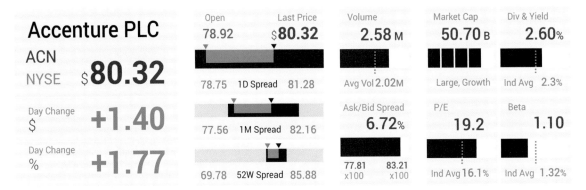

Figure 5.12 **Quote—Nested Time Bars**

Each performance view is connected to the next by keeping and layering the day's spread. The black triangle points out the current price in all displays, whereas the gray triangle shows the open price. The teal color across the quote shows the positive day change, the black indicates today's price spread, whereas the light gray bar corresponds to the timeframe's spread. This type of historical connection shows you the current price point and current day's movement in relative terms to the month and year. The significance of the day's change is put into multiple time-based perspectives.

Perspective is also introduced with averages. Averages are shown in the quote with a dashed line to mark average volume and various industry averages for all others that apply. The revised quote (refer to Figure 5.12) uses graphical elements that support historical and industry-based perspectives to show the significance of a value.

Another method of showing context is connecting the current price in relative terms to time intervals. Figure 5.13 provides the relative perspective of time by percentage change.

Quote Redesigned - Iteration 2

Figure 5.13 **Quote—Discrete Time Bars**

As a discrete interval, a day, month, or year is a defined time frame in which gains and losses can be tracked. Figure 5.13 shows a contextual connection to the historical data by displaying the percentage change mapped to full period spreads. *Is the stock up or down for the day, month, or year? And by how much? And how does that compare to the spread for that time period?* The perspective of the display shows that today's price is down for the month by 1.23% but significantly up, by 12.98%, for the 52-week change.

The same data display can be organized differently to fit different space and size requirements. For example, Figure 5.14 adopts a linear row layout.

The linear form factor shown in Figure 5.14 allows multiple quotes to be stacked and added to a collection of quotes. This is accomplished by keeping the key text values. Additionally, market fluctuations can be communicated with more than just the changing numbers of a data screen. Figure 5.15 introduces a new marker to track the change in price and emphasize the dynamic nature of the stock's change in price.

Quote Redesigned - Iteration 2, Simplified

Figure 5.14 **Single Row Layout**

Quote Redesigned - Iteration 3

Quote Redesigned - Iteration 3, Simplified

Figure 5.15 **Horizontal Contrail**

Similar to an aircraft with vapor trails, the performance change markers are attached to trails that show directional movement for each spread. The black circle end of the trail marks the current state, whereas the color tail-end marks the value at the beginning of the set period. Across the quote, color is consistently applied to indicate an increase or decrease in value. You can scan the display and see that the Div & Yield % has increased, whereas the P/E ratio has decreased over the past quarter.

By organizing the orientation of the display from left to right or top to bottom, you can produce results that impact not just the quote layout but also the inferences of the data. The next visualization changes the orientation of the contrail display. Figure 5.16 connects your verbal language associations of the terms up and down with your visual associations of how those terms should be shown.

Vol **2.58** M   Ask/Bid **6.72%**   M Cap **50.7** B   Div & Yield **2.60%**   P/E **19.2**   Beta **1.10**

52W Change	Open	Volume		Ask/Bid Spread	Market Cap	Div & Yield	P/E
+12.98%	**71.09**	**2.58** M		**6.72%**	**50.70** B	**2.60%**	**19.2**
69.78	85.88	Avg Vol	2.02M	77.81 x100 83.21 x100	Large Ind Avg **2.3%**		Ind Avg **16.1%**

+12.98%   Vol **2.58** M   Ask/ Bid   **6.72%**   Mrkt Cap **50.7** B   Div & Yield **2.60%**   P/E **19.2**

The vertical orientation of the quote (refer to Figure 5.16) illustrates what is up and what is down in a visually intuitive way. You can track the black circle across the indicators and see what is above or below average and by how much. A combination of technical and fundamental indicators is incorporated into the display. By creating a simple representation of the data's dynamic nature, the display opens the possibility of including technical indicators that otherwise are typically shown as separate charts. This version of the quote benefits from exploring *1) How should historical and industry context be shown? 2) How should changes across indicators be shown? 3) How can you connect verbal and visual language associations? 4) How should numeric values be incorporated into the visualization?*

Quote Redesigned - Iteration 4

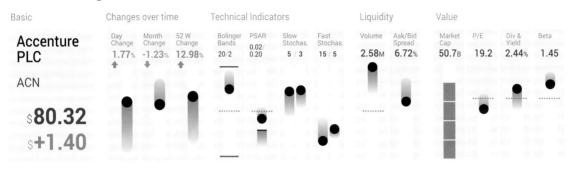

Quote Redesigned - Iteration 4: Interactive State

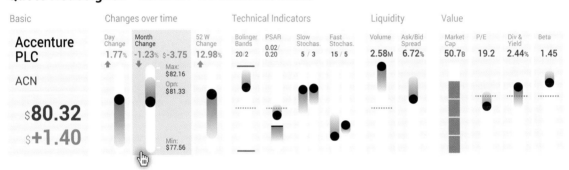

Figure 5.16 **Vertical Contrail**

Key Take-Aways

This section provides a step-by-step approach to the redesign of the quote to provide a cohesive solution that can apply to varying-sized quotes with different data points. At the start, three varying sizes of quotes are presented, each of which contain different amounts and types of data points. The uniting factor within each quote indicator is the continuous change in value. This section evolves the contrail marker as the uniting visual element that shows the continuous change across all indicators.

Watchlist

Most watchlists are tables of data with lists of values organized into columns. If a security is worth watching, chances are you are tracking it in your watchlist. Since the point of a watchlist is to monitor and be well informed on key indicators for a security, the displays have to be at once comprehensive and pointed to show significant changes. This section continues from the previous section by using many of the same visual elements from the quote to help you answer: *How can you display the security data for easy comparison? How can you display a large amount of watchlist data within a single view?* Our intent is twofold: 1) to make it easier to analyze one security in the context of many and 2) to provide a birds-eye view across the collection.

Similar to both the ticker and the quote, this section provides an evolutionary redesign of the watchlist with several iterations to explain the process. First, Figure 5.17 illustrates a typical watchlist populated with just a few stocks to present the sample data.

Watchlist

Symbol	Name	Last Price	Open	Day Change		Day Range	52W Change		52W Range	Volume	Average Volume	Ask/Bid	M Cap	Div & Yield	P/E	Beta
ACN	Accenture PLC	$80.32	$78.92	$1.40	1.77%	$78.75 → $81.28	$9.23	12.98%	$69.78 → $85.88	2.58M	2.02M	6.72%	50.70B	2.60%	19.2	1.10
INFY	Infosys Ltd ADR	$17.99	$17.99	$0.17	0.91%	$17.98 → $18.23	$2.54	16.26%	$14.50 → $18.68	3.41M	4.21M	3.13%	41.10B	1.97%	17.9	1.73
HTHIY	Hitachi Ltd ADR	$60.32	$60.99	$-0.67	-1.10%	$60.32 → $61.19	$-15.08	-20.00%	$80.50 → $60.32	0.35M	0.28M	7.92%	29.50B	0.83%	5.8	0.47

Figure 5.17 **Watchlist Data Table**

Next, Figure 5.18 repurposes the Horizontal Contrail Quote (refer to Figure 5.15) by stacking the quote to create the watchlist. Since a typical watchlist has the capability to show leaders and laggers, Figure 5.18 organizes the display to focus on the change %. By aligning the visual display to the opening price across both the Day Change and 52W Change columns, you can create a leader or lagger list either by sorting the short-term returns for the day or the longer-term returns for the year.

Watchlist - Period Change

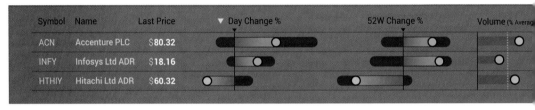

Figure 5.18 Contrail—Day Change Alignment

Watchlist - Period Change with Spread

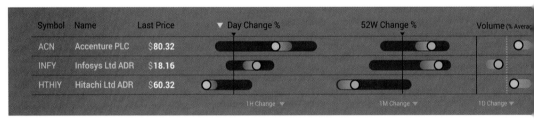

Watchlist - Period Change with Spread and Recent Change

Figure 5.19 Contrail with Spread

In the foreground a simple blue/orange color filled circle indicates an increase or decrease for each respective time period. Notice how well the colors stand out, making it so that the blue/orange circles are easily tracked across the display. The industry averages within the watchlist further support your understanding of a value's significance. The small but impactful addition of industry

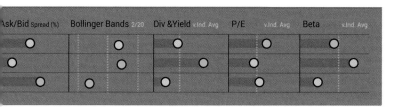

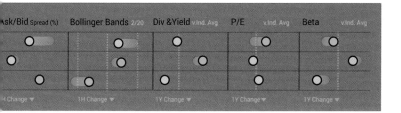

averages to Div & Yield, P/E, and Beta is layered into the background of the display with a white dotted line.

Although Figure 5.18 enables easy comparison of leaders and laggers, the day's price spread is missing. Hence, Figure 5.19 adjusts the display to include the day's spread.

Watchlist – Period Change with Spread (refer to Figure 5.19) shows you the relative nature of a day change and how that relates to the year. By incorporating the period spread into a dark gray background, the Day Change and 52 Week Change columns include the volatility for each stock.

Watchlist - Period Change with Spread and Recent Changes visually addresses the need to see recent changes within the hour across the indicators. The ability to select a specific "Change" timeframe is provided at the bottom of each column. *Did the Ask/Bid spread % increase or decrease and by how much?* In addition to the price change, introducing the trail markers to the Volume and Ask/Bid columns provide immediate perspective on liquidity. For longer time horizon changes of P/E, Dividends, Yield, and Beta, the trail markers show trends in the fundamentals. The trail markers concisely provide more information to the visual display. For example, the inclusion of movement and direction provides a simplified assessment of the current price point dynamics within the Bollinger bands channel.

What is the Dividend Yield spread across my watchlist? And how does it compare to the industry average? The dot plot (shown in Figure 5.20) is added to the top of each column to provide a condensed view of what's below. The dot plot display presents the full data collection vertically sorted by value with markers colored according to the direction of the period change. Below the dot plot is the stock list of dividend and yield values, each listed within their own row as color dots.

The current selection of 3.9% is one of the few in the watchlist that has made it beyond the 2.3% industry average marker. The ability to make this connection and others like it provide many benefits:

▶ **Concise**—Tracks the same watchlist in a fraction of the space.

▶ **Range context**—Displays the distribution of the watchlist items.

▶ **Placement context**—The highlighted dot is shown within the sequential order of all the rest.

Watchlist Dividends & Yield

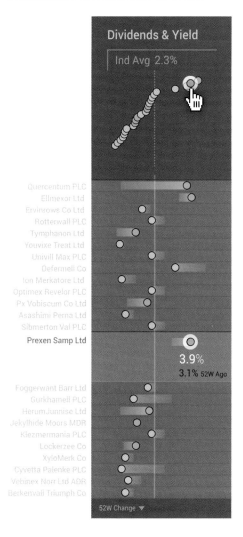

Figure 5.20 Dot Plot Column Summary

▶ **Increase/decrease context**—The collection of color dots shows you if the indicator has experienced an increase or decrease and what the respective split is between the two.

▶ **Industry average context**—Where applicable, the average line divides and shows above or below average results.

The column summary not only provides a perspective of the column contents but it also highlights the selected stock across the indicators. For example, Figure 5.21 shows a 52-week gain paired with a high Beta rating. The column summaries are interesting to see, and as an interactive system, you can query the display to see the relative placements across other securities. Actually, the more you review the column summary, the more you realize how your attention gravitates toward the top and dissipates from reviewing the column

Watchlist - Iteration 1

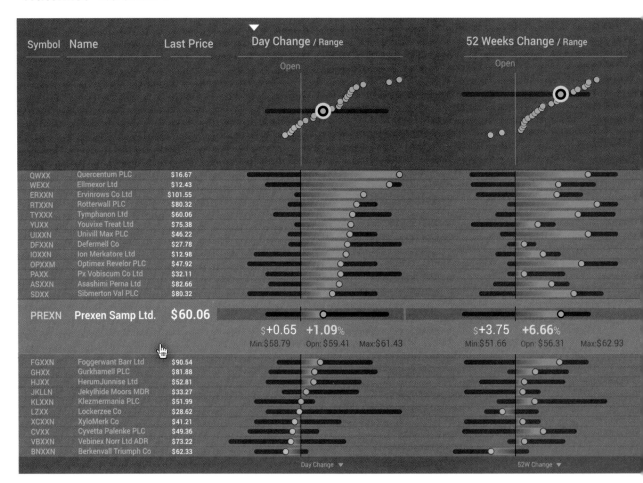

Figure 5.21 **Dot Plot and Horizontal Contrail**

contents in detail. The redundancy of the dot plot view into the column contents lessens your need to closely review the detail column data. The sheer list of data points across all columns can become overwhelming even in an organized visual display. You could argue that displaying all the columns overloads the display with too much information. Although the display is largely visual and easier to track trends and outliers, the details of each column divide your focus.

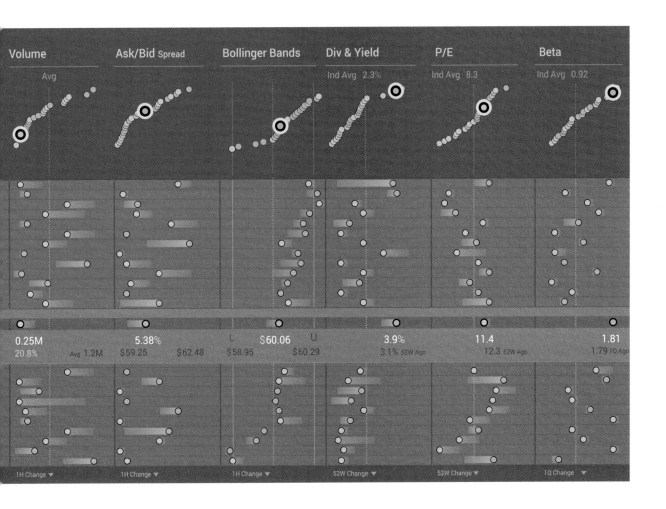

The next iteration (Figure 5.22) examines what can be done to hone your attention and remove distractions. *What should be done to the display to create greater focus?*

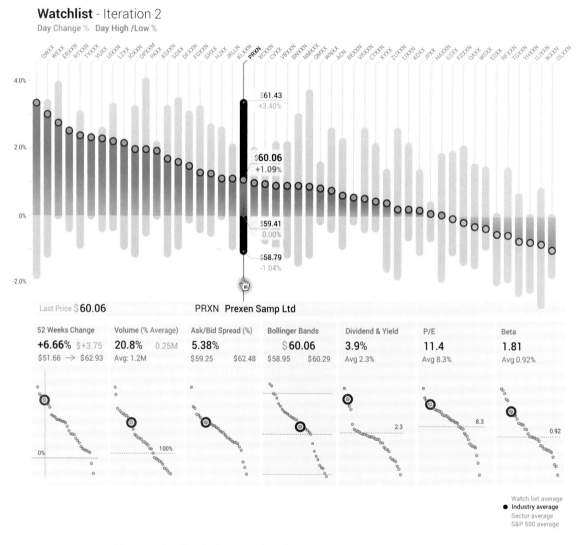

Figure 5.22 Vertical Contrail with Dot Plot Summary – Alignment by Change

Figure 5.22 resolves the issue of competing attention by constraining the representation of the remaining seven data dimensions to a collection of concise column summary views. The visualization shows the summary results across all indicators but provides focus to only one. Removing the column details improves the display and provides the space to include other details to augment the focus.

With a larger summary display, you can layer in the values connected to each indicator and compare those values against the benchmark. These additions add to the flexibility of the display to see more and do more with the data. You can see more securities and compare those securities against a list of benchmarks. You might have noticed the display includes twice the amount of securities when compared to the previous watchlist. The previous watchlist contained 24 securities, whereas this version's vertical layout compactly lists 48.

This iteration connects the summary and detail data, and as an interactive display, it provides the option to navigate the data by selecting from the indicators or the stock list. Visual techniques show the connections between the detail and summary level data: The highlighted ticker, bold stock name, black fill, and line gray connectors work together to improve the legibility, selection, and connection between the displays.

The next two figures use the same display and examine a different alignment. The detailed data display shown in Figure 5.23 is organized to align the day's spread against the zero line. Even without resetting the sort order, the view shows the variability of the day's price across the watchlist.

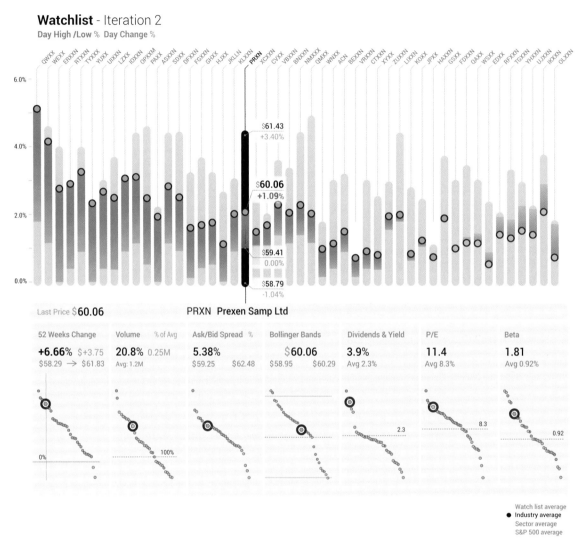

Figure 5.23 Vertical Contrail with Dot Plot Summary – Alignment by Spread

Watchlist - Detail and Summary

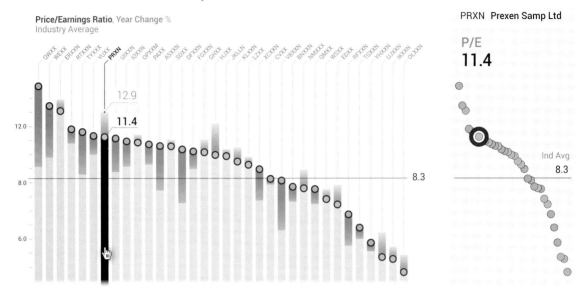

Price/Earnings Ratio, Year Change %
Industry Average

PRXN Prexen Samp Ltd

P/E
11.4

Figure 5.24 **Detail Contrail versus Summary Dot Plot**

To understand this iteration of the watchlist, Figure 5.24 presents the detail and summary view of the P/E ratio. The detail view on the left is akin to a zoomed-in version of the summary view on the right. Aside from the stock list, the detail view (visual on the left) provides the contrail and associated numeric values. Otherwise, the two views represent the same numeric values and visual perspective of the data. The similarity in the display and overlap in the data sets makes one view redundant and is not required in the display. For this reason, when the detail view is introduced, the interactive display removes the summary view to eliminate duplication.

Key Take-Aways

Our goals in redesigning the watchlist were to allow analysis of a stock within the context of a collection, and to provide an aerial view of all the securities in that watchlist. Our new watchlist design meets these goals and amends a few others, providing various types of context. The range and distribution of values in an ordered list, the placement of each stock within this range, and the performance of each stock in the list offer relative contexts to the watchlist group. However, the watchlist also provides context outside the group with industry, sector, index, and watchlist benchmark comparison. It also provides the context of time: A contrail shows recent changes across all the indicators.

Our new watchlist is both more concise and consistent. It provides various forms of context with aerial summary views of the indicators and doubles the list of stocks in the watchlist. It adheres consistently to our previously established visual elements of the ticker and quote by applying the contrail to the watchlist.

Visual System: Ticker, Quote, and Watchlist

Concise, information-rich displays can help you monitor and assess price movements, leading indicators, or comparative placement. The key purpose of the ticker, the quote, and the watchlist is to stay informed about changes in key performance indicators. For this reason, the solutions show change, communicate quickly, and work across different tools. The vertical contrail is the visual element that effectively communicates change and unites these three tools together. By encapsulating the following questions, the contrail element compactly and accurately communicates:

▶ **Where are we now?** The dot (either white, black, or colored-in) indicates the current value. Purposefully set to the highest contrast, the current value is meant to stand out in the foreground.

▶ **Where were we earlier?** The color tail of blue or orange shows the recent increase or decrease. As a fading tail, the end point of the color tail is meant to differentiate between the most recent changes in a darker color to least recent in a lighter color.

▶ **How quickly are we changing?** The length of the trail in the quote and watchlist indicates either a quick change with a long trail or slow change with a short trail.

The final set of the redesigned ticker, quote, and watchlist is shown in Figure 5.25.

Ticker

LAPE +0.37%   AAPE -0.35%

Quote

Basic

Accenture PLC

ACN

$**80.32**

$**+1.40**

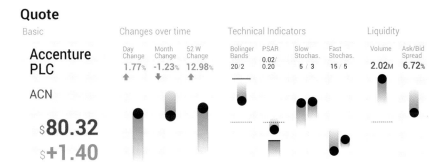

Changes over time			Technical Indicators				Liquidity	
Day Change	Month Change	52 W Change	Bolinger Bands	PSAR	Slow Stochas.	Fast Stochas.	Volume	Ask/Bid Spread
1.77%	-1.23%	12.98%	20/2	0.02/ 0.20	5 / 3	15 / 5	2.02M	6.72%

Watchlist

Day Change %   Day High /Low %

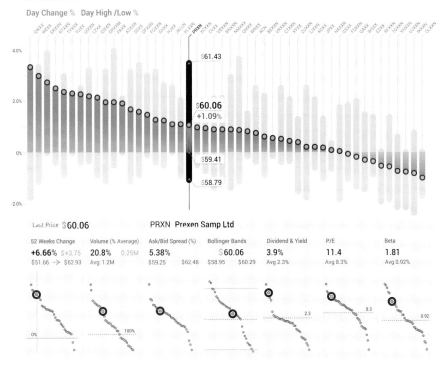

Last Price $60.06   PRXN Prexen Samp Ltd

52 Weeks Change	Volume (% Average)	Ask/Bid Spread (%)	Bollinger Bands	Dividend & Yield	P/E	Beta
+6.66% $+3.75	**20.8%** 0.25M	**5.38%**	$**60.06**	**3.9%**	**11.4**	**1.81**
$51.66 → $62.93	Avg: 1.2M	$59.25 $62.48	$58.95 $60.29	Avg 2.3%	Avg 8.3%	Avg 0.92%

$61.43

$60.06
+1.09%

$59.41

$58.79

Figure 5.25 **Visual System**

Summary

Tickers, quotes, and watchlists are some of the most widely used yet unchanged set of tools in the industry. These heavily text-based tools can be improved upon by asking, *1) Which data points are interesting to showcase? 2) How should you represent this data to make it actionable?* This chapter provides new versions of each tool by answering those two questions and iterating through various designs. With each iteration we give you the thought process behind its design decisions to reveal how the final versions are derived.

Our final versions of the ticker, quote, and watchlist share a uniting visual element that makes the three tools relatable to each other. As the key visualization, the contrail is incorporated into the final version of each tool.

VISUALIZATION	DESCRIPTION	FIGURE
Contrail	Current and past values relative to a time period represented with a circle for the current value, a connected color trail shows past values; The range is set by the time period.	5.25

Although each tool has been redesigned separately, the underlying purpose, to show a change in price, unites all the visualizations. Therefore, each of the tools can be used either independently or together as a complementary system that supports your trading tasks. As you become more accustomed to the contrail, you'll rely on it to monitor securities. You can extend the application of the contrail and integrate it into other trading tools such as the trade ticket or trade alerts.

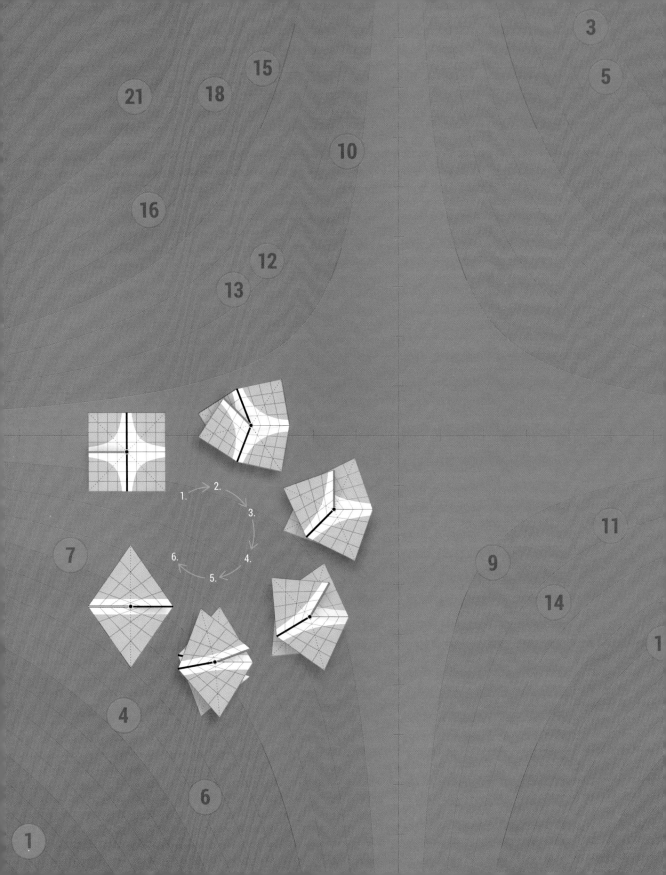

6

Performance Measurement

A key part of the Investment Process involves tracking and analyzing the overall investment performance of a portfolio—both in absolute terms and also relative to the fluctuations of the broader markets. A thorough analysis of market and portfolio performance can teach members of the investment firm important lessons that, as a feedback loop, can be used to update both the Security Assessment and the Portfolio Construction work that has come before. For example, performance attribution can give insights to the sources of the returns and the risks that have been experienced. If the reality experienced by the portfolio *ex post* does not conform to the estimates calculated on an *ex ante* basis, changes, updates, and reallocations to the portfolio might be in order.

The visualization examples in this chapter are designed for multiple audiences—those who monitor, conduct, and present the measurement and analysis of investment performance. Analyst teams, independent of the investment function, typically perform these types of Performance Measurement and Analysis. Teams in the investment firm's back office, usually calculate Performance Measurements, whereas the firm's middle office typically conducts Performance Analysis—that is, Performance Attribution. Although those in the back and middle offices conduct the analysis, those in the front office (i.e., portfolio managers) and the firm's clients make the actual investment decisions. They use the output of Performance Analysis in the form of reports and presentation materials. This chapter spans the front, middle, and back office functions of Performance Measurement and Analysis to benefit all parties, including clients, with improved visualizations.

This chapter offers reviews for three forms of Performance Measurement and Analysis data. First, we look at direct observations of market performance and their impact on an investment firm's funds and its portfolio managers' set of portfolios. Our analysis of Performance Measurements shows how to apply the same visualization techniques to charts targeted to three different audiences. Second, we discuss profit and loss as revealed in a portfolio statement and a firm composite. For the firm composite, the standards set by Global Investment Performance Standards (GIPS) are assumed to have been reviewed and followed by the investment firm. Third, we see how the performance of both markets and the portfolio over time can be broken out into individual contributory factors of Attribution. These *ex post* data results can then be compared to *ex ante* return and risk assumptions made by the investment firm. We end the chapter with a review of performance and risk attribution to reflect upon how to display the priority of changes and updates that may be in order.

NOTE

All the data in this chapter is hypothetical data and is representative of what is provided in the marketplace.

Market Performance

How is the market performing right now? Which sectors are doing well? How are the influential large cap securities performing? Martin Wattenberg, an American artist and scientist who creates visual explorations of culturally significant data, designed and introduced the Map of the Market in 1999 to provide a holistic answer to the question *"How is the market doing?"* His visualization became a well-regarded method to stay informed about the market throughout the day. The Map of the Market (Figure 6.1) introduced heatmaps and treemaps as new chart types and influenced others to use these innovative techniques. *Treemaps* present a hierarchy of nested data in rectangles and are often paired with *heatmaps* that use color to denote another quantitative variable.

Map of the Market

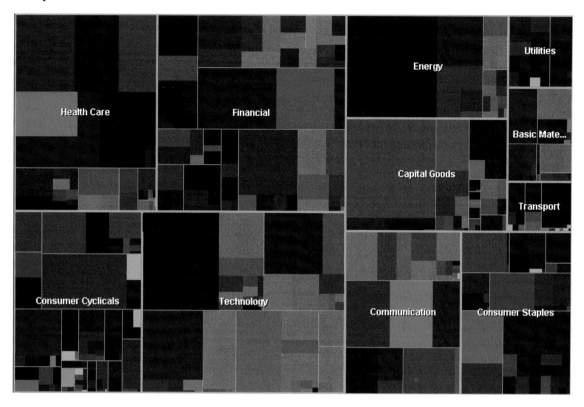

Figure 6.1 **Heat and Tree Map**

The Map of the Market is a representation of the current performance of publicly traded companies in one chart, usually a set of companies that are contained in a given index of the market. Each company is represented as a rectangle. The size of the rectangle corresponds to market capitalization, and its color indicates gains or losses in the price since the previous market close: Red indicates a drop in the price, and green an increase.

Wattenberg's insight in creating The Map of the Market was to adapt an older visualization first introduced by Ben Shneiderman, an American computer scientist and professor at the Human Computer Interaction Lab at the University of Maryland College Park. His treemap technique displayed hierarchy in the form of nested rectangles. The treemap, in combination with Wattenberg's heatmap, rapidly direct the user's attention toward areas of significant change. The Map of the Market is a powerful way to see the performance of the entire market. Despite these benefits, the chart has a few shortcomings. To better assess market performance, the data can be presented in a more structured way.

The next set of charts displays the same market data and further organizes how the data are presented. Similar to the Map of the Market, these charts are purely visual and omit numeric values. They can be augmented with a display panel that lists values of selected holdings.

The Marimekko Chart in Figure 6.2 represents similar data to the Map of the Market, but it represents sectors as columns and companies as horizontal slices within each column. A Marimekko chart is a stacked bar chart used to represent two variables that are illustrated as the height and width of each bar. In Figure 6.2, the size of each slice corresponds to the market capitalization of the company it represents, with the best performing companies listed at the top and the worst at the bottom. As shown in the legend, this creates a gradient ranging from white to yellow to orange, indicating positive, neutral, and negative performance, respectively.

Within a market, you can also assess which sectors are experiencing gains and which are experiencing losses. The gradients are scaled to provide you with an overall sense of market performance and show if there are more gains than losses or if a day is mixed. Color gradient changes and gravitate more of your attention toward those sectors that are experiencing losses. Because the chart is organized vertically, side-by-side comparisons can be more direct. For example, Figure 6.2 shows contrasting gains and losses with gains in the financial sector and heavy losses in the technology sector.

You can apply a similar approach to visually represent assets under management of an investment firm's managed funds, or to separately managed portfolios. Next, Figure 6.3 applies a similar visualization method to show how an investment firm can monitor how their funds are performing.

Market Sector Performance

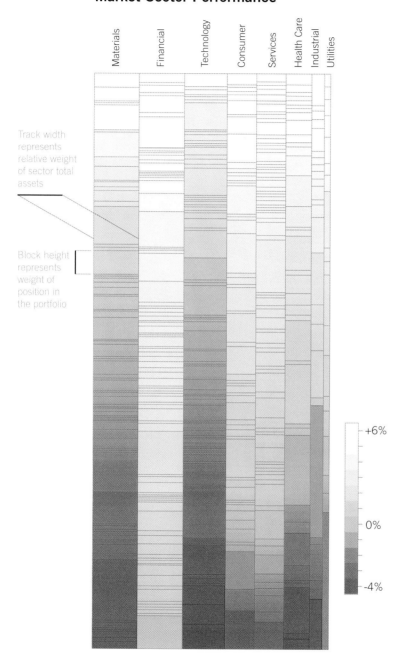

Track width represents relative weight of sector total assets

Block height represents weight of position in the portfolio

+6%

0%

-4%

Figure 6.2 Marimekko Chart – Monochromatic Gradient Unidirectional

Firm Performance

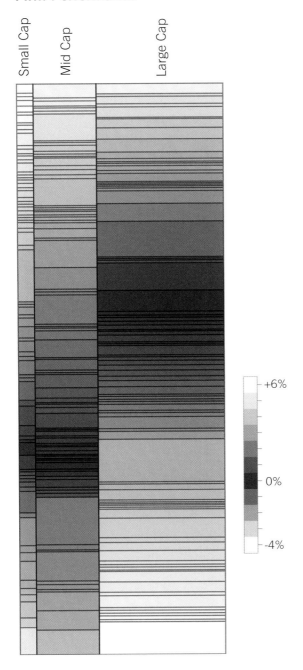

Figure 6.3 **Marimekko Chart – Monochromatic Gradient Centered**

The Firm Performance chart in Figure 6.3 shows how the investment management firm's funds are performing within a specified time frame. It applies a similar chart structure as Figure 6.2, but to market cap categories. In addition, the Firm Performance chart uses unique specification details. First, it uses a different color scheme to draw your attention toward the centered zero marker. The darkest gradient at the zero mark helps to split each column into its own negative and positive performance ranges. Just by tracking the zero marker across the categories you can see which category of funds produce more gains than losses. Second, the width of each fund category represents the relative percentage of total assets. Third, the height of each fund rectangle represents the relative assets under management within the firm.

Next, the Marimekko chart in Figure 6.4 applies slightly different specification details to review performance across many portfolios. The Marimekko Chart – Polychromatic Gradient applies the same visual methods as the previous two charts and only alters 1) the category groups to reflect the underlying data; and 2) the color scheme to closely track changes in performance. Using multiple gradients of color creates a highly differentiated color mapped scale which can reveal more specific percentage changes through color alone. Although our chart introduces more color bands, it purposefully limits the bands to three colors (including white) that are blended one to the next. Introducing too many colors into the scale would make it more difficult to decode which color was mapped to which value on the scale. (For more guidance on color use see Chapter 11, which discusses design principles.)

Key Take-Aways

The Marimekko Chart solution provides visual techniques to display performance status across investments that are categorized either by sectors in the market, funds at an investment management firm, or by separate client portfolios managed by investment managers. Performance, relative size of asset categories, and quantities of assets in a side-by-side layout provide a good way to compare all three.

Portfolio Performance

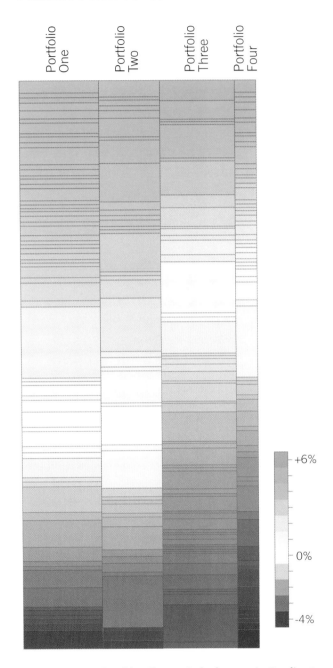

Figure 6.4 **Marimekko Chart – Polychromatic Gradient**

The color scale you use directly impacts the details you would like to communicate. Although our examples apply certain gradients to certain types of data sets, these assigned gradients are not intended to be prescriptive. Depending on the color scale you select, you can emphasize different data points in the scale and distinguish performance changes. Table 6.1 lists color scheme options that can help you make a color scale selection.

SCHEME	DESCRIPTION	BENEFITS	FIGURE
Monochromatic - Unidirectional	Color gradient based on progressive changes between light and dark shades of a single color	Emphasizes negative percentages and draws your attention toward the darker shades of the color	6.2
Monochromatic – Centered	Color gradient using a single color with the darkest shade showing the middle mark of a scale, separating the column into two sets of values	Emphasizes the zero mark; draws your attention to the divide that separates top and bottom performers or negative and positive values	6.3
Polychromatic	Transitional color gradients that mark a percentage change with two or more color bands	Enables you to identify groups of percentage change with color bands	6.4

Table 6.1
Gradient Color Scheme Options

Investment Firm Composite

Global Investment Performance Standards (GIPS) set global guidelines for measuring, calculating, and reporting performance data. The established standards allow for a direct comparison of performance regardless of region or country and follow the guiding principle of providing full disclosure and fair representation. For detailed information about GIPS, visit http://www.gipsstandards.org/.

A *composite* as defined by the GIPS handbook is "an aggregation of one or more portfolios into a single group that represents a particular investment objective or strategy." One key portion of the GIPS standards applies to composites. It enables you to investigate a firm's performance track record or compare one firm's performance gains over another firm. Because the standards are set at a global level, U.S. and non-U.S. firms that are GIPS-compliant can be compared and evaluated equally, on a level playing field. The data used in this section represents a sample investment firm's composite and applies the following definitions as defined by GIPS:

- **Composite Gross Return (%)**—The total rate of return of an investment before the deduction of any fees or expenses associated with the underlying investment expenses, management fees (transaction expenses and administrative expenses), and carried interest.

- **Composite Net Return (%)**—The total rate of return of an investment that reflects the deduction of all underlying fees and expenses, including management fees (transaction expenses and administrative expenses), performance fees, and accrued carried interest.

- **Custom Benchmark Return**—The total rate of return results taken from published sources on the relevant reference.

- **Composite 36 Month St Dev (%)**—The 3-year annualized standard deviation measures the variability of the composite *ex post*.

- **Benchmark 36 Month St Dev (%)**—The 3-year annualized standard deviation measures the variability of the selected benchmark *ex post*.

- **Number of Portfolios in the Composite**—The number of portfolios managed according to a similar investment mandate, objective, or strategy and or type (for example, segregated or pooled, taxable versus tax exempt). The minimum portfolio size for inclusion in the composite is disclosed in the presentation notes that must be provided with the composite, as per GIPS.

- **Internal Dispersion (%)**—A measure of the spread of the annual returns of individual portfolios within a composite.

The GIPS Data Table, shown in Figure 6.5, is a representative data set sample of a GIPS-compliant table. This representative GIPS example is limited to the table data and does not include the corresponding notes and disclosures outlined in the *GIPS Handbook* that would make the composite complete.

Firm Composite

	Composite Gross Return (%)	Composite Net Return (%)	Custom Benchmark Return (%)	Composite 36 Month St Dev (%)	Benchmark 36 Month St Dev (%)	Number of Portfolios	Internal Dispersion (%)	Composite Assets ($ M)	Firm Assets ($ M)
2002	−10.5	−11.4	−11.8	8.9	7.5	31	4.5	165	236
2003	16.3	15.1	13.2	6.2	3.1	34	2	235	346
2004	7.5	6.4	9.9	5.4	7.2	38	5.7	344	529
2005	1.8	0.8	0.3	4.9	4.6	45	2.8	445	695
2006	11.2	10.1	12.2	8.9	6.5	48	3.1	520	839
2007	6.1	5	7.1	7.1	8.5	49	2.8	505	1,014
2008	-17.3	-18.1	-20.9	12.6	10.2	44	2.9	475	964
2009	16.5	15.3	14.7	4.1	5.3	47	3.1	493	983
2010	10.6	9.5	13	6.6	7.1	51	3.5	549	1,114
2011	2.7	1.7	0.4	7.8	7.4	54	2.5	575	1,236

Figure 6.5 **GIPS Data Table**

Because it's a simple table, deriving the information from it may seem simple as well. There are only ten years of data and seven columns: *70 data points is not a lot—or is it?* Within one composite, you can track whether the composite produced positive or negative returns—both gross and net—and compare those returns to the benchmark.

Instead, consider reviewing the data to observe the firm's performance trends. The Firm Composite Interlocking Blocks, Figure 6.6, replaces the table text values with a variation of a bar chart.

Under GIPS standards, the proposed visualization may supplement but not replace the data table in presentations to clients or prospective clients. Internal communications are under no such obligations.

NOTE

Firm Composite

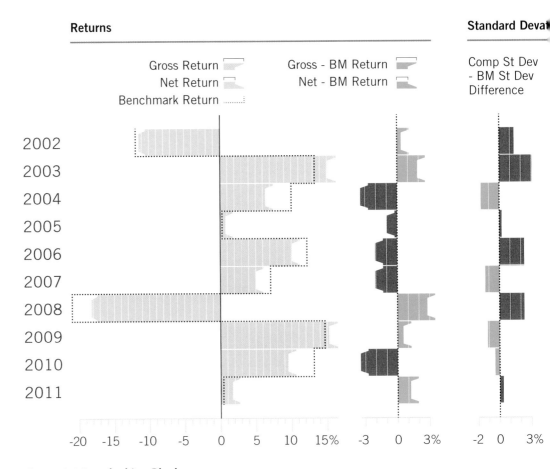

Figure 6.6 **Interlocking Blocks**

Imagine Figure 6.6 is your internal standard to display composite data. Immediately, data definition standards paired with visualization standards provides you with a better way to quickly compare composites. Stacking up and comparing one block composite to another becomes more direct. You can identify and see:

▶ The net returns above the benchmark

▶ How those returns relate to the standard deviation

▶ How risk exposure has evolved over the years

Composite/Firm Stats

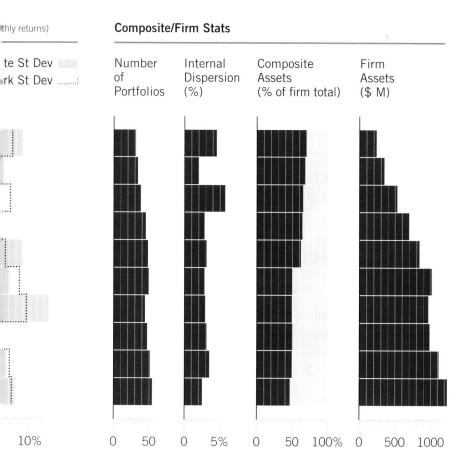

Number of Portfolios	Internal Dispersion (%)	Composite Assets (% of firm total)	Firm Assets ($ M)

10%   0   50   0   5%   0   50   100%   0   500   1000

The blocks, marked at the 1% and 5% interval, are filled in a neutral light shade of blue and are shaped with Lego-like profile cutouts showing the difference between gross and net returns. The first column consolidates three data sets: Gross Return, Net Return, and Benchmark Return. The benchmark dotted line tracks excess and shortage in the first column, while the second column visually presents these variations across the years with cutouts that provide a direction comparison. For example, the second column tracks the offset from the benchmark and shows that 2002 and 2003 produced greater returns relative to the benchmark, whereas 2004–2007 produced lower returns relative to the benchmark.

The Standard Deviation columns use similar but simplified visualization methods as the Returns columns. A side-by-side view of columns 2 and 3 make it easier to compare the risk and reward results. A few additional and notable techniques include:

▶ **Column structure**—A category and subcategory column pairing creates hierarchy and visual structure. Reading seven columns versus three simplifies and improves comprehension. Grouping data columns that contain related data sets improves comparison. Combining these related data sets into one chart column enables you to see the relationships.

▶ **Integrated legends**—The proximity of the legend to the visual element can impact how easy or difficult it is to understand the chart. The closer the legend is connected to the implementation, the easier it is for you to make a visual connection to ultimately identify and use. A legend that is connected to subheaders lessens the decoding required to understand each visual element.

▶ **Connected scales**—Each chart column is associated with a scale located at the bottom of the chart that is centered on the zero line. This zero line is used as the anchor point to make the chart easier to reference both within and across various chart columns.

▶ **Color highlights**—Color is used to emphasize different aspects of the data. Light gray and light blue are used to explain the results, and the blue/red combo is used to show the results. Reserving color to highlight key data helps direct your attention.

The use of column structure, integrated legends, connected scales, and color highlights are visualization techniques that when combined can make your charts more effective.

Key Take-Aways

The firm's composite data aims to answer how well a firm's investment strategy has performed. Standards, such as GIPS, create common data structure and measurement methods to facilitate comparisons. They enable you to investigate a firm's performance track record and compare one firm's performance gains over another's. Figure 6.6 extends the fair representation principle to a visual solution that adheres to standards that improve understanding.

Portfolio Gain/Loss

The data behind gain/loss performance reporting contain valuable bits of information that, however important, present challenges to the individual tasked with representing them clearly. Contributions, redemptions, market value additions and subtractions, realized gain versus unrealized gain, realized versus unrealized loss, and paid dividends are some of the main aspects of the data that require tracking. The Portfolio Gain/Loss (G/L) Table (Figure 6.7) shows a representative data set of total gain/loss data generated from a sample portfolio.

The Portfolio G/L Table tracks dividends collected, realized and unrealized gain/loss, and total gain/loss for 57 securities. The unrealized data track the paper profits or losses on open positions, while the realized data show closed positions' gains or losses based on the sale price minus the purchase price. Sorted in descending order, the Total Gain/Loss column prioritizes the list as the simple addition of the dividends and realized and unrealized gains and losses.

The next set of charts represents the same data set displayed as distinctly arranged bar charts. Both charts are valid solutions and can be used according to the level of detail you would like to show. One chart presents the summary level data in a horizontal layout; the other presents summary and detail data in a vertical layout. Figure 6.8 presents the former.

The Portfolio G/L Summary chart consolidates the long list of securities into a condensed bar chart. The rows list aggregate dividends, gains, losses, subtotals, and totals, while the columns split the data into bars that represent realized and unrealized gains and losses. Centered along the zero line, each section within each bar represents a corresponding dollar amount. Color, then, reinforces the impact of both realized and unrealized losses.

Portfolio Gain/Loss

	Dividends Collected	Realised Gain/Loss	Unrealised Gain/Loss	Total Gain/Loss
First REIT	$5,002.80	$2,477.35	$8,486.44	$15,966.59
Starhub	$3,550.00	$2,974.89	$5,592.86	$12,117.75
UMS	$940.00	($162.53)	$9,217.27	$9,994.73
Straco	$297.50	$0.00	$7,334.13	$7,631.63
China Merchant Pacific	$2,530.00	$761.75	$3,904.93	$7,196.69
Singtel	$438.00	$2,893.40	$0.00	$3,331.40
Keppel Corp	$260.00	$2,425.00	$0.00	$2,685.00
Boustead	$240.00	$0.00	$2,015.83	$2,255.82
Kingsmen Creatives	$320.00	$0.00	$1,519.74	$1,839.74
Aims Amp Industrial REIT	$1,458.05	($86.16)	$306.85	$1,678.74
Ascendas REIT	$697.50	$957.69	$0.00	$1,655.19
Mapletree Logistic Trust	$471.60	($42.66)	$993.66	$1,422.60
Singapore Shipping Corp	$0.00	$0.00	$1,342.16	$1,342.16
Global Investments Limited	$600.00	$721.58	$0.00	$1,321.58
Mapletree Greater China Commercial Trust	$0.00	$1,198.00	$0.00	$1,198.00
Singapore Post	$300.00	$423.47	$456.68	$1,180.15
Parkway Life REIT	$134.40	$970.85	$0.00	$1,105.25
SembCorp Industries	$0.00	$938.00	$0.00	$938.00
Kian Ann	$42.70	$887.83	$0.00	$930.53
Second Chance Properties	$422.00	$0.00	$420.38	$842.38
M1	$480.00	$350.47	$0.00	$830.48
SIA Engineering	$560.00	($967.50)	$1,232.50	$825.00
Singapore Press Holdings	$70.00	$694.48	$0.00	$764.48
Adampak	$40.00	$577.35	$0.00	$617.35
Frasers Centerpoint Trust	$622.90	($71.21)	($2.93)	$548.76
Macquarie International Infrastructure Fund	$1,573.50	($1,147.45)	$0.00	$426.05
Riverstone	$24.65	$0.00	$388.84	$413.49
Valuetronics	$0.00	$409.33	$0.00	$409.33
Asia Enterprise Holdings	$73.50	$294.00	$0.00	$367.50
Lippo Malls Indonesia Retail Trust	$48.80	$153.75	$0.00	$202.55
Soilbuild Business Space REIT	$68.10	($16.30)	$139.35	$191.15
Pertama	$31.70	$158.78	$0.00	$190.48
Cache Logistic Trust	$480.82	($315.00)	$0.00	$165.82
CH Offshore	$15.00	$142.16	$0.00	$157.16
Nikko STI ETF	$76.50	($40.62)	$103.60	$139.48
Karin Technology	$79.62	$55.39	$0.00	$135.01
Stamford Land	$0.00	$0.00	$134.17	$134.17
ARA	$0.00	$53.47	$45.55	$99.02
CapitaCommercial Trust	$0.00	$84.86	$0.00	$84.86
Sabana REIT	$543.80	($474.00)	$0.00	$69.80
Wheelock Properties	$60.00	$6.74	$0.00	$66.74
APTT	$41.30	$0.00	($6.96)	$34.34
Golden Agri	$0.00	$19.37	$0.00	$19.37
Neratel	$0.00	($6.24)	$0.00	($6.24)
Sing Investments	$7.70	$0.00	($15.00)	($7.30)
Mapletree Industrial Trust	$49.40	($63.64)	$0.00	($14.24)
Yangzijiang	$90.00	($140.49)	$0.00	($50.49)
Sarin Technologies	$95.16	($151.91)	$0.00	($56.75)
CDL Hospitality Trust	$108.20	($169.09)	$0.00	($60.89)
Nam Lee Pressed Metal	$0.00	($80.57)	$0.00	($80.57)
GRP	$240.00	($350.00)	$0.00	($110.00)
Olam	$0.00	($218.00)	$0.00	($218.00)
STI ETF	$88.00	($150.50)	($178.88)	($241.38)
IFS	$239.25	($631.79)	($129.11)	($521.65)
Plato Capital	$0.00	$0.00	($534.00)	($534.00)
Food Junction	$705.00	($1,364.36)	$0.00	($659.36)
Pteris	$30.00	$0.00	($1,311.00)	($1,281.00)

Figure 6.7 **G/L Data Table**

Portfolio Gain/Loss Summary

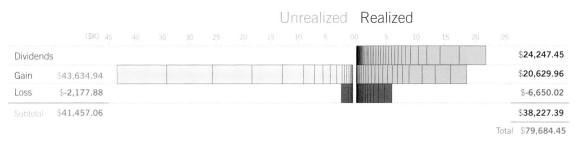

Figure 6.8 **Segmented Butterfly**

The chart represents all 57 securities in one compact graphic. At a glance, you can compare realized and unrealized gains and losses with the relative size of each security's gain/loss represented as a segment in each bar. Although this summary view displays no details, the next solution does. Figure 6.9 not only provides both a summary and detail view, but in addition, it rearranges the layout to make it easier to connect the summary with details.

In this version, the columns list unrealized, realized, and dividends data as stacked blocks while the rows list the numeric values for gains, losses, subtotal, and total. The color blue is used to show gains while red bars and text is used to show losses. You can interact with the chart to highlight the unrealized, realized, and dividends across the chart while simultaneously displaying the detail security data.

Many reports and interactive systems combine summary and detail views. Figure 6.9 illustrates an interactive system that provides details on demand. Within the first view, the system shows high-level data patterns that provide context to your questions without extraneous detail. Selecting or momentarily rolling over certain areas of the chart with your cursor can provide those details and fold them back when you're through. This organization of data allows for just in time (JIT) data delivery, which increases efficiency and decreases visual waste by providing the data only when needed. To successfully apply this approach, understand that the goals and various use cases for your audience need to be closely considered and evaluated.

Portfolio Gain/Loss Summary Details

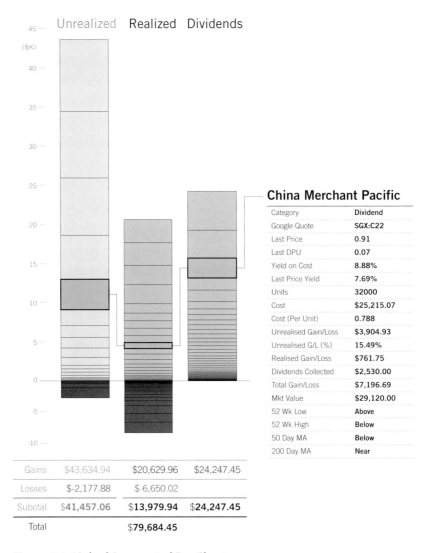

China Merchant Pacific

Category	Dividend
Google Quote	SGX:C22
Last Price	0.91
Last DPU	0.07
Yield on Cost	8.88%
Last Price Yield	7.69%
Units	32000
Cost	$25,215.07
Cost (Per Unit)	0.788
Unrealised Gain/Loss	$3,904.93
Unrealised G/L (%)	15.49%
Realised Gain/Loss	$761.75
Dividends Collected	$2,530.00
Total Gain/Loss	$7,196.69
Mkt Value	$29,120.00
52 Wk Low	Above
52 Wk High	Below
50 Day MA	Below
200 Day MA	Near

Gains	$43,634.94	$20,629.96	$24,247.45
Losses	$-2,177.88	$-6,650.02	
Subotal	$41,457.06	$13,979.94	$24,247.45
Total		$79,684.45	

Figure 6.9 Linked Segmented Bar Chart

NOTE

JIT is a well-known inventory strategy for companies. The goal of JIT is to increase efficiency and decrease waste by supplying data, services, or products as needed in a production process. JIT is a commonly used approach in the manufacturing industry.

Attribution

It is well known that investment professionals debate the proper way to calculate and present both Return and Risk Attribution, leaving these issues still lacking in consensus. Some of the debate centers around identifying which underlying factors influence the active returns (or) risk. Other debates turn on more arcane aspects of how certain attribution analyses should be properly aggregated across portfolios or over time. In any event, we have chosen certain accepted methodologies in order to illustrate our visualizations. We neither support nor are we ideologically tied to a selected industry methodology. Instead, we have chosen examples based on wide distribution and common practices. You may subscribe to different attribution methodologies and models. If that's the case, you may still be able to apply the principles and techniques we offer for visualizing your data.

Return Attribution

Return Attribution data sets focus on the *level* of periodic investment returns of a portfolio, usually relative to the level of periodic investment returns of a stipulated benchmark, to explain the impact of the portfolio management investment decisions. This section reviews quarterly sector weighting and security selection effects based on a portfolio's quarterly returns to attribute these two investment decisions.

The report methodology follows the Brinson, Hood, and Beebower (BHB) principles published in 1986. A key part of the methodology includes a quadrant table framework referred to as The Simplified Framework for Return Accountability.

NOTE

The BHB principles are published in "Determinants of Portfolio Performance" by Gary P. Brinson, L Randolph Hood, and Gilbert L. Beebower, in *Financial Analyst Journal*, July–August 1986, pp.39–44.

This section expands on the quadrant table introduced by BHB to display return attribution data. A series of tables and schematic diagrams are used to visually explain revised charts. Step by step, each figure shows how the final visualization is derived. To start, Figure 6.10 illustrates the original BHB framework and shows how it is applied to a sample report.

Attribution Weighting Effects by Sector

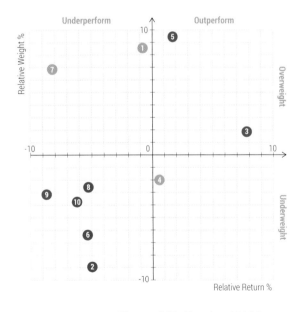

		Weight +/-\n%	Return +/-\n%	Effect\nbps
1	Consumer Discretionary	8.51	-0.79	-6.72
2	Consumer Staples	-8.88	-5.02	44.58
3	Energy	1.84	7.80	14.39
4	Financials	-1.97	0.56	-1.10
5	Health Care	9.40	1.72	16.17
6	Industrials	-6.34	-5.39	34.19
7	Information Technology	6.82	-8.20	-55.89
8	Materials	-2.54	-5.31	13.46
9	Telecom Services	-3.12	-8.73	27.25
10	Utilities	-3.72	-6.25	23.23

Figure 6.10 **Quadrant Table**

The Quadrant Table displays sector weights and returns with the x-axis dedicated to returns and the y-axis to sector weights. The quadrants that result in positive effects are filled in blue and the negative effect results are shown in yellow. Although the data seems simple and the quadrant approach seems straightforward, it can be tough to see the weight impact, rank the investment choices, see how good or bad those investment decisions are, or identify areas to learn from and adjust. Figure 6.11 uses the quadrant framework but improves upon the weighted impact in each sector.

Attribution Weighting Effects by Sector

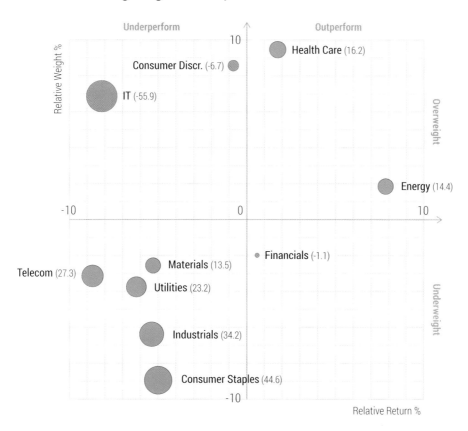

Figure 6.11 **Weighted Bubbles**

The size of the bubbles within the quadrants correlates to the effect value. You can see that IT has the greatest impact with a negative effect of −55.9bps, while the Financial sector has the smallest impact of −1.1bps. The weighted bubbles further inform you of the size and impact of certain investment choices. However, the rank order of the effect value is still difficult to grasp. Comparing the circle size and assessing which one is larger than another is even more difficult to do when the sizes are relatively close to one another.

To further improve this visualization, the next visual maintains the framework principles but reconstructs the underlying grid. A hyperbola in which $y=k/x$ such that k is the value of the sector effect, x remains the returns, and y is the relative weights constructs the new grid. This new grid can make it easier to detect if the attribution results are comparable and within the same effect track. Although the table can list the calculated effect values, Figure 6.12 provides a coordinate system that shows you the location of each effect value.

Attribution Weighting Effects by Sector

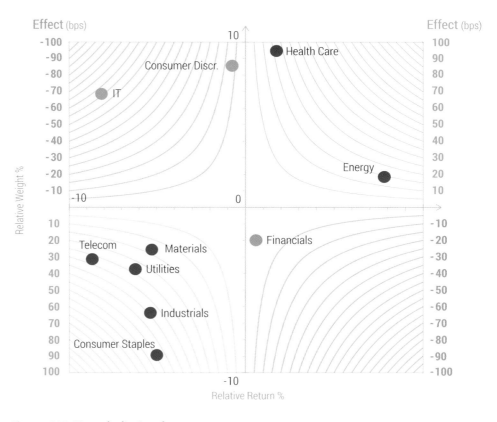

Figure 6.12 **Hyperbolic Quadrants**

Applying a hyperbolic grid to the quadrants is useful because it shows you the coordinate value of effect in bps. You don't have to rely on the size of the bubble or the quadrant coordinates; instead you can simply reference the effect track. For example, you can see that both Energy and Materials are within the same 10–20 bps effects track.

The next iteration, as shown in Figure 6.13, presents the hyperbolic quadrant with a gradient to make the tracks more visible.

Attribution Weighting Effects by Sector

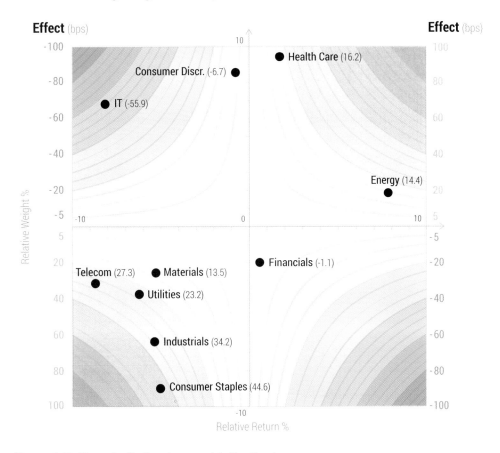

Figure 6.13 **Hyperbolic Quadrants with Gradient**

To complement the values, a color-fill gradient highlights the positive and negative effect values and groups the results into bands. This version of displaying attribution data joins the gradient bands, effect values, and sector labels to further assess rank order.

One shortcoming of Figure 6.13 is the constant band comparison between the blue and orange quadrants. To assess the rank order of the sector relative returns, the chart requires you to track each sector one by one across the four quadrants. Instead, a simplified rank order can be displayed to eliminate the tracking across quadrants and bands. The next set of visuals illustrates how to apply an alternative value axis layout to replace the curvilinear effect scale. Figure 6.14 explains this space modification applied to the standard quadrant model.

Space Conversion

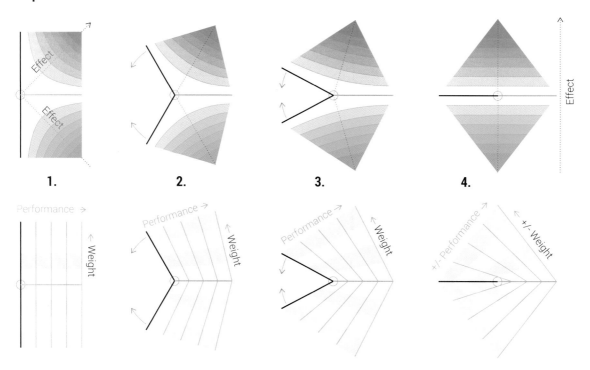

Figure 6.14 **Coordinate System Diagram**

Figure 6.15 provides a step-by-step illustration of how stretching the space as suggested in Figure 6.14 will lead to consolidations of quadrants. The two blue ("Good Quadrants") and two orange ("Bad Quadrants") overlap and thus create simplified bipolar areas.

Both Figures 6.14 and 6.15 visually describe the new coordinate system, which supports a rank view of effect. Visual gradients remain in the effect diagram to show the groups of positive and negative effects. With the three coordinates present and explained, you can now incorporate the attribution weighting effects.

Quadrant Overlap

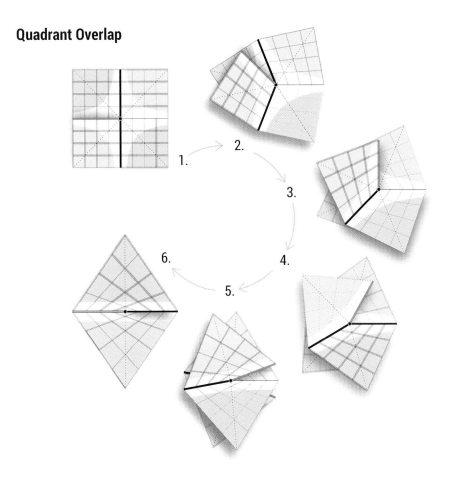

Figure 6.15 **Quadrant Fold Diagram**

The results of the combined quadrant produce a simplified plane that plots the effect in rank order from high- to low-ranking effect values. The circular color fill differentiates overweight versus underweight selections. In Figure 6.16, it is interesting to see that all the negative effect values can be attributed to overweight choices.

Attribution Weighting Effects by Sector

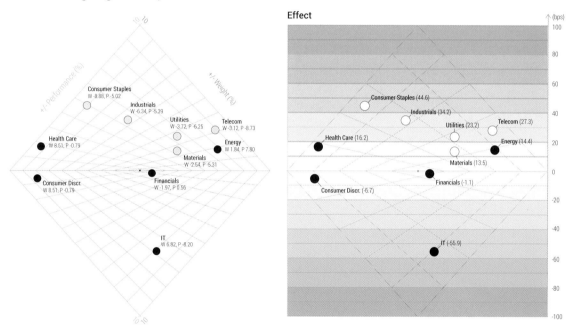

Figure 6.16 **Hyperbolic Plane**

Another part of attribution reporting often includes security selection. The next set of figures applies the same grid structure and hyperbolic plane composition to the securities in a portfolio. To start, Figure 6.17 presents the list of securities within the BHB quadrant table.

The quadrant table can easily accommodate this list of securities and include many more. The security list is numbered, color-coded, and sorted by the effect value. Next, Figure 6.18 presents the data within the effect tracks and Figure 6.19 maps the security effect values to the hyperbolic plane.

Attribution Security Selection

Selections	Weight +/- %	Return +/- %	Effect bus
① Kering	-4.21	-8.71	36.67
② Carnival	3.37	8.8	29.66
③ Starbucks	4.06	4.62	18.76
④ Liberty Media	-2.86	-6.4	18.30
⑤ Tesla Motors	3.56	4.97	17.69
⑥ Swatch Group	-3.68	-4.5	16.56
⑦ Compass Group	-1.39	-6.8	9.45
⑧ Continental	-0.69	-3.81	2.63
⑨ eBay Inc	-1.32	2.3	-3.04
⑩ CBS	2.81	-1.12	-3.15
⑪ Denso	-0.95	5.06	-4.81
⑫ Nike	1.72	-2.98	-5.13
⑬ Renault	1.42	-3.8	-5.40
⑭ Ford Motor	-1.72	3.73	-6.42
⑮ General Motors	3.65	-3.08	-11.24
⑯ Alibaba Group	2.23	-5.82	-12.98
⑰ Bridgestone	-2.13	6.32	-13.46
⑱ Fujitsu General	3.39	-4.22	-14.31
⑲ Home Depot	-2.14	7.28	-15.58
⑳ Hermès Int.	-1.91	8.67	-16.56
㉑ Walt Disney	3.36	-6.15	-20.66
㉒ Sirius XM	-3.05	9.19	-28.03
㉓ Amazon	-4.02	9.71	-39.03

Figure 6.17 **Quadrant Table**

Attribution Security Selection

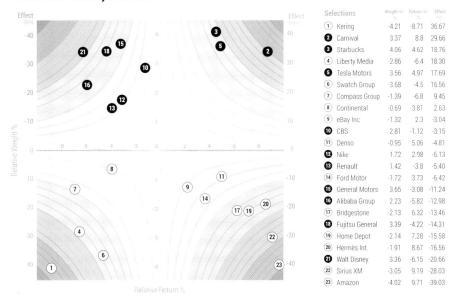

Selections	Weight +/- %	Return +/- %	Effect bus
① Kering	-4.21	-8.71	36.67
② Carnival	3.37	8.8	29.66
③ Starbucks	4.06	4.62	18.76
④ Liberty Media	-2.86	-6.4	18.30
⑤ Tesla Motors	3.56	4.97	17.69
⑥ Swatch Group	-3.68	-4.5	16.56
⑦ Compass Group	-1.39	-6.8	9.45
⑧ Continental	-0.69	-3.81	2.63
⑨ eBay Inc	-1.32	2.3	-3.04
⑩ CBS	2.81	-1.12	-3.15
⑪ Denso	-0.95	5.06	-4.81
⑫ Nike	1.72	2.98	-5.13
⑬ Renault	1.42	-3.8	-5.40
⑭ Ford Motor	-1.72	3.73	-6.42
⑮ General Motors	3.65	-3.08	-11.24
⑯ Alibaba Group	2.23	-5.82	-12.98
⑰ Bridgestone	-2.13	6.32	-13.46
⑱ Fujitsu General	3.39	-4.22	-14.31
⑲ Home Depot	-2.14	7.28	-15.58
⑳ Hermès Int.	-1.91	8.67	-16.56
㉑ Walt Disney	3.36	-6.15	-20.66
㉒ Sirius XM	-3.05	9.19	-28.03
㉓ Amazon	-4.02	9.71	-39.03

Figure 6.18 **Hyperbolic Quadrants**

The resulting display of the security selection on a hyperbolic plane presents an ordered list and introduces a greater understanding of placement and distribution. *Which band has the largest clusters and are those clusters over or underweight?*

Attribution Security Selection

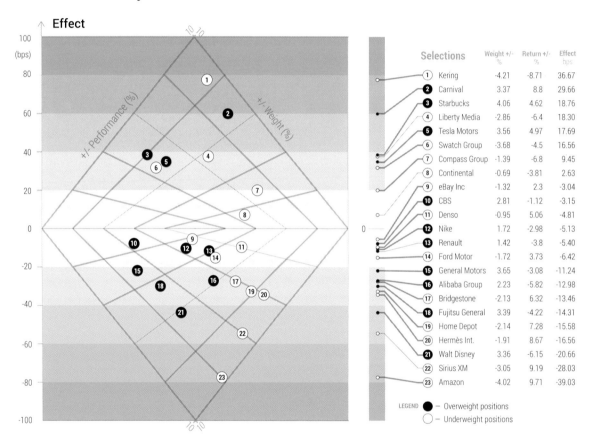

Selections	Weight +/- %	Return +/- %	Effect bps
1 Kering	-4.21	-8.71	36.67
2 Carnival	3.37	8.8	29.66
3 Starbucks	4.06	4.62	18.76
4 Liberty Media	-2.86	-6.4	18.30
5 Tesla Motors	3.56	4.97	17.69
6 Swatch Group	-3.68	-4.5	16.56
7 Compass Group	-1.39	-6.8	9.45
8 Continental	-0.69	-3.81	2.63
9 eBay Inc	-1.32	2.3	-3.04
10 CBS	2.81	-1.12	-3.15
11 Denso	-0.95	5.06	-4.81
12 Nike	1.72	-2.98	-5.13
13 Renault	1.42	-3.8	-5.40
14 Ford Motor	-1.72	3.73	-6.42
15 General Motors	3.65	-3.08	-11.24
16 Alibaba Group	2.23	-5.82	-12.98
17 Bridgestone	-2.13	6.32	-13.46
18 Fujitsu General	3.39	-4.22	-14.31
19 Home Depot	-2.14	7.28	-15.58
20 Hermès Int.	-1.91	8.67	-16.56
21 Walt Disney	3.36	-6.15	-20.66
22 Sirius XM	-3.05	9.19	-28.03
23 Amazon	-4.02	9.71	-39.03

LEGEND ● – Overweight positions
○ – Underweight positions

Figure 6.19 **Hyperbolic Plane**

Key Take-Aways

This section provides two related solutions to identify and rank return attribution data. Both solutions display the effect data within a hyperbolic grid to provide a simplified ranking system, and both solutions can be applied to sector and security-level attribution reporting. The hyperbolic quadrants (Figures 6.13 and 6.18) maintain the original BHB quadrant system and apply the gradient color-fill to distinguish effect rank. This in turn (Figures 6.16 and 6.19) creates a ranked positive to negative effect value list.

Each visualization within this section has some merit. For example, the hyperbolic quadrant solution (Figures 6.12 and 6.18) has the advantage of resembling the original BHB quadrant system. The quadrant system shows attribution pertaining to the four combinations of weight and returns. The familiarity of this visualization can make it more readily understandable. In contrast, the hyperbolic plane (Figures 6.16 and 6.19) introduces a new coordinate system to provide a simplified ranking system. The new solution removes the quadrants and replaces these with a consolidated plane that shows the distribution and clusters of the effect values.

Risk Attribution

Risk attribution focuses on the *volatility* of a portfolio's periodic investment returns relative to the benchmark's investment returns. This section charts multi-factor risk model data to evaluate *ex post* risk at a firm-wide level. The following charts show you how to display risk model results, and answer: *Is a certain fund riskier than its peer and by how much? What is the relative volatility of the invested fund?* A clear understanding of this data enables you to make informed decisions based on the relative volatility of a firm's funds.

The Risk Attribution Table (Figure 6.20) displays the results of sample risk models. As you review the data table, consider how you would answer the questions related to peer relative risk. Note that the models are representative and can easily be replaced with other vendor models or your own proprietary models to track active risk, beta, and % factor risk. The Risk Attribution Table is a useful tool that provides 1) valuable data based on a range of calculation results; 2) organized data groups; and 3) a look-up table used to reference and pinpoint certain data points. Yet there are several barriers that limit you from gaining insights from the data.

Portfolio Risk Attribution

	Active Risk Global	-1 Yr Active Risk Global	Active Risk US	-1 Yr Active Risk US	Beta Global	-1 Yr Beta Global	Beta US	-1 Yr Beta US	% Factor Risk Global	-1 Yr % Factor Risk Global	% Stock Risk Global	-1 Yr % Stock R... G
Large Cap Growth												
LM Growth	3.68	4.74	3.78	4.54	1.11	1.18	1.08	1.19	60	76	40	
Controlled US Growth	1.92	2.16	2.17	2.35	1.07	1.1	1.06	1.02	24	36	76	
Pragmatic Growth	4.34	4.91	4.26	5.38	1.14	1.23	1.19	1.23	75	80	25	
Merit Growth	3.91	5.38	4.23	5.26	1.16	1.2	1.17	1.23	64	78	36	
Varied Growth	2.00	2.11	2.37	2.09	1.04	1.02	1.04	1.02	18	25	82	
Tactical Growth	3.04	3.70	3.32	3.40	1.11	1.1	1.08	1.06	48	63	52	
Active Growth	5.49	6.16	6.29	5.89	1.20	1.25	1.23	1.23	75	79	25	
Growth Longitude	4.48	4.32	5.26	4.77	1.19	1.15	1.20	1.21	65	69	35	
Large Cap Value												
Merit Value	1.86	2.26	2.48	2.99	0.92	0.93	0.94	0.89	55	63	45	
Varied Core/Value	1.80	2.41	1.86	2.47	0.95	0.95	1.00	0.96	52	60	48	
Merit Equity	1.64	2.10	1.79	2.46	0.98	0.98	1.02	0.95	26	35	74	
DG Capital Appreciation	4.50	4.43	4.77	5.93	1.18	1.06	1.23	1.15	76	66	24	
Pragmatic Value	3.80	4.40	3.84	5.23	1.08	1.11	1.09	1.10	66	70	34	
Value	1.78	1.78	1.95	2.26	0.98	1.01	0.99	0.96	25	28	75	
Value - Dividends	2.81	3.62	3.42	5.09	0.91	0.87	0.87	0.81	70	80	30	
DG Value	3.51	4.09	4.13	6.22	0.83	0.83	0.86	0.74	74	87	26	
Controlled US Value	1.68	1.76	1.84	2.11	1.02	1.00	0.97	1.02	18	22	82	
DG Basic Value	3.33	3.05	2.85	2.63	1.06	1.06	1.09	1.05	68	69	32	
Mid Cap												
Mid Cap OM	2.74	2.96	3.06	3.14	0.95	0.95	0.94	0.98	26	19	74	
Select Mid Cap Growth	4.21	5.45	4.18	5.68	1.08	1.11	0.99	1.12	18	34	82	
Mid Cap Value	3.00	3.36	3.25	3.40	1.01	1.00	0.95	0.94	35	39	65	
Select Mid Cap Value	4.50	4.81	4.68	4.96	1.03	0.97	1.00	1.04	33	24	67	
Mid Cap Growth	4.58	7.25	4.26	6.89	1.12	1.23	1.17	1.15	61	79	39	
Mid Cap Growth Longitude	4.04	5.65	4.80	5.37	1.18	1.15	1.11	1.18	64	72	36	
MG Cap Value	3.14	3.67	3.86	5.27	0.91	0.92	0.86	0.83	44	37	56	
Small Cap												
Small Cap Value	3.71	4.23	4.42	5.89	0.94	0.87	0.89	0.85	53	45	47	
Small Cap Openings	3.80	4.07	4.44	5.62	1.07	1.09	1.10	1.13	45	55	55	
Emerging Companies	3.85	3.97	5.60	5.03	0.97	0.90	1.04	1.01	37	51	63	
Small Cap Growth	3.04	3.10	3.25	3.25	1.03	1.06	1.00	0.99	21	15	79	
Select Small Cap Growth	4.03	4.78	4.34	4.79	0.96	1.09	1.02	1.02	15	23	85	
Small Cap Openings	3.01	3.78	3.59	4.53	1.01	1.07	1.05	1.08	23	39	77	
SW Micro Cap	6.62	8.26	6.51	7.42	0.82	0.82	1.02	0.91	48	61	52	
Controlled Small Cap Equity	2.30	2.22	2.34	2.39	0.96	1.00	0.93	0.97	34	18	66	
US Small Cap Growth	2.35	2.33	2.18	2.45	0.97	1.07	0.94	1.01	19	12	81	
US Smaller Cap TA	3.66	3.56	4.77	4.22	1.00	1.05	1.07	1.08	17	27	83	
US Focus												
Choice Growth	8.09	9.61	8.42	10.44	1.35	1.28	1.25	1.38	78	89	22	
Choice Value Growth	8.74	8.17	8.15	9.66	1.39	1.22	1.36	1.33	80	70	20	
All Cap Pragmatic	11.79	15.19	13.04	17.58	1.49	1.56	1.50	1.67	75	90	25	
Choice Intrinsic Value	5.06	6.31	6.01	6.89	1.04	1.08	1.01	1.07	23	27	77	
CM Specialty Growth	5.06	5.75	6.02	6.96	1.13	1.13	1.23	1.24	66	78	34	
Focused Equity	3.53	3.71	4.05	3.53	1.10	1.08	1.00	1.02	44	42	56	
Choice Merit Equity	3.47	3.44	3.82	4.18	0.89	0.97	0.91	0.96	40	27	60	
CM Choice	3.79	4.88	4.89	7.41	1.00	1.08	0.98	1.10	29	43	71	

Figure 6.20 **Risk Data Table**

Although the table is an effective look-up tool, it is not effective for comparison. Across 43 funds and 12 different calculated results, you are presented and tasked to make sense of 516 different numeric data points. It is difficult to scan the table to compare and analyze how various funds have trended over the past year. It is also difficult to calculate the differences among multiple models. For example, to analyze a fund's active risk, you need to review and calculate four data points: two models and those two models 1 year back. *What is the active risk of our funds across models and what is the magnitude of change? How does the Active Growth funds compare to other funds in its category of Large Cap Growth?*

Instead, consider an approach that maintains the three original benefits of the table (range of calculation results, organized group structure, look-up method) while removing the calculation efforts. The following set of figures are all part of one solution introduced in small parts. A small slice of the data is shown in Figure 6.21.

Figure 6.21 **Bar Chart**

This mini chart (Figure 6.21) is a simple start to compare active risk across the eight funds with ease.

With the baseline data well represented, the next chart, Figure 6.22, layers in time as another element of the chart.

Figure 6.22 **Bar Delta**

Color-filled triangles attached to each bar show movement changes over a one-year period to track funds and their corresponding direction and rate of change for the labeled risk model. As shown in the legend, the tip of the triangle represents the current value, and the base of the triangle represents the values one year back. All triangle tips are attached to the ends of the bars, while all triangle bases float to the right or left of the bar. To further enforce an increase or decrease in active risk orange (a warning color) indicates increases in the risk, whereas blue (a cool calming color) shows decreases.

The resulting Figure 6.22 consolidates two data columns into one. This slice of the data set represents 16 risk values, and can answer the following questions: *Which funds experienced an increase in active risk over the past year? Which funds were the most stable? Which fund decreased the most over the past year?* These questions are relatively easy to answer using our visual system. In contrast, numeric representations, as shown in the original table, require 120 calculations to be made to answer these same questions. Figure 6.23 consolidates more data and incorporates another slice of the data into the chart.

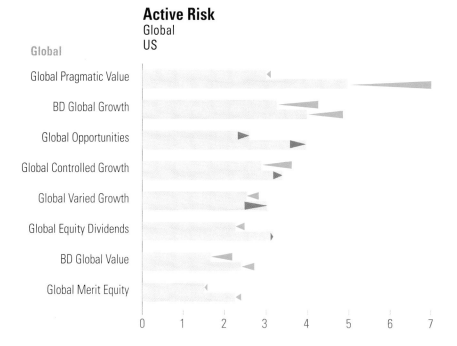

Active Risk
Global
US

Global

Global Pragmatic Value

BD Global Growth

Global Opportunities

Global Controlled Growth

Global Varied Growth

Global Equity Dividends

BD Global Value

Global Merit Equity

0   1   2   3   4   5   6   7

Figure 6.23 Bar Delta Stacks

As shown in Figure 6.23, two stacked bars encourage direct comparison between the risk models. This data slice includes 32 distinct values—calculated as eight funds, two models, and two points in time—all within one column. As a result of the consolidation to one column, the small differences across the data set can surface.

The efficiency gains the chart provides through quick comprehension (without calculations) outweigh the effort required to learn the visual system. However once learned, the chart can use multiple triangle markers and provide a comprehensive view across more funds and more attributes.

Figure 6.24 applies these similar techniques and approaches to the remaining data set, transforming the original data table into one visual communication.

Portfolio Risk Attribution: Active, Beta, Factor and Stock Risk

Figure 6.24 **Bar Delta Columns**

The original twelve columns of data—for active, beta risk, factor, and stock risk—are reduced to three columns. And while the table no longer shows the numeric values, accommodations can be made to incorporate and layer those details as needed. As in previous visuals, when numeric values are needed, they can be displayed in a panel to the right of the chart.

Key Take-Aways

As a comprehensive review of a full fund list, the Portfolio Risk Attribution chart pinpoints funds or groups of funds with significant increases or decreases in risk. The ability to parse the data with ease is made possible by employing the following methods:

▶ **Direct comparison**—Replacing numeric values with bars makes it easy to compare funds, risk models, or years. An enriched set of horizontal stacked bar charts facilitates comparisons across the 43 funds.

▶ **Data consolidation**—Folding four columns into one unites related data sets. For example, all four data columns that represent active risk are consolidated into one chart column.

▶ **Triangle markers**—Triangle markers visually illustrate the rate of change for each fund. *Which funds experienced the quickest decrease in active risk? Which fund group faced the most increase in beta risk?* The triangle markers quickly answer these questions.

Figure 6.24 has been constructed to optimize your comprehension of the change in risk data to directly compare related data and discover trends guided by the triangular markers.

Summary

In this chapter, you have seen data sets composed of market level data with the market map, firm level data with the composite and risk attribution example, and portfolio level data with gain/loss and return attribution.

Across each of these use cases, you have seen visualization techniques that show you how to:

▶ Reorganize data for better comparison as shown in the market map

▶ Group-related data sets as shown in the GIPS composite table

▶ Provide data delivery on demand as shown in portfolio gain/loss report

▶ Map data to a different grid system as shown in return attribution

Aside from these visualization techniques, this chapter has also introduced new chart types. The following table lists the visualization ideas we have applied to performance measurement data. They represent new versions of each chart type that best represent the data. The Marimekko chart is the only commonly used chart type that has been refined to showcase performance data. The other chart types introduce adjustments to emphasize different aspects of the data.

VISUALIZATION	DESCRIPTION	FIGURE
Marimekko Chart	Vertically organized rectangles in which the height and width represents quantity and the columns represent categories.	6.2, 6.3, 6.4
Interlocking Blocks	Two sets of blocks; one represents the quantities of three values, while another represents the net results of two values.	6.6
Linked Segmented Bar	Two or more stacked bar charts linked so that when one section is selected the corresponding sections are highlighted, showing location and other attributes of the entity.	6.9
Hyperbolic Quadrants	A quadrant grid system based on a hyperbolic formula in which $y=k/x$ (k is the product of x and y), x is the value on the x-axis and y the value on the y-axis.	6.12, 6.13, 6.18
Hyperbolic Plane	Consolidated hyperbolic quadrants such that positive and negative planes are combined to show the rank order of the mapped items.	6.16, 6.19

VISUALIZATION	DESCRIPTION	FIGURE
Bar Delta	A bar with an isosceles triangle attached to the end. The attached vertex indicates the same bar quantity, whereas the edge parallel to the bar end indicates another quantity.	6.22, 6.23, 6.24

This chapter introduced new visualization techniques largely based on existing visual methods. Treemaps, stacked bars, quadrants, and single bar charts are all widely used methods to display data. However, adjusting the treemap from a set of nested rectangles to vertically organized rectangles improves comparison. And simply attaching interlocking blocks and triangles to a bar provides additional information about net results and the rate of change. Each of these visualizations builds on the familiarity of an existing chart type, then adds an improvement. Building upon prior knowledge makes each new visualization easier to interpret and learn and recognize as an improvement.

PART 3

Showcasing Data for Effective Communications

▶ **Chapter 7:** Financial Statements

▶ **Chapter 8:** Pension Funds

▶ **Chapter 9:** Mutual Funds

▶ **Chapter 10:** Hedge Funds

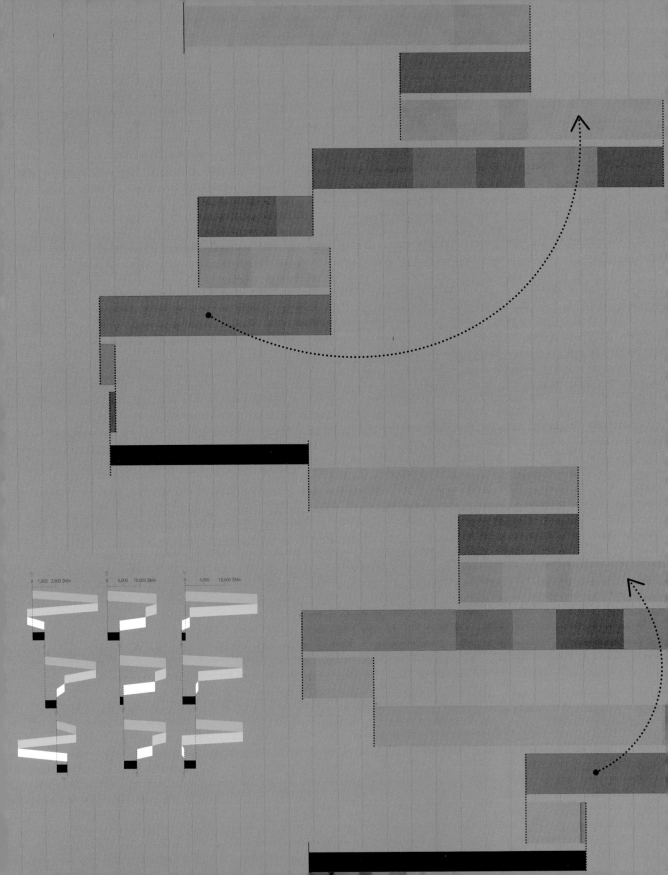

0 1,000 2,000 $Min   0 5,000 10,000 $Min   0 5,000 10,000 $Min

7

Financial Statements

Accounting standards set the expectations, scope, and definitions of the data in financial statements. In an annual report, hired auditors are expected to review data and presentation materials to ensure accuracy and honesty across all pages. Annual reports, 10-K SEC filings, and established practices in compliance with generally accepted accounting principles (GAAP) have well-documented principles, policies, and procedures to ensure integrity and a common understanding in the practice of organizing and presenting financial data.

As the industry recognizes accuracy as a baseline requirement, transparency and accessibility to the details of the data becomes important as well. This chapter explores visualization ideas that maintain conventional standards of financial statements while answering the following questions about how you might improve and augment the data display to be more transparent and easily accessible to answer: *How do the operating expenses compare to the revenues? What comprises investment cash flows and how does it compare to operational cash flows? How can you show the connection between the statement of financial position and cash flows or operating budget?*

Each section within the chapter reviews a fundamental aspect of financial statements including the statement of cash flows, statement of activities, and operating budget. Within each of these financial statements, we aim for accuracy, transparency, and accessibility, all the while showing you how to apply and embed those principles into charts. All the examples in this chapter start with the traditional text and numeric value table list and evolve into a set of visual representations. Each set begins with a chart that communicates the core data points and then extends the chart to incorporate more details or more capabilities in later examples. You learn how to further tailor the display by selecting from a range of visual techniques to enrich your review of the statement of cashflows, financial activity, and operating budgets.

NOTE   The data set used in the chapter is sourced from the annual reports of both nonprofit and for-profit organizations. Although the visuals are sourced and designed for print, a few are also shown as interactive displays.

Statement of Cash Flows

Knowing how cash moves in and out of an organization provides crucial insights into how an organization operates. Views that highlight cash flows focus on incoming flows for operation, investment, or finance and outgoing expenditures and investments. This data shown in a cash flows statement helps you answer questions such as: *How well can this organization generate cash? How do incoming flows compare to outgoing cash flows?* To help you see and better understand the answers to those questions, this section provides various data visualization techniques for statement of cash flows of both nonprofit and for-profit organizations.

Nonprofit Organizations

The statement of cash flows for a nonprofit organization resembles that of a for-profit organization. The differences lie not in the structure of the statement but in the focus and results, showing how they manage cash flows. Nonprofit organizations focus on how little they require to operate and how generously they fund services that support their community. The visualization that follows the data table in Figure 7.1 can serve this focus. But first, we review a standard nonprofit cash flows statement (Figure 7.1).

Smith College
Statements of Cash Flows
June 30, 2013 and 2012   (In Thousands of Dollars)

Cash Flows From Operating Activities	2013	2012
Change in net assets	155,174	(37,557)
Adjustments to reconcile increase in net assets to net cash used in operating activities:		
Depreciation and amortization	19,774	18,757
Unrealized (gain) loss in market value, interest, and fees on interest rate swap agreements	(11,739)	16,668
Net unrealized and realized gains on investments	(203,653)	(28,232)
Actuarial change in life income obligation	(729)	508
Contributions restricted for long-term investment	(4,345)	(2,653)
Contributions of property and securities	(4,722)	(4,460)
Net change in operating assets and liabilities:		
Receivables, net and other assets	2,316	5,504
Accounts payable, accrued liabilities, and asset retirement obligation	1,804	1,124
Deferred income, deposits, and agency funds	1,209	(290)
Net cash used in operating activities	**(44,911)**	**(30,631)**
Cash Flows From Investing Activities		
Purchases of plant and equipment	(17,557)	(20,142)
Funds held by bond trustee	27	13
Short-term investments	(8,813)	21,124
Proceeds from student and other loan collections	1,538	2,005
Student and other loans issued	(1,086)	(1,365)
Purchases of investments		(89,980)
Sales and maturities of investments	388,839	133,039
Net cash provided by investing activities	**28,412**	**44,694**
Cash Flows From Financing Activities		
Contributions restricted for long-term investment	4,345	2,653
Payments on long-term debt	(2,635)	(2,510)
Net cash provided by financing activities	1,710	143
Net change in cash and cash equivalents	(14,789)	14,206
Cash and cash equivalents, beginning of year	32,737	18,531
Cash and cash equivalents, end of year	**17,948**	**32,737**
Supplemental disclosure:		
Interest paid	6,488	6,614
Gifts in kind	1,643	2,952
Purchases of plant and equipment increasing (decreasing) accounts payable	1,264	(297)

Figure 7.1 **Statements of Cash Flows**

As it stands, the Statements of Cash Flows table (Figure 7.1) presents a string of positive and negative numbers, subtotals, and totals. The numbers easily blend in from one line item to another and do not show the impact and size of each line item. Although each section provides a net amount, you still need to inspect individual line items to understand the extent and direction of the flows. *Does one large positive flow counter the remaining negative flows? Or instead is there more of a balance?* Augmenting the details of the flows with visual indicators enables you to make better sense of the data to see how the organization is spending. Figure 7.2 visualizes the data, so the previous questions can be quickly answered.

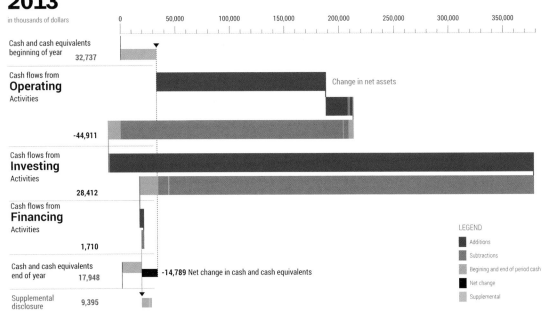

Figure 7.2 **Summary Waterfall**

As an organization, where did your cash level start at the beginning of the year, where did you spend, and how did you arrive at the current balance? Waterfall bar charts such as the one in Figure 7.2 show how movement of individual flows can impact a derived value. This type of chart is well-suited to display the cash flows data in Figure 7.1. To help track the operating versus investing activities, the vertical line that starts at 32,737 provides a constant reference point as cash flows in and out of the organization. The line shows how close or far away from the starting point the flows reach.

If you compare the order and values of the data in Figure 7.2 to the original Statements of Cash Flows (Figure 7.1) you may notice some differences. First, the order of the data has been altered to show the beginning and ending balance in the beginning and ending of the chart. Second, Figure 7.2 aggregates the values for each section. Next, Figure 7.3 expands the data set and includes all the values listed in the original cash flow table.

The Detail Waterfall (Figure 7.3) introduces the full data set while still maintaining the same structure as the previous cash flows chart. The aggregations of positive cash flows (detailed in shades of blue) versus negative cash flows (shades of orange) reorganize the detail data into two categories of positive and negative. The color variations within each bar correspond to the listed line item amounts; some are too small to see or appear only as faint lines. For example, Funds Held by Bond Trustees listed as 13 (thousand) is too small of an amount to see as a color block, whereas the next listing of Short-Term Investments is a sizeable amount at 21,124 (thousand) and represented as the next color block. The color blocks provide more visual information about the varying amounts within each section. As a result, the waterfall chart provides three levels of hierarchical exploration:

▶ **Top-level aggregates**—Results of top-level aggregates for operating, investing, and financing activities. For example, operating activities list −30,631 as the aggregate value.

▶ **Grouped items**—Grouped additions are shown as blue bars and the subtractions are shown in orange bars. To reinforce the grouping, the text items appear in the corresponding color of the bars.

▶ **Individual items**—Individual line items are listed within each group.

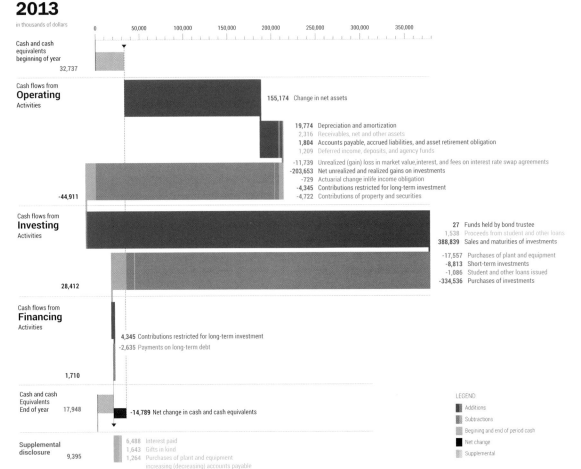

Figure 7.3 **Detail Waterfall**

The Waterfall chart can grow to include more years of summary and detail data as time unfolds. Figures 7.4 and 7.5 show two ways to illustrate two years of cash flow data into one chart.

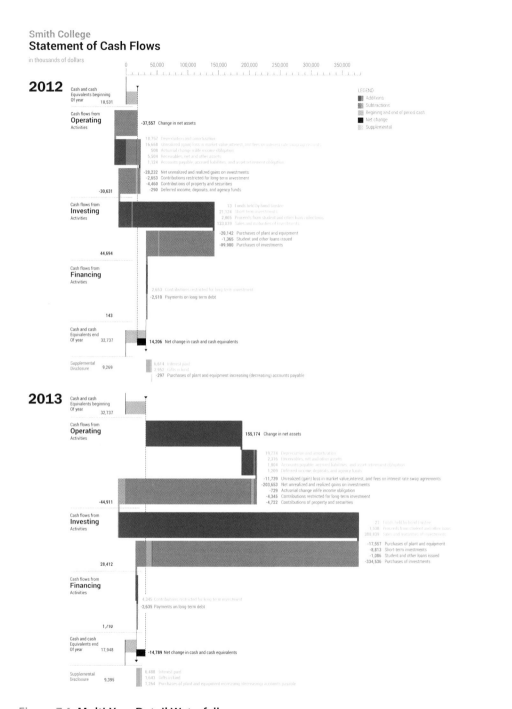

Figure 7.4 **Multi-Year Detail Waterfall**

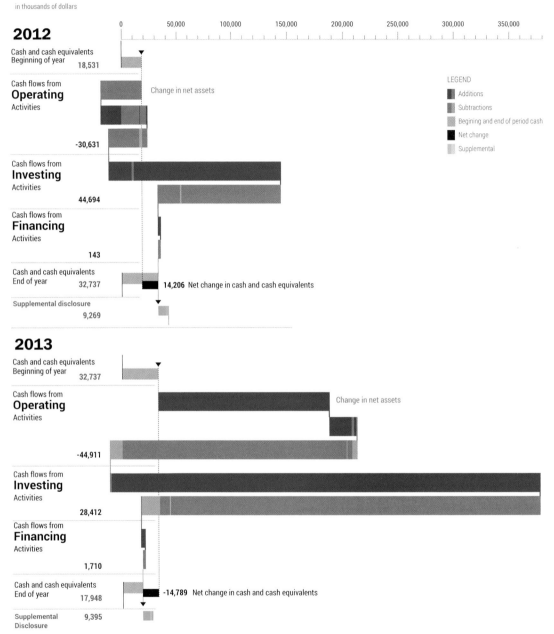

Figure 7.5 **Multi-Year Summary Waterfall**

The benefit of the Waterfall chart is that it can expand from year to year and seamlessly connect one year's flows into another. Detail or summary, two years or four, the Waterfall chart can expand or contract in both details and years. Observations of the data can include trends that point to long-term or short-term cash flow strategy stated by the organization. For example, Figure 7.5 shows a two-year trend of consistently allocating small Financing Activities paired with an increase in Investing Activities. As years are added to the chart, you can view more trends that connect organizational accomplishments set to a multi-year strategy.

Key Take-Aways

Cash flows data can be well represented with the Waterfall chart. It shows how cash or cash equivalents move in and out of an organization using a series of bars describing how individual cash flows impact a derived value. Waterfall charts are flexible enough to represent summary, detail, and multi-year cash flows. These multi-year cash flows reveal if there are trends in how cash is used and if the goals are supported with a cash flows strategy. Later in this chapter, you will see additional benefits to and variations on the Waterfall chart. It can be applied to other types of financial statements, and other visualizations can be integrated into the Waterfall chart.

For-Profit Organizations

For-profit organizations typically aim to show how well they manage their money to impress current and potential investors. Some may want to present healthy starting/ending cash amounts to prove they have sufficient working capital; and others may wish to demonstrate that they can generate cash to grow their business. In either case, the Waterfall chart can fulfill these goals. Figure 7.6 represents for-profit data and applies the Waterfall chart to visualize this data.

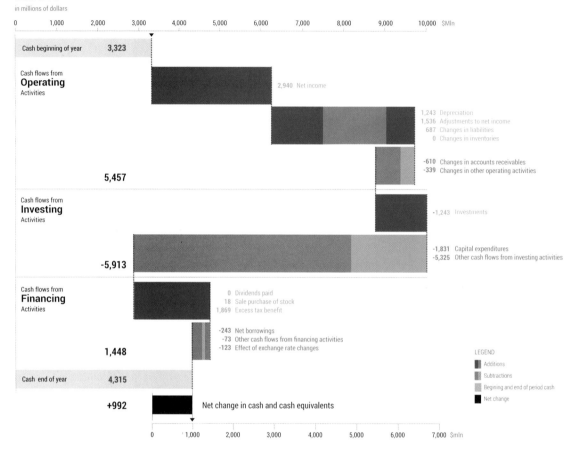

Figure 7.6 Detail Waterfall

Although the data and goals of for- and nonprofit organizations may differ substantially, the detailed Waterfall cash flows visualization technique can work equally well for both. The same visualization techniques of displaying cash flows data in Detail, Summary, or Multi-year Waterfalls can be applied. But some may wish to visually distinguish the components of their cash flows by tweaking the style of the Waterfall visualization as in Figure 7.7.

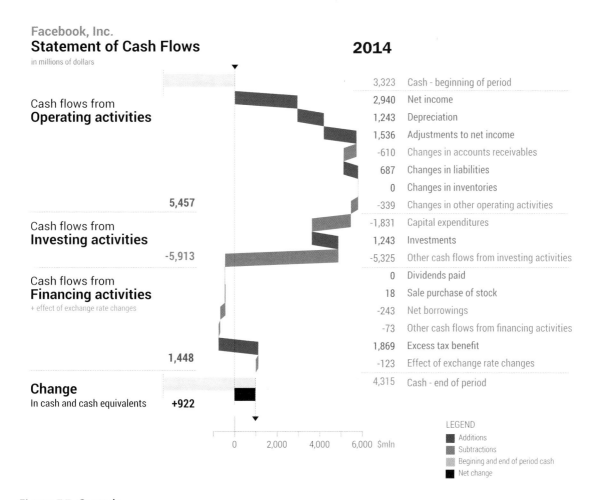

Facebook, Inc.
Statement of Cash Flows
in millions of dollars

2014

	3,323	Cash - beginning of period
Cash flows from **Operating activities**	2,940	Net income
	1,243	Depreciation
	1,536	Adjustments to net income
	-610	Changes in accounts receivables
	687	Changes in liabilities
	0	Changes in inventories
5,457	-339	Changes in other operating activities
Cash flows from **Investing activities**	-1,831	Capital expenditures
	1,243	Investments
-5,913	-5,325	Other cash flows from investing activities
Cash flows from **Financing activities** + effect of exchange rate changes	0	Dividends paid
	18	Sale purchase of stock
	-243	Net borrowings
	-73	Other cash flows from financing activities
	1,869	Excess tax benefit
1,448	-123	Effect of exchange rate changes
	4,315	Cash - end of period
Change In cash and cash equivalents **+922**		

LEGEND
- Additions
- Subtractions
- Begining and end of period cash
- Net change

Figure 7.7 **Cascade**

The slight slant to each bar reinforces the positive or negative direction of its cash flows. Slanting to the right or left visually links starting and ending points of each bar. This minor adjustment enables you to easily track the flows and removes the need to bundle positive and negative flows into undifferentiated groups. The Cascade chart's fixed order of items, listed in a table format, allows for a more reliable year-to-year comparison of variations in cash flows components. Figures 7.8 and 7.9 present three years of side-by-side cash flows data.

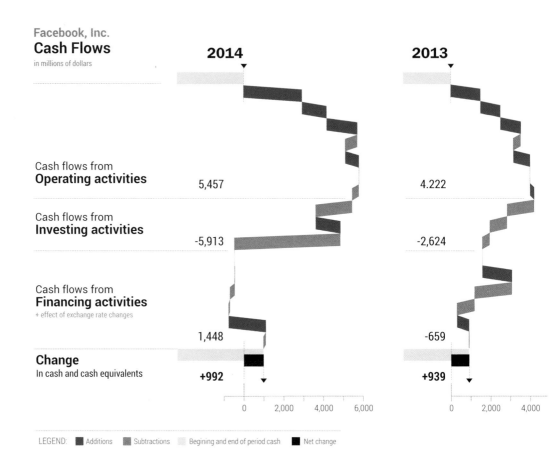

Facebook, Inc.
Cash Flows
in millions of dollars

	2014	2013
Cash flows from **Operating activities**	5,457	4.222
Cash flows from **Investing activities**	-5,913	-2,624
Cash flows from **Financing activities** + effect of exchange rate changes	1,448	-659
Change In cash and cash equivalents	**+992**	**+939**

LEGEND: ■ Additions   ■ Subtractions   ▢ Begining and end of period cash   ■ Net change

Figure 7.8 **Multi-Year Cascade**

2012

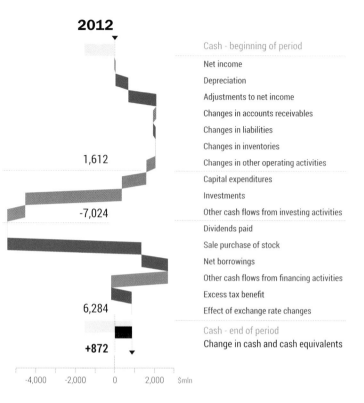

Cash - beginning of period

Net income

Depreciation

Adjustments to net income

Changes in accounts receivables

Changes in liabilities

Changes in inventories

Changes in other operating activities

1,612

Capital expenditures

Investments

-7,024

Other cash flows from investing activities

Dividends paid

Sale purchase of stock

Net borrowings

Other cash flows from financing activities

Excess tax benefit

6,284

Effect of exchange rate changes

Cash - end of period

+872

Change in cash and cash equivalents

-4,000   -2,000   0   2,000 $mln

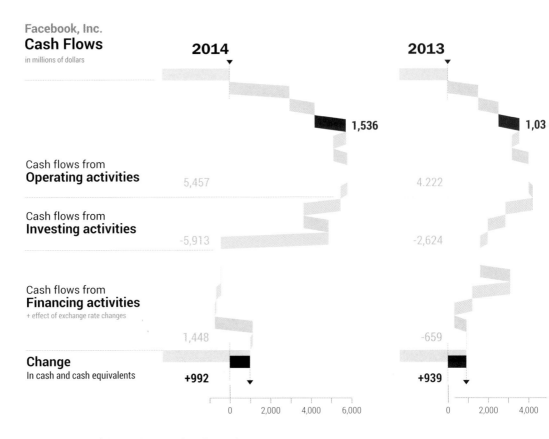

Figure 7.9 Multi-Year Interactive Cascade

Depending on your needs, you can select from any of the Cascade chart variations. For example, Figures 7.8 and 7.9 show two variations of the Cascade chart. Figure 7.8 shows aggregate values with a list of underlying items and assumes a static image or print and an audience that does not need to review the underlying numeric values for each line item. In contrast, Figure 7.9 lists aggregate values with access to those specific values. It assumes an interactive display that can present the detail values on demand. Another way to join summary and detail cash flows is shown in Figures 7.10 and 7.11, respectively.

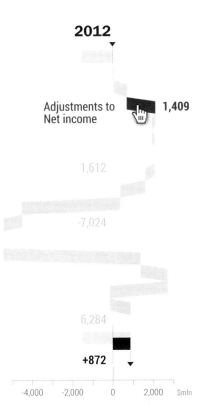

2012

Adjustments to
Net income   1,409

1,612

-7,024

6,284

+872

-4,000   -2,000   0   2,000 $mln

The detail display (Figure 7.10) provides all 66 values across three years within
one view. In contrast, the summary display (Figure 7.11) is abbreviated and shows
only 12 data points. Another variation applied to the Cascade chart is the use of
color. Because the bar slant communicates the direction of the cash flows, the
bars can use color for another purpose. Color distinguishes the groupings in
Figures 7.10 and 7.11 as opposed to the direction of the flows.

Cash Flows Facebook, Inc
in millions of dollars

2014

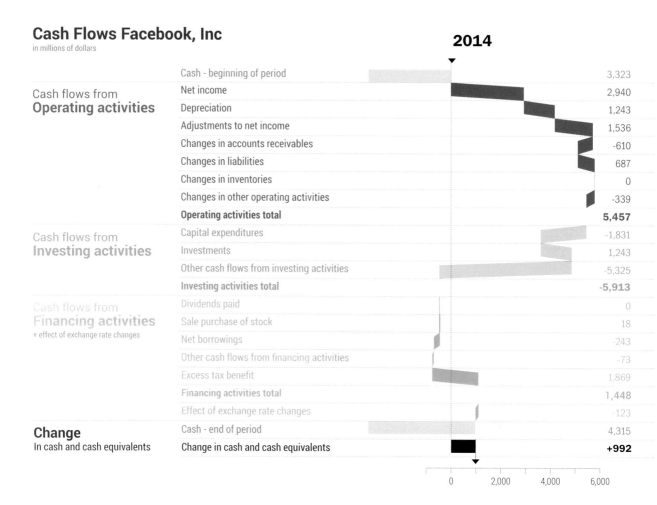

	Cash - beginning of period	3,323
Cash flows from Operating activities	Net income	2,940
	Depreciation	1,243
	Adjustments to net income	1,536
	Changes in accounts receivables	-610
	Changes in liabilities	687
	Changes in inventories	0
	Changes in other operating activities	-339
	Operating activities total	**5,457**
Cash flows from Investing activities	Capital expenditures	-1,831
	Investments	1,243
	Other cash flows from investing activities	-5,325
	Investing activities total	**-5,913**
Cash flows from Financing activities + effect of exchange rate changes	Dividends paid	0
	Sale purchase of stock	18
	Net borrowings	-243
	Other cash flows from financing activities	-73
	Excess tax benefit	1,869
	Financing activities total	1,448
	Effect of exchange rate changes	-123
Change In cash and cash equivalents	Cash - end of period	4,315
	Change in cash and cash equivalents	**+992**

0   2,000   4,000   6,000

Figure 7.10 **Multi-Year Detail Cascade**

The next set of figures introduces comparison techniques to the Cascade charts. For example, comparing the cash flows of publically traded companies within the same industry can provide a helpful perspective to investors. Figures 7.12 and 7.13 show two types of comparative analysis.

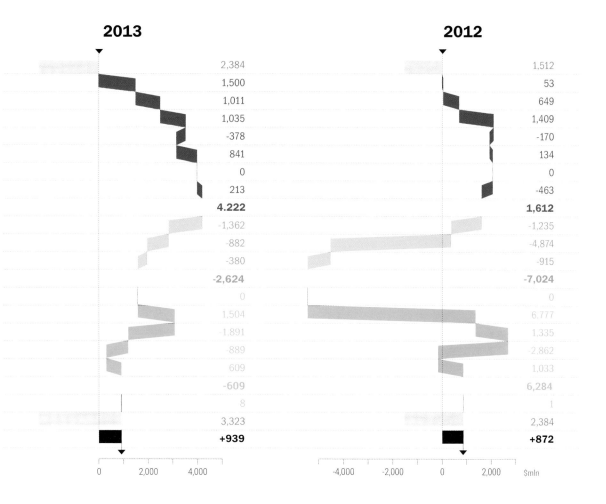

2013		2012	
	2,384		1,512
	1,500		53
	1,011		649
	1,035		1,409
	-378		-170
	841		134
	0		0
	213		-463
	4.222		**1,612**
	-1,362		-1,235
	-882		-4,874
	-380		-915
	-2,624		**-7,024**
	0		0
	1,504		6.777
	-1,891		1.335
	-889		-2.862
	609		1.033
	-609		6,284
	8		1
	3,323		2,384
	+939		**+872**

| 0 | 2,000 | 4,000 | | -4,000 | -2,000 | 0 | 2,000 | $mln |

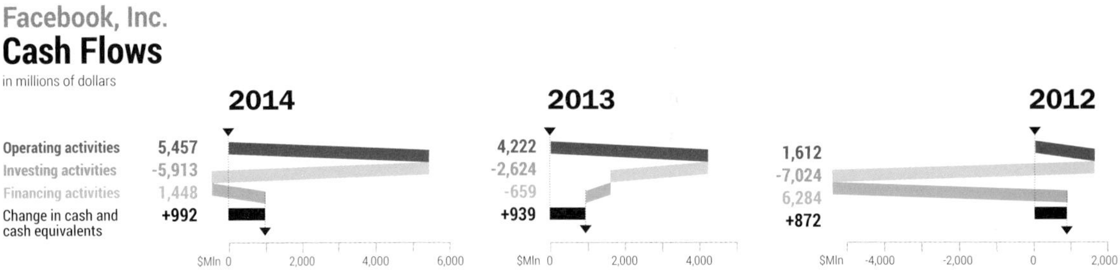

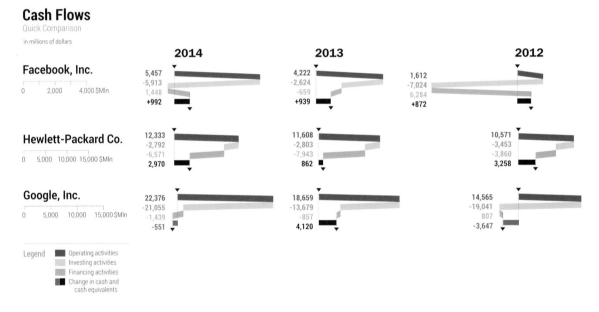

Figure 7.11 Summary Cascade

Figure 7.12 Comparison Cascade by Year

You can customize both the level of data aggregation from summary to detail and the specifics of how you render the data using color. If you want to emphasize the groupings, you should mimic how color is used in Figure 7.10 and Figure 7.11. If you would rather showcase the positive and negative flows, apply the color encoding as shown in Figure 7.8. Aligning your communication needs with the variations and customizations of the chart is part of the selection process.

Compact summary views enable you to include a list of cash flows data across both years and firms (Figures 7.12 and 7.13). Figure 7.12 shows a year-centric view with the rows dedicated to a list of different firms, whereas Figure 7.13 provides a firm-centric view with its rows dedicated to listing different years. In either case, the layout can scale to include more years and firms. You can pick the orientation of the data to align the flows by year or by firm.

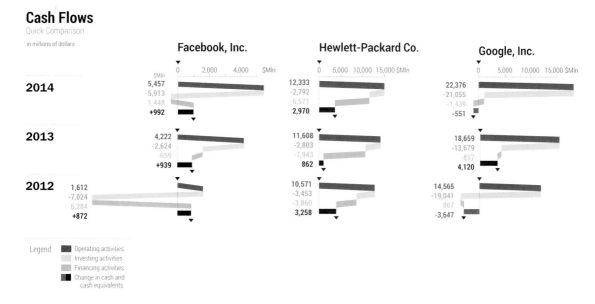

Figure 7.13 **Comparison Cascade by Firm**

Both Figures 7.12 and 7.13 introduce red and black colors to highlight the change in cash and cash equivalents. This is yet another example of how you can select from various aspects of the chart structure.

Key Take-Aways

This section reuses the Waterfall chart and introduces the Cascade chart to represent cash flows data for for-profit organizations. Like variations on a theme, this section shows how to apply the Cascade chart technique to a variety of use cases. From Waterfall to Cascade, Summary to Detail, Single to Multi-year, each variation is tailored to serve different needs. Both the

Waterfall and Cascade charts each augment a series of numbers with recognizable shapes that encode basic properties of yearly flows. The variety of Cascade chart types provides a selection of visualization techniques that you can mix and match to suit your needs. Say you want to present a multi-year approach to financing activities. In this case you may elect to 1) use a three-year interactive data display, 2) include each numeric cash flows value, 3) use color to group the activities, and 4) point out a positive or negative ending results in cash/cash equivalents with the red/black color code. Each of these choices tailors the data presentation to match your narrative.

Statement of Financial Activity

The Statement of Financial Activity is a key financial statement for nonprofits and is similar to the Income Statement for for-profit organizations. Although this section focuses on the Statement of Financial Activity data, the same visualization techniques can be applied to an Income Statement or any statement that describes how movement of individual flows impacts a derived value. Both statements present the income and expenses of an organization for a stated period of time. The Statement of Financial Activity shows the effects financial choices make on the net assets of an organization. Figure 7.14 shows the typical approach to presenting the Statement of Financial Activity as a table.

Similar to cash flows data, the data listed in the Statement of Financial Activity (Figure 7.14) is composed of positive and negative flows across three groups including unrestricted, temporarily restricted, and permanently restricted activities. With a similar data structure and purpose seen in the Statement of Cash Flows, Figure 7.15 applies the Waterfall chart to the Statement of Financial Activity.

In Figure 7.15, an arrow points out net assets released from restrictions which makes it the only change this detailed Waterfall has from the original. Reusing a chart type like this across a set of financial statements creates consistency and builds upon any previously learned knowledge of how the chart works. The arrow visually connects two related objects within the chart to show the transfer of assets between the referenced line items.

Smith College
Statements of Activities
June 30, 2013 and 2012

(In Thousands of dollars)

Changes in Unrestricted Net Assets	2013	2012
Operating Revenues and Other Additions		
Student income: Tuition and other fees	127,112	123,372
Residence and dining fees	35,683	34,407
Student aid	(62,796)	(59,120)
Student income, net	**99,999**	**98,659**
Gifts and grants	22,573	25,630
Investment return supporting operations	23,022	19,116
Other income	13,288	13,184
Net assets released from restrictions	60,353	61,695
Total operating revenues and other additions	**219,235**	**218,284**
Operating Expenses		
Instruction	90,261	86,454
Academic support	29,608	28,620
Student services	22,696	22,063
Auxiliary enterprises	35,717	33,280
General and administrative	33,038	30,034
Total expenses	**211,320**	**200,451**
Operating subtotal	**7,915**	**17,833**
Non-Operating Revenues and Other Changes		
Unrealized gain (loss), interest, and fees on interest-rate swap agreements	7,413	(21,091)
Net investment return increasing (decreasing) long-term investments	30,091	(9,785)
Non-operating revenues and other changes	**37,504**	**(30,876)**
Increase (decrease) in unrestricted net assets	**45,419**	**(13,043)**
Changes in Temporarily Restricted Net Assets		
Gifts, grants and change in donor intent	(1,138)	14,337
Investment return	148,399	21,029
Change in life income funds	1,836	(585)
Net assets released from restrictions	(60,353)	(61,695)
Increase (decrease) in temporarily restricted net assets	**88,744**	**(26,914)**
Changes in Permanently Restricted Net Assets		
Gifts, grants and change in donor intent	17,935	3,962
Investment return	1,000	(175)
Change in life income funds	2,076	(1,387)
Increase in permanently restricted net assets	21,011	2,400
Total increase (decrease) in net assets	155,174	(37,557)
Net assets, beginning of year	1,761,704	1,799,261
Net assets, end of year	**1,916,878**	**1,761,704**

Figure 7.14 **Statement of Financial Activity**

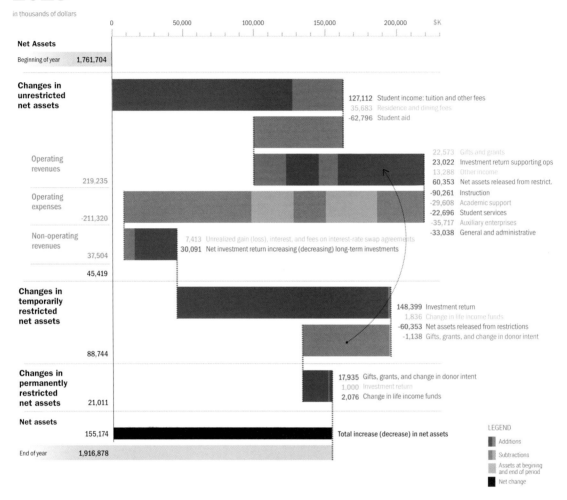

Smith College
Statements of Activities
2013

in thousands of dollars

Net Assets

Beginning of year   1,761,704

Changes in unrestricted net assets

127,112	Student income: tuition and other fees
35,683	Residence and dining fees
-62,796	Student aid

Operating revenues   219,235

22,573	Gifts and grants
23,022	Investment return supporting ops
13,288	Other income
60,353	Net assets released from restrict.

Operating expenses   -211,320

-90,261	Instruction
-29,608	Academic support
-22,696	Student services
-35,717	Auxiliary enterprises
-33,038	General and administrative

Non-operating revenues   37,504

7,413	Unrealized gain (loss), interest, and fees on interest-rate swap agreements
30,091	Net investment return increasing (decreasing) long-term investments

45,419

Changes in temporarily restricted net assets

148,399	Investment return
1,836	Change in life income funds
-60,353	Net assets released from restrictions
-1,138	Gifts, grants, and change in donor intent

88,744

Changes in permanently restricted net assets   21,011

17,935	Gifts, grants, and change in donor intent
1,000	Investment return
2,076	Change in life income funds

Net assets

155,174   Total increase (decrease) in net assets

End of year   1,916,878

LEGEND
- Additions
- Subtractions
- Assets at begining and end of period
- Net change

Figure 7.15 Detail Waterfall – Connected Values

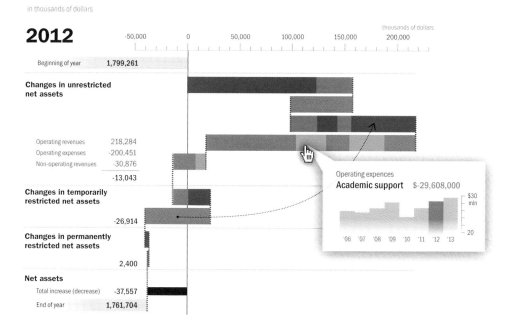

Smith College
Statements of Activities
in thousands of dollars

2012

Beginning of year	1,799,261

Changes in unrestricted net assets

Operating revenues	218,284
Operating expenses	-200,451
Non-operating revenues	-30,876
	-13,043

Changes in temporarily restricted net assets

	-26,914

Changes in permanently restricted net assets

	2,400

Net assets

Total increase (decrease)	-37,557
End of year	1,761,704

Operating expences
Academic support $-29,608,000

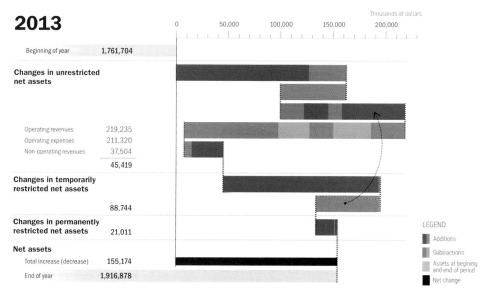

2013

Beginning of year	1,761,704

Changes in unrestricted net assets

Operating revenues	219,235
Operating expenses	-211,320
Non-operating revenues	37,504
	45,419

Changes in temporarily restricted net assets

	88,744

Changes in permanently restricted net assets | 21,011 |

Net assets

Total increase (decrease)	155,174
End of year	1,916,878

LEGEND
- Additions
- Subtractions
- Assets at begining and end of period
- Net change

Figure 7.16 Integrated Waterfall

This version of the Interactive Waterfall (Figure 7.16) provides breadth and depth to the data—with multiple years' worth of data providing breadth, and the pop-up display panel of detailed operating expenses providing depth. Questions regarding changes in the financial activity can be posed and answered by calling up the interactive display panel. *How do the operating expenses compare to the revenues? Historically, what has been spent on academic support?* To answer these types of questions, this Interactive Waterfall chart integrates two data sets—the Statement of Financial Activity and the Operating Budget—and two chart types.

Key Take-Aways

This section illustrates how to use the Waterfall chart in other financial statements, and how to integrate data from two financial statements into one interactive chart. For example, the Interactive Waterfall chart (Figure 7.16) introduces the concept of integrating the Statement of Financial Activity and Operating Budget, thereby clarifying the connections between the two data sets. The interactive display provides a cohesive experience, contextually links the data, and explains each aggregate value with a historical perspective.

Operating Budget

This section reviews a ten-year operating budget and suggests a way to provide a better grasp of how monies are allocated in an organization. Using consistent methods to present the same items across the years enables the user to compare changes in operating costs over the years. *Which costs are consistently increasing or decreasing? How do these adjustments impact future planning?* Figure 7.17 shows a sample ten-year operating budget to address these questions.

Wellesley College
Ten-Year Operating Budget
June 30, 2013 and 2012

											(in thousands of dollars)	(Average annual %)	
Operating revenues	2004	2005	2006	2007	2008	2009	2010	2011	2012	2013	Nominal	Real
Tuition and fees	62,928	66,989	71,431	79,298	83,447	86,543	90,400	96,402	96,702	100,075	5.30%	3.20%
Room and board	17,214	18,489	19,867	21,070	22,289	23,958	24,859	26,759	27,436	28,224	5.70%	3.60%
Financial aid grants	-26,757	-29,732	-31,818	-34,754	-36,212	-41,215	-44,687	-50,317	-49,947	-52,616	7.90%	5.80%
Net student charge revenue	53,385	55,746	59,480	65,614	69,524	69,286	70,572	72,844	74,191	75,683	4.00%	1.90%
Distribution from endowment - operations	60,522	65,919	67,762	72,595	75,392	79,155	83,196	78,304	75,007	77,848	2.90%	0.80%
Restricted gifts for current use	6,930	6,071	5,429	6,377	6,769	7,051	6,341	4,757	4,282	5,905	-0.30%	-2.40%
Unrestricted gifts and bequests	10,589	12,024	10,049	10,606	10,671	10,741	10,825	11,274	12,282	11,537	1.20%	-0.90%
Federal, state grants & contracts - restricted	10,965	8,979	8,048	8,789	8,322	8,567	9,896	8,609	9,740	10,382	0.10%	-2.00%
Sales and services of auxiliary enterprises	7,010	7,290	7,561	8,312	7,811	6,174	6,423	6,239	6,439	5,207	-2.70%	-4.80%
Other	3,556	3,661	5,316	6,467	6,716	4,619	3,308	4,040	4,414	4,832	6.10%	4.00%
Total revenues	152,957	159,690	163,645	178,760	185,205	185,593	190,561	186,067	186,355	191,394	2.60%	0.50%
Operating expenditures												
Instruction and departmental	48,802	51,503	54,892	60,763	65,219	64,508	68,114	66,988	69,005	70,001	4.20%	2.10%
Sponsored research and other programs	12,873	11,104	10,167	10,712	10,672	10,433	10,354	9,569	10,492	11,072	-1.40%	-3.50%
Library	5,602	5,922	6,094	6,247	6,458	6,632	5,798	5,638	5,739	5,704	0.30%	-1.80%
Student services	24,199	25,330	28,538	29,713	31,743	28,567	28,666	29,971	29,886	31,153	3.00%	0.90%
General administration	7,533	8,310	8,680	12,611	13,164	15,513	12,856	10,714	10,309	10,703	5.40%	3.30%
General institutional	21,237	21,558	21,178	22,647	23,470	24,441	22,986	25,644	26,263	26,366	2.50%	0.40%
Maintenance and operations	11,746	13,089	16,123	15,038	15,542	15,970	14,104	14,409	13,099	12,596	1.30%	-0.80%
Debt service	7,082	7,513	7,078	7,907	7,135	7,163	6,831	6,098	6,547	10,136	5.50%	3.40%
Major maintenance and capital expenditures	6,416	7,678	5,003	6,916	5,596	5,280	6,680	5,841	6,113	6,855	3.20%	1.10%
Auxiliary enterprise expenditures	7,467	7,681	5,889	6,199	6,205	7,081	7,243	7,138	8,450	8,303	1.80%	-0.30%
Total expenditures	152,957	159,688	163,642	178,753	185,204	185,588	183,632	182,010	185,903	192,889	2.70%	0.60%

Figure 7.17 **Ten-Year Operating Budget**

With a total of 284 numeric values, the ten-year operating budget provides historical context behind current values. The trajectory of data across all items in the operating budget can provide context of scale. *Relative to federal and state grants, how much has been provided in financial aid grants? How divergent or convergent are the revenues from Tuition to expenditures in Instruction?* The next set of charts, starting with Figure 7.18, provides direct ways to represent the 284 data points.

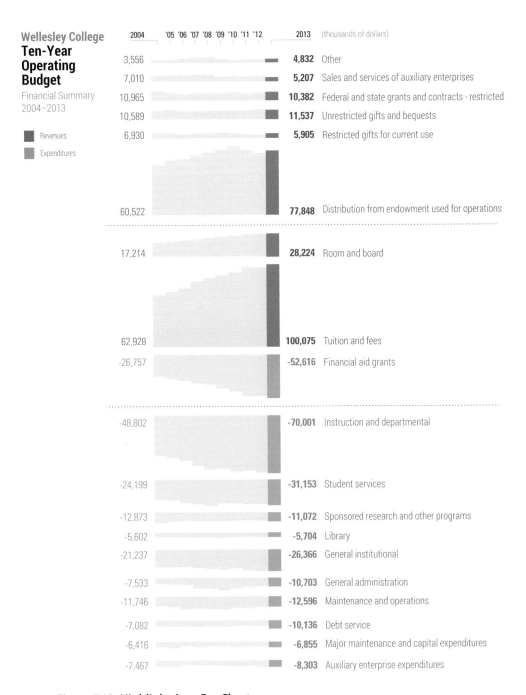

Wellesley College
Ten-Year Operating Budget
Financial Summary 2004–2013

■ Revenues
■ Expenditures

(thousands of dollars)

2004	2013	
3,556	**4,832**	Other
7,010	**5,207**	Sales and services of auxiliary enterprises
10,965	**10,382**	Federal and state grants and contracts - restricted
10,589	**11,537**	Unrestricted gifts and bequests
6,930	**5,905**	Restricted gifts for current use
60,522	**77,848**	Distribution from endowment used for operations
17,214	**28,224**	Room and board
62,928	**100,075**	Tuition and fees
-26,757	**-52,616**	Financial aid grants
-48,802	**-70,001**	Instruction and departmental
-24,199	**-31,153**	Student services
-12,873	**-11,072**	Sponsored research and other programs
-5,602	**-5,704**	Library
-21,237	**-26,366**	General institutional
-7,533	**-10,703**	General administration
-11,746	**-12,596**	Maintenance and operations
-7,082	**-10,136**	Debt service
-6,416	**-6,855**	Major maintenance and capital expenditures
-7,467	**-8,303**	Auxiliary enterprise expenditures

Figure 7.18 Highlight Area Bar Chart

Area Bar charts provide a straightforward method to show quantity rank information in a data set. To emphasize the current year, a combination of darker color bars and bold numbers bring your attention to the right of the chart. Color is used consistently for both the visual area Bar chart and text values to reiterate and fully distinguish the revenue versus expenditure data. You may have noticed the individual items have been reordered within the groups. To balance the chart, the larger budgets are placed toward the middle area of the chart and smaller budgets are moved toward the outskirts. The reordering of the list shows a semi-sorted view of top revenues and expenditures within closer proximity of each other. In addition, two vertical dotted lines group together the top three items from the original table. These types of order and grouping adjustments help compare the data more efficiently.

Next, Figure 7.19 changes the Area Bar chart to highlight the last several years.

A gradual shift of attention is attained with the Gradient Area bar chart example. The gradient technique communicates that the lighter color blocks are simply background information, whereas the stronger, darker color blocks are more relevant to the present and require most of our attention. Associations of past to present and informational to important are in harmony with the implementation of the gradient.

Figures 7.18 and 7.19 primarily focus on the most-recent years of the data. Instead of placing your attention on recent years, Figure 7.20 introduces a different version of the chart to emphasize the change in quantities relative to the starting point of ten years previous to the current data.

The Offset Area Bar chart uses a benchmark approach to illustrate past, current, and future budgets. With the level set at year 2004, all budgets are measured as deviations from that starting point. This chart enables you to see which budgets have increased and which budgets have decreased and by how much.

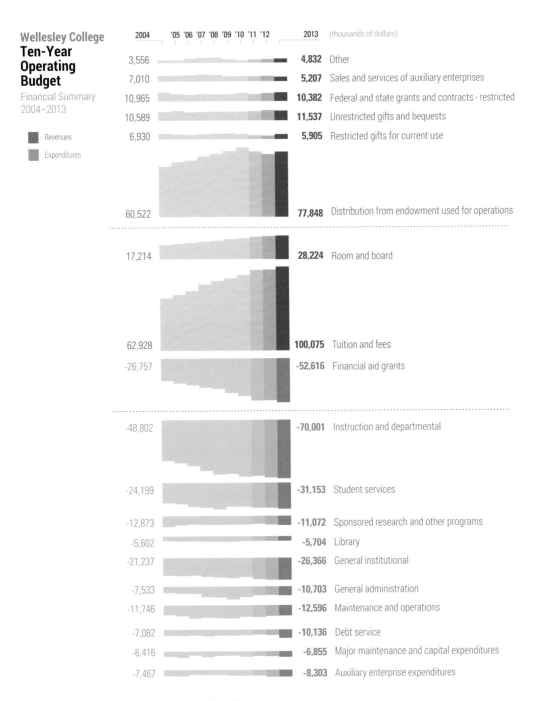

Figure 7.19 **Gradient Area Bar Chart**

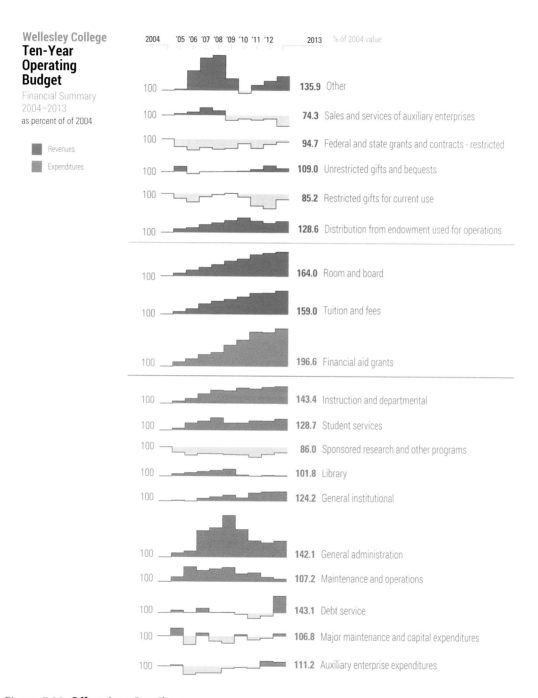

Wellesley College
**Ten-Year
Operating
Budget**
Financial Summary
2004–2013
as percent of of 2004

■ Revenues
■ Expenditures

| 2004 | '05 '06 '07 '08 '09 '10 '11 '12 | 2013 | % of 2004 value |

100   **135.9** Other

100   **74.3** Sales and services of auxiliary enterprises

100   **94.7** Federal and state grants and contracts - restricted

100   **109.0** Unrestricted gifts and bequests

100   **85.2** Restricted gifts for current use

100   **128.6** Distribution from endowment used for operations

100   **164.0** Room and board

100   **159.0** Tuition and fees

100   **196.6** Financial aid grants

100   **143.4** Instruction and departmental

100   **128.7** Student services

100   **86.0** Sponsored research and other programs

100   **101.8** Library

100   **124.2** General institutional

100   **142.1** General administration

100   **107.2** Maintenance and operations

100   **143.1** Debt service

100   **106.8** Major maintenance and capital expenditures

100   **111.2** Auxiliary enterprise expenditures

Figure 7.20 **Offset Area Bar Chart**

Key Take-Aways

All three operating budget charts provide straightforward area chart views to show the trends and changes in a budget. Key lessons have been incorporated into each of these charts. First, the order of the operating revenues and expenditures is reorganized to improve the comparison of the large budget items. Second, the charts show visualization techniques that emphasize quantities in dollars or emphasize the relative changes in percentage from a given starting point. The benchmark of a starting year drives the comparison for all future years, providing a quick review of budget changes. Third, the ten-year operating budget data can be integrated into other statements (Figure 7.16). You can select which operating budget chart to use depending on whether you wish to emphasize quantities or percentage change.

Summary

The visualizations in this chapter focus on the need for transparency and accessibility in the highly standardized world of financial statements. Transparency increases when readers can see the source details of an aggregated value, and accessibility increases when they can easily get to the details. Each visualization reveals the size and impact of each line item. For example, the Summary Waterfall chart (Figure 7.2) shows how investment and operational cash flows compare in size and how they impact the year ending cash balance.

These visualizations also link statements together. The Integrated Waterfall chart (refer to Figure 7.16) incorporates part of the operating budget data into an integrated view. Integrating the two statements makes the data more accessible to those who wish to review past budgets in context.

Financial statements are known for accuracy and attention to detail and employ a uniform method to gather and present data. The examples in this chapter maintain conventional standards of financial statements while introducing visuals to augment the standard tables. The visualizations reflect the direct and accurate stance of financial statements with the use of straight lines to indicate precise aggregate levels, negative and positive flows, and quantity changes across the years.

The following is a list of the visualizations in this chapter:

VISUALIZATION	DESCRIPTION	FIGURE
Summary Waterfall	A series of connected bars organized in a grid to show how negative and positive quantities can impact a derived value. Only the subtotal values display with the corresponding bar.	7.2
Detail Waterfall	A series of connected bars organized in a grid to show how positive and negative quantities can impact a derived value. Both the subtotals and individual underlying values display with the corresponding bar.	7.3, 7.6, 7.15
Multi-year Waterfall	A series of connected bars organized in a grid by year and used to illustrate how positive and negative quantities can impact a derived year-end value.	7.4, 7.5
Summary Cascade	A series of connected parallelograms organized in a grid to show direction and impact of positive and negative quantities on a derived value. Only the subtotal values display with the corresponding bar.	7.11, 7.12, 7.13
Detail Cascade	A series of connected parallelograms organized in a grid to show direction and impact of positive and negative quantities on a derived value. Both the subtotal aggregates and individual values display with the corresponding bar.	7.7, 7.10

VISUALIZATION	DESCRIPTION	FIGURE
Multi-year Cascade	A series of connected parallelograms organized in a grid by year to show direction and impact of positive and negative quantities on a derived year-end value.	7.8, 7.9
Highlight/ Gradient Area Bar	Quantity indicated with color fill from the axis lines. A combination of darker color bars and bold numbers emphasize particular years.	7.18, 7.19
Offset Area Bar	A change in quantity from a given starting point is indicated with color fill from the axis lines. Darker color fill indicates an increase in quantity and lighter color fill shows a decrease.	7.20

The visualizations introduced in this chapter are all variations on a single theme. That theme is reuse; and the Waterfall chart provides one useful example. We reapply one basic concept to both nonprofit and for-profit organizational objectives, and to two different financial statements with summary, detail, and multiple year versions. We explain reuse through other examples such as:

▶ How to reuse the Cascade chart to expand the data set to compare one organization with others.

▶ How to reuse an Area Bar chart and integrate it with another type of chart.

▶ How to reuse visual techniques, such as color or groupings, from any of the charts to tailor your narrative.

For this reason, many of the charts are similar in structure, yet distinct in how they reveal specifics. The chapter includes several versions of the same chart type: seven Cascade, and three Area bar charts. Each version reuses the basic chart structure yet displays detailed data, interactions, and groupings in distinct ways. Although the financial statements in this chapter have been limited to three, you can reuse these charts in other financial statements or data sets that require a similar purpose.

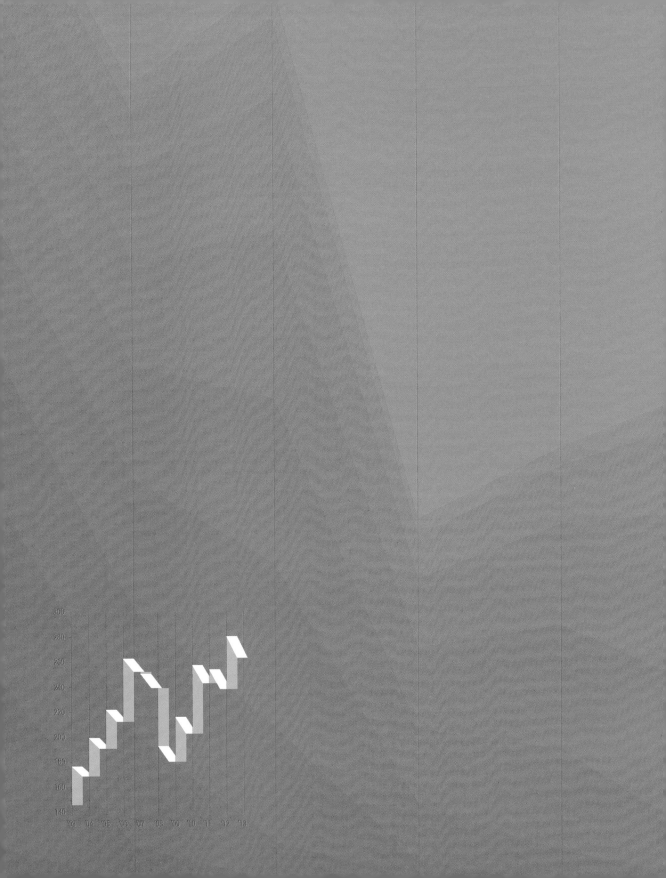

8

Pension Funds

Pension funds are the largest managed pooled investment and represent $36.1 trillion worldwide (according to the 2015 Towers Watson annual Global Pension Assets Study of 16 major markets). Many pension funds have significant funding gaps, and with greater market volatility, longer life expectancies, population bulges, and inflation, they continue to face adversity. Over the years, plan sponsors have made a number of changes to reduce their deficits including decreasing benefits, increasing employee contributions, increasing the retirement age, and shifting toward defined contribution plans. Given the changing landscape and the impact to millions of active participants in pension plans worldwide, a close review of the data is called for to tell a clear story of the current state of the funds and to help make accurate predictions about their future directions.

The California Public Employees' Retirement System (CalPERS) represents the fifth largest pension in the world (Bloomberg data, 2014). Managers of this complex fund produce a 250-page annual report that incorporates numeric data to explain details within the current status of the fund. The report holds the majority of the data in tables and uses only seven charts to display the financial overview and fund performance, making it difficult to extract meaningful conclusions from the data. More can and should be done to show clearly the state of the fund to the 1.7 million CalPERS members. With $262 billion on the line, this fund has every reason to provide better representation and understanding of the data to all interested parties.

This chapter focuses on three major areas within the CalPERS fund: 1) plan members and their profiles; 2) contributions versus benefits; and 3) the ultimate position of the fund as seen in the funding ratio. We use the Public Employees' Retirement Fund (PERF) from the annual report, as it covers nearly all CalPERS retirement benefits. Examples from these three focus areas can be used in presentations to the board or conversations between the investments, funding, and financial departments of the fund. All the ideas can be applied to future annual reports as a way to improve pension communications to plan members. Although the examples in this chapter are not embedded in the investment process to actively manage pension funds, the examples provide fund status and can be used to assess current state.

Plan Members

Visualizations in this section provide a brief overview of the plan participants in the fund and review current and historical data points to reveal trends in member populations. The demographic trend data displays what the fund needs to support and ultimately where the fund is headed with various member levels. For example, the member make-up with population segmentation, number of members, and change in members over a ten-year period are all views into the pension fund's future requirements.

Throughout this section, we start with the full data table to create a visual representation of the entire data set. Next, the visualizations evolve and become more selective in the data used from the tables to make different points and emphasize one perspective or data set over another. We introduce new techniques and variations of existing chart types to improve how we communicate the information.

The data in this section is taken from a few of the CalPERS annual report tables including Exhibit G: Members in Valuation, Exhibit D: Sample Non-Economic Assumptions, and Membership & Retirement Data. We have chosen these tables because they describe the member profile and are representative of others in the section; the first represents nine tables and the last four. The existing data set for actuarial member section is more expansive; the explorations are a start to what can be done with the data as we transform tables of data into usable charts.

Members in Valuation

The Members in Valuation data set provides subtotal and total quantities for age groups and years of service. A chart can be structured to emphasize one data set over another: Individual values, cumulative values, or rank order are all perspectives the data sets can reveal. In this section, you see how different chart types can showcase individual values over cumulative values or rank order.

First, review the existing data set. Figure 8.1 is a re-created table taken from CalPERS Comprehensive Annual Financial Report. The data and organizational structure of the table is a straight replica of what is presented in the report with eight similar tables that follow.

Members in Valuation

State Miscellaneous First Tier | By Attained Age & Years of Service – June 30, 2012

Age Group	Distribution of Active Members by Age & Service Years of Service at Valuation Date						Total	Total Payroll
	0-5	5-10	10-15	15-20	20-25	25+		
15-24	1,300	8	0	0	0	0	1,308	39,011,397
25-29	6,494	1,261	34	0	0	0	7,789	327,231,868
30-34	6,877	4,228	1,416	45	0	0	12,566	635,190,729
35-39	5,392	4,571	4,251	623	43	0	14,880	865,546,250
40-44	4,770	4,810	6,029	2,145	1,060	81	18,895	1,177,744,251
45-49	4,303	4,209	6,099	2,797	3,761	1,393	22,562	1,462,722,249
50-54	4,031	3,856	6,203	3,023	4,579	5,583	27,275	1,796,534,147
55-59	3,185	3,347	4,955	2,540	3,748	6,572	24,347	1,626,013,132
60-64	1,869	2,186	2,911	1,575	2,145	3,356	14,042	957,810,740
65+	909	988	1,353	640	692	1,138	5,720	394,805,269
Total	39,130	29,464	33,251	13,388	16,028	18,123	149,384	9,282,610,032

Figure 8.1 Valuation Table

If you were to take this table and directly transfer the data points to a Line chart, the results could look like Figure 8.2.

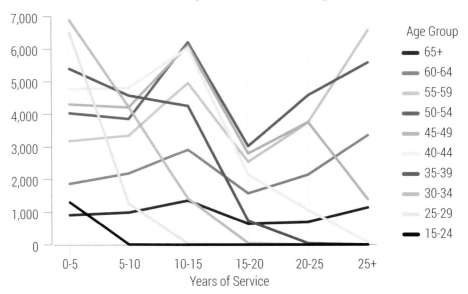

Number of Members in Valuation
State Miscellaneous First Tier | By Years of Service & Attained Age – June 30, 2012

Age Group
- 65+
- 60-64
- 55-59
- 50-54
- 45-49
- 40-44
- 35-39
- 30-34
- 25-29
- 15-24

Years of Service

Figure 8.2 **Color-Coded Line Chart**

This unreadable Line chart (Figure 8.2) represents how some may depict the data. The ten color-coded age group lines cross over each other and create a tangled canvas. You could trace each line to see the individual age group results, but together the ten points seem meaningless and unrelated. Instead, you may need to see the details of each group, as well as the summary across all; you may need to provide an individual age group result, as well as a view across all the age groups.

The next chart, shown in Figure 8.3, separates the age groups. You can notice immediate benefits. This separation detangles the groups and shows a clear profile to the years in service for each group.

It is easy to see a pattern emerge from Area Comparison (Figure 8.3). The combined series of charts enable you to see the changes in volumes as each age group incrementally expands into more years of service. Although the ten sequential charts reveal individual patterns, the chart shown in Figure 8.4 reveals cumulative patterns.

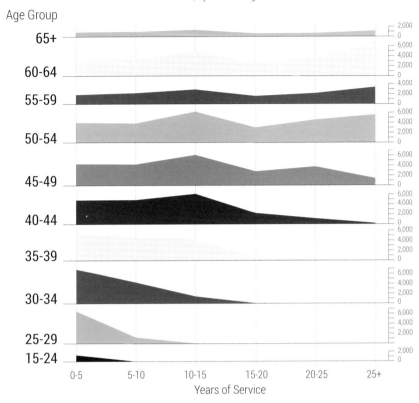

Number of Members in Valuation

State Miscellaneous First Tier | By Attained Age & Years of Service – June 30, 2012

Figure 8.3 **Area Comparison Chart**

The stacked area approach to the chart (Figure 8.4) provides four major benefits: 1) each age group is clearly shown; 2) group patterns emerge; 3) cumulative member trends are presented; and 4) the data is consolidated into one chart. The primary distinguishing factor between Figures 8.3 and 8.4 is the values; the former shows values as individual age groups and the later as cumulative. Both charts are readable and provide different perspectives of the data to make different points. An additional perspective to the data can be the rank order by age group. Next, Figure 8.5 charts both totals and percentage to present rank.

Number of Members in Valuation
State Miscellaneous First Tier | By Attained Age & Years of Service – June 30, 2012

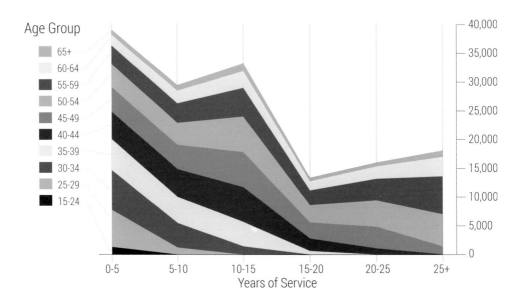

Figure 8.4 **Stacked Area Chart**

Members in Valuation
State Miscellaneous First Tier | By Attained Age & Years of Service – June 30, 2012

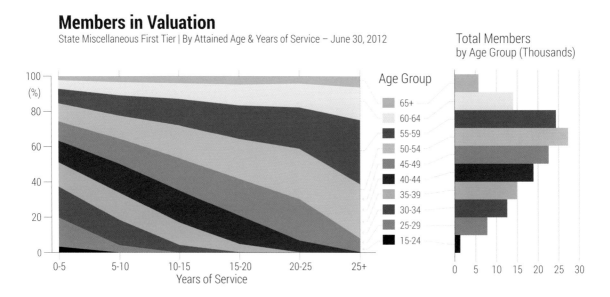

Figure 8.5 **Area and Bar Combo Chart**

Across the years of service, what is the rank order of the members by age group? You could estimate it based on the Area chart. But instead the Bar chart provides a more accurate account of rank order. The two charts address this question with relative and absolute ranked charts. The y-axis percentage provides the age group relative view, whereas the Bar chart provides the absolute number of members. The Combo chart presents five benefits: 1) each age group is represented; 2) group patterns emerge; 3) relative member trends are presented; 4) actual group ranks are linked; and 5) the data is consolidated into a Combo chart that shares labels across the two charts.

Next, the age group-focused chart (the bottom chart of Figure 8.6) creates a more organized view of the data that makes it easier to evaluate. It displays how the number of members peak and then together decrease to converge around a stabilized level. This is a perspective brought about by pivoting the data. The reorganized structure of the chart reveals the overall pattern across age groups; it is easy to see there exists a rise and fall to the number of members in valuation.

With the new pivoted view, we can ask the similar questions we answered with our previous charts: *Which years of service group has the most distributed age group?* A chart of individual groups can illustrate this view (Figure 8.7). *Which age group has the largest population?* A chart that accumulates the values can present this answer (Figure 8.8).

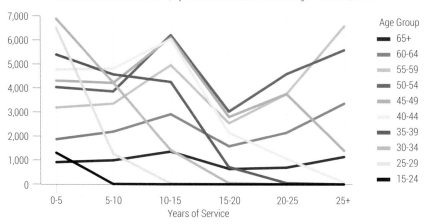

Number of Members in Valuation
State Miscellaneous First Tier | By Years of Service & Attained Age – June 30, 2012

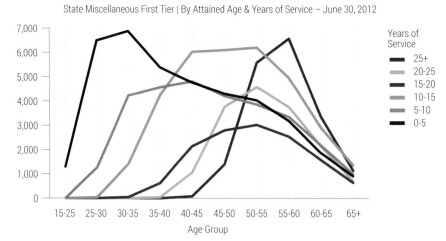

Number of Members in Valuation
State Miscellaneous First Tier | By Attained Age & Years of Service – June 30, 2012

Figure 8.6 Color-Coded Line Chart

The charts show the technique of individual or cumulative values; sequential individual charts (Figure 8.7) provide individual attention to the year of service ranges, whereas the cumulative (Figure 8.8) presents peak member volumes across all. Each chart features and emphasizes different data points. For example, the Area Comparison chart shows individual values, the Stacked Area chart highlights cumulative values, and the Area & Bar Combo emphasizes rank. Figure 8.9 applies the same Area & Bar Combo chart to show rank order of members by years of service.

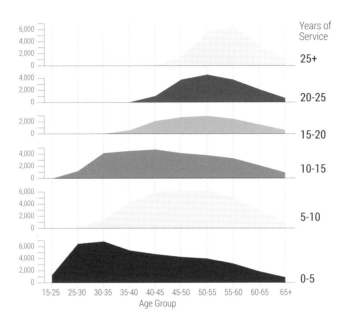

Figure 8.7 Area Comparison Chart

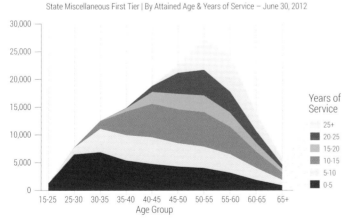

Figure 8.8 Stacked Area Chart

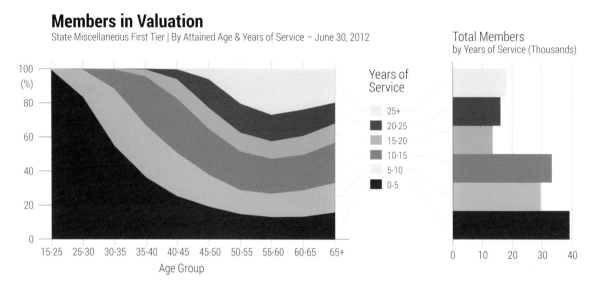

Members in Valuation
State Miscellaneous First Tier | By Attained Age & Years of Service – June 30, 2012

Total Members
by Years of Service (Thousands)

Years of Service

25+
20-25
15-20
10-15
5-10
0-5

Age Group

Figure 8.9 Area & Bar Combo Chart

Combo charts can emphasize one perspective solely or present a major and a minor emphasis. Figure 8.9 provides a major and minor emphasis: relative and absolute rank of years of service rank as the major perspective and separate age group values as the minor. Actually, both Figures 8.5 and 8.9 use the same chart structure to emphasize rank with greater accuracy and individual values as a secondary focus. In Figure 8.9, the chart secondarily shows the overall pattern to years of service relative to age group. This perspective is possible with the individual years of service values presented as a percentage.

Key Take-Aways

Transforming a data table into a chart requires some careful decision-making. If you decide to display all the data sets in one chart, you may end up with a spaghetti effect that communicates little. You may find it more effective to isolate each quantity either into separate charts or within a main chart with its own color fill. Alternative charts that follow our spaghetti example emphasize different aspects of the data, including individual quantities, aggregate totals, and relative and rank quantities. You can tell a different story with each chart or present them all together to show all sides.

In addition to deciding what chart type to use, you have to choose what the x-axis and y-axis represent. Re-assigning the x- and y- axes as in Figures 8.5 and 8.9 show the same chart type and data with different results because the data has been pivoted. The existing nine tables of Members in Valuation data can be easily overlooked. However, replacing them with Figures 8.5 and 8.9 emphasizes some interesting patterns in the data.

Post Retirement

The next data set extends the age group to move beyond years of service and into post retirement. The post retirement numbers are presented in groups of male versus female, healthy versus disabled within bracketed age groups from 50–100. This section reviews these different groups and explores how to present the data so that it best suits the needs of forecasting the pension. Figure 8.10 displays the post retirement data provided by CalPERS.

Post-Retirement Mortality

Rates vary by age and gender

Age	Healthy Recipients		Non-Industrially Disabled		Industrially Disabled	
	Male	Female	Male	Female	Male	Female
50	0.00239	0.00125	0.01632	0.01245	0.00443	0.00356
55	0.00474	0.00243	0.01936	0.01580	0.00563	0.00546
60	0.00720	0.00431	0.02293	0.01628	0.00777	0.00798
65	0.01069	0.00775	0.03174	0.01969	0.01388	0.01184
70	0.01675	0.01244	0.03870	0.03019	0.02236	0.01716
75	0.03080	0.02071	0.06001	0.03915	0.03585	0.02665
80	0.05270	0.03749	0.08388	0.05555	0.06926	0.04528
85	0.09775	0.07005	0.14035	0.09577	0.11799	0.08017
90	0.16747	0.12404	0.21554	0.14949	0.16575	0.13775
95	0.25659	0.21556	0.31025	0.23055	0.26108	0.23331
100	0.34551	0.31876	0.45905	0.37662	0.40918	0.35165

Figure 8.10 **Mortality Table**

The table shown in Figure 8.10 is one of the many tables within Exhibit D: Sample Non-Economic Assumptions from the CalPERS actuarial section. The next set of charts, starting with Figure 8.11, use this data set to track and plot mortality rates across populations and gender.

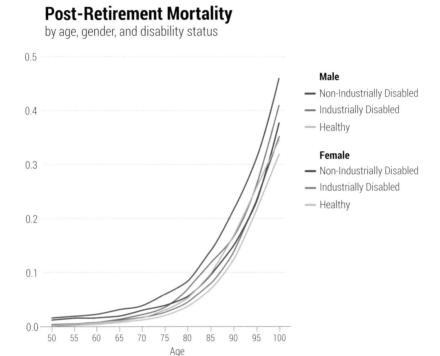

Post-Retirement Mortality
by age, gender, and disability status

Figure 8.11 **Color-Coded Line Chart**

As a starting point, a line chart (Figure 8.11) shows each column of data with similar trend lines and variations in the male/female populations. As such, distinction is given to these two populations through color sets: Blues for males and red/orange for females. Although the color line groupings provide some distinguishing factors between male/female and disabled/healthy variances, overlaps in the lines make it hard to clearly see the rates they represent.

Aside from problems with the visibility of interwoven lines, the perspective of the chart itself also bears rethinking. Its current perspective, similar to the table data, revolves around mortality rates; however, the fund needs to plan to cover members who receive benefits. Figure 8.12 flips the perspective and reviews the survival rates as an alternative.

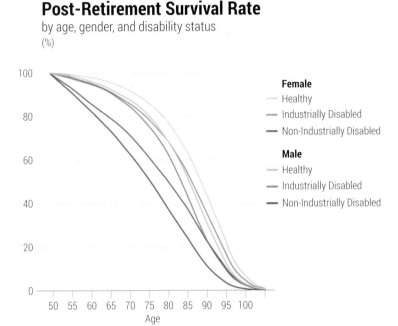

Post-Retirement Survival Rate
by age, gender, and disability status
(%)

Figure 8.12 **Color-Coded Line Chart**

Figure 8.12 is the result of recalculating the mortality rate table data into one that focuses on survival percentages. It reveals a greater variation between the populations and shows a direct read of lower survival rates as time progresses. The chart aligns the legend order to the new perspective of healthy populations at the top. There is still more you can do to improve clarity and readability. To avoid population lines overlapping, you need to separate it into two fully revealing charts. Gender turns out to work well as a criterion by which to divide the data, as shown in Figure 8.13.

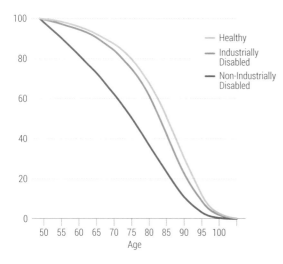

Male Post-Retirement Survival Rate
by age and disability status
(%)

Healthy
Industrially Disabled
Non-Industrially Disabled

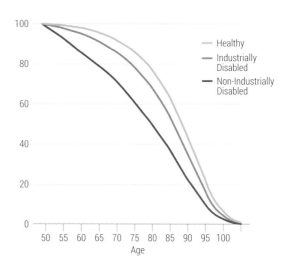

Female Post-Retirement Survival Rate
by age and disability status
(%)

Healthy
Industrially Disabled
Non-Industrially Disabled

Figure 8.13 **Dual Line Chart**

This technique of separating the data into two charts makes it easier to see the two population rates. The technique greatly improves your ability to read the chart and focuses your attention to the data sets you want to compare. In addition, this technique of separation opens up the possibility to change the pairing into other sets, as shown in Figure 8.14.

The three sets of female/male pairing, as shown in Figure 8.14, uncovers similar trend lines and variations in longevity, with females living consistently longer than men. We learn more about how CalPERS should plan ahead, knowing that today's survival rates are projections into tomorrow's funding needs.

Drastic changes are not always required to make a point. Figure 8.15 uses the color fill of an Area chart to communicate the volume of coverage the plan needs to consider. The small difference between a Line chart and Area chart adds weight and therefore gravitas to the area below the curve. In addition, the chart purposefully fills in the larger quantity to emphasize these are the topline numbers the pension needs to plan for.

Post-Retirement Survival Rate

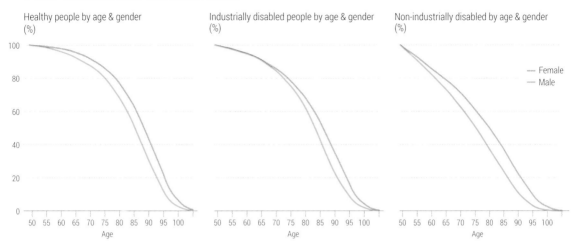

Figure 8.14 **Paired Line Charts**

Post-Retirement Survival Rate

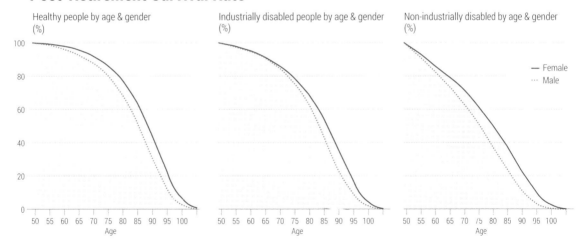

Figure 8.15 **Paired Area & Line Chart**

Key Take-Aways

Although the original data focuses on mortality rates, the final chart reconsiders the main purpose of the data. It flips the perspective from mortality to survival rates in order to emphasize the needs of the pension. The key take-away is that you should always question the data set's perspective and ask what the data isn't telling you that you should know. In this case, an aging population reveals that the pension should reflect how people are living longer lives. The survival rates chart provides this perspective.

The second take-away is that you should untangle the data and make it more easily consumable by splitting it across multiple charts to make each data set more readable and easier to follow. For example, you can split the data into pairs to compare and contrast the statistics from different groups like we did here with male and female groups.

Retirement Programs

The next plan membership data shifts from population segments of current values to population segments over a ten-year period of membership and retirement data. The amount of data in the table opens the doors to a mix of charts. The first set of charts address the totals for each population segment. The second set of charts addresses important ratios in the data. Last, a new technique is introduced to closely inspect and distinguish changes in the population and ratio charts.

The Membership and Retirement Data Table (Figure 8.16), taken from the Statistical Section of the annual report, tracks how the various member populations change over the years. With this data you uncover what these changes mean and contrast the data sets to see the balance of members to recipients. From one detail table to a detail chart, Figures 8.17 and 8.18 transfer the table line items to chart line items.

Membership & Retirement Data – Retirement Programs
Public Employees' Retirement System | 10-Year Review

	Members Group	2004	2005	2006	2007	2008	2009	2010	2011	2012	2013
State Members	Miscellaneous	227,096	219,919	214,721	219,101	222,806	224,966	224,084	223,251	228,667	227,291
	University of California	92	127	111	103	93	81	56	49	45	44
	Industrial	10,607	11,032	11,695	10,815	11,862	12,822	13,624	13,732	13,734	13,038
	ARP	0	0	13,955	16,608	19,086	19,422	16,477	13,972	9,491	12,160
	Highway Patrol	10,236	11,359	6,968	6,987	7,133	7,471	7,589	7,573	7,565	7,556
	Safety	16,714	21,750	23,129	26,099	28,763	29,911	29,305	29,402	28,935	28,878
	Peace Officer / Firefighter	44,740	46,485	46,605	48,722	51,371	51,260	49,437	48,243	47,162	45,116
	Total State Members	**309,485**	**310,672**	**317,184**	**328,435**	**341,114**	**345,933**	**340,572**	**336,222**	**335,599**	**334,083**
Public Agency Members	Schools	372,614	380,374	394,911	409,675	426,686	432,383	427,211	425,186	428,117	430,865
	Cities	158,884	161,515	166,192	171,546	175,240	173,315	167,994	163,430	160,253	158,649
	Counties	87,468	88,717	92,013	95,177	98,395	97,188	95,122	93,651	93,468	94,980
	Districts & Other Public Agencies	73,616	75,704	78,595	82,067	84,698	85,578	85,145	84,937	85,003	85,660
	Total Public Agency Members	**692,582**	**706,310**	**731,711**	**758,465**	**785,019**	**788,464**	**775,472**	**767,204**	**766,841**	**770,154**
	Total Active & Inactive Members	**1,002,067**	**1,016,982**	**1,048,895**	**1,086,900**	**1,126,133**	**1,134,397**	**1,116,044**	**1,103,426**	**1,102,440**	**1,104,237**
Benefit Recipients	Service Retirement	341,348	353,212	367,737	380,162	393,328	408,428	428,821	450,263	464,601	486,625
	Disability Retirement	42,064	41,857	42,383	42,965	42,813	43,074	43,090	43,347	43,626	43,857
	Industrial Disability Retirement	29,320	30,025	31,157	32,081	32,757	33,453	33,951	34,733	35,495	36,493
	Industrial Death	958	972	995	1,013	1,039	1,045	1,056	1,070	903	894
	1957 Survivor Benefit	2,881	2,960	3,074	3,164	3,246	3,398	3,535	3,626	3,831	3,698
	1959 Survivor Benefit	2,880	2,875	2,295	2,985	3,069	3,115	3,170	3,195	3,171	3,192
	Total Benefit Recipients	**419,451**	**431,901**	**447,641**	**462,370**	**476,252**	**492,513**	**513,623**	**536,234**	**551,627**	**574,759**
	Total Members	**1,421,518**	**1,448,883**	**1,496,536**	**1,549,270**	**1,602,385**	**1,626,910**	**1,629,667**	**1,639,660**	**1,654,067**	**1,678,996**

Figure 8.16 **Retirement Programs Table**

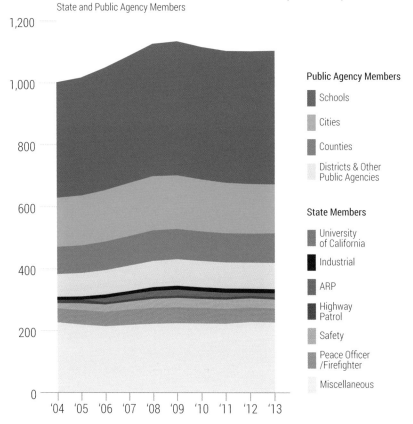

Figure 8.17 Stacked Area Chart

Roughly 1.7 million members are represented in three different color areas with Figures 8.17 and 8.18 to distinguish and reinforce the three groups from the table data. Aside from seeing the sheer volume of member data, the stacks show the profile of active/inactive members and benefit recipients. The chart profile visually shows us:

▶ The make-up of each group with proportional representations of the data

▶ Cumulative growth over the years with a direct indication of the change in volume

▶ The balance of those that are adding into the fund versus those that are receiving from the fund

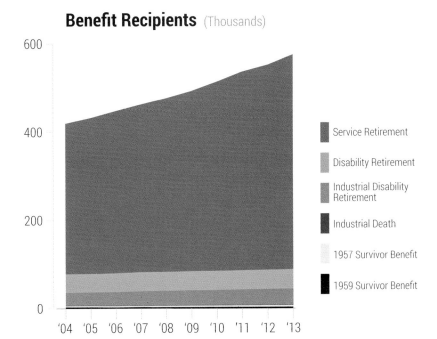

Benefit Recipients (Thousands)

Service Retirement

Disability Retirement

Industrial Disability Retirement

Industrial Death

1957 Survivor Benefit

1959 Survivor Benefit

Figure 8.18 **Stacked Area Chart**

Stacking the data sets shows the accumulation and total member values, yet you may also want to compare the stacks. You may want to examine the balance of members across the groups. As a system of inputs and outputs, you may want to highlight contributors to and consumers of the fund, known as members and recipients, and the balance of these two entities within the system. In Figures 8.19 and 8.20, each member group is displayed as a tally of subtotals.

Total Members

(Thousands)

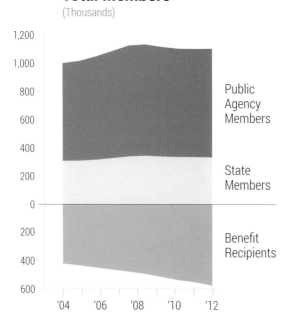

Public Agency Members

State Members

Benefit Recipients

Figure 8.19 **Stacked Area Chart**

Total Active & Inactive Members
(Thousands)

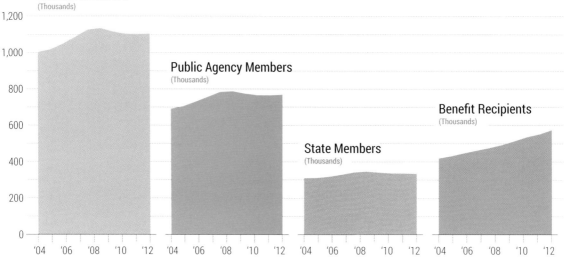

Public Agency Members
(Thousands)

Benefit Recipients
(Thousands)

State Members
(Thousands)

Figure 8.20 **Area Comparisons Chart**

These figures remove the details to compare changes in volume across the member groups clearly. Changing the display from stacking the groups (Figure 8.19) to lining them up (Figure 8.20) enables you to focus your attention on the curve lines across groups. You can observe how the public and state agency members flatten while the benefit recipients rise steadily. Because you have the measurements for each group, you can see how the curve lines move in unison or diverge. Figure 8.21 shows the relationship between these two groups of recipients and members.

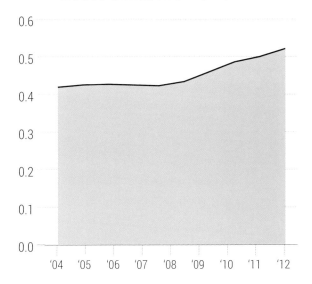

Ratio of Benefit Recipients to Active & Inactive Members

Figure 8.21 **Ratio Area Chart**

At times you may need to go beyond the table data and create your own calculations to understand relationships between two data sets. Figure 8.21 shows an example of this case: The plot of two populations as a ratio can get to the core of understanding the balance of members to recipients. The ten-year plot of the ratio produces a directional view into where the ratio may head if the conditions remain the same. Because a curve is the best indicator of change, Figure 8.22 focuses more attention on the profile of the curve line.

Total Active & Inactive Members

(Thousands)

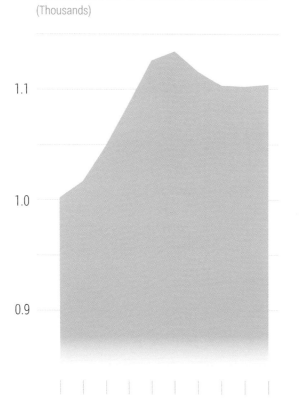

Figure 8.22 **Zoom Chart**

A close inspection of the line profile of the all members reveals more details to the changes over time. The zoom view is paired up with the full Area chart view to disclose the full context of the chart. In Figure 8.22, you can review the changes to member numbers with a more granular scale and still see the magnitude of size. As concentrated views, the Zoom chart highlights the changes. Similar to time-lapse photography that highlights movement and change of a seemingly motionless event, these concentrated views of the data do the same to bring forth changes.

A comparison across member groups uncovers the magnitude of change in member populations. Figure 8.23 uses the same technique of zooming into the y-axis to discover the significance in member changes.

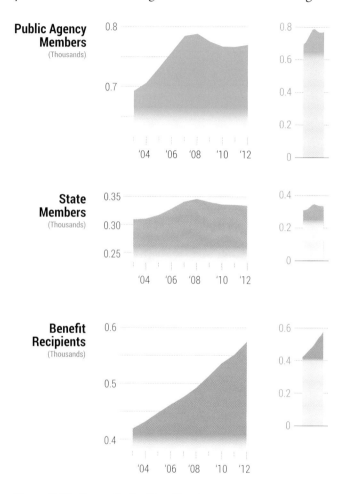

Figure 8.23 **Zoom Collection Chart**

As a set, you can compare each graph and see that the public agency members show a slight upward turn while state members stabilize. Benefit recipient numbers have climbed, and continue to rise. The Zoom chart provides the type of resolution you need to detect small hiccups and bends in benefit recipients' upward climb. The power of the Zoom chart is its capacity to call attention to specific data points, making the unnoticed noticed. Figure 8.24 illustrates this point.

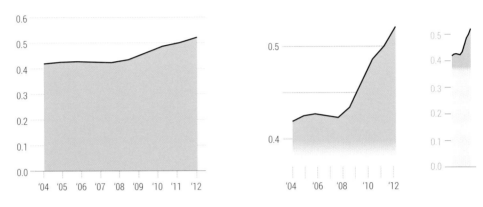

Ratio of Benefit Recipients to Active & Inactive Members

Figure 8.24 **Ratio Zoom Chart**

Consider the ratio curve of recipients to members through the zoom lens. Figure 8.24 shows the original ratio on the left as a contrast to the zoomed-in version on the right. The differences are clear. The Zoom chart provides you an acute awareness of the ratio changes and similar to the previous Zoom charts, each one is paired with a full Area chart to show volume.

Key Take-Aways

Temporal data that show totals and subtotals such as Plan Membership data can first be shown with basic Area or Line charts. Such simple representations of the data ground your knowledge about the membership groups. From here, you can start to inquire and adjust the charts to reveal changing ratios and other comparative details of change over time.

This section introduced the Zoom chart, which provides a detailed view of a fluctuating area in a chart and thereby renders small variations more visible. The accompanying thumbnail of the full chart shows these variations in relation to total value.

Contributions versus Benefits

As a priority, participants want to see their accrued benefits to understand what to expect from their payments. Participants also want to understand the health of the contributions that provide those benefits. In a payment-centric view, charts can be used to evaluate the net of both the contributions and deductions. This section reviews how those numbers impact the average allowance by reviewing and comparing fund profiles and member salary data.

Additions by Source

This section transforms data tables into charts by starting with a simple depiction of the data as a Bar chart. Across these simple depictions you find that the full data table is not always represented. The first visualizations in this section incorporate the full table of data but those that follow do not. Instead, the other charts use subtotals within the table to focus on different aspects of the data set.

This section uses data from two tables, as shown in Figure 8.25: The Additions by Source table is the detail breakdown of the Additions column in the Changes in Net Position table. Relationships between these two tables are illustrated in Figure 8.26 and represent a ten-year economic review of the fund.

Additions by Source

Ten-Year Review, in Thousands of Dollars

	Member Contributions	Employer Contributions	Investment Income	Miscellaneous Income	Total
2003/04	2,266,445	4,261,347	24,265,850	6,723	30,800,365
2004/05	3,176,781	5,774,120	21,893,728	473	30,845,102
2005/06	3,080,879	6,095,029	22,041,265	0	31,217,173
2006/07	3,262,699	6,442,384	40,748,261	9,119	50,462,463
2007/08	3,512,075	7,242,802	-12,499,110	6,202	-1,738,031
2008/09	3,882,355	6,912,376	-57,367,054	3,155	-46,569,168
2009/10	3,378,867	6,955,049	25,567,295	10,234	35,911,445
2010/11	3,600,089	7,465,397	43,904,425	3,011	54,972,922
2011/12	3,598,437	7,772,913	-203,084	7,070	11,175,336
2012/13	3,896,078	8,123,833	30,284,807	7,176	42,311,894

Changes in Net Position

Ten-Year Review, in Thousands of Dollars

	Additions	Deductions	Net Change	Beginning of Year	End of Year
2003/04	30,800,365	7,978,972	22,821,393	144,762,706	167,584,099
2004/05	30,845,102	8,798,320	22,046,782	167,584,099	189,630,881
2005/06	31,217,173	9,657,253	21,559,920	189,630,881	211,190,801
2006/07	50,462,463	10,530,582	39,931,881	211,190,801	251,122,682
2007/08	-1,738,031	11,469,172	-13,207,203	251,122,682	237,915,479
2008/09	-46,569,168	12,446,428	-59,015,596	237,915,479	178,899,883
2009/10	35,911,445	13,432,880	22,478,565	1,791,375,091	201,616,074
2010/11	54,972,922	14,827,205	40,145,717	201,616,074	241,761,791
2011/12	11,175,336	15,955,182	-4,779,846	241,761,791	236,981,945
2012/13	42,311,894	17,303,935	25,007,959	236,981,945	261,989,904

Figure 8.25 **Additions and Changes Tables**

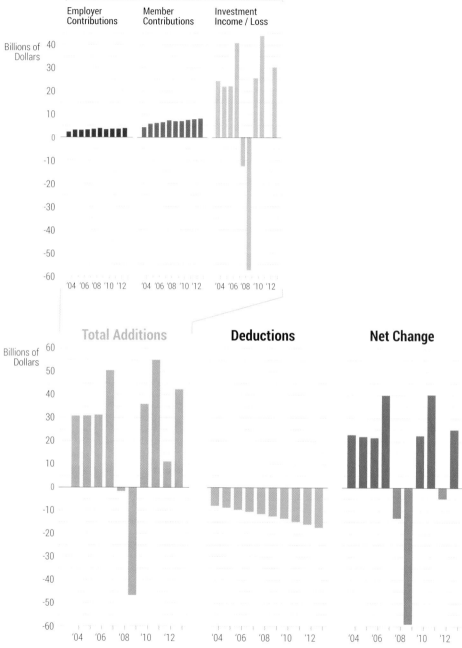

Figure 8.26 Bar Charts

Standard Bar charts like those in Figure 8.26 generally make comparisons easy and direct. The shared y-axis makes the comparison even more directly relatable. The word "direct" is key, and means that references and look-ups can be eliminated. You could present each column of data as its own chart, as shown in Figure 8.26; however doing so would require the eyes of your readers to scan across bar heights to compare them. A review of Employer Contribution to Investment Income/Loss across ten years becomes tedious. Instead, you can provide a visual representation that eliminates not only references and look-ups but also the need for rulers to compare values across the years, as shown in Figure 8.27.

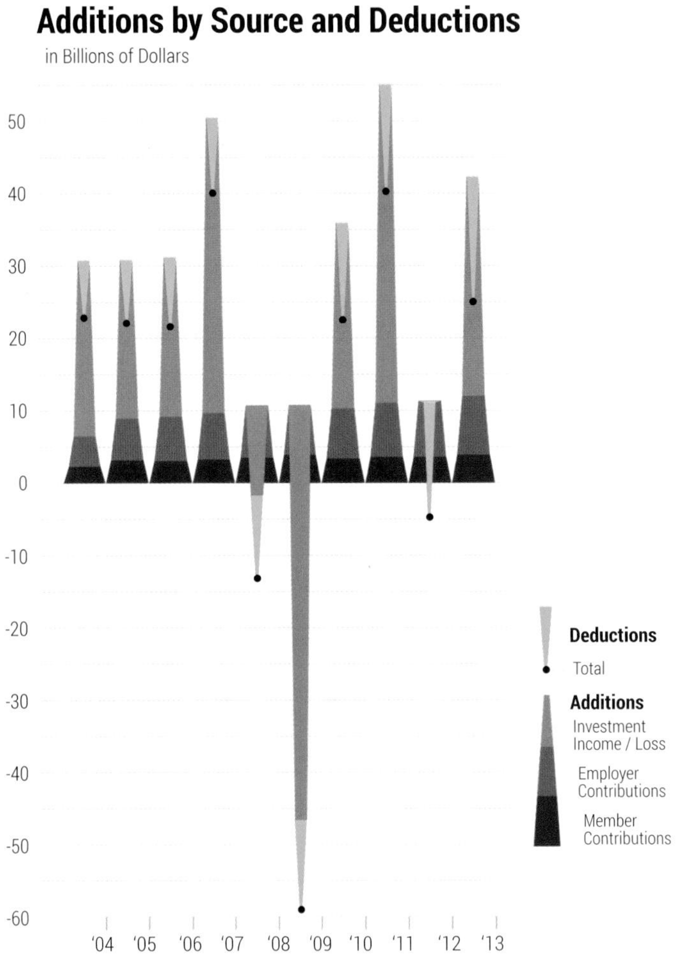

Figure 8.27 **Fold-Over Stack Chart**

To reduce the distance from one data set to another, simply remove the distance. You can align data sets around year markers, obviating the task of tracing to compare different data sets across the years. The Fold-Over Stack (Figure 8.27) consolidates six data sets into one chart: The stacked additions, shown in three shades of blue, incorporate the Additions by Source table. In addition, the triangular shape has the flexibility to accumulate either positive or negative values. The inverted yellow triangle provides a dual indicator of deductions and the net change.

Consolidating six charts into one not only saves space but presents relationships efficiently. The techniques used in the chart include:

- **Alignment**—Layering and aligning the data sets to yearly markers.

- **Stacking**—Stacking the data within the triangular bar. Part Area chart, the volume of blues and yellow add and subtract to the net.

- **Folding**—Capping the positive values by bending the triangle down. The fold separates the positive and negative values.

- **Pointing**—The tip of the triangle acts as a pointer to the resulting net change.

As you've seen in previous examples in this chapter, charts can emphasize one point over another. Figure 8.28 changes the perspective of the storyline to emphasize the net change.

Figure 8.28, augments the yellow points that end in the net change amounts with solid black bars to bring these values to the fore. Although the chart emphasizes net change, it deemphasizes the additions and deductions by placing them in the background as shadows. The Bar Shadow chart shows you the changes each year and describes how those changes were derived. If only net changes are of interest, this chart removes details from the previous chart to bring focus to the year over year changes. However, if instead the year end results are of interest then Figure 8.29 provides this emphasize.

Net Change
in Billions of Dollars

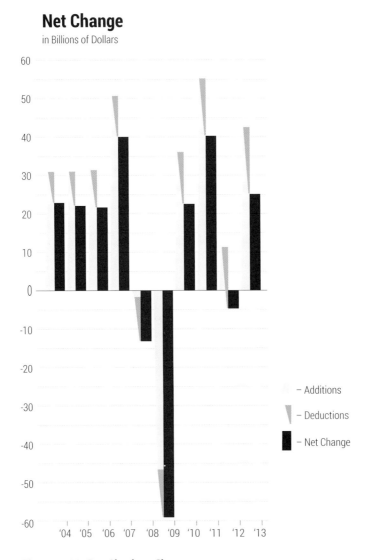

Figure 8.28 Bar Shadow Chart

The solid black bars in Figure 8.29 still dominate the chart. It not only tells the position at the end of each year but, as in Figure 8.28, also explains why. The net can be derived, but the main point of the chart is the net position. The chart emphasizes each year's endpoint and uses color connectors to link one year to the next. They form paths of positive or negative addition and deduction events, whose angle shows whether this year's position is above or below the previous year.

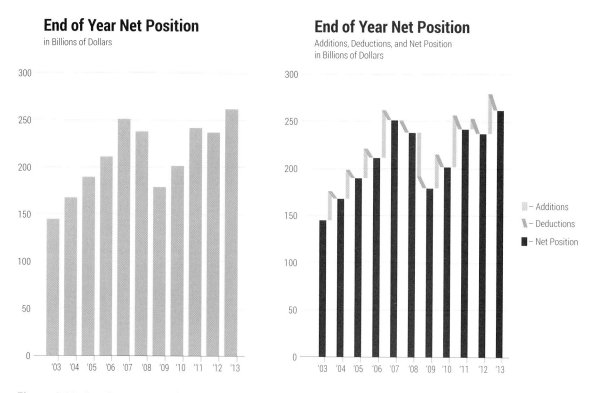

Figure 8.29 **Bar Connectors Chart**

Large sums, significantly and consistently above $100 billion at the end of each year, make details of additions and deductions harder to see. The next chart (Figure 8.30) solves this, still showing the full scale without sacrificing details.

Typical Waterfall charts present connected bars with negative or positive movement, commonly shown as color bars. The synchronized positive movement of an addition and negative movement of a deduction is presumed in most Waterfall charts but is not the case with the CalPERS data set. The net position data set is slightly more complex with cases of negative additions. For this reason, the standard Waterfall chart is slightly updated. The Directional Waterfall chart (Figure 8.30) uses color to denote additions and deductions but then also uses embedded arrows to reinforce the direction of the net position.

End of Year Net Position

Additions, Deductions, and Net Position
in Billions of Dollars

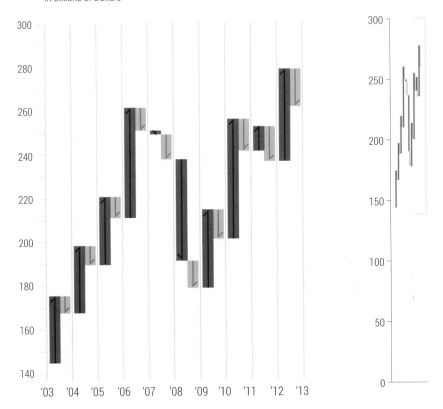

Figure 8.30 Directional Waterfall Chart

The additional benefit of Figure 8.30 is the "divide and conquer" approach of the two charts. Each chart is used for a specific need, and when paired together, the charts display a close-up view and understanding of the full context. The chart on the left enables you to see a close-up view of the net position, whereas the chart on the right provides you context of scale. The context of scale chart shows just how much the net position has changed over the years and how that change compares to the overall size of the fund. The full y-axis starting at the zero mark makes the fund size more comparable to the net position change.

Next, Figure 8.31 continues to use the dual chart approach yet focuses more attention on net positions.

End of Year Net Position
Additions, Deductions, and Net Position
in Billions of Dollars

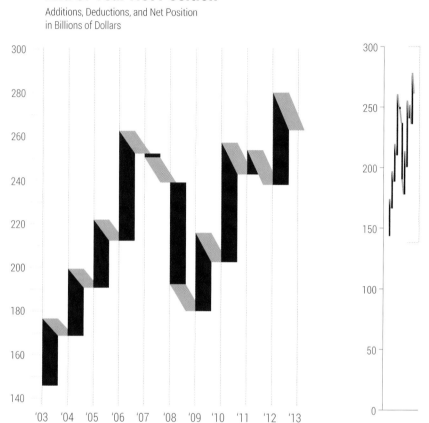

Figure 8.31   **Folded Bar Chart**

The Folded Bar (Figure 8.31) chart is like a folded strip of paper that is creased to point up or down. It readily communicates an increase or decrease and points out inconsistencies in the alternating up/down pattern. The Folded Bar is a 2D chart that has been influenced by the look of a physical 3D object. Yellow bars drawn at an angle reinforces this perspective.

Key Take-Aways

This section builds on the strengths of the Bar chart and introduces variations on it to map data with a mix of positive and negative values. The Fold-Over, Bar Shadow, Bar Connectors, Directional Waterfall, and Folded Bar charts are all variations of the Bar chart that can show year-to-year changes.

Each chart displays a slightly different perspective of the data. The Fold-Over chart includes more details about cumulative additions and deductions. The Bar Shadow chart emphasizes the composition to derive the net change, while the Bar Connectors show the connections between year-end net positions. The Directional Waterfall and Folded Bar charts both show cumulative results of each year's additions and deductions.

Both easy to create and to read, the Bar chart is probably the most widely used chart type. Introducing these new techniques to the Bar charts is therefore relatively easier than introducing a completely new type of data visualization.

Changes in Retirees & Beneficiaries

The Retirees & Beneficiaries data set takes a closer look into the deductions side of the equation with a review of the number of retirees added and removed each year. In addition to the "added to" and "removed from" yearly rolls, comparisons in annual allowances (as shown in Figure 8.32) present the profile of the fund.

CalPERS annual report Exhibit H presents us with a schedule of Retirees & Beneficiaries Added to/and Removed from Rolls to end the actuarial section. The original table provides a 6-year review of four funds. In contrast, Figure 8.32 represents a 6-year review of one fund, PERF. This data reuses a previously presented chart with a different data set: Figure 8.33 shows you how to simplify the previously introduced Fold-Over chart.

Retirees & Beneficiaries Added to/and Removed from Rolls

Year Ended	Added to Rolls		Removed from Rolls		Rolls - End of Year		% Increase in Annual Allowances	Average Annual Allowance
	Number	Allowances	Number	Allowances	Number	Allowances		
6/30/07	29,821	$828,676,000	15,881	$251,559,000	461,624	$10,421,160,000	8.7 %	$22,575
6/30/08	30,462	911,182,000	16,228	267,867,000	475,858	11,422,808,000	9.6	24,005
6/30/09	31,929	1,006,450,000	16,168	275,138,000	491,619	12,506,735,000	9.5	25,440
6/30/10	37,566	1,265,188,000	17,323	299,011,000	511,862	13,751,737,000	10.0	26,866
6/30/11	40,596	1,318,290,000	17,298	319,210,000	535,160	15,032,305,000	9.3	28,089
6/30/12	39,729	1,286,891,000	19,412	381,443,000	555,477	16,126,912,000	7.3	29,033

Figure 8.32 **Retirees & Beneficiaries Table**

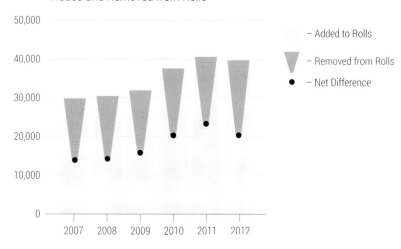

Figure 8.33 **Added & Removed Fold-over Chart**

The general rule to reuse this chart pattern is based on its purpose to show additions, subtractions, and net. If the data type supports this purpose, the Fold-Over chart design can be applied. Figure 8.33 largely focused on the first half of the table including added and removed rolls to derive the net. Figure 8.34 focuses on the second half of the table data starting with rolls at the end of the year. It uses the last four columns of the table data but shows two funds for comparison.

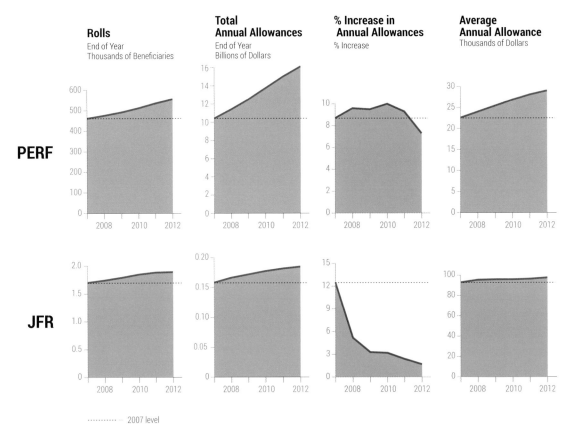

Figure 8.34 Area Comparison Chart

Figure 8.34 is another example of reusing a familiar chart type with a small twist. In general, Area charts are useful for showing the volume and profile of data. Figure 8.34 capitalizes on those benefits and accentuates them through additional tweaks to the chart. The Area Comparison chart collection improves the profile comparison of each chart by incorporating four additional alignment techniques:

▶ **Horizontal dotted line**—A horizontal dotted line is introduced to support the readers' ability to compare the progress across the years from the starting point.

- ▶ **Vertical placement**—The vertical placement of the dotted line is aligned and consistently situated across all charts.

- ▶ **Matrix layout**—The layout of column and row headers and aligned year labels provides an organized framework for comparison and growth. The framework can grow and include more funds if needed.

The three techniques are small details that, when combined, improve your ability to see and compare variances. Unless explicitly pointed out, you may not know to re-create these small alignment details into your chart. However, when you do they will be valuable and used by your audience.

Key Take-Aways

The charts in this section are all examples of previous charts you can repurpose and apply to different data sets. Both the Fold-Over and the Area Comparison charts have been slightly modified to adapt to specific needs. For the Fold-Over chart, details were removed until the data represented subtotals of Added and Removed Rolls. For the Area Comparison charts, details were added to make the charts easier to compare across a collection.

History of Member Salary

To contrast the allowances provided by the fund, the next data set reviews member salary. From one type of payment to the next, the following historical table data of salaries includes a standard ten-year span (Figure 8.35).

Exhibit F: History of Member Salary of CalPERS is a small table listed among a series of reference tables. Listed on page 145 of the annual report, this is the type of table that may easily be skipped over and missed. The Salary Table (Figure 8.35) is selected to illustrate how the data can tell contrasting stories. Figure 8.36 shows these parallel stories by reviewing the profile of the quantities.

History of Member Salary Data

Valuation Date	Number of Active Members	Annual Covered Payroll (in Millions)	Average Annual Salary	% Increase in Average Pay
6/30/03	778,203	34,784	44,697	4.3
6/30/04	760,498	35,078	46,126	3.2
6/30/05	756,234	36,045	47,664	3.3
6/30/06	767,127	38,047	49,597	4
6/30/07	793,164	40,864	51,521	3.9
6/30/08	813,474	44,236	54,379	5.5
6/30/09	812,864	45,053	55,425	1.9
6/30/10	794,138	44,984	56,645	2.2
6/30/11	779,481	43,901	56,321	-0.6
6/30/12	762,459	42,599	55,871	-0.8

Figure 8.35 **Salary Table**

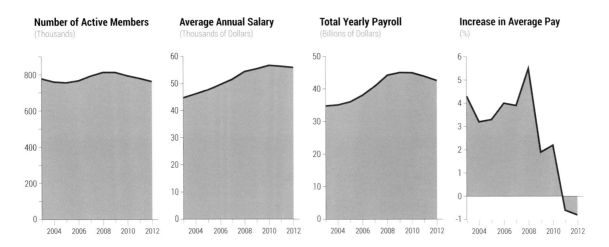

Figure 8.36 **Area Comparison Chart**

Area charts rely on the top line to project a profile of continuous data across the designated timeframe. A review of Figure 8.36 shows you three cases of yearly incremental changes and one case of extreme shifts in the data sets. However, each of the data sets has a designated y-axis scale. The data is not directly linked by type; one data set covers individuals, two use dollars, and the fourth percentage. Despite these variations in incremental and extreme shifts, scales, and data types, you still need to learn from the data and understand:

▶ How the member salaries have developed over the past decade

▶ The pace of change between data sets

▶ The relationships are between these developments

Essentially, you want to link the data sets in order to relate one data set to another. The next chart applies the previously introduced alignment technique. Figure 8.37 shows when and how to combine data sets and when/why to separate data sets into two views.

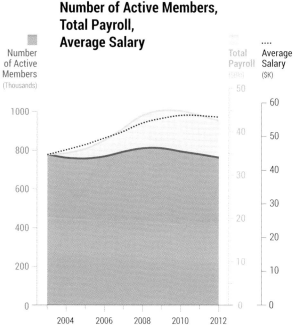
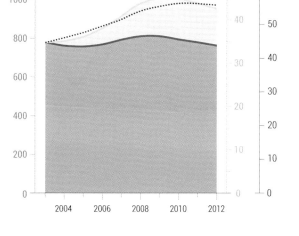
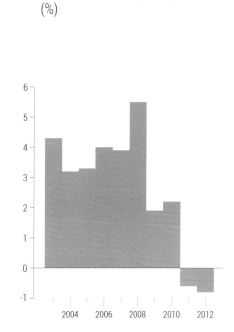

Figure 8.37 **Area Charts – Line and Bar Chart**

The key to relating one data set to another is alignment of similar data points. In the case of the salary data, the connection to all the data sets is time. In Figure 8.37, all four data sets are aligned around the yearly markers, starting in 2003 and ending in 2012 together—so even though the line chart shows three y-axes, you can relate the three values to changes over the same time period. As the average salary continues to rise, the number of members and the total payroll amounts fall; these are the types of direct observations that can be made with an aligned and layered line chart.

The two area charts shown in Figure 8.37 present the profile of a line and bar chart and are essentially extensions of a line and bar chart with added fill. The use of the two charts in this solution may elicit a key question: *Why elect to use a line over a bar chart with the provided data set?* A line chart is a useful method to uncover trends, layer more than one data set, and display up to three y-axes, whereas a bar chart's strength lies in showing precise differences. Figure 8.37 makes use of each of the chart's strengths and illustrates each case.

Key Take-Aways

This short section shows an example of when and how to combine data sets into one chart and points out when to use a Line or Bar chart for time series data. If you want to closely track relationships between two data sets and the data sets have shared points, combining charts can be a viable technique. However, combining data sets that have more than three y-axes can become difficult to label let alone read. The key is to keep the data sets to three and visually create a shared starting point to compare and contrast changes.

Time-series data is typically displayed as a Line chart, but there are some cases in which it is best to display as a Bar chart. The question is: *How do you pick which one to use?* A Line chart tracks the path of a moving point with an explicitly defined direction. In contrast, a Bar chart points out the stops along the path. To summarize, use a Line chart to point out trends in the data and use a Bar chart to show discrete changes and more precisely track variations in those changes.

Funding Ratio

Fund managers are tasked with mitigating liability exposures and improving funding ratios. The funding ratio data and the data sets related to funding ratio are a main focus of pension funds. This section provides useful funding ratio charts to showcase how you should display funding data and what types of data combinations improve your ability to analyze how the fund is doing. One data table is used to help shape the answers to this question: Exhibit A, Funding Progress in the CalPERS Annual Report includes the data for all the funds. This section focuses on one fund, the PERF, and uses a part of the Funding Progress table (Figure 8.38). The same techniques introduced in this section can be used to represent the remaining funds.

Funding Progress – Unfunded Liability & Funded Ratios

Actuarial Valuation Date	Actuarial Value of Assets ($ Mln)	Actuarial Accrued Liability ($ Mln)	Unfunded AAL (UAAL) (AVA Basis) ($ Mln)	Funded Ratio – (AVA Basis)	Annual Covered Payroll ($ Mln)	UAAL as a % of Covered Payroll	Market Value of Assets ($ Mln)	Unfunded AAL (UAAL) (MVA Basis) ($ Mln)	Funded Ratio (MVA Basis)
6/30/03	158,596	180,922	22,326	87.7	34,784	64.2	144,330	36,592	79.8
6/30/04	169,899	194,609	24,710	87.3	35,078	70.4	167,110	27,499	85.9
6/30/05	183,680	210,301	26,621	87.3	36,045	73.9	189,103	21,198	89.9
6/30/06	199,033	228,131	29,098	87.2	38,047	76.5	211,188	16,943	92.6
6/30/07	216,484	248,224	31,740	87.2	40,864	77.7	251,162	-2,938	101.2
6/30/08	233,272	268,324	35,052	86.9	44,236	79.2	238,041	30,283	88.7
6/30/09	244,964	294,042	49,078	83.3	45,100	108.8	178,860	115,182	60.8
6/30/10	257,070	308,343	51,273	83.4	44,984	114	201,632	106,711	65.4
6/30/11	271,389	328,567	57,178	82.6	43,901	130.2	241,740	86,827	73.6
6/30/12	282,991	340,429	57,438	83.1	42,599	134.8	236,800	103,629	69.6

Figure 8.38 **Funding Progress Table**

Ten years of funding data in the Funding Progress Table (Figure 8.38) provides 100 data points (including dates). There are multiple ways to combine 100 data points into representative illustrations. However, you need to first consider that these data points are essential to representing the overall health of a fund. The communication for this data set needs to showcase independent points yet also combine data sets to compare and contrast.

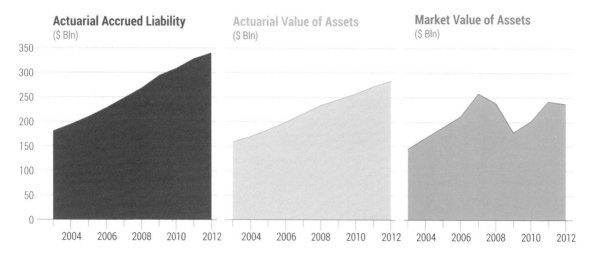

Figure 8.39 Area Comparison Chart

Line charts can be simple and powerful tools. The immediate understanding of time series data as a simple line makes this type of chart frequently used. These area charts represent three columns of the table and could be extended so that every column in the table would be presented as an area chart. As the critical part of the pension fund story, each of the table columns could command their own chart. Assets, liabilities, and the market value of assets need to be shown. However, you can go beyond these straight representations and overlay the data sets, as shown in Figure 8.40.

Two charts combined into one makes for easier comparisons. Stacked Area charts, such as Figure 8.40, layer assets on top of liabilities and share a y-axis to reinforce and enable a direct comparison of the data sets. The primary consideration to creating these charts is to thoughtfully select the pairing options. *Which column headers in the table should be paired? Which values should be set to the background and which to the foreground?* Area Layer charts succeed when you consider the pairing of two data sets, such as assets and liabilities. The next charts, as shown in Figure 8.41, pair the remaining data sets with a slight variation in technique.

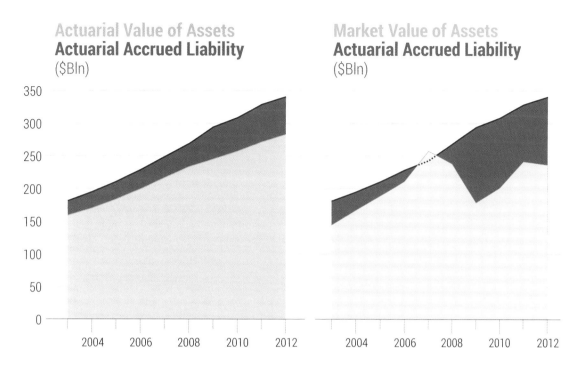

Actuarial Value of Assets
Actuarial Accrued Liability
($Bln)

Market Value of Assets
Actuarial Accrued Liability
($Bln)

Figure 8.40 **Stacked Area Charts**

A part of delivering a clear visual representation is identifying the data sets that need to be bundled and communicated as a package. However, when layering data, the views can become obstructed and therefore compromised. Area and Line Charts in Figure 8.41 provide a simple solution that reveals crucial aspects of the two data sets without obstructions. The combination of an Area chart in the background with a Line chart in the foreground is simple yet should be executed with a few important details in mind:

▶ **x-axis and y-axis**—In order to pair charts, the x-axis data should be shared. When possible, you should aim to pair data sets that can also share the y-axis. If the y-axis is shared, gray grid lines can be introduced. This approach not only simplifies the comparison, but also creates a pairing that is inherently compatible to relate.

▶ **Background versus foreground**—Use the background for context and the foreground to convey your primary message. The top layer should display the data set that your audience needs to focus on and follow closely.

▶ **Line treatment**—Change the line treatment to show areas of overlap. This small detail helps to delineate when the primary data set is within the boundaries of the secondary set.

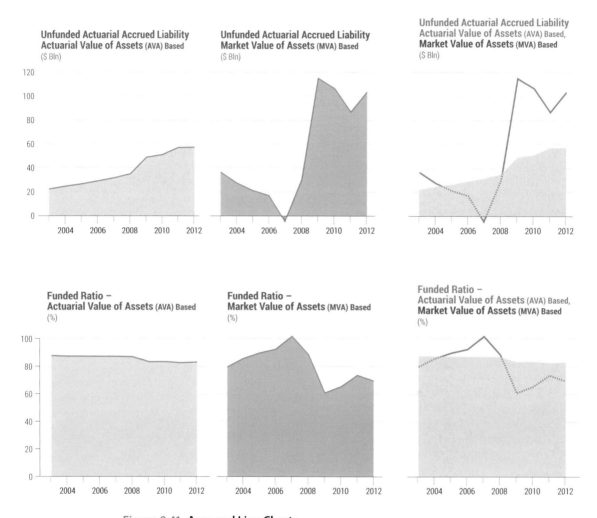

Figure 8.41 **Area and Line Charts**

These details are small, yet when combined improve the representation of the data sets. In the quest to clearly represent the data, the next charts, as shown in Figure 8.42, apply the previously introduced zoom technique to see more details in the data set.

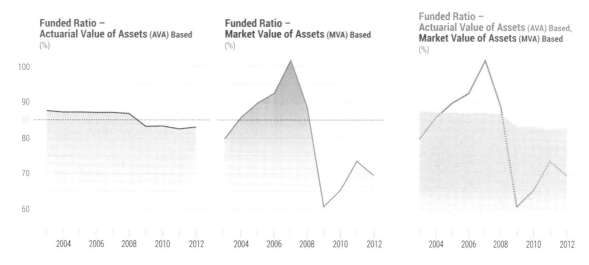

Figure 8.42 **Ratio Zoom Chart**

A close-up view of the funded ratio provides details to better evaluate the data. The Ratio Zoom Chart (Figure 8.42) accentuates the variations in value between the AVA and MVA data sets. You can clearly see the 25% difference between the values in 2009 and contrast this difference with a 0% difference just a year prior.

Next, Figure 8.43 presents an example of combining data sets that do not share a y-axis. This chart shows you both when and how to combine data sets that may not seem comparable.

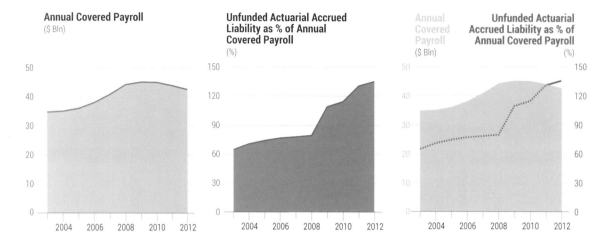

Figure 8.43 Area and Line – Dual Axes Charts

The Area and Line – Dual Axes charts (Figure 8.43) is an example of how you can juxtapose two different data sets and contrast the movement of one value against another. These two sets are particularly interesting because the subject of Annual Covered Payroll is present in both and the units provide insights into each data set. The presence of both dollars and percentage provide both absolute and relative context. For example, you can review the 2011 Annual Covered Payroll in billions while seeing the percentage of Unfunded Actuarial Accrued Liability for the same year.

Combined views, such as those shown next in Figure 8.44, transform the entire table data into five charts. Mirroring the table data with paired data sets is a technique you can use to tell mini stories about the data. The collection shows a consistent correlation between Actuarial Value of Assets and Actuarial Accrued Liability, which continues to increase year over year. In contrast, when reviewing the Actuarial Value of Assets relative to the Market Value of Assets, there is a downward trend in the Funded Ratio when reviewing the ten-year span.

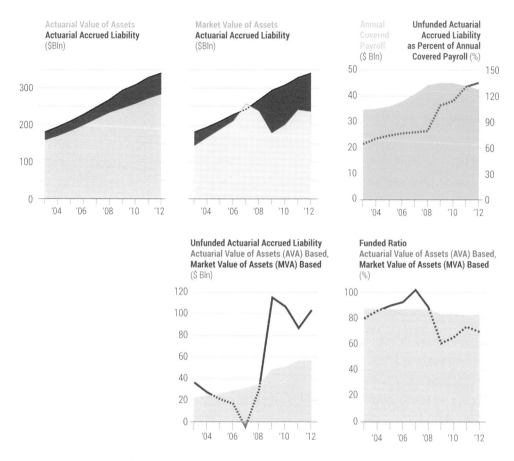

Figure 8.44 **Area and Line Chart Collection**

Key Take-Aways

The goal for this section is to showcase key data sets surrounding the funding ratio and to identify how best to present and combine data views. Consolidating two data sets into one view by combining area and line chart enables easy comparison while preserving clear differentiation. The result of these paired charts is that you can compare, contrast, and/or correlate two data sets. The act of pairing key data sets shows your audience a perspective they may not realize on their own. If you do not provide these combined views, your audience may easily overlook or not carefully evaluate the data in this way.

Summary

This chapter explored a few data sets within the CalPERS fund to better understand the members, payments, and funding ratio of the plan. Although our data set focuses on these three areas, the chart types focuses on two—the Line and Bar charts. This chapter expands on the standard Line and Bar chart to review how they can be separated, combined, and enhanced to create a more understandable story of the data. Bar and Line charts are the most frequently used charts, and an understanding of how to extend and when to use each can be powerful.

Throughout, the charts provide ways to untangle data and emphasize individual quantities, paired quantities, aggregate totals, and relative and absolute rank quantities. New types of Bar charts are introduced to show how to emphasize a different aspect of the data. They represent constituents of payments as additions, deductions, net change, and year-end net position. The full list of visualization solutions include these:

VISUALIZATION	DESCRIPTION	FIGURE
Area Comparison	Separate Area charts presented in one view.	8.3, 8.7, 8.34, 8.36, 8.39
Stacked Area	Represents cumulative totals. Based on a Line chart, color represents the amount between the axis and the line.	8.4, 8.8, 8.17, 8.18, 8.19, 8.40
Area and Bar Combo	Dual views of the quantities as an Area and Bar chart.	8.5, 8.9, 8.20
Area and Line	Combined Area and Line representation in one chart.	8.15, 8.41, 8.42, 8.43, 8.44
Zoom	A method to show detailed results of an Area or Line chart.	8.22–8.24
Fold-Over Stack	A visual method to show the net results of multiple quantities.	8.27, 8.33

VISUALIZATION	DESCRIPTION	FIGURE
Net Change Bar Shadow	Three discrete quantities that emphasizes the net change. Net change is shown in the foreground as a Bar chart, whereas the two quantities are shown in the background.	8.28
Net Position Bar Connectors	Resulting yearly quantities shown as a Bar chart with color-coded bars to link one year to another.	8.29
Net Position Directional Waterfall	Cumulative effect of sequentially introducing positive and negative values with an embedded arrow to show the direction.	8.30
Net Position Folded Bar	Cumulative effect of sequentially introducing positive and negative values with linked bars to show the starting and ending values.	8.31

This chapter skims the surface of the CalPERS data set in order to introduce new chart types and techniques listed in the preceding table. With a review of historical demographic, payment, and funding ratio data to help project, the charts are all meant to carefully assess the state of the pension fund for future planning. Each chart shows how to curate visualizations by combining and contrasting data sets, emphasizing different perspectives, and at times showing what the data isn't directly telling you.

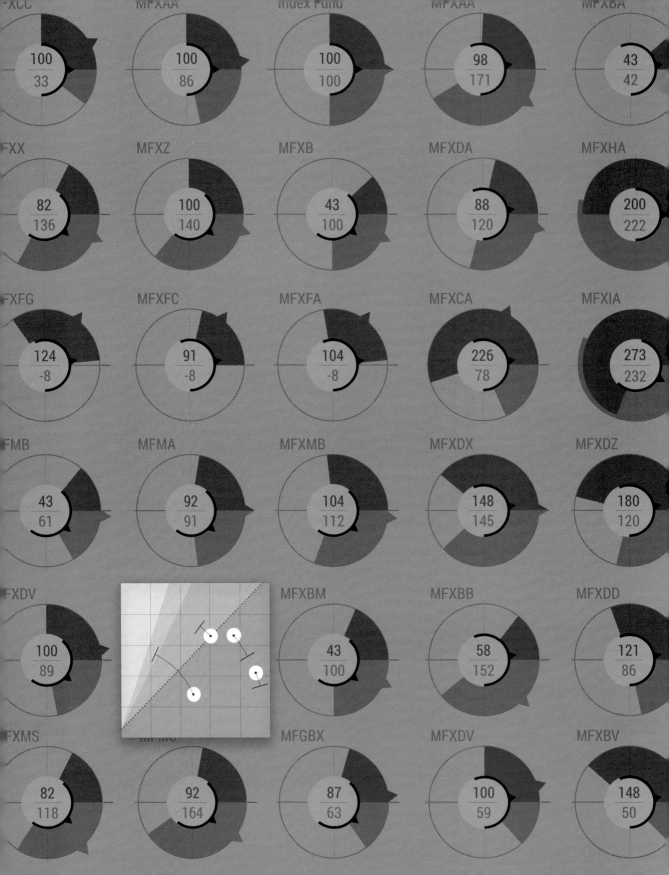

9

Mutual Funds

According to the International Investment Funds Association, total worldwide mutual fund assets have reached an all-time high, approximately $31 trillion (at the start of 2015), up $7.58 trillion over the previous 3 years. The majority of the mutual fund investors (approximately 82%) in the United States invest through employer-sponsored retirement plan accounts, and more than 7,900 funds raise assets via employer-sponsored retirement programs (source: Investment Company Institute, 2014).

In addition, investors are provided with a range of documentation materials to make their mutual fund choices. Available documentation on mutual funds ("Standard Fund Documentation") typically includes the following:

- ▶ Fund fact sheet
- ▶ Summary prospectus
- ▶ Prospectus
- ▶ Statement of additional information
- ▶ One or more annual reports
- ▶ One or more semiannual reports
- ▶ One or more shareholder updates
- ▶ One or more holdings reports

With data that points to growth in assets under management, growth in number of investors, and growth in number of funds, documenting and displaying fund data in clear, relative terms has never been more crucial.

This list grows if you also include fund analysis provided by third parties such as Morningstar, MarketWatch, Bloomberg, and others. This abundance of mutual fund choices combined with an overabundance of documentation can overwhelm investors. For this reason, visualizations in this chapter are designed for 401k plan sponsors and third-party providers to present fund data clearly and simply through various digital channels. Mutual fund companies may also use the proposed visualizations to portray specific aspects of their funds.

This chapter analyzes the range of communication methods used to describe a mutual fund. We distill these methods to a core set of component visualizations for the fund's allocation profile, fees, performance, and risk. Then we suggest how to share these core component visualizations for online digital formats. Specifically, we discuss how to apply these visualizations to the context of a new type of educational fund fact sheet and suggest how to make use of them in an interactive digital display.

We close the chapter with a system for better comparison across a collection of funds. We look at core components and fund documentation from a historical perspective. Finally, we offer a comparative graphic study that embeds data visualizations into an existing table with varying time intervals. Such embedded visualizations can be used to highlight outliers and rank funds. Because today's investment choices are based on a fund's capability to provide returns, these types of assessments bring clarity to fund comparison and selection.

NOTE All the data in this chapter is hypothetical and is representative of what is provided in the marketplace.

Core Components

Components essential to mutual fund communications include allocations, performance, and risk. All fund documents include them. Investment websites often uses charts to explain them. The shared presence of these data components across the various documents, 401k plan sponsor websites, and third-party providers makes it practical to use a component-based approach to visualizations.

You can design these data visualizations once and reuse them, disseminating them across all of your communications. Because the components can be distributed across multiple communications, it becomes more important to think through the core components and carefully craft each one. The component visualizations suggested in this section provide design iterations to highlight improvements of a previous chart or highlight alternative options you can use to make a different point or to reveal variations between investment schemes.

Allocation Profile

A fund's investment style and philosophy result in allocating holdings that reflect different percentages for market cap, sector, and region. This allocation profile helps to describe where the fund is invested and what you can expect to see in terms of its risks and returns. In this way, the allocation profile of the mutual fund (shown in Figure 9.1) introduces the fund and sets the stage for comparisons. The chart provided compares allocations between a real world equity fund we have chosen for illustration (ticker MFSMP) and the average of funds in its peer category.

Market Cap Allocations

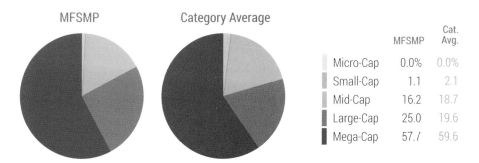

	MFSMP	Cat. Avg.
Micro-Cap	0.0%	0.0%
Small-Cap	1.1	2.1
Mid-Cap	16.2	18.7
Large-Cap	25.0	19.6
Mega-Cap	57.7	59.6

Figure 9.1 **Pie Chart**

The most popular, but not always the most useful, method to graphically represent allocations is through the use of pie charts (Figure 9.1). This representation may suffice when all that's needed is a rough allocation assessment, there is no need for comparison, and there are a limited number (fewer than four) of slices to show. In most cases, however, allocations include more than four categories, and their graphic representation must reveal internal variations and comparisons with category averages or benchmarks. As Figure 9.1 illustrates, pie charts fall short when it comes to revealing slight variations. The same data can be displayed with perhaps more success using a stacked bar chart (Figure 9.2).

Is the fund heavily weighted in consumer staples or utilities? What are its market cap allocations? Which sectors and regions does it represent? How do its allocations compare with benchmarks and category averages? The Stacked Bar with Table chart (Figure 9.2) provides these answers by aligning visual elements for comparison and providing text for explanation. The combination of image and text provides speed and precision in one view.

Of the three allocations, the regional allocations in Figure 9.2 could be represented more directly with a map. Simple geometric forms can replace cartographic details if all you need is to categorize by continents, which in the next example (Figure 9.3) are conveyed through their familiar spatial relationships.

As shown in Figure 9.3, showing proportional distributions in the form of colors on a rough map (in this case of the continents of North America, Latin America, Greater Europe, and Asia) reveals regional variations at a glance. *Is there an equal or unbalanced distribution across the regions? Is the fund within developed or emerging markets?*

Regional allocation data have the flexibility to be displayed within the Stacked Bar chart or the Geometric Map; but with this flexibility come a few trade-offs.

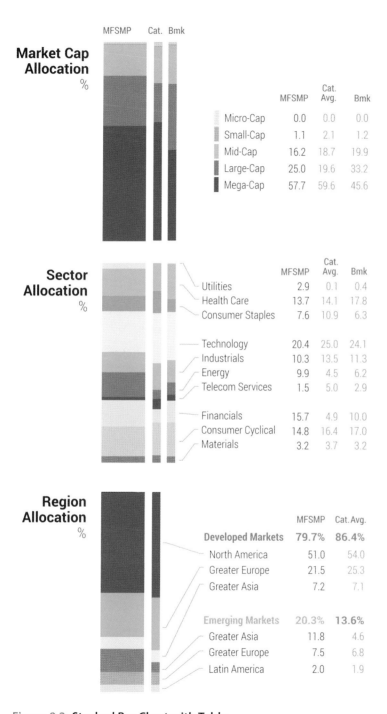

Market Cap Allocation %

	MFSMP	Cat. Avg.	Bmk
Micro-Cap	0.0	0.0	0.0
Small-Cap	1.1	2.1	1.2
Mid-Cap	16.2	18.7	19.9
Large-Cap	25.0	19.6	33.2
Mega-Cap	57.7	59.6	45.6

Sector Allocation %

	MFSMP	Cat. Avg.	Bmk
Utilities	2.9	0.1	0.4
Health Care	13.7	14.1	17.8
Consumer Staples	7.6	10.9	6.3
Technology	20.4	25.0	24.1
Industrials	10.3	13.5	11.3
Energy	9.9	4.5	6.2
Telecom Services	1.5	5.0	2.9
Financials	15.7	4.9	10.0
Consumer Cyclical	14.8	16.4	17.0
Materials	3.2	3.7	3.2

Region Allocation %

	MFSMP	Cat. Avg.
Developed Markets	**79.7%**	**86.4%**
North America	51.0	54.0
Greater Europe	21.5	25.3
Greater Asia	7.2	7.1
Emerging Markets	**20.3%**	**13.6%**
Greater Asia	11.8	4.6
Greater Europe	7.5	6.8
Latin America	2.0	1.9

Figure 9.2 Stacked Bar Chart with Table

Region Allocation

MFSMP

MFSMP

>50%

<5%

Figure 9.3 **Geometric Map**

The Geometric Map (Figure 9.3) uses color saturation to provide a quick at-a-glance understanding of the regional allocations. The simplified triangulated shapes of the continents are well-suited for scaling down and can convey the regional allocations even when considerably reduced in size. In contrast, the use of the Stacked Bar chart for the regional data, as shown in Figure 9.2, provides consistency across the other data points of market cap and sectors. It also provides numeric values and the ability to directly compare specific allocations with category averages.

 In order to offer a historical perspective of the allocations, another option to the Geometric Map can provide direct comparisons. Figure 9.4 shows how various allocations have changed over time.

The Historical Stacked Bar chart (Figure 9.4) is a natural extension of the Stacked Bar chart (Figure 9.2) and shows how a fund's allocations change over time. An interactive display might juxtapose these figures to show connections, for example, between current and previous allocations. Each block's height marks its percentage allocation, revealing steps up or down over time in its individual assignment.

The next example (Figure 9.5) shows how ten sector allocations vary over time.

Historical Allocations

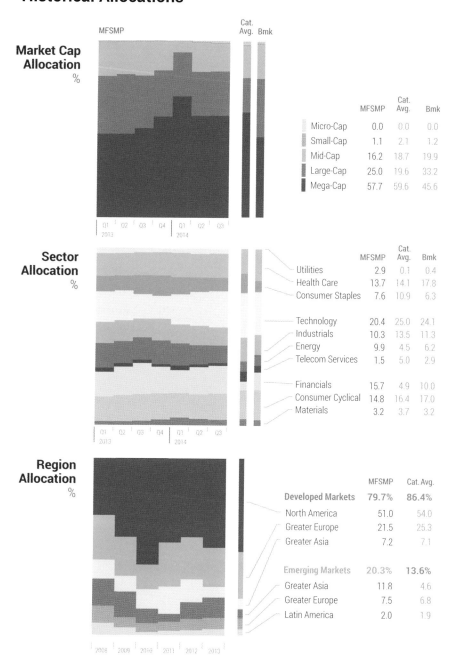

	MFSMP	Cat. Avg.	Bmk
Micro-Cap	0.0	0.0	0.0
Small-Cap	1.1	2.1	1.2
Mid-Cap	16.2	18.7	19.9
Large-Cap	25.0	19.6	33.2
Mega-Cap	57.7	59.6	45.6

	MFSMP	Cat. Avg.	Bmk
Utilities	2.9	0.1	0.4
Health Care	13.7	14.1	17.8
Consumer Staples	7.6	10.9	6.3
Technology	20.4	25.0	24.1
Industrials	10.3	13.5	11.3
Energy	9.9	4.5	6.2
Telecom Services	1.5	5.0	2.9
Financials	15.7	4.9	10.0
Consumer Cyclical	14.8	16.4	17.0
Materials	3.2	3.7	3.2

	MFSMP	Cat. Avg.
Developed Markets	**79.7%**	**86.4%**
North America	51.0	54.0
Greater Europe	21.5	25.3
Greater Asia	7.2	7.1
Emerging Markets	**20.3%**	**13.6%**
Greater Asia	11.8	4.6
Greater Europe	7.5	6.8
Latin America	2.0	1.9

Figure 9.4 **Historical Stacked Bar Chart**

Sector Allocation
Last 7 Quarters

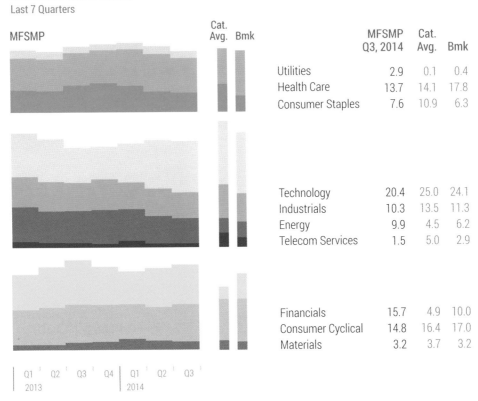

	MFSMP Q3, 2014	Cat. Avg.	Bmk
Utilities	2.9	0.1	0.4
Health Care	13.7	14.1	17.8
Consumer Staples	7.6	10.9	6.3
Technology	20.4	25.0	24.1
Industrials	10.3	13.5	11.3
Energy	9.9	4.5	6.2
Telecom Services	1.5	5.0	2.9
Financials	15.7	4.9	10.0
Consumer Cyclical	14.8	16.4	17.0
Materials	3.2	3.7	3.2

Figure 9.5 **Stacked Bar Groups Chart**

Separating the sectors into defensive, sensitive, and cyclical sector groups (from top to bottom) enables one to review each allocation more accurately. Figure 9.5 gives more information about sector allocations than Figure 9.4 and here's why:

▶ **Comparative allocation at a category level**—Small sets of subcategories in each group rely on vertical order to associate graph layers and table row labels, avoiding awkward callout lines.

▶ **Alignment to the benchmark and category**—Distinct groupings provide clearer comparisons with benchmarks and category averages.

- ▶ **Reestablished baselines**—Maintaining smaller sets of row headers in each of the groups' bar charts resets the starting point for each one. In Figure 9.4, 10 sectors must track across 7 points in time, with only a single baseline of zero. Giving each sector a different baseline turns allocations into constantly moving targets. Figure 9.5 alleviates this tracking problem.

Together, these two views can complement each other. You can provide allocation data both at the summary level (refer to Figure 9.4) as well as the detail level (refer to Figure 9.5), or combine them in an interactive solution. The next set of charts (Figure 9.6) shows an additional perspective that can be incorporated into each of the allocation data sets.

One method to extend your audiences' understanding of the fund allocations is to show offsets from the benchmark and category average. The sorted views organize the data display making it easier for you to see what is over-, under-, or closely aligned to the benchmark. The varying timeframes of year versus quarter are taken into consideration in Figure 9.6. As you zoom in and out of the visualization, the treatment of quarters and years stack up to cleanly reveal the time interval. Although such variations do not typically appear in present-day documents, this is an example of how extending the data view can provide an enriched perspective and reveal how a strategy has performed over time.

Market Cap Allocation
Difference between MFSMP and Benchmark

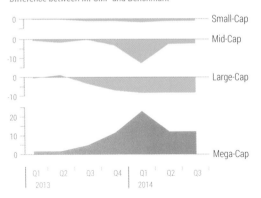

Market Cap Allocation
Difference between MFSMP and Category Average

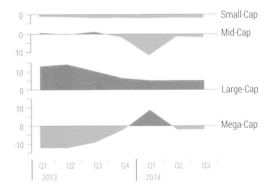

Sector Allocation
Difference between MFSMP and Category Average

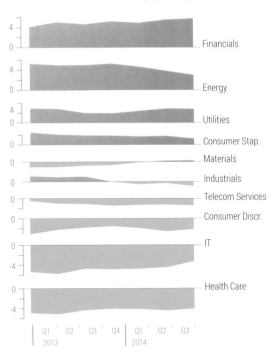

Region Allocation
Difference between MFSMP and Category Average

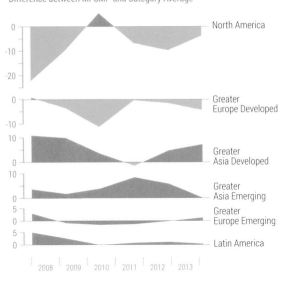

Figure 9.6 **Surface Area Variations Chart**

Key Take-Aways

This section questions the traditional method of showing allocations with pie charts and instead introduces the Stacked Bar chart, the Geometric Map, and the Surface Area Variations to explain the allocation profile of the fund. These alternative charts are interoperable and can be used individually or as a set. In addition, they can scale beyond market cap allocations and represent additional views of sector and region.

Fees

Fees have become top of mind for many as the market expands the number of mutual fund offerings and investors look for value. This growing sensitivity to fee levels results in selective investors carefully reviewing and comparing fee structures. Overall cost structures that include service, transaction, sales load, and distribution fees as part of the expense ratio can be a strong marketing tool for those with favorable numbers. In this section, we provide various options to display fee data. Selecting one version over another will depend on the details your audience requires.

Fund Operating Expenses

The next set of examples examines fund operating expenses in detail. You examine how to show fees in comparison to other share classes, category averages, and category quartiles.

Fund operating expenses are typically listed as a table of numbers. In Figure 9.7, a combined view of such a table along with a Stacked Bar chart displays each number in both text and visual format.

While breaking down expenses provides useful details, the "net fees" value remains the most important number to note. Hence, the net fees are listed in bold as the Total Operating Expenses. To further emphasize total expenses, the chart adjusts the starting point, taking reimbursements into consideration. This enables you to visually reveal actual total operating expenses in the Stacked Bar charts and still provide a net result. Figures 9.8 and 9.9 show ways to simplify the fees view and introduce context relative to a peer group of fund classes.

Fund Operating Expenses

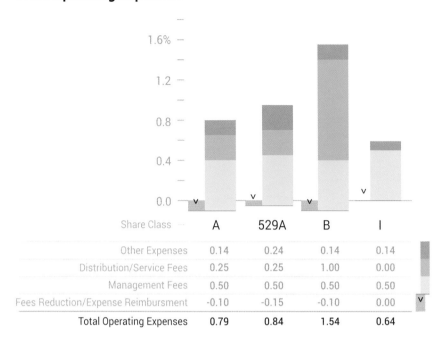

Share Class	A	529A	B	I	
Other Expenses	0.14	0.24	0.14	0.14	
Distribution/Service Fees	0.25	0.25	1.00	0.00	
Management Fees	0.50	0.50	0.50	0.50	
Fees Reduction/Expense Reimbursment	-0.10	-0.15	-0.10	0.00	
Total Operating Expenses	**0.79**	**0.84**	**1.54**	**0.64**	

Figure 9.7 **Net Bar Chart with Table**

Fund Operating Expenses

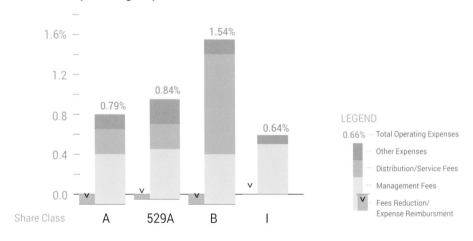

Figure 9.8 **Net Bar Chart**

The data shown in the Net Bar chart (Figure 9.8) focuses your attention to the total operating expenses. The numbers in percentage listed at the top of each bar provides you with a direct answer to the totals. This simplified view removes the details and can be suited for a summary view of the data. If presented in a digital format, the chart view can expand and show the table details on demand. Because share classes are targeted toward different types of investors, investors would rather see the details that are pertinent to them. Our next example (Figure 9.9) is targeted to show the details of one share class.

Fund Operating Expenses
Share Class B

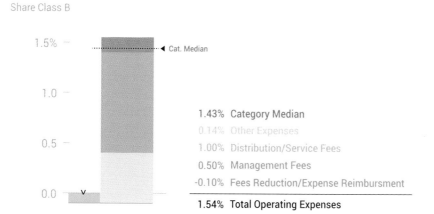

Figure 9.9 **Net Bar Chart with Data Labels**

Are the fees above or below the peer group and by how much? The Net Bar Chart with Data Labels (Figure 9.9) shows the details of the Fund Operating Expenses for one share class and how it compares to the peer group. The Median marker to the right of the chart introduces relative context of the category median, whereas the black dotted line shows that it is above the median for operating expenses. Figure 9.9 can be presented as a stand-alone component or a detail view of the previous Figure 9.8. Given these two choices, adding the summary level view will depend on your audience and type of documentation required.

Expense Ratio

The expense ratio of a fund distills the fund's operating expenses to one number. Without context, that one number can seem out of line with expectations or experience. A simple way to add perspective and context to the expense ratio is by incorporating previous years' fees, category averages, and category quartiles. The next set of charts explores how to best incorporate context to the expense ratio number. First, Figure 9.10 provides the historical perspective by including the previous years' expense ratio.

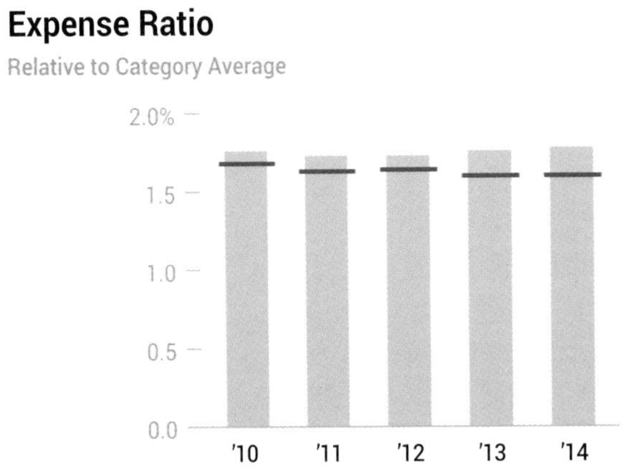

Expense Ratio
Relative to Category Average

	'10	'11	'12	'13	'14
Expense Ratio	1.76	1.73	1.73	1.76	1.78
MC Category Average	1.68	1.63	1.64	1.6	1.6

Figure 9.10 **Context Bar Chart with Stepped Averages**

Figure 9.10 shows a simple bar chart that incorporates two data points across 5 years. *How stable is the expense ratio? How does it compare to the category average?* You can expand these basic questions to incorporate more context. Figure 9.11 shows you how to layer more data into the chart. However, rather than layering information to the foreground, the next examples layer information into the background.

Expense Ratio
Relative to Category Quartiles

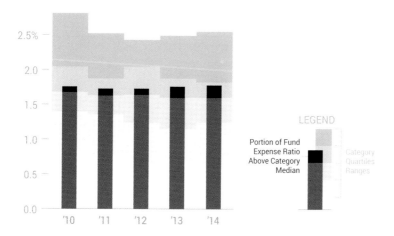

Figure 9.11 **Context Bar Chart—Quartile Background**

Figure 9.11 uses a combination of foreground and background effects to provide more perspective and better comparison. Category quartiles, defined as a peer category, are represented by graduated blues in the background, giving the sense that they provide context to the expense ratio ranges in the foreground. The top quartile shown in the darkest blue indicates category data in the top 25%. It answers, *What is the range of the highest expense ratios for the category?* The bottom quartile in light blue shows the ranges of the category data below the 25% mark of the expense ratio data. It answers, *What is the range of the lowest expense ratios for the category?*

The foreground bar chart emphasizes the category average by filling in the above average section in black, whereas the below average sections are left as dark gray. *Is the expense ratio increasing or decreasing? How does it compare to the category average and top quartiles?* Both of these questions can be answered with these two types of treatments as additional data points are introduced to the foreground and background.

The next two charts (in Figure 9.12) experiment with different foreground markers to show how each one can communicate a different point.

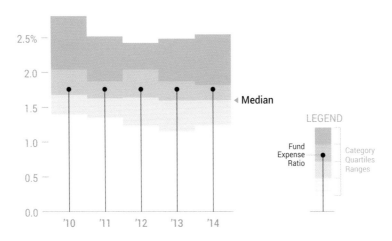

Expense Ratio
Relative to Category Quartiles

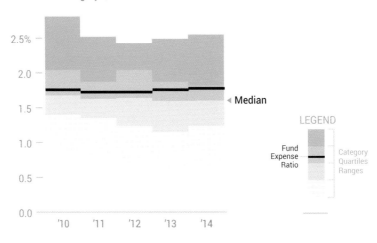

Expense Ratio
Relative to Category Quartiles

Figure 9.12 Context Levels Chart—Quartile Background

Different markers can emphasize different points to help you to see the data differently. The bar markers (shown in Figure 9.11) emphasize the height and variation from the median. The stem markers (reference Figure 9.12) call attention to the expense ratio points, whereas the step markers identify the levels with more precision. Because the steps are connected end to end, tracking the variation across the years becomes easier to do. Figure 9.13 highlights all three: 1) the variation from the median, 2) the expense ratio points, and 3) greater precision and tracking across the years. It flips the question and changes the perspective from one of absolute percentage to one that concentrates on relative placement.

Expense Ratio
by Category Quartiles

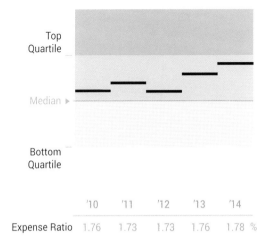

Figure 9.13 Context Levels Chart—Quartile Bands

The background quartiles, as shown in Figure 9.13, are now aligned and mark the expense ratio in context to the quartiles. The previous Figure 9.12 uses the y-axis to show percentage, aligns the quartiles to that axis, and results in an absolute marked view of the data. In contrast, Figure 9.13 uses the y-axis to list the quartiles, layers the percentage within the quartiles, and results in a relative perspective of the data. In this way, the relative perspective shows you the variation from the median. The next example, Figure 9.14, shows a simple adjustment to show the trending data.

Expense Ratio
by Category Quartiles

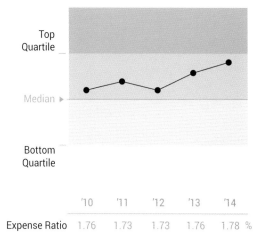

	'10	'11	'12	'13	'14	
Expense Ratio	1.76	1.73	1.73	1.76	1.78	%

Figure 9.14 **Context Line Chart—Connected Dots on Quartile Bands**

The replacement of the step markers with connected dots enables you to see the connections and trends between each point. In addition, Figure 9.14 illustrates the variation from the median and the expense ratio points. In relative terms, the expense ratio has increased over the course of 5 years in comparison to the peer group. Yet in absolute terms, the actual increase is .02%. This example shows that both perspectives of the absolute and relative values are useful to review. The two perspectives create a fuller, more informed picture that combines the actual expense ratio and the shifted view relative to category quartiles.

Key Take-Aways

This section reviews both the total operating expenses and the expense ratio across 5 years. From an aggregate list to a historical perspective, the different data sets require different visual techniques. For example, individual numbers seen in this Fees section provide a mix of negative and positive values that impact the total operating expenses. Because of this, the chart begins by establishing the negative values as the starting point. You can reuse this technique in cases in which you need to show the net results. In contrast, the expense ratio data enables you to track trends in context of the category quartiles. Relative and absolute values can provide two perspectives on your data. You can apply backgrounds such as the quartile background or quartile bands to provide a fuller context to your charts.

Performance

Fund performance is tracked across years to show the enduring ability of the fund management team to generate returns. *How does the fund's performance returns compare to the category average? What is the 10-year growth of $10K invested in the fund?* This section goes beyond these typical questions and introduces additional relevant data points to your charts. The sales charge, load, and no load category quartiles are additional data points that will be included. First, this section starts with one of the most commonly shown charts—Figure 9.15 shows a line chart.

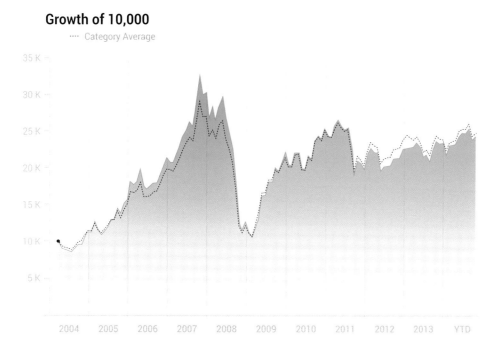

Figure 9.15 **Context Line Chart—$10K 10YR Performance**

This rolling ten-year view is common, simple to understand, and often combined with a benchmark, noted in Figure 9.15 as the category average. Without a word, you can see how well the fund rebounded after the 2008 crisis. No text is required to analyze the alignment in performance to the category average. Minimal values are required to orient, see coordinates, and track trends. The classic line chart presents time series data well. As a successful communication display, the chart is a foundational data visualization that has been in use for centuries.

The familiarity and simplicity of the line chart enables you to do more and introduce additional data points for a richer display. *How does the sales charge decision for your fund impact its growth of investment vis a vis that of the category average?* This question is answered in the following Line chart (Figure 9.16).

The top line chart in Figure 9.16 uses three lines to differentiate the no load, load, and category performance, whereas the bottom line chart uses the orange fill to highlight the gap between the load and no load. The fill technique simplifies the display and makes it easier for you to track one line instead of three. The same data points are shown in both charts, but the messiness of three lines (top chart) is replaced with one (bottom chart). Next, Figure 9.17 incorporates category context into the chart.

By using the fill technique in this figure, the quartile data is stacked in the background for additional context and shows a full category perspective of the fund's growth. You can see how close a fund tracks to the category average as well as the range of the other quartiles. The next example (Figure 9.18) adjusts the coordinate system of the chart with different values in the y-axis.

Growth of 10,000

No-Load Fund Performance
Fund Performance Accounting for Load
Category Average

-1.00%
Deferred
Sales
Charge

-4.75%
Sales
Charge

Growth of 10,000

No-Load Fund Performance
Fund Performance Accounting for Load
Category Average

-1.00%
Deferred
Sales
Charge

-4.75%
Sales
Charge

Figure 9.16 **Context Line Chart—Highlight Spread**

Figure 9.17   Context Line Chart—Quartile Background

Figure 9.18 uses the same data points as Figure 9.17 yet both provide different perspectives. The former delineates the contextual data with an absolute perspective of the data, whereas the latter does so with a relative perspective. If you would like to see the variation the fund experienced from the average, Figure 9.18 shows a clearer depiction of the data. If you would rather compare the variation of the fund to its peer quartiles, Figure 9.17 shows a better communication tool.

The next series of charts apply the same techniques to trailing return data. The visualizations, starting with Figure 9.19, builds on the commonly used bar chart. *How well has the fund performed in the last month, year, or 5 years? How do these returns compare to the category average?* You can answer both of these questions with Figure 9.19.

Growth of 10,000
by Category Quartiles

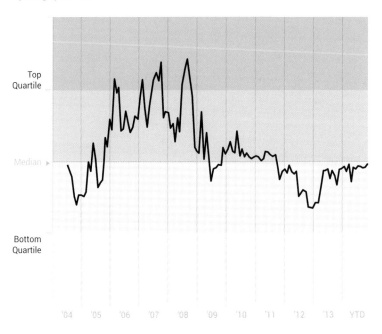

Figure 9.18 **Context Line Chart—Quartile Bands**

Trailing Returns (Monthly)
···· Category Median

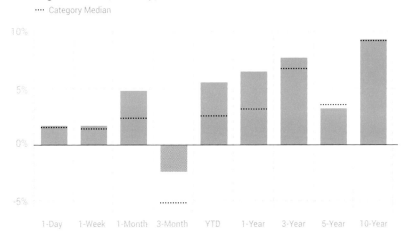

Figure 9.19 **Context Bar Chart—Trailing Returns**

With a large number of funds to select from, the data points shown in Figure 9.19 are not enough. You need more context and a more well-rounded view of the returns. Yet again, the visualizations can provide more context by using the same approach shown in the Growth of $10,000 chart and the Expense Ratio chart. The next example (Figure 9.20) incorporates more data into the background of the chart to accurately show how the fund compares to its peers.

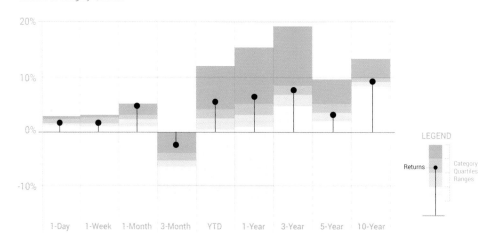

Trailing Returns (Monthly)
Relative to Category Quartiles

Figure 9.20 Context Bar Chart—Quartile Background

Similar to a map that layers streets in the context of terrain, Figure 9.20 layers returns in the context of category quartiles. The chart displays the returns and the context of the rank of those returns. For example, although the fund provided negative returns in the 3-month time mark, the quartile perspective shows it performed within the top quartile during that time. All funds delivered negative returns in the recent 3-month timeframe and positive returns across the longer 10-year periods. You can show both how the fund performs and how well it performs in context to all others. With the percent returns on the y-axis, the chart is a return-centric view of the data. You can see the fund's actual returns. In contrast, Figure 9.21 maps the trailing returns to the quartile bands.

Trailing Returns (Monthly)
by Category Quartiles

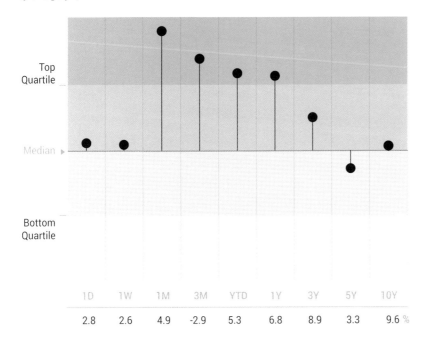

	1D	1W	1M	3M	YTD	1Y	3Y	5Y	10Y
	2.8	2.6	4.9	-2.9	5.3	6.8	8.9	3.3	9.6 %

Figure 9.21 **Context Level Chart—Quartile Bands**

Both Figures 9.20 and 9.21 are useful in evaluating the actual returns in comparison to the peer relative returns, and together the charts provide a more complete perspective of the fund's performance. There is no doubt that the peer group context is important to include as the mutual fund market bids for attention. As a communication tool, a collection of charts (Figure 9.22) can be used to compare, explain, and even perhaps justify results.

Absolute vs. Relative Values Comparison

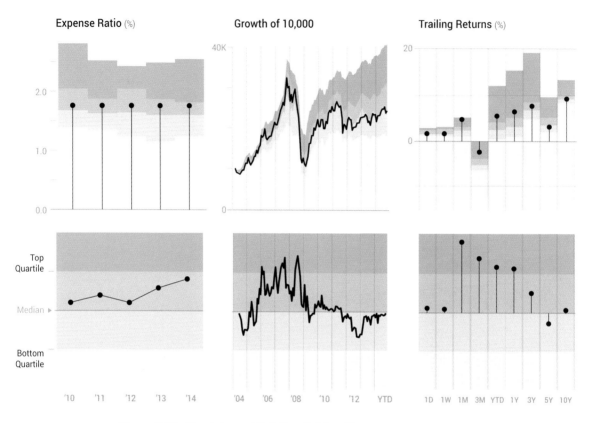

Figure 9.22 **Absolute and Relative Pairing Chart**

Across fees, 10-year growth, and trailing returns, the charts introduced category data as quartiles and produced views to showcase the numeric values in absolute terms and relative terms. As a collection, the Absolute & Relative Pairing (Figure 9.22) can be used to tell a multifaceted story. Visualizing and placing both absolute and relative charts into one view ensures a well-rounded perspective is provided.

▶ **Absolute Context:**

   ▶ Provides actual values for each time period

   ▶ Shows the placement of the actual value within the quartiles

- ▶ Displays the trends of the values across the years/time periods

- ▶ Shows the values and ranges of the quartiles per time period

- ▶ Shows the trends of the category average in relation to the % values

- ▶ Shows the trends of the category quartiles in relation to the % ranges

- ▶ **Relative Context:**

  - ▶ Shows the placement of the actual value within the quartiles

  - ▶ Shows the variation from the median

  - ▶ Shows the trend of the fund's rank across quartiles

  - ▶ Shows the frequency of the fund's rank within quartiles

  - ▶ Shows above or below average results

Key Take-Aways

The benefits listed in each type of visualization show how coupling absolute and relative views can provide a richer perspective of the data. In Figure 9.22 the charts not only juxtapose absolute and relative views, but also ground them with the same reference bands of the category quartiles. By using the quartile backdrops in both sets of visuals, you can orient and compare absolute and relative values. As noted, both views show the placement of the actual value within the quartiles to be compared and contrasted.

Although the charts (Figures 9.15–9.22) use a category average comparison data point, you can elect to use other comparison data points. For example, you can compare the fund data to a market benchmark with the same visualization techniques as shown in Figure 9.22.

Risk

Volatility, upside/downside capture, beta, Sharpe Ratio, R2 levels and other statistical measurements are some of the numeric tools you can use to evaluate investment risk in a mutual fund. This section addresses these key risk indicators that are typically presented in documentation materials distributed to the public. You can improve the visuals to track risk in context of the category average, benchmark, and market for better comparison. *With the market upside capture set to 100 by virtue of it being the benchmark, how might we show the fund's upside and downside capture ratio of the market's movements? How might we show the capture ratio data across the years?* This section investigates and resolves these questions.

Upside/Downside Capture

The upside capture ratio shows how much of the market gain the fund captured when the market rose while the downside capture shows how much of the market loss the fund suffered when the market declines (i.e., *did the fund provide some downside protection?*). However, if you compare a fund across years or if you compare a set of funds for the same year, you may have additional questions. *Which fund/year provides a greater tendency toward a beneficial upside or downside capture ratio? How closely aligned is the fund to similar capture experiences of the category average?* Figure 9.23 shows the fund and market reference points to compare above or below market capture.

Upside/Downside Capture

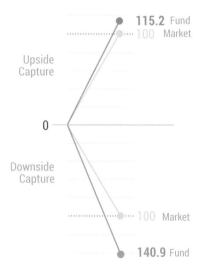

Figure 9.23 **Pointer Chart**

Similar to a laser pointer, the Upside/Downside Capture Points chart (Figure 9.23) projects both the angle and the end points onto a marked graph background. The combination of both the points and the angle enables you to assess just how far above or below the capture point the fund lies. The color use and labels provide the details to distinguish the fund from the index representing market movements. Figure 9.24 illustrates how you can include category average into the chart.

Upside/Downside Capture

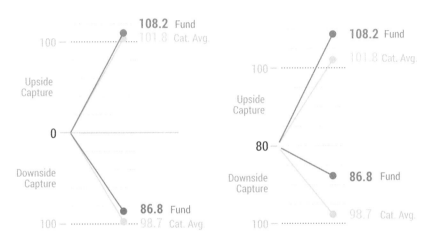

Figure 9.24 **Pointer Chart—Zoom**

If you zoom into the display, (as shown with the image on the right of Figure 9.24) you can clearly see the relative size of the upside and downside. The chart provides details only a zoomed-in display can provide. From a distance, both captures look similar, but upon closer inspection, the gaps stand out easily. The next visual inspects how the upside and downside capture has changed over time. Figure 9.25 shows side-by-side views of the years' captures to compare how a fund has adjusted and responded.

FLCSX

Upside/Downside Capture   FLCSX v. Category

	1 Year	3 Years	5 Years	10 Years
Upside Capture	94.1	112.6	112.7	117.0
Category	92.4	97.4	97.2	99.0

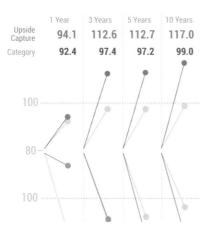

Figure 9.25 **Pointer Collection**

Again, the zoomed-in technique across the years enables you to see the differences more clearly. The category average points are rendered in gray and shadow the upside capture in blue and downside capture in orange. By presenting the data with foreground and background colors, you can focus your attention on the changes year over year. *Where are the capture points across the years and what are the overall trends or tendencies of the fund?* Figure 9.25 answers our questions regarding historical capture points but falls short on visualizing the trend data.

The next set of visualizations explores how to show both trends and tendencies so that we see not only the capture points across the years, but we also see the overall capture tendency of the fund in one view. Figure 9.26 uses the dial metaphor and replaces the capture points with measurement levels.

Dials, knobs, meters, and gauges are measurement tools that can show levels of various amounts. The Dial Gauge visually answers the upside and downside capture question and introduces a third and fourth question: *What level is the midpoint of the capture? And does the midpoint fall to the north or south of the zero line?* The arrow marks the midpoint to indicate the fund's capture tendency. Next, Figure 9.27 shows how to include additional data points for further reference.

Upside/Downside Capture

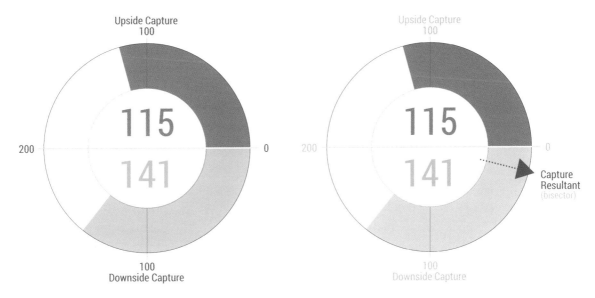

Figure 9.26 **Dial Gauge Chart**

Upside/Downside Capture
vs. Category Average

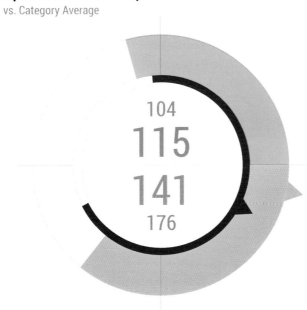

Figure 9.27 **Comparison Dial Chart**

Figure 9.27 improves on Figure 9.26 by layering in category average data points. The inner black radius line reveals upside, downside, and midpoint captures for the category average. The visual now incorporates six total data points and explicitly labels four of them. Gray numerals label the category upside and downside capture points, and color ones label the fund data.

The six dial data points afford better comparison. For example within the fund you can see the ranges and midpoints. In addition, you can use a collection of Comparison Dials (as referenced in Figure 9.28) to compare and quickly show capture results.

The dials (refer to Figure 9.28) can be read from the outside moving toward the center; the outside provides more summary level information, whereas the center lists the detail information.

- ▶ **Summary level**—The outside notch shows trend data of where the capture midpoint falls. So from the outset, you can assess the fund as a down or up capture fund. The colors reinforce the upside and downside levels, and overall the system is flexible enough to show below zero and beyond 200.

- ▶ **Midlevel**—The category radius line (shown in black) provides comparison to the category average data. The fund's midpoint notch shows alignment or misalignment to the category.

- ▶ **Detail level**—The center provides the reader with the details to the actual numeric values. As reinforcement to the visuals, the text shows the exact upside and downside values that are harder to extract from the chart alone.

The next visualization (Figure 9.29) layers in more details to show a historical perspective of the capture data. It incorporates yearly details within the Comparison Dial to see a clearer view of past captures. This new treatment transforms the Comparison Dial visualization and grows six data points in Figure 9.27 to show 16 data points in Figure 9.29.

Upside/Downside Capture Comparison

Figure 9.28 **Comparison Dial Collection**

Upside/Downside Capture

Multiple Time Periods

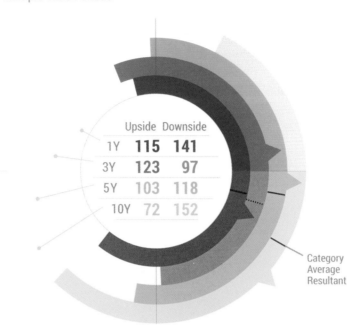

	Upside	Downside
1Y	**115**	**141**
3Y	**123**	97
5Y	103	118
10Y	72	152

Category
Average
Resultant

Figure 9.29 **Temporal Dial Chart**

The blue gradients (refer to Figure 9.29) progressively show how the captures have evolved across the time periods. Complemented with category midpoint markers (dotted lines), the marked directive arrows help you answer: *Does the fund tend to fall within the downside or upside capture across the years?* Holistically, the chart enables you to assess the capture profile of the fund. The reference points of time, peer comparison, and midpoints together create the overall capture profile to better track trends.

Although Figure 9.29 is comprehensive, it may take time to review. The next visualization aims to provide you with a simplified version. The quadrants approach (Figure 9.30) consolidates the upside/downside capture points and replaces the midpoint.

Upside/Downside Capture
FAMKX vs. Category Average

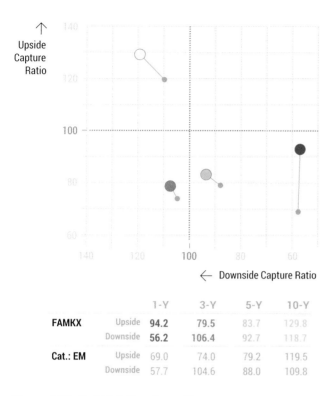

		1-Y	3-Y	5-Y	10-Y
FAMKX	Upside	**94.2**	**79.5**	83.7	129.8
	Downside	**56.2**	**106.4**	92.7	118.7
Cat.: EM	Upside	69.0	74.0	79.2	119.5
	Downside	57.7	104.6	88.0	109.8

Figure 9.30 **Dot Link Quadrant Chart**

Mapping the upside and downside capture within quadrants, as shown in Figure 9.30, removes the need to mark the midpoint. Instead, you need to review only the quadrant placement and movement across the years. The upside and downside quadrant location is complemented with the associated values listed within the table. The quadrant approach enables you to notice the following:

▶ **Rank**—The quadrant system makes it easy to identify best and worst outcomes to distinguish top and bottom rank.

▶ **Tendency**—The consistent or inconsistent placement across the four sections is an indicator of the fund's tendency. If the captures map consistently to the same quadrant, you can say the fund has a tendency toward the identified section.

▶ **Offset**—The lines that connect the fund to the category average show you just how offset the two are from each other. You can analyze how the fund closely aligns, forges ahead, or trails behind the category average.

Rank, tendency, and offset are the significant attributes you can track with the Capture Quadrants chart. To improve the prominence of these attributes even further, you can tilt the chart (as shown in Figure 9.31) to make the results indisputable.

Upside/Downside Capture
FAMKX vs. Category Average

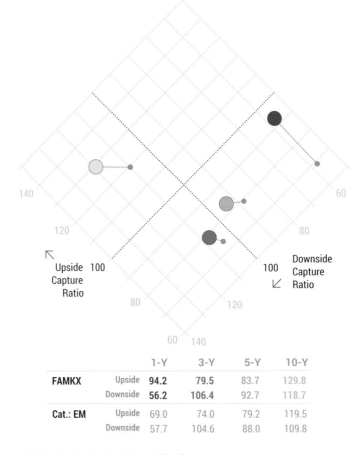

		1-Y	3-Y	5-Y	10-Y
FAMKX	Upside	**94.2**	**79.5**	83.7	129.8
	Downside	**56.2**	**106.4**	92.7	118.7
Cat.: EM	Upside	69.0	74.0	79.2	119.5
	Downside	57.7	104.6	88.0	109.8

Figure 9.31 Dot Link Quadrant Tilt Chart

What year yielded the best capture ratio combination? And how did it compare to the category average? The 45-degree tilt (Figure 9.31) conveys the top captures by emphasizing the top center as the best. You can decide to be more preferential or sensitive to downside or upside capture. Marks to the right show a preference toward aversion to risk, whereas marks to the left show a preference toward greater opportunity gains. Therefore, the Quadrant Tilt becomes a useful tool for seeing how stable the fund is and if the fund has more of a tendency to provide up or downside capture.

Alpha, Beta, Sharpe Ratio, and Sortino Ratio Combination

Alpha, Beta, Sharpe Ratio, and Sortino Ratio are key risk metrics that are often listed in a fund's marketing materials. As a set, the metrics provide a more holistic view of a fund's risk profile. However, similar to previous examples in this chapter, the visualizations, like Figure 9.32, work best with the addition of relevancy.

Risk Levels

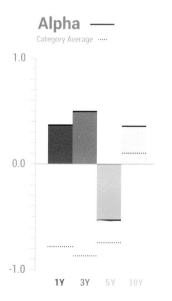
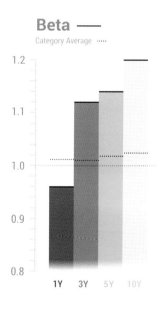
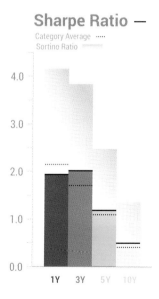

Figure 9.32 **Context Bar Chart**

Figure 9.32 shows two levels to each Bar chart: One level marks the fund's risk level, and the other marks the category average level. Although the Alpha and Beta charts track two levels, the Sharpe/Sortino ratio tracks three levels each year. The Sortino Ratio is shown as a background fill for context. Figure 9.33 illustrates how you can integrate a stronger indicator to highlight the difference between the risk and category average levels.

Risk Levels Variations

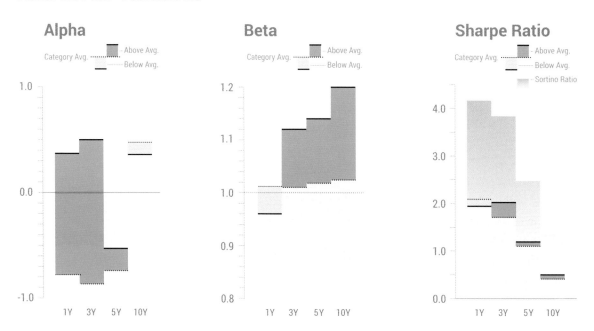

Figure 9.33 **Context Bar Chart—Highlight Spread**

How aligned is the fund's risk level to the category average? How wide is the spread? Which spreads are above the industry average, and which spreads are below? Figure 9.33 not only shows the spreads but also shows the direction of the spread. You can scan the chart just to see what is above or below the benchmark. Contrasting color shows the direction (blue for above average and yellow for below average) and height shows the size of the spread, removing your effort to make those assessments.

R² levels

The R² levels can explain the degree to which movements in the fund are attributed to movements in the benchmark index. Figure 9.34 uses a pie chart to show just how closely aligned they are to the benchmark across different timeframes.

R² Levels

Figure 9.34 **Pie Fill Chart**

Why show the R2 levels in a radial format over a linear format? As a single number (refer to Figure 9.34), the radial form provides you with a better understanding of each year's offsets from the benchmark. For example, the high correlation of 98 shows a thin sliver of a gap, whereas the low correlation of 43 shows the level has not made it beyond the 50 mark. The white space in the pie shows the gap and how far off the fund is to the benchmark. The turn in the pie beyond the 50 mark is important to note and easy to see in a radial format. Your eyes can detect straight lines versus lines drawn at an angle; the Pie Fill takes advantage of this capability. In contrast, a square shape would not easily show a fill slightly over or under the 50% mark. The Pie Fill visualization enables you to see if the value is slightly over or under the 0, 25, 50, 75, and 100% mark. Your ability to detect straight edges and accurately estimate the percentage is the reason why R² levels are best shown in a radial format.

Sharpe Ratio

The next set of charts study the Sharpe Ratio more closely and provide comparison points to the benchmark, risk free rate, and time, as well as categorical success metrics. This section starts by showing how the Sharpe Ratio is commonly graphed (Figure 9.35). In this example, funds are mapped to a coordinate system of standard deviation on the x-axis and returns on the y-axis.

Sharpe Ratio
MFSMP vs. S&P 500

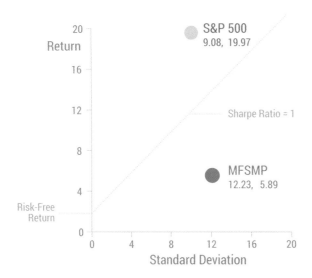

Figure 9.35 **Dot Plot Chart**

Is the fund and benchmark above or below the Sharpe Ratio = 1 line? With the familiar Return/Standard Deviation coordinate system (refer to Figure 9.35), the chart places the fund's ratio and benchmark ratio in context of the risk-free rate. Figure 9.35 is a primer for incorporating a historical perspective to the next visualization. The Dot Link Temporal Collection (Figure 9.36) enables you to inspect the time continuum with the benchmark values for each year.

Over time, which fund shows better returns for the same risk? The line indicating the Sharpe Ratio of 1 is drawn in the background and provides a consistent reference line across all funds. The story for each fund varies but the setting remains the same. The progression over the years, 10, 5, 3, and 1 from the light blue to dark blue highlights the most current time frame of 1 year in dark blue and the 10-year time frame as light blue. The MFSPM chart (within Figure 9.36) tells the story of how the fund has increased its risk metric in comparison to the benchmark. In contrast, the FLCSX chart (within Figure 9.36) shows how the Sharpe Ratio has improved over time and aligned consistently to the benchmark.

Sharpe Ratio Temporal Tracking

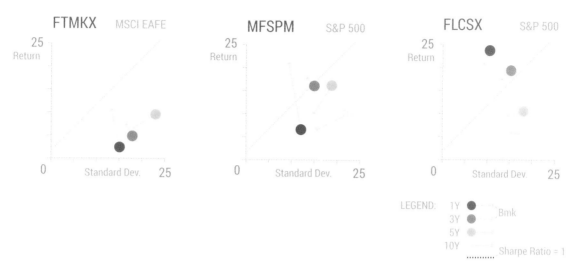

Figure 9.36 **Dot Link Temporal Collection**

Figure 9.37 shows another method to compare the fund to the benchmark. It is a schematic explanation of how the fund Sharpe Ratio is connected to the benchmark Sharpe Ratio.

Sharpe Ratio Arc
MFSMP vs. S&P 500

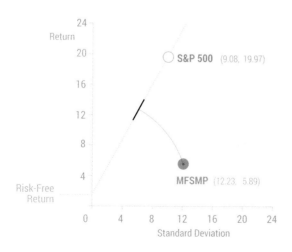

Figure 9.37 **Arc Schematic Chart**

To gain a proper understanding of the fund-to-benchmark ratio relationship, you need to be aware that in this coordinate system (Figure 9.37), the ratio is represented as an angle. The chart explains:

▶ **Benchmark line**—The position of the benchmark and the risk-free rate determines the corresponding Sharpe ratio benchmark line. The benchmark line is marked with a short, bold black line.

▶ **Connected arc**—The benchmark line is connected to the fund ratio with an arc. The arc shows the difference between the respective benchmark (S&P500) and Fund (MFSMP).

Relative to the fund ratio, how does the benchmark compare? If the fund followed the same benchmark threshold, what is the ratio the fund should strive to beat? These questions can be answered with the Sharpe Ratio Arc. Another way to explain the answer to these questions is through Figure 9.38, Arc Connection.

Sharpe Ratio Arc Construction

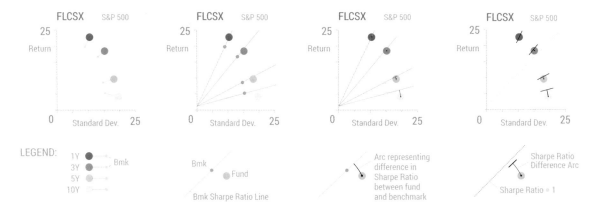

Figure 9.38 **Arc Construction**

Figure 9.38 shows the connection between the fund ratio, benchmark ratio, and corresponding benchmark line. The illustrated sequence shows how the benchmark ratio (indicated as a dot) determines the corresponding benchmark line.

These lines are consequently reduced to connected arcs and concisely represent the difference between the fund and the benchmark Sharpe ratios.

Next, Figure 9.39 shows the Sharpe Ratio Arc approach applied to three funds.

Sharpe Ratio Comparison

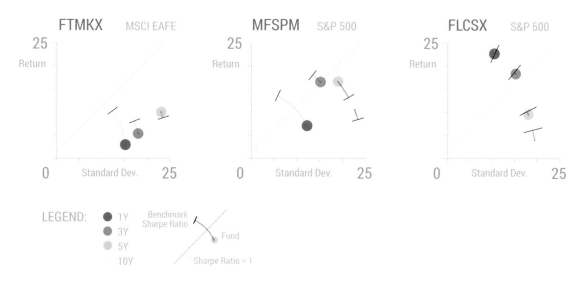

Figure 9.39 **Arc Collection**

A review of three fund's Sharpe Ratios shows a clearer connection to the benchmark. Similar to the previous two charts, Figure 9.39 illustrates the ratio benchmark line as an anchor to join the connected arc. The Sharpe Ratio Arcs answer key questions:

▶ Does the fund have a history of being above or below the Sharpe Ratio equal to 1 line?

▶ Does the fund benchmark have a history of being above or below the Sharpe Ratio equal to 1 line?

▶ Is the fund positioned better relative to the Sharpe Ratio equal to 1 line than its benchmark?

- ▶ How close is the fund tracking to the benchmark?

- ▶ How do the funds compare to each other?

Yet, although the chart can answer these types of relative questions, you can still layer in more context into the background. Figure 9.40 illustrates this point.

Sharpe Ratio Comparison

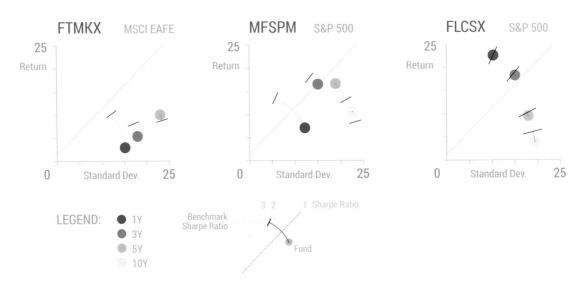

Figure 9.40 **Sharpe Ratio Arc Bands Collection**

Did the fund make it into the good, very good, or excellent bands of risk adjusted returns? The Sharpe Ratio Arc Bands (Figure 9.40) adds these three aspirational categories to the background of the chart. The fill between 1–2 represents a good Sharpe Ratio, 2–3 very good, and greater than 3 represents excellent with the lightest blue band. Because the color bands represent one-half the chart, it makes it much clearer to see if the fund made or missed the threshold.

Risk Components

Your perception of how well a fund is managing risk can largely be based on your understanding of the data. Although the previous section focuses on charting ideas for each risk metric, this section focuses on combining those risk charts (as shown in Figure 9.41).

Risk Components
LCSX - Large Cap Stock

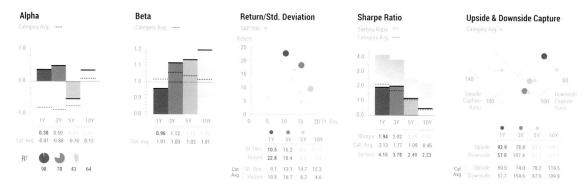

Figure 9.41 Multiple Views Collection

Multiple views of key risk metrics in one display can provide you with a wider understanding of how the fund is managing risk. The historical views across alpha, R^2, beta, returns/standard deviation, Sharpe Ratio, and upside and downside capture can help you expand your view further to track trends and compare against the category average. The collection paints a more complete story of how the various risk metrics are congruent or point toward an exception. You can review the exceptions in the story to inspect and ask, "Why this result?" The Multiple Views approach is a good start to assessing and managing risk for a fund. It collects multiple charts all centered on one aspect of the fund, in this case, risk. The approach is flexible and scalable to display different risk metrics or include more risk metrics to make the display more comprehensive.

Key Take-Aways

The variety of risk metrics covered in this section produce a variety of data visualization solutions. The upside/downside capture metric is illustrated with Pointer, Dial Gauge, and Dot Line Quadrant charts to show the capture tendency of the fund. R^2 values are shown as a Pie Fill. Alpha, beta, and Sharpe Ratio are illustrated with a Context Bar to highlight spreads from the category average. This section reviewed the Sharpe Ratio more closely, resulting in the Arc chart that provides a comparable benchmark target. The techniques vary because purposes and data differ. Study each risk metric. Perhaps the most powerful visualization is the Multiple Views (Figure 9.41): A compilation of key risk metrics provides a more complete assessment of risk.

Fund Fact Sheets

Fund fact sheets are one of the most commonly viewed documents and are often listed as the first document to reference online. Once accessed, readers will find that the two-page document is challenged to succinctly communicate the basic fund information. The data within the fund fact sheet overlaps with many other documents and, as marketing material, it is typically the most visual. The next fact sheet examples use the existing data, replace charts with new components, and update the layout to enhance the readability of the quantitative information. The new educational fund fact sheet embraces transparency and includes visual components that explain the fund.

The existing Fund Fact Sheets (Figure 9.42) reference the data sets in tables and text and use just a few basic charts to display the data. As blocks of content, the fact sheets mix both graphics and text in no particular order across the pages.

One fund fact sheet may present the top ten holdings and sector weights on the first page; another fact sheet will present these on the second page. One fund fact sheet will present data in a table; another will present the same data as a chart. Despite variations between fact sheets, most use the same types of data and charts. In general, they tend to limit the visualizations. The fund sheet examples in Figure 9.42, for example, show 1–2 charts per fact sheet.

Figure 9.43 replaces a few content blocks of a typical fund fact sheet with the newly designed components presented earlier in the chapter.

Existing Fund Fact Sheets

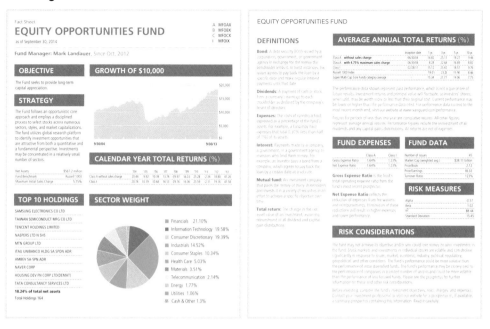

Figure 9.42 **Fund Fact Sheet Examples**

Fund Fact Sheets   Integrated Components

Figure 9.43 **Fund Fact Sheet – Integrated Components**

While you cannot completely replace text with visuals, the document as shown in Figure 9.43 replaces text blocks with integrated components, each of which includes both visuals and values. Instead of one chart, the fund fact sheet now shows 11. Each component is independent and can be replaced without a big impact on the overall layout. The only caveat is that the component dimensions should match.

The layout and location of each of the data sets (in Figure 9.43) has not changed from the previous fund fact sheet. Within the same allocated space, the layout augments the data with supporting charts to tell a richer story of the fund. You can see the fund profile and understand the risk metrics. Each component attracts your attention and encourages you to inspect the information more closely.

The modular system of swapping out text blocks with integrated components can continue even further. Without much disruption to the rest of the fund fact sheet, you can change how you design and communicate a data set. Figure 9.44 shows a slight update to a component, using the modular system approach.

Fund Fact Sheets   Modified Components

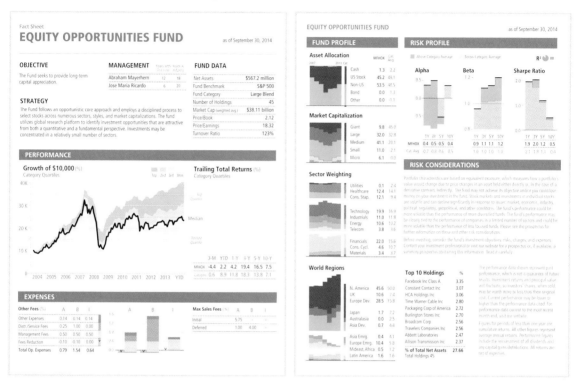

Figure 9.44 Fund Fact Sheet – Updated Components

Exactly what has changed between Figures 9.43 and 9.44? It is hard to tell. The updated components in the fund fact sheet maintain the order and integrity of the layout. Figure 9.44 simply uses different components for Sector Weightings and World Regions. The slight change is not disruptive to the layout.

The next Fund Fact Sheet design (Figure 9.45) suggests an alternative layout to the fund fact sheet so that you can follow the content in an orderly way. It does disrupt the layout by rethinking it all together and considers this question: *What might be a better way of designing the overall layout of the fund fact sheet so that it works better on paper and in a future digital solution?*

Fund Fact Sheets Page 1

EQUITY OPPORTUNITIES FUND

as of September 30, 2014

FUND DATA

Net Assets	$567.2 million
Fund Benchmark	S&P 500
Fund Category	Large Blend
Number of Holdings	45
Market Cap (weighted avg.)	$38.11 billion
Price/Book	2.12
Price/Earnings	18.32
Turnover Ratio	123%

OBJECTIVE

The Fund seeks to provide long-term capital appreciation.

MANAGEMENT

	Years with The Firm	Years in Industry
Abraham Mayerhern	12	18
Jose Maria Ricardo	6	20

STRATEGY

The Fund follows an opportunistic core approach and employs a disciplined process to select stocks across numerous sectors, styles, and market capitalizations. The fund utilizes global research platform to identify investment opportunities that are attractive from both a quantitative and a fundamental perspective. Investments may be concentrated in a relatively small number of sectors.

Summary of Results

For the twelve months ended October 31, 2013, Class A shares of the Equity Opportunities Fund provided a total return of 41.3% ❶ at net asset value. This compares with a return of 32.4% for the fund's benchmark, the S&P 500 Index.

Contributors to Performance

Strong stock selection in the special products & services sector was a positive factor for performance relative to the S&P 500 Index. Within this sector, an overweight position in payment solutions provider Core Technologies ❷ and the fund's holdings of education service provider Grand Laurel Education boosted relative results as both stocks turned in strong performance over the period. Bronco Technologies traded higher during the period, led by sales and earnings growth which exceeded 20% for the sixth consecutive quarter. The growth was partly attributed to successful acquisitions, including New Zealand based CardLink, and strong partnerships with firms such as Shell's Global Commercial Fleet business.

Detractors from Performance

Stock selection in the energy sector hindered relative performance. Within this sector, the fund's timing of ownership in shares of petroleum refining and transportation company Marathon Oil ❸ and independent oil refiner Bolerro Energy weakened relative performance. In addition, holdings of oil company Energy XXI (Bermuda) held back relative results. ❹

Stocks in other sectors that held back relative results included the fund's holdings of air cargo and aircraft operation solutions provider Atlas Worldwide Holdings, an overweight position in television and internet provider Border Communications ❺, holdings of sports apparel retailer Cumiez and an overweight allocation early in the period to infrastructure management software developer Solarwinds. Early in the period, Border Communications reported lower-than-expected earnings due to a decline in voice revenues which appeared to have driven the stock lower. During the reporting period, the fund's relative currency exposure, resulting primarily from differences between the fund's and the benchmark's exposures to holdings of securities denominated in foreign currencies, was another detractor from relative performance. All of The Firms investment decisions are driven by the fundamentals of each individual opportunity and as such, it is common for our funds to have different currency exposure than the benchmark.

The performance data shown represent past performance, which is not a guarantee of future results. Investment returns and principal value will fluctuate, so investors' shares, when sold, may be worth more or less than their original cost. Current performance may be lower or higher than the performance data cited. For performance data current to the most recent month-end, visit our website.

Figures for periods of less than one year are cumulative returns. All other figures represent average annual returns. Performance figures include the reinvestment of all dividends and any capital gains distributions. All returns are net of expenses. Performance results do not include adjustments made for financial reporting purposes in accordance with U.S. generally accepted accounting principles and may differ from amounts reported in the financial highlights.

PERFORMANCE

Growth of $10,000 (%)
Category Quartiles

Top 2nd 3rd Btm

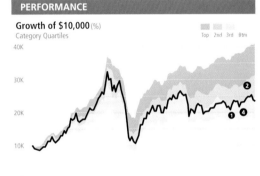

Trailing Total Returns (%)
Category Quartiles

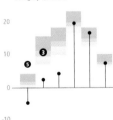

	3-M	YTD	1-Y	3-Y	5-Y	10-Y
MFHOX	-4.4	2.2	4.2	19.4	16.5	7.5
Category	0.6	8.9	11.8	18.3	13.8	7.1

EXPENSES

Other Fees (%)

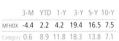

	A	B	I
Other Expenses	0.14	0.14	0.14
Distr./Service Fees	0.25	1.00	0.00
Management Fees	0.50	0.50	0.50
Fees Reduction	-0.10	-0.10	0.00
Total Op. Expenses	0.79	1.54	0.64

Max Sales Fees (%)

Initial	5.75	-	-
Deferred	1.00	4.00	-

Figure 9.45 **Fund Fact Sheet**

Fund Fact Sheets Page 2

EQUITY OPPORTUNITIES FUND

FUND PROFILE

Asset Allocation

2007	2013 Cat.		MFHOX	Cat. Avg.
		Cash	1.3	2.2
		US Stock	45.2	49.1
		Non-US	53.5	48.5
		Bond	0.0	1.3
		Other	0.0	-1.1

Market Capitalization

2007	2013 Cat.		MFHOX	Cat. Avg.
		Giant	9.8	45.0
		Large	32.0	32.8
		Medium	41.1	20.1
		Small	11.0	2.1
		Micro	6.1	0.0

Sector Weighting

		MFHOX	Cat. Avg.
	Utilities	0.1	2.4
	Healthcare	12.4	14.1
	Cons. Stap.	12.1	9.4
B	Technology	19.9	16.9
	Industrials	11.0	11.8
	Energy	10.6	10.2
	Telecom	3.8	3.6
A	Financials	22.0	15.6
	Cons. Cycl.	4.6	10.7
	Materials	3.4	3.7

World Regions

	MFHOX	Cat. Avg.
N. America	45.6	50.0
UK	10.6	7.4
Europe Dev.	28.5	15.8
Japan	1.7	7.2
Australasia	0.0	2.5
Asia Dev.	0.7	4.4
Asia Emrg.	0.4	4.1
Europe Emrg.	10.4	5.8
Mideast, Africa	0.5	1.2
Latin America	1.6	1.6

Top 10 Holdings (% of total assets)

	1. Facebook Inc Class A	3.35	6. Burlington Stores Inc	2.70
	2. Constant Contact Inc	3.07	**D** 7. Broadcom Corp	2.56
	3. HCA Holdings Inc	3.06	**E** 8. Travelers Companies Inc	2.56
C	4. Time Warner Cable Inc	2.80	9. Abbott Laboratories	2.47
	5. Packaging Corp of America	2.72	**F** 10. Bank of America Corp	2.37
	Total Holdings 45		% of Total Net Assets	27.66

RISK PROFILE

■ Above Category Average   Below Category Average R^2 ◔ 88

Alpha

	1Y	3Y	5Y	10Y
MFHOX	0.4	0.5	-0.5	0.4
Cat. Avg.	-0.7	-0.8	-0.6	0.5

Beta

	1Y	3Y	5Y	10Y
MFHOX	0.9	1.1	1.1	1.2
	1.0	1.0	1.0	1.0

Sharpe Ratio

	1Y	3Y	5Y	10Y
	1.9	2.0	1.2	0.5
	2.1	1.8	1.1	0.4

Fund Manager Commentary

Looking back at the fiscal year, we outperformed a very strong 19% return for the S&P 500 with leading performance from the financials and information technology sectors. We still find these two sectors to be attractively valued, and they currently represent a combined 47% of our portfolio **A**. For the fiscal year, 26 of the Oakmark Fund's holdings gained over 30%, and only Apple declined by more than 20%. Despite Apple's poor full fiscal year performance, it was one of the Fund's top two performers for the third quarter, gaining 21%. After a period of skepticism surrounding the company's ability to create compelling new products, Apple is once again experiencing strong demand for its recently introduced iPhones **B**. We remain pleased that the company is allocating more of their $145B cash balance to share repurchases and dividends **C**. Throughout the market, even as equity valuations have increased, we are still finding attractive opportunities in businesses with strong balance sheets **D E**, high free cash flow, and a management committed to return a substantial portion of excess capital to shareholders through dividends and share repurchases.

Strategic and Tactical Allocations

Although equity markets moved higher in the quarter, we found opportunities to make new additions to the Fund, adding three U.S. and two European holdings. The first name alphabetically is Bank of America **F**. For years, Bank of America was the poster child for all that was troubling about banks. But like the industry as a whole, we believe Bank of America has made tremendous progress simplifying and "de-risking" its business. For instance, in just the past few quarters it has gone from being one of the worst capitalized big banks to one of the best. (For perspective, the company's tangible common equity ratio is 64% higher than it was in 2006, which was before the crisis). Management also took advantage of lowered investor expectations as an opportunity to invest heavily in systems technology and rationalization. Investors have rewarded the company for its progress and brought the stock up from its lows. However, it is still being valued at a sizeable discount to its peers. In our view, the discount derives both from stale perceptions of the relative risk profile, but also because Bank of America's near-term earnings are more depressed than its peers. We expect this discount to close with time, as investors reevaluate the "new" Bank of America and its profitability catches up.

Risk Considerations

Portfolio characteristics are based on equivalent exposure, which measures how a portfolio's value would change due to price changes in an asset held either directly or, in the case of a derivative contract, indirectly. The fund may not achieve its objective and/or you could lose money on your investment in the fund. Stock markets and investments in individual stocks are volatile and can decline significantly in response to issuer, market, economic, industry, political, regulatory, geopolitical, and other conditions. **H** The fund's performance could be more volatile than the performance of more diversified funds. The fund's performance may be closely tied to the performance of companies in a limited number of sectors and could be more volatile than the performance of less focused funds **G** Please see the prospectus for further information on these and other risk considerations.

Before investing, consider the fund's investment objectives, risks, charges, and expenses. Contact your investment professional or visit our website for a prospectus or, if available, a summary prospectus containing this information. Read it carefully.

The newly designed Fund Fact Sheet (Figure 9.45) now has both updated components and layout. The communication is now organized for you to review the quantitative data to the left and the qualitative data to the right. The numerated markers (black circles) within the set connect the two points and provide you with the linked connection points between the visual on one side and the text on the other. This provides you with the opportunity to review each component independently and read the associated explanation. Although the layout has a distinct two-column structure, the organizing principle supports the traditional flow of a left to right, top to bottom structure. In addition, the layout still enables you to reorder or replace and update components without disrupting the layout.

Key Take-Aways

The redesigned educational fund fact sheet provides more flexibility for both the producer and the consumer of the information. As the producer, you can replace or add components without a disruption to the layout. You can create your own visual story of the fund. As a consumer of the sheet, you can scan through the charts without interference, or alternate between viewing the charts and reading the text. The two columns that separate the visuals from the text permit this flexibility.

Mutual Fund Comparison

This section takes spreadsheets and tables of fund return data and transforms them into tables with embedded visualizations. The chief investment officer (CIO) can showcase a review of the firm's capacity to provide returns to its investors by investing client assets in well-chosen mutual funds. A third-party analysis provider can confidently share a short-listed set of funds. The investor can review a set of funds. Across these three audiences, the focus of the analysis is largely a comparative one. In one case, comparison helps to rank the fund list and create a short list of fund candidates, and in another case, you can

make a selection. Because comparison is the goal, this section incorporates new techniques for comparing total returns and expense ratios as well as returns in comparison to a benchmark.

Total Returns

Total annual returns are the main focus of many mutual fund investments, and when paired with the expense ratio, you have a balanced view of value. In this section we discuss both of these data sets and show how to incorporate each one into a table. *How do you track total returns as they relate to YTD, 1YR, 5YR, and 10YR data? How do you include expense ratio data?* Figure 9.46 illustrates a prototypical reproduction of a mutual fund list that neatly organizes 10 columns of data and 43 funds into 3 categories of Stock Funds, Asset Allocation Strategies, and Global/International Funds.

The Mutual Fund Table (Figure 9.46) is a perfect candidate for incorporating data visualization techniques to make the assessment process less painful and possible. For example, if the four data points within the Average Annual Total Returns (%) were visualized in terms of average annual total percentage returns, the core data set could become more comprehensible. Figure 9.47 shows how this might be done. It introduces the Ribbon technique to mark the average annual returns for each time marker.

The Ribbon is a flexible visual technique that provides you with an informative view of the return data points. The blue Ribbon (shown in Figure 9.47) marks the 1Y, 5Y, and 10Y timeframes, whereas the black dot marks YTD. As shown in the second row of Figure 9.47, the Ribbon can and does fold on top of itself to mark a directional change. With the wide point at the 10Y mark and the tip at the 1Y mark, the Ribbon also doubles as a tool to see trends and point directional movement. The length of each Ribbon segment is another indicator of how much the fund has moved between the time spans.

Mutual Fund Comparison Sheet

	Class A Inception Date	Max Sales Charge	AVERAGE ANNUAL TOTAL RETURNS (%)				EXPENSE RATIOS (%)		
			YTD	1 yr.	5 yrs.	10 yrs.	Gross	Net	Waiver End Date
STOCK FUNDS									
Aberdeen Investors Trust	07/15/24	5.75	2.54	-4.40	-0.20	4.63	0.78	0.78	–
Aberdeen Growth Stock Fund	01/01/35	5.75	1.73	-3.14	1.61	4.32	0.81	0.81	–
Blended Research Core Equity Fund	08/07/97	5.75	2.27	-3.63	-0.92	5.24	1.64	0.90	01/31/14
Core Equity Fund	01/02/96	5.75	1.93	-4.27	-0.64	5.09	1.18	1.18	–
Equity Opportunities Fund	08/30/00	5.75	2.19	-7.49	-2.11	5.37	1.32	1.32	–
Growth Fund	09/13/93	5.75	2.74	-2.15	2.03	6.29	1.18	1.18	–
Mid Cap Growth Fund	12/01/93	5.75	1.60	-9.56	-3.50	2.99	1.28	1.28	–
Mid Cap Value Fund	08/31/01	5.75	1.12	-8.36	-1.10	6.07	1.22	1.22	–
New Discovery Fund	01/02/97	5.75	5.40	-14.51	3.16	6.01	1.36	1.34	12/31/13
New Discovery Value Fund	05/26/11	5.75	5.26	-2.26	4.66	-2.24	1.26	1.26	–
Research Fund	10/13/71	5.75	2.69	-2.69	0.03	5.20	0.93	0.93	–
Technology Fund	01/02/97	5.75	2.27	0.24	2.93	8.01	1.52	1.52	–
Total Return Fund	10/06/70	5.75	-0.75	-2.97	0.19	4.42	0.77	0.77	–
Utilities Fund	02/14/92	5.75	-1.17	-4.66	1.31	12.65	1.04	1.04	–
Value Fund	01/02/96	5.75	1.74	-3.81	-1.85	4.95	0.94	0.94	–
ASSET ALLOCATION STRATEGIES									
Conservative Allocation Fund	06/28/02	5.75	-1.11	-2.68	3.36	5.08	1.07	1.07	–
Moderate Allocation Fund	06/28/02	5.75	-0.19	-4.34	1.93	5.52	1.11	1.11	–
Growth Allocation Fund	06/28/02	5.75	0.77	-6.35	0.15	5.73	1.18	1.18	–
Aggressive Growth Allocation Fund	06/28/02	5.75	1.24	-8.67	-1.68	5.19	1.25	1.25	–
Balanced Allocation 2010 Fund	09/29/05	5.75	-1.84	-2.39	3.69	4.83	1.34	0.97	08/31/12
Balanced Allocation 2020 Fund	09/29/05	5.75	-0.38	-4.07	0.80	3.91	1.25	1.06	08/31/12
Balanced Allocation 2030 Fund	09/29/05	5.75	0.83	-7.06	-1.30	2.79	1.40	1.15	08/31/12
Balanced Allocation 2040 Fund	09/29/05	5.75	1.16	-7.99	-1.83	2.42	1.51	1.17	08/31/12
Balanced Allocation 2050 Fund	09/15/10	5.75	1.21	-7.69	3.10	5.27	6.17	1.18	08/31/12
Balanced Allocation Income Fund	09/29/05	5.75	-1.86	-2.32	4.39	4.75	1.24	0.97	08/31/12
Absolute Return Fund	03/30/11	4.75	-4.93	-7.29	-5.74	-3.84	1.59	1.15	12/31/12
Diversified Income Fund	05/26/06	4.75	1.98	1.32	4.54	5.88	1.10	1.10	–
Diversified Target Return Fund S6	12/20/07	5.75	-1.01	2.60	-5.11	-0.51	2.03	1.40	02/28/14
Global Multi-Asset Fund	03/30/11	5.75	-5.56	-14.49	-6.46	-10.25	1.76	1.44	10/31/12
GLOBAL / INTERNATIONAL FUNDS									
Asia Pacific ex-Japan Fund	09/15/10	5.75	-2.76	-18.90	-4.96	-3.29	14.69	1.70	11/30/12
Emerging Markets Equity Fund	10/24/95	5.75	-0.52	-19.22	-2.55	11.85	1.76	1.76	–
European Equity Fund	09/15/10	5.75	-0.56	-18.22	-7.94	-1.97	15.12	1.55	11/30/12
Global Equity Fund	09/07/93	5.75	2.22	-9.29	-0.86	6.64	1.37	1.37	–
Global Growth Fund	11/18/93	5.75	0.88	-9.89	-1.70	5.83	1.53	1.53	–
Global Leaders Fund	09/28/11	5.75	3.19	-1.67	7.64	8.76	2.72	1.45	12/31/12
Global New Discovery Fund	12/16/11	5.75	6.10	-3.87	2.98	8.86	3.25	1.50	12/31/12
Global Total Return Fund	09/04/90	5.75	-1.17	-4.53	1.80	6.79	1.30	1.25	02/28/14
International Diversification Fund	09/30/04	5.75	-0.39	-14.26	-3.49	6.03	1.35	1.35	–
International Growth Fund	10/24/95	5.75	0.14	-14.69	-2.58	7.26	1.37	1.37	–
International New Discovery Fund	10/09/97	5.75	3.95	-11.08	-1.67	9.80	1.39	1.39	–
International Value Fund	10/24/95	5.75	-0.10	-8.01	-2.08	8.02	1.27	1.27	–
Latin American Equity Fund	09/15/10	5.75	0.56	-20.57	-3.26	-6.60	10.55	1.65	11/30/12
Research International Fund	01/02/97	5.75	-2.64	-18.54	-5.81	5.53	1.20	1.20	–

Figure 9.46 **Mutual Fund Table**

Mutual Fund Returns

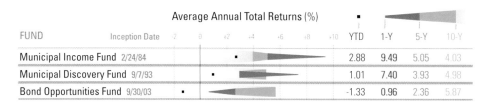

Figure 9.47 Ribbon

You may have noticed the Ribbon is also used as a column header to columns 1-Y, 5-Y, and 10-Y. This technique is just one example of label consolidation. There are other ways and reasons to consolidate. Figure 9.48 points out a few more ways to consolidate and the results of doing so.

Mutual Fund Comparison

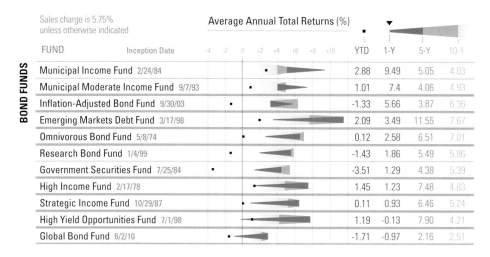

Figure 9.48 Label Consolidation

There are a number of tactical label adjustments that have been made to the table to consolidate and streamline the table data. Figure 9.48 adjusts labels to:

▶ **Remove redundancies**—The original Max Sales Charge column is a data set with largely repetitive data. The table has removed this repeated local value with a global note at the top left stating that the Sales charge is 5.75%. This results in one less column.

▶ **Relocate and readjust**—The fund category label has been removed as a row header and relocated to the left of the fund list. Shown at 90 degrees, the Bond Funds label is still legible. This results in three fewer rows.

▶ **Reuse and reduce**—The fund column incorporates the inception date of the fund as secondary data to consolidate two columns into one. In addition, the column header for each time period serves as the dot and Ribbon legend—to serve as a legend and a column header— and a dual-purpose label.

The effort to consolidate has provided more space to incorporate visuals into the data table. In addition, you can focus your attention on the core data points and simply be aware of other data points as needed. Although the label consolidation effort is a tactical redesign effort, it is an essential one to integrate the Ribbon visualization.

Now you may notice that the expense ratio data columns have not been incorporated. Next, the full data set is combined to show the expense ratios as embedded visuals into a table. With the addition of this data, the table (Figure 9.49) is complete and useful for the firm's management, third-party providers, or investors to compare and rank.

Mutual Fund Comparison Sheet

Sales charge is 5.75%
unless otherwise indicated

Average Annual Total Returns (%)

As of June 30, 2012

Expence Ratios (%)

FUND	Inception Date										YTD	1-Y	5-Y	10-Y			Net	Gross	Waiver End Date
STOCK FUNDS																			
Technology Fund 1/2/97											2.27	0.24	2.93	6.01			1.52	1.52	–
Growth Fund 9/13/93											2.74	-2.15	2.03	6.29			1.18	1.18	–
New Discovery Value Fund 5/26/11											5.26	-2.26	4.66	2.24			1.26	1.26	–
Research Fund 10/13/71											2.69	-2.69	0.03	5.20			0.93	0.93	–
Total Return Fund 10/6/70											-0.75	-2.97	0.19	4.42			0.77	0.77	–
Investors Growth Stock Fund 1/1/35											1.73	-3.14	1.61	4.32			0.81	0.81	–
Research Core Equity Fund 8/7/97											2.27	-3.63	-0.92	5.24			0.90	1.64	01/31/14
Value Fund 1/2/96											1.74	-3.81	-1.85	4.95			0.94	0.94	–
Core Equity Fund 1/2/96											1.93	-4.27	-0.64	5.09			1.18	1.18	–
Aberdeen Investors Trust 7/15/24											2.54	-4.40	-0.20	4.63			0.78	0.78	–
Utilities Fund 2/14/92											-1.17	-4.66	1.31	12.65			1.04	1.04	–
Equity Opportunities Fund 8/30/00											2.19	-7.49	-2.11	5.37			1.32	1.32	–
Mid Cap Value Fund 8/31/01											1.12	-8.36	-1.10	6.07			1.22	1.22	–
Mid Cap Growth Fund 12/1/93											1.60	-9.56	-3.05	2.99			1.28	1.28	–
New Discovery Fund 1/2/97											5.4	-14.51	3.16	6.01			1.34	1.36	12/31/13
ASSET ALLOCATION STRATEGIES																			
Diversified Target Return Fund* 12/20/07											-1.01	2.60	5.11	0.51			1.40	2.03	2/28/14
Diversified Income Fund 5/26/06											1.98	1.32	6.24	5.88			1.10	1.10	–
Balanced Allocation Income Fund 9/29/05											-1.86	-2.32	4.39	4.75			0.97	1.24	8/31/12
Balanced Allocation 2010 Fund 9/29/05											-1.84	-2.39	3.69	4.83			0.97	1.34	8/31/12
Conservative Allocation Fund 6/28/02											-1.11	-2.68	3.36	5.08			1.07	1.07	–
Balanced Allocation 2020 Fund 9/29/05											-0.38	-4.07	0.80	3.91			1.06	1.25	8/31/12
Moderate Allocation Fund 6/28/02											-0.19	-4.34	1.93	5.52			1.11	1.11	–
Growth Allocation Fund 6/28/02											0.77	-6.35	0.15	5.73			1.18	1.18	–
Balanced Allocation 2030 Fund 9/29/05											0.83	-7.06	-1.30	2.79			1.15	1.40	8/31/12
Absolute Return Fund* 3/30/11											-4.93	-7.29	-5.74	-3.82			1.15	1.59	12/31/12
Balanced Allocation 2050 Fund 9/15/10											1.21	-7.69	3.10	5.27			1.18	6.17	8/31/12
Balanced Allocation 2040 Fund 9/29/05											1.16	-7.99	-1.83	2.42			1.17	1.51	8/31/12
Aggressive Growth Allocation Fund 6/28/02											1.24	-8.67	-1.68	5.19			1.25	1.25	–
Global Multi-Asset Fund 3/30/11											-5.56	-14.49	-6.46	-10.25			1.44	1.76	10/31/12
GLOBAL / INTERNATIONAL FUNDS																			
Global Leaders Fund 9/28/11											3.19	-1.67	7.64	8.76			1.45	2.72	12/31/12
Global New Discovery Fund 12/16/11											6.10	-3.87	2.98	8.86			1.50	3.25	12/31/12
Global Total Return Fund 9/4/90											-1.17	-4.53	1.80	6.79			1.25	1.30	02/28/14
International Value Fund 10/24/95											-0.10	-8.01	-2.08	8.02			1.27	1.27	–
Global Equity Fund 9/7/93											2.22	-9.29	-0.86	6.64			1.37	1.37	–
Global Growth Fund 11/18/93											0.88	-9.89	-1.70	5.83			1.53	1.53	–
International New Discovery Fund 10/9/97											3.95	-11.08	-1.67	9.80			1.39	1.39	–
International Diversification Fund 9/30/04											-0.39	-14.26	-3.49	6.03			1.35	1.35	–
International Growth Fund 10/24/95											0.14	-14.69	-2.58	7.26			1.37	1.37	–
European Equity Fund 9/15/10											-0.56	-18.22	-7.94	-1.97			1.55	15.12	11/30/12
Research International Fund 1/2/97											-2.64	-18.54	-5.81	5.53			1.20	1.20	–
Asia Pacific ex-Japan Fund 9/15/10											-2.76	-18.90	-4.96	3.29			1.70	14.69	11/30/12
Emerging Markets Equity Fund 10/24/95											-0.52	-19.22	-2.55	11.85			1.76	1.76	–
Latin American Equity Fund 9/15/10											0.56	-20.57	-3.26	6.60			1.65	10.55	11/30/12

*Maximum sales charge for this fund is 4.75%

Figure 9.49 **Ribbon Comparison**

Figure 9.49 lets you scan, review, and understand the data with minimal effort. The table consolidates 10 columns into three groups, emphasizes the visuals over the text, and communicates the same data points more effectively. Although the fund list is presented as a table, the solution could be made into an interactive one. Because the focus of the analysis is largely a comparative one, interactivity enables you to explore the data and look for trends. For example, the black triangle above the 1Y column is a sort indicator. As an interactive display, you could select another column header to sort and the Ribbon display would adjust and reorder the funds.

Key Take-Aways

One advantage to applying visual representation to a dense data set is the familiarity of the table structure. You can embed similar visualizations into your own tables to improve your ability to quickly analyze the data. The embedded visualization transforms each cell in the table into a connected Ribbon that makes comparison possible. The strong benefit is the synchronicity of understanding the overall big picture view of the data while still retaining the granularity of the original input. The solution does not sacrifice the detail but rather enhances it and makes comparison of multiple variables a possibility.

Ranking Against Benchmarks

A common practice for many firms is to review fund performance against the benchmark to rank and assess value. Benchmark returns require a combination of market data and internal company data to be brought together into one view. The ability to compare funds across various time intervals provides you with strong reference points for better assessment.

The Category Returns vs. Benchmark, as shown in Figure 9.50, is an example of past performance of funds as they relate to risk adjusted alpha, % of the fund, and average returns. The purpose of this table is to highlight funds that exceed thresholds within alpha as well as % ahead of index.

Returns vs. Benchmark

Category / Global/International/Regional	Index	3 Month			1 Year			3 Years			5 Years			10 Years		
		Average Return	Alpha	% Ahead of Index	Average Return	Alpha	% Ahead of Index	Average Return	Alpha	% Ahead of Index	Average Return	Alpha	% Ahead of Index	Average Return	Alpha	% Ahead of Index
Global Large Cap Core	World Index	8.51	0.07	47	19.66	1.16	59	14.31	0.53	38	4.32	1.15	79	9.13	1.62	91
Global Large Cap Core	All Country World Index	8.51	2.38	89	19.66	3.14	83	14.31	1.87	81	4.32	1.56	83	9.13	1.32	88
Global Large Cap Growth	World Growth Index	7.71	0.30	48	18.93	2.50	84	14.99	0.89	74	4.22	1.29	81	9.21	1.96	84
Global Large Cap Value	World Value Index	9.63	0.15	41	21.96	1.34	57	13.61	0.17	57	3.92	0.54	60	8.50	0.81	61
Global Multi Cap Core	World Index	6.89	-1.54	47	17.21	-1.30	55	12.61	-1.17	48	3.97	0.82	66	8.14	0.62	75
Global Multi Cap Core	All Country World Index	6.89	0.77	66	17.21	0.68	68	12.61	0.17	62	3.97	1.23	68	8.14	0.33	41
International Large Cap Core	EAFE Index	3.09	-1.19	16	17.44	-0.93	27	10.57	0.44	72	0.24	0.39	49	8.37	0.55	56
International Large Cap Core	All Country World ex US Index	3.09	2.83	87	17.44	3.87	85	10.57	2.43	91	0.24	0.58	74	8.37	-0.36	27
International Multi Cap Core	EAFE Index	3.34	-0.95	38	17.25	-1.12	37	10.41	0.28	48	0.71	0.86	58	8.42	0.59	50
International Multi Cap Core	All Country World ex US Index	3.34	3.08	78	17.25	3.68	73	10.41	2.27	84	0.71	1.04	60	8.42	-0.32	24
International Multi Cap Growth	EAFE Growth Index	5.36	0.12	60	20.75	0.99	69	11.23	-0.22	55	3.20	1.45	88	10.94	1.36	84
Europe Equity	Europe Index	4.29	1.71	74	22.26	3.47	77	12.64	1.87	74	0.82	1.50	68	9.62	1.84	74
Emerging Markets	Emerging Markets Index	-6.56	2.46	63	6.04	2.94	63	4.95	1.38	67	0.22	0.33	56	14.35	0.89	61
Equal-Weighted Average Results		4.81	0.57	56	17.85	1.35	62	11.70	0.76	64	2.28	0.98	68	9.26	0.84	63

Figure 9.50 Category Returns vs. Benchmark Table

The Category Returns vs. Benchmark data table is a representative sample of simulated fund data. A full data set may have multiple category headers to list the funds. Instead, the sample table includes one category, shown in bold, with corresponding funds listed below the header "Global/International/Regional."

Each time interval lists secondary headers: Average Return, Alpha, and % Ahead of Index, which are then repeated five times for each time interval. The Average Return column is a simple equal weighted average return calculation that is annualized for periods greater than 1 year for each fund. Here alpha is defined as the difference between a fund's actual performance and the performance that might have been expected given its volatility relative to the benchmark index. The percentage Ahead of Index is defined as the percentile ranking of the fund ahead of the index. The current Category Returns vs. Benchmark visualization is dedicated to answer the following:

▶ Across all funds, which fund produced positive or negative alpha?

▶ Which fund results in a higher or lower threshold of positive or negative returns against the identified benchmark(s)?

▶ How consistent has this performance been for each fund?

The visual aids of red and tan color-coded cells highlight some of the textual data to call out instances that exceed a threshold. The hue-based indicator system employs a method of layering visual information on top of the text. In this case, tan is used to indicate instances of positive alpha (> 1.00) and % ahead of index > 77, whereas red is used to indicate negative alpha (< -1.00) with a % ahead of index < 50.

The challenge with the Category Returns vs. Benchmark table is that although the data is organized as a list of funds, the column structure does not help to organize your own analysis. The table forces you to scan and read various parts of the table to make your own connections. Each value within the cells stands alone as a discrete value, and you are left to attempt to create a continuous system of tracking and linking the data points. The two main focus areas for improvement include a repetitive column system and use of color to highlight thresholds.

Similar to other reports organized in spreadsheets, the Category Returns vs. Benchmark table repeats a serial list of column headers. The repeated header system is seen in cases in which there is a primary and secondary header. The shortfall of this table set-up is that you cannot easily compare "Average Return" against all time intervals or "Alpha" or "% Ahead of Index," for that matter. Instead you are obligated to track textual information in the first cell to textual information in the tenth cell to compare the category average return within "YTD" to "5 Years."

You are forced to rely on the text inside the color cell to understand how much the threshold has been breached by reading each value. As an alternative, consider a mechanism to easily identify, calculate, and compare. The goals of the next set of visual tools (starting with Figure 9.51) aims to do the following:

- Help you identify a threshold breach either in a positive or negative direction as well as see the extent of the breach.

- See rather than read and calculate a value.

- Compare and track performance.

In Figure 9.51, the visual table illustrates numerical data as a series of bars that indicate defined threshold incidents in positive or negative returns.

Returns - Historical Span

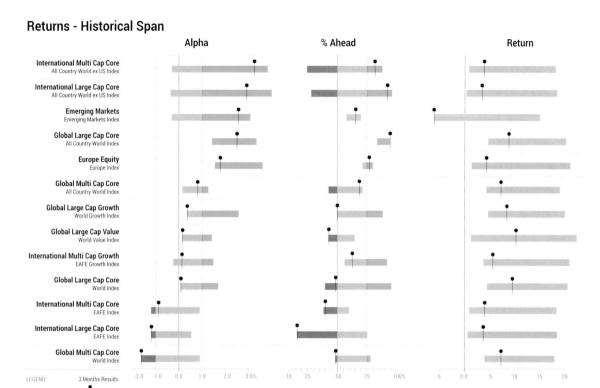

Figure 9.51 Bar and Pin Chart

The table structure maintains the row headers listed as funds and the columns headers for historical returns specifically within Alpha, % Ahead, and Return. However, the table emphasizes Alpha. It lists alpha first and is sorted in descending order of Alpha. A reference scale at the base of the table is presented to indicate the numerical values across each column header. The zero vertical lines connect the reference scale at the base of the table up to the column headers. As shown in the legend, the pin marker references 10 Year historical returns while taking note of the 3M return.

The visual treatment used in Figure 9.51 emphasizes the display of historical spread and then marks the YTD performance as additional information. This version of the data is useful if you are interested in seeing or communicating long-term performance over short-term performance. However, you can also consider the reverse. *What if you would rather emphasize the short-term performance?*

Next, consider another approach (Figure 9.52) that puts more focus on short-term performance.

3 Months Returns

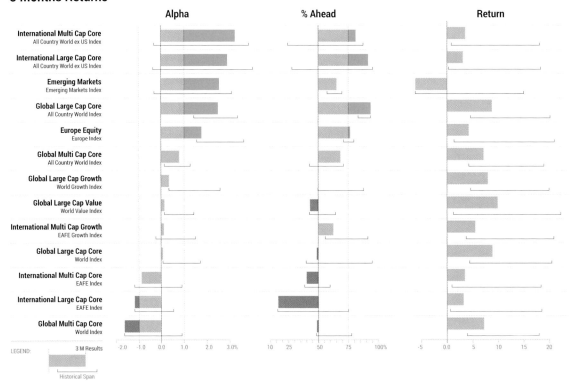

Figure 9.52 **Bar Bracket Chart**

This alternative chart (Figure 9.52) places more emphasis on the short-term performance while still maintaining the context of the historical performance back to the 10-year timeframe. In this version of the same data, you can get an understanding of how the list of funds has performed across different time intervals. Alignment with the number line below shows the range of how consistent or inconsistent a fund has performed over the years. You can quickly see if the current performance is within or outside of the fund's "typical path" or if the fund has been making incremental progress toward the current performance.

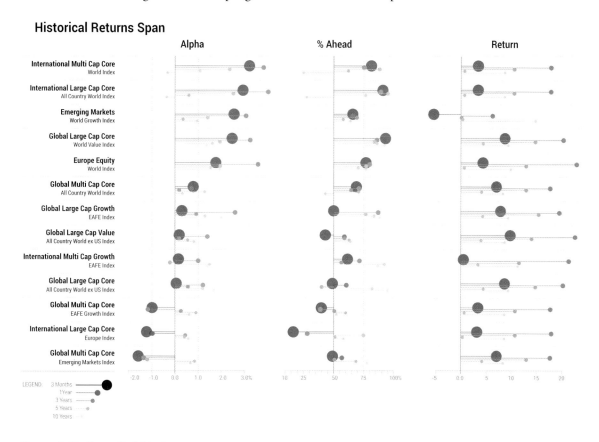

Figure 9.53 **Stem/Bubble Steps**

The Stem/Bubble Steps uses varying elements of color, size, and shape to communicate each time period. As the legend indicates, each circle progressively grows in both size and color saturation as time nears. Each line and circle is anchored to a vertical line to indicate how much of a deviation there is from the centerline. And similar to musical notes on a page, the stem and bubble combination accentuate their location and can be described as how far above or below middle C they are on a keyboard. Anything played above or below a certain octave can be alerting and noted as a breach to the predefined threshold.

The benefits of Figure 9.53 are threefold. First, the use of both size and color gives prominence to the current value. Second, each stem and bubble pairing presents historical points, each as independent value representations. Third, the circle shape communicates motion and depicts performance as dynamic.

Despite these benefits, instead you may need to emphasize the threshold range with a more simplified chart (shown in Figure 9.54).

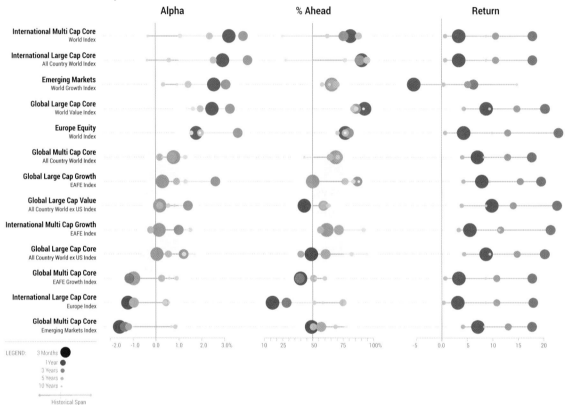

Figure 9.54 **Bubble Trace**

Figure 9.54 extends the benefits of the predecessor by introducing two concepts: visual simplification and visual reinforcement. The first concept of visual simplification asks this question: *What can be removed from the chart without compromising the intended communication?* As a subtractive method, the goal of simplification is to remove visual noise from the chart to focus on the data results. Simplification of a visual removes additive hindrances, blocks, or barriers that cause you to pause without the benefit of greater understanding. Figure 9.54 uses a single horizontal line to anchor the performance markers. Eliminating the extra horizontal lines, referenced as stems in the chart, enables you to focus on the circles.

Visual reinforcement asks the following question: *What can be added to the chart to improve, extend, or supplement the intended communication?* As supportive aides to a chart, visual reinforcements are typically not primary or prominent in a chart; rather these reinforcements are generally subtle and rendered in the background of a chart. In Figure 9.54, the light gray vertical block is rendered as a background fill and is used as a visual aid to clearly define the threshold points. The gray vertical block is a subtle introduction to the chart that improves your ability to read the chart.

Key Take-Aways

Charts within the Category Returns vs. Benchmark collection (Figures 9.51–9.54) emphasize certain time period over others. For example, the Bar and Pin Chart (Figure 9.51) focuses on long-term performance, whereas the Bar Bracket Chart (Figure 9.52) highlights more recent performance. The Stem/Bubble Steps (Figure 9.53) and the Bubble Trace (Figure 9.54) introduce a visual system that shows individual time period. Although the charts emphasize different points, their core purposes remain unchanged. They remain capable of helping you to identify a threshold break, to see (rather than read and calculate) a value, and to compare and track performance across different time intervals. Which chart(s) you use depends on what needs you need to address.

Summary

This chapter discusses the redesign of core component visualizations and shows how to integrate them within qualitative information and quantitative tables. The Fund Fact Sheet, for example, combines these redesigned visual components with textual description to convey qualitative information. In contrast, the quantitative table shown in the "Mutual Fund Comparison" section provides a column of visualizations next to corresponding numeric values to compare a short list of funds. In the former case, visualizations vary and represent different data sets with comparison points within the fund. In the latter, the visualizations are consistent and repeat for comparison across a list of funds. Both of these use cases produce a diverse set of mutual fund data visualizations:

VISUALIZATION	DESCRIPTION	FIGURE
Stacked Bar Chart	A segmented Bar chart uses height to represent amount.	9.2, 9.4, 9.5
Geometric Map	Geometric shapes represent continents with color fill to represent a percentage value.	9.3
Surface Area Variations	Color fill is used to represent a quantity within a grid.	9.6
Net Bar	Cumulative value is represented as a bar that first considers the negative values.	9.7–9.9
Context Bar, Level, Line	Values represented with a bar, level, or line are complemented with a comparative value in relative and absolute terms.	9.10–9.22, 9.32, 9.33
Pointer Chart	A projected line indicates an amount; both the angle and endpoints of the projected line on the grid indicate a value.	9.23–9.25
Dial Gauge	Measures a value with a circular array.	9.26–9.29

VISUALIZATION	DESCRIPTION	FIGURE
Arc	Identifies a distance between two points along the circumference of a circle.	9.37–9.40
Ribbon	A graduated color band can fold and expand in length and width to indicate time-frame and value.	9.47–9.49
Bar and Pin	Within a bar chart a pin marks a related timeframe.	9.51
Bar Bracket	Within a bar chart a bracket marks a related timeframe.	9.52
Stem/Bubble Steps	Multiple stem/bubble pairs mark a related timeframe.	9.53
Bubble Trace	A single stem pairs a bubble to a timeframe.	9.54

As sales and marketing tools, component visualizations and fund lists provide benefits not just for public relations but also for internal tools. For example, you could use visual components from the fund fact sheet section for your own monitoring needs. A visual component is a standalone element, and you can employ as many or as few components as you need. You can create your own dashboard or set of dashboards using a collection of components. To display a table data, for example, you could reuse the Ribbon technique when you need to show the change in value across different discrete time intervals. The description of each visualization listed here can help to identify which visual technique you can reuse and how.

10

Hedge Funds

Every hedge fund investors' primary question is, *"Can this hedge fund produce absolute returns?"* It is the job of the hedge fund manager to ensure this question can be answered with a resounding "Yes;" positive returns using alternative investment management techniques can be achieved. Although we cannot predict if a fund will produce absolute returns, data visualizations can surface patterns and behaviors of funds based on their characteristics to better analyze strategies.

This chapter focuses on evaluating hedge funds from the perspective of the investor and the investment consultant who advises fund investors. We examine two important sets of hedge fund data to compare funds and strategies, starting with data from an individual fund and ending with data for the industry overall. Neither set of data is unique or proprietary to a specific firm's methodology and instead is available publicly, providing a glimpse into the hedge fund world.

The chapter begins by reviewing an example of exposure breakdowns for a fund to reveal the long/short aspects that are seen in many funds. The ability to employ a range of trading strategies of long and short positions in traditional and nontraditional markets can markedly influence fund performance. The visualization examples explore how these market exposures present patterns and correlate to market movements. Contrasting the fund returns based on market exposure against a provided index is one means for investors and consultants to evaluate funds and determine if the fund manager is adding value.

The second part of this chapter uses an industry-wide performance rankings data set. Here, we take a look at the hedge fund world as a whole and review data that uncovers top performing strategies and their respective ranking history over the post financial crisis period. We also review strategies and size in AUM (assets under management) for both the fund and firm to provide context to the strategy, fund, and rank order. Finally, we close with a cross-industry view of what it means to be top rank. Our review of the top 100 funds unveils the capability of strategies, funds, and firms to maintain top rank. Although the hedge fund industry aims for absolute returns, the visualizations reveal several of the top 100 funds are not consistently ranked and do not provide absolute returns.

NOTE The individual fund data within the first three sections of this chapter is hypothetical data and is representative of what is provided in the marketplace, whereas the source data for the top 100 funds is from Barron's.

Long/Short Positions

This section uses equity hedge strategy data that combines long and short positions. As one of many hedge fund strategies, this particular strategy uses a market neutral strategy with a corresponding index to benchmark the strategy. The equity long/short fund data includes exposure breakdown by various categories, highlights net exposure, and compares these points across a set of funds. Firms can look inward and compare how various funds perform individually, as a fund of funds, or as a complete collection; consultants can review a set of funds; and investors can more readily see the variation of each fund.

First, begin by looking at exposure data for one fund, as illustrated in Figure 10.1. This chart shows you a simple method to present long and short positions.

The Butterfly chart (refer to Figure 10.1) shows both long and short positions across different groups within the fund. The bar charts are organized around a zero mark with long and short positions in percentage. The short position bars (in orange) are defined as the market value of the short position divided by the total short market value. Similarly, the long position bars (in blue) are defined as the market value of the long position divided by the total long market value.

The benefit of the Butterfly chart is that it consolidates two data sets of long and short positions into one continuous bar by expanding the scale. Color is used to distinguish the long versus the short positions, and you can generally see how positions are balanced. For example, the chart enables you to review either the symmetrical or asymmetrical exposure to long/short positions within a set of categories. *Organizing the data around the zero mark begins to show a mirror image like a butterfly, but exactly how symmetrical are those exposures?* The chart does not make it easy for you to answer if the long and short positions are equal, or if not equal, by how much. The next chart (Figure 10.2) includes visual queues to indicate asymmetrical exposures to show how much of an exposure actually exists with netted values.

Fund Exposures

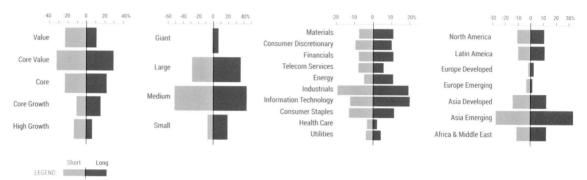

Figure 10.1 **Butterfly**

Net Fund Exposures

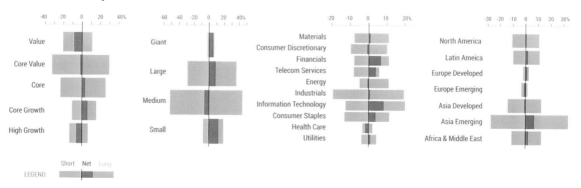

Figure 10.2 **Butterfly Net Bar**

The Butterfly Net Bar chart (refer to Figure 10.2) layers in the differences between the long and the short positions. The netted value displays a darker translucent bar chart on top of the existing bar chart to identify how much exposure there is and where it is greater or equal. Each individual chart stands alone as its own visual entity. *However, what if you want to associate these fund exposures to a fund?* There are two possible ways: You could achieve this with text and provide a label to be read, or you could achieve this visually in the chart. Figure 10.3 shows several exposure attributes of one fund combined into one visual entity.

Fund Exposures

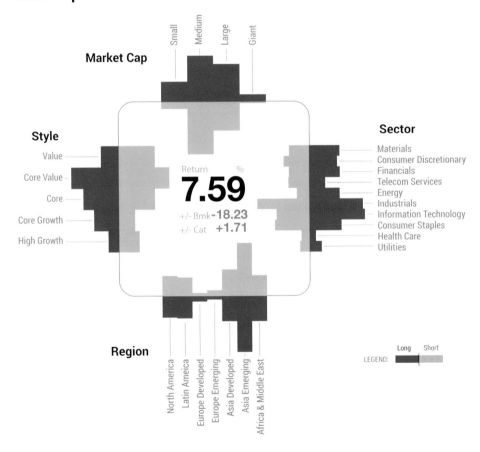

Figure 10.3 **Grouped Butterfly Bars**

Combining the charts into a lassoed group presents you with one chart; the color bars, lasso line, and centered return value of 7.59 percent creates a grouped structure.

There are advantages and disadvantages to showing the full set of details in the Grouped Butterfly Bars. The advantages are, of course, the specifics that each detail level exposure provides. The disadvantages are the different amount of segments across the four groups; market cap has four segments, sector has ten, region has seven, and style has five. The variation makes it more difficult to assess and compare exposure across the four groups. For you to visually compare the four groups within this fund or to another, you first need to objectify the visual. The representation of the same visual can be somewhat tweaked to produce a visual symbol. The Butterfly Bar Glyph (Figure 10.4) introduces a standardized number of segments for better comparison.

As a symbol embedded with meaning, each bar mark within the glyph indicates the long/short position, exposure, and net. You can see the net of each long/short position shown as a black line that travels across each bar.

Figure 10.4 introduces the concept of representing a fund through the vessel of a glyph. Glyphs are recognizable symbols that are created to represent a specific meaning. For example, each letter in the alphabet is a glyph. The symbols used to represent each letter are simple geometric lines that children learn to read and write by the age of 5. Glyphs are instantly recognizable because they are simplified.

The Butterfly Bar Glyph uniquely applies the strengths of a glyph to identify characteristics of a fund. For example, the groups have been reduced in complexity to show you overall exposure within three segments. The three segments are exhaustive and mutually exclusive with 100% of the sector information represented in three segments. The standardized number of segments enables you to instantly recognize the coded values without repeated dependence on legends or keys.

Fund Exposures

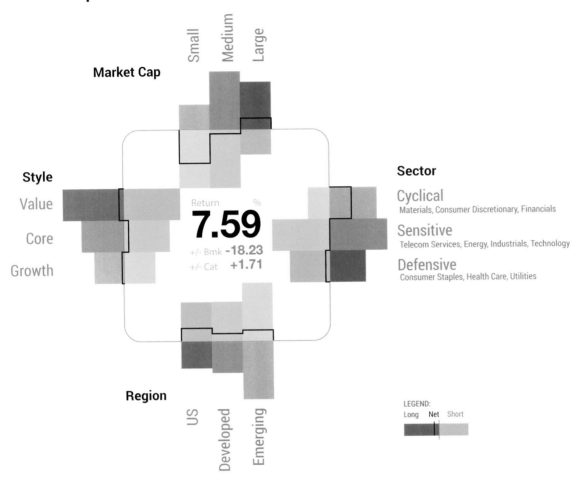

Market Cap

Small · Medium · Large

Style

Value · Core · Growth

Return   %

7.59

+/- Bmk -18.23
+/- Cat +1.71

Sector

Cyclical
Materials, Consumer Discretionary, Financials

Sensitive
Telecom Services, Energy, Industrials, Technology

Defensive
Consumer Staples, Health Care, Utilities

Region

US · Developed · Emerging

LEGEND:
Long   Net   Short

Figure 10.4 **Butterfly Bar Glyph**

Removing the details down to the essential features of the fund makes it easier for you to compare the exposures within and across funds. The next chart tests what can be displayed as essential features by scaling down the glyph. The scaled-down mini version abstracts the data set for you to call out the characteristics even further. Figure 10.5 shows you how these mini glyphs can be both abstract and detailed by providing an unobstructed view of each exposure with the specifics of exposure as needed.

Fund Exposures
Interactive

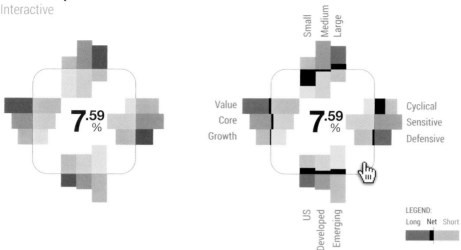

Figure 10.5 **Mini Glyphs**

Figure 10.5 displays the same Mini Glyph chart twice; to illustrate the interactive states in which the details of the labels and long/short netting are added only on mouse-over. This layer technique provides you the benefits of both the visual data and text label data. It also enables you to consume the data into two logical steps: The symbolized quintessential essence of the fund and supportive detail labels of each long/short pairing. The added benefit of the scaled down glyphs is space. As shown in Figure 10.6, the mini glyphs take up less space, which makes it easier to compare with other funds.

Fund Exposures Comparison

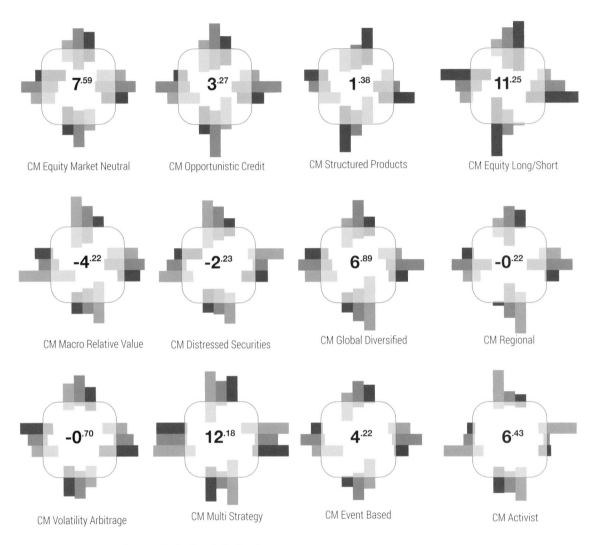

Figure 10.6 **Glyph Collection**

Since losses can be infinite with short sells, a display like Figure 10.6 makes it easier for you to identify funds with short selling risk. As a set, the Mini Glyphs enables better comparison by using techniques of consolidation, organization, scale, and standardization:

- ▶ **Standardization**—The glyph as a system introduces a set of consistent marks as standards. For example, the glyph has been standardized to three bars within each group. Standardization across all visual marks is an important gate into comparison.

- ▶ **Consolidation**—The benefit of a glyph is the compact delivery of information that combines four charts into one. Figure 10.6 shows you the consolidation of 40 charts into 10 small-sized glyphs.

- ▶ **Scale**—The collection of glyphs (refer to Figure 10.6) efficiently reduces the chart footprint even further with the introduction of the Mini Glyph. Scaling down the glyphs enables the collection to physically fit within a smaller footprint and enables you to compare more glyphs in one view.

- ▶ **Organization**—The organization and placement of each Mini can help you in the task of comparison. Sequential order of the Mini Glyphs by specific fund exposure can help you to review and compare the set. Other larger glyph collections organized by returns, geography, or by internal company structures may be used to reveal patterns.

Central to each glyph are the fund returns. The single bold text values stand out and are easy for you to scan across the collection. Exactly how you decide to organize, sort, or group the collection can improve scanning and analyzing the collection even further.

Key Take-Aways

The glyph is a useful visualization method to display multivariate data in a simple and concise format. This compactness provides quick side-by-side comparison of several entities, in this case funds, based on multiple properties. As a visualization vessel, the glyph can be used to support different data use cases. For example, you can take the same glyph design and display the return percentage in the center in context of the performance attribution data. Or you could project future fund performance in context of the current exposures. Either way, the glyph can display 39 data sets (calculated with 4 groups of 3 bars with 3 data points each, plus the 3 data points in the middle of the glyph) within a small footprint.

Long Positions and Benchmarking

As stated earlier, not all strategies use short positions. The next set of visualizations helps you quickly assess long-only funds with a stronger presence of the benchmark numbers. Figure 10.7 reuses the glyph concept and introduces more color coding into the glyph to elevate differences in market exposure. In addition, this section shows how to visually incorporate each fund's alignment or misalignment from the benchmark.

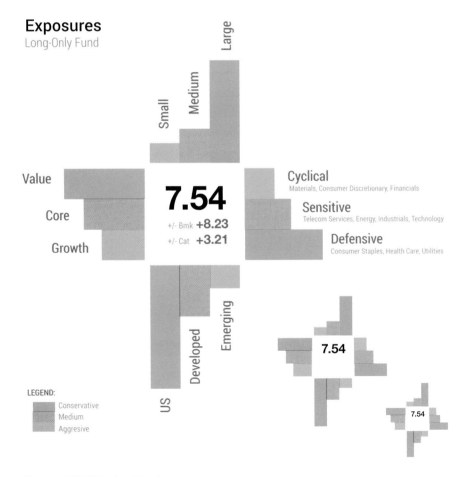

Figure 10.7 Tricolor Glyph

As the name suggests, the Tricolor Glyph introduces color to distinguish invest-ment style within each group. Teal is reserved for the conservative characteris-tics of large cap, defensive sectors, U.S. region, and value style. Purple denotes moderate characteristics and orange indicates aggressive characteristics. As a long-only fund of data, the chart's bars grow outward exclusively. A few scaled-down versions of the Tricolor Glyph, as shown in the bottom right, are used to test the readability of a miniature version.

The benefit of the tricolor system is that it provides you with more distinguish-ing qualities across all characteristics of the fund. For this reason it can help you answer questions such as, *Is the fund highly conservative?* The dominating teal bars make it easy for you to see that's the case. Despite the small scale of the minis, the solid block colors are distinguishable. However, you can also include details in the Mini Glyphs. The next sets of solutions (Figures 10.8 and 10.9) explore a few possibilities of how to incorporate details.

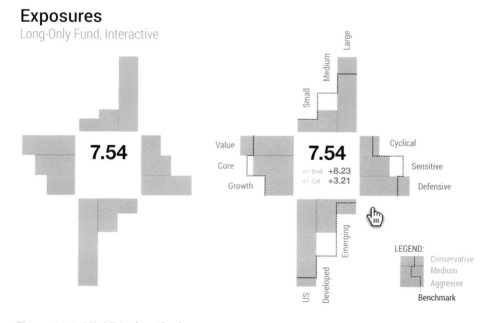

Figure 10.8 **Mini Tricolor Glyph**

Similar to the Mini Glyph (Figure 10.5), the Mini Tricolor Glyph illustrates an interactive application of the visual. The details shown in the interactive Mini Tricolor Glyph example, however, are different. Instead of showing you the short/long netted amount, you can now see the benchmark's outline of market exposure. You can compare each fund characteristic to the benchmark by using the black dotted line drawn on top of each bar. This enables you to see each fund's alignment or off-set from the benchmark. In addition, the fund, benchmark, and category return values are placed in the center of the glyph for comparison.

You can depict an entire collection of funds by using the mini form of the Tricolor Glyph. Figure 10.9 illustrates a *set* of funds for you to compare and contrast by using the tricolor technique.

Comparing and contrasting the collection of glyphs, as shown in Figure 10.9, is easier for you to do with the use of the tricolor system. You can spot conservative funds highlighted as blue bars versus aggressive funds with dominant orange bars. The third example shows a moderate fund with dominant purple bars. More interesting, motion is also now introduced as an element to the charts. Both the length and the dominant color influences in each chart have a flare of rotational pull. The rotational pull of the conservative fund creates a pinwheel that appears to rotate to the left, whereas the rotational pull of the aggressive fund creates a pinwheel that rotates to the right. In contrast, the moderate fund does not communicate motion and instead seems to balance in the center. Finally, the fund with mixed characteristics no longer has a rotational pull and stands out for that reason.

Exposures Comparison
Long-Only Funds

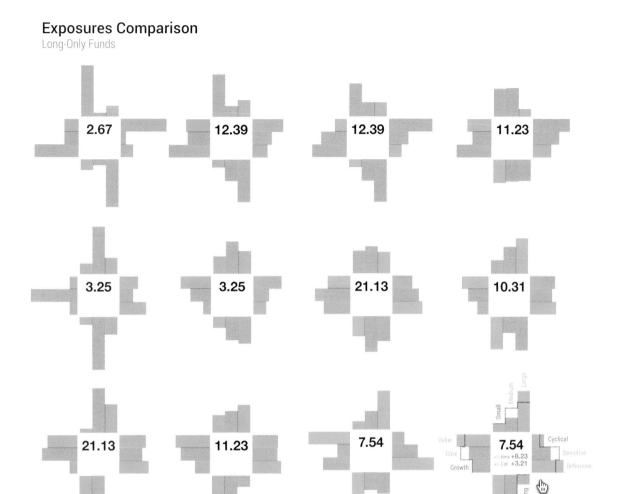

Figure 10.9 **Tricolor Glyph Collection**

The benefit of the Tricolor Glyph collection is that it surfaces the overall characteristic even further than the previous glyph example (refer to Figure 10.9). You can recognize each glyph as a pattern; the rotational direction provides the ability for you to recognize the pattern and proves the strength of a glyph as a symbol embedded with meaning. Primarily designed for pattern recognition, glyphs typically do not lend themselves to details or explanations. However, the interactive mouse-over states listed on the third row (of Figure 10.9) do provide details.

Although the mouse-over technique is useful for you to briefly see the details and offset from the benchmark, the inherent brevity makes it difficult to compare the benchmark offsets across all funds. In addition, it is hard for you to visualize the underweight and overweight exposures. The next glyph collection (Figure 10.10) introduces an indicator that clearly shows underweight and overweight exposures when compared to the benchmark.

Overweight and Underweight v. Benchmark
Exposures Comparisons of Long-Only Funds

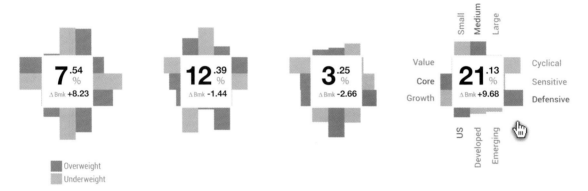

Figure 10.10 **Glyph Benchmark**

You can clearly see the fund/benchmark net in the Glyph Benchmark collection (Figure 10.10). The color bars show areas of investment and interest with overweighted exposures, whereas the gray shown as negative space cutouts draw attention to areas with underweighted exposures. As a result, the glyph emphasizes the active management aspects of fund strategy for each parameter; the glyph's bar shows you only the divergence from the benchmark and, in the center, a numerically represented tracking error.

The benefit of the Glyph Benchmark is that it works together as a system with the previous chart, Figure 10.9, to provide you another perspective to the same funds. The fund/benchmark active result uses the same visual layout to maintain consistency between the charts. You can extend your understanding of the fund performance by introducing this data set as another layer of information or by sorting the collection by exposure, performance, or benchmark.

Key Take-Aways

The strength of the Tricolor Glyphs (Figures 10.7–10.10) is that they uncover distinct patterns and enable you to quickly recognize fund characteristics. The long-only data provides the ability to distinguish patterns and focus on benchmark comparison. Aggressive or conservative characteristics of a fund can stand out. Localized overweights and underweights in comparison to the benchmark can also stand out. These noticeable characteristics that stand out are possible through the visual system (Figures 10.7–10.10) that compares funds across a collection.

Fund Characteristics

In the previous glyph designs, the simple bar and line charts are combined to explain the fund's exposures. Each glyph is encoded with the same basic element of a bar chart to show amount. This next section starts to coalesce around a different approach to the glyph: *What if you used an already recognizable object seen in nature to describe the fund characteristics? How would you describe these characteristics into an already familiar object?* The next examples use an encoded glyph, defined as a familiar object that uses the object's characteristics to represent a specific meaning. The Chernoff Fish shown in Figure 10.11 explores the idea of relying on a fish's attributes to be the vessel of fund characteristics.

Similar in concept to Chernoff faces, the Chernoff Fish maps multiple characteristics to a highly recognizable object, a fish. Statistician Herman Chernoff (who held teaching posts at MIT and Harvard) introduced the idea of showing multivariate values via the features of a person's face. The eyes represent one value, the nose another value, and mouth a third value, and so on. Chernoff's faces are symmetrical and show the front view of the face. Unlike Chernoff's faces, the asymmetrical characteristics of a fish's side profile reduce redundancy of pairs and can be used to show you more variables. The schematic diagram in Figure 10.11 shows the well-appointed characteristics of a fish as a logical link to a fund's characteristics. As the center of attention, the eyes show performance with the pupil representing the fund's returns and the outline showing the top fund performance within the same category. The mass of the fish is depicted with the market cap for the belly and style for the back. The fins are reserved to show exposure across various regions and sectors.

Fund Characteristics Legend

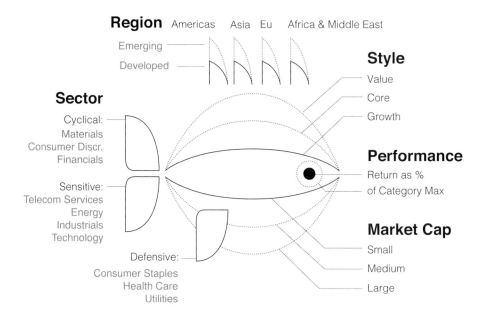

Figure 10.11 **Chernoff Fish**

It is important for you to encode the right set of fund characters to fish characteristics to make the glyph both logical and powerful. A sensible mapping of characteristics makes decoding the fish more memorable. As an example, it is easy to remember the pupil is mapped to performance as a major focus point to the fund. Encoding the market cap and style to the body creates a more powerful analysis of the investment style of the fund. The next illustration shows you how well-appointed characteristics impact a collection of funds.

Encoding a fund's characteristics impacts how well you can evaluate the entire collection. Good encoding practices enables you to answer the following questions: *As a collection, how does the school of funds compare? How recognizable are the various funds and strategies employed? Do the conservative funds stand out?* The School of Funds chart shown next, Figure 10.12, presents a collection of funds for further evaluation. Here, the chart illustrates how well the encoding practices work.

Fund Comparison

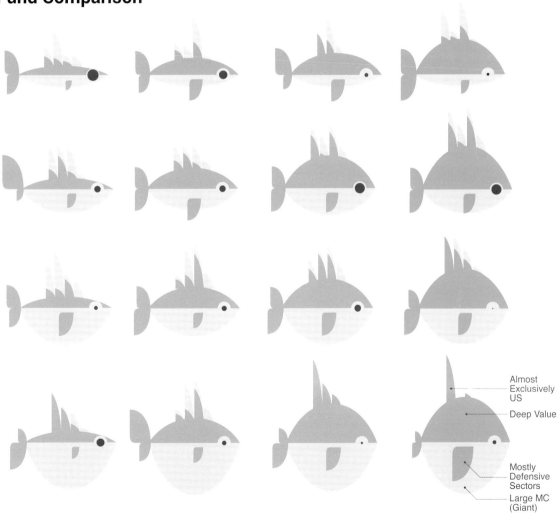

Figure 10.12 **School of Funds**

How do you distinguish the flounders from the barracudas? The School of Funds chart organizes 16 funds primarily by the fish's mass characteristics. The funds are sorted horizontally by style and vertically by market cap. As you review each fund individually or scan the set, you will notice the variations are well noted and distinguishable both within and across the set. Although somewhat whimsical as a data visualization, there is rigor and strength in the approach. The benefits of the School of Funds chart include attributes analysis, pattern recognition, and ranking:

- **Attributes analysis**—*How well can you identify and spot differences and similarities?* Each fund's features are translated into fish attributes that can help you explain the fund's characteristics. Attributes analysis enables you to understand the characteristics to compare and contrast funds. Using the visual system based on individual fish characters, the overall understanding of the fish's behaviors and positioning becomes a personality that naturally appears. For example, the agility of the small cap growth funds over the longevity of the large cap value funds becomes an extended part of the fund's personality.

- **Pattern recognition**—*How well can you recognize and foresee a recurring behavior?* Pattern recognition is the ability to predict outputs based on learned inputs. Decoding the fish's features into fund characteristics and behaviors establishes the ability to provide potential next steps based on existing information.

- **Ranking**—*Which fund has performed the best?* Ranking establishes order in the collection by using the pupil size to identify greater than or less than returns against its peers. Comparing the fish eyes quickly highlights which funds are top ranked versus bottom ranked.

The School of Funds visualization pushes beyond the conventional fund evaluation and creates a new lexicon of how you can describe funds. Each fund has the potential to become more memorable as the combined fish characteristics produce a persona on their own. To extend the characteristics to a persona, the Long/Short Fund Strategies, as shown in Figure 10.13, illustrates how to distinguish the predominately long strategy funds from the funds that mainly use short strategies.

Long/Short Fund Comparison

Long   Short

Figure 10.13 **Directional Chernoff Fish**

Both color and orientation identify the fund's short versus long strategies. As shown in the Directional Fish (Figure 10.13), funds dominated with short strategies are orange and swim left, whereas funds dominated with long strategies are blue and face right. Or the long/short fund characteristics are shown as a set of two complementary strategies and can describe a market neutral fund with both long and short positions. Shorted investments are represented as an orange fish facing left, whereas the opposite-facing blue fish shape encodes the long exposures strategy. Yet more detailed characteristics can be added to the fish, as shown in Figure 10.14.

Fund Characteristics Legend
Detailed Sector Information

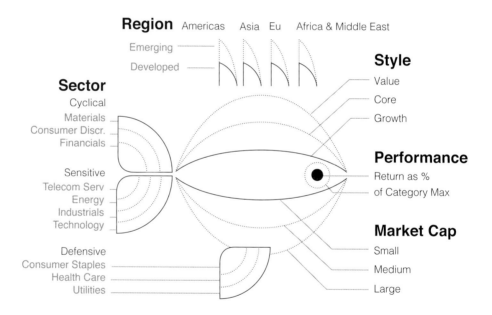

Figure 10.14 Detailed Chernoff Fish

The Detailed Chernoff Fish schematic adds sector details to the previous schematic (refer to Figure 10.11). Details can either enhance or detract from analyzing the main points of a visualization. Depending on the visualization, it can accommodate more details and present the details well or compromise the communication. The question becomes: *Do these added details help or hurt the communication?* The next chart, Detailed School of Funds (Figure 10.15) tests the limits of adding details to the original Chernoff Fish. As you review the school of fish, also review the added sectors and evaluate if the details are a useful addition to the fish.

Fund Comparison
Detailed Sector Information

Figure 10.15 **Detailed School of Funds**

The full sector list, in the Detailed School of Funds, appears in the tail and pectoral fins. Both the presence and market exposure across the sectors is drawn with the color and thickness of the individual arches. Color saturation distinguishes the sectors, whereas the size of each arch shows the percentage value of the market exposure.

The drawback with the sector details is that they are not as legible or as memorable as the original implementation of School of Funds (see Figure 10 12). First, the list of 10 sectors and 16 other characteristic initially requires you to reference the schematic and decode the shades of blue to one of the characteristics. Partly a numbers game, you are required to remember the placement and order of 26 characteristics in total. Next, you have to closely inspect and compare each feature to one another. The 10 similarly depicted sectors may constrain your ability to identify and distinguish the detailed sector characteristics. Lastly, the combination of the amount and type of details makes it more difficult for you to recall.

If not used often, this chart lobbies for the argument of simplification. In this case, simplification improves the visualization, making it both memorable and easier to decode for the infrequent audience. However, if frequently used, you would learn these details over time. You would be able to quickly decode the details and have access to more information from the features.

Key Take-Aways

Glyphs are not just visual marks of lines created to symbolize data. As discussed in this section, glyphs can also be familiar objects in our environment that can be encoded to represent data. In both cases, successful glyphs are simple and standardized. Simplified glyphs make it easier for you to map characteristics of the glyph to a data value. The glyphs that work are those that are standardized to compare the data's attributes, patterns, and ranking. Although this section uses a fish as the glyph to communicate fund data, you can decide to use another familiar object. If you do have multivariate data to display, selecting an object that is asymmetric efficiently supports more data points per display area.

Strategy Rank

Each year, the inquisitive and competitive hedge fund industry publishes a list of top-ranking hedge funds, fund manager performance, and fund manager salaries. In a high-stakes industry with large sums to invest, peers and investors want to know how well a certain fund performed in comparison to others. Or how well managers performed compared to their peer group. The industry draws attention from outsiders and the media. Well-known publications such as *Bloomberg* and *Barron's* grab the public's attention with their annual reports that provide a ray of light into an otherwise opaque closed-doors world. In this section we take advantage of those publications to get a comprehensive view of the industry.

Although the source data for this section is provided by Barron's, the strategy categories for each of the funds has been provided by the authors.

The annual data set shows the results of a year's worth of active investment decisions on behalf of the investment team to produce the top 100 performing funds based on a 3-year annualized gain. *Did the team's day-to-day decisions work? How well did its investment strategies do? How long can top-performing strategies hold top-ranking status?* This section explores these questions in a series of visual methods to show investment strategies' rank, performance, fund size, and firm size across the post-financial crisis period of 2008–2013. We start to answer these questions with the Stacked Area chart (Figure 10.16) that shows you the strategy categories used across those years.

Percent of Hedge Funds in Each Strategy
(Ordered by 2013 Size)

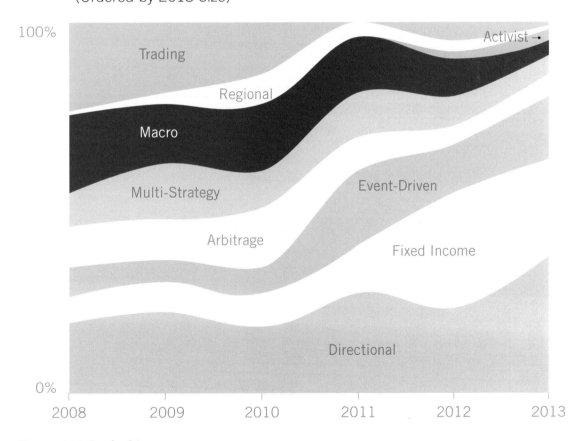

Figure 10.16 **Stacked Area**

The Stacked Area chart shown in Figure 10.16 represents the market share of the top 100 performing hedge funds, grouped by strategy. The 173 investment approaches within the full data sample were categorized into nine strategies: trading, regional, activist, macro, multi-strategy, arbitrage, event-driven, fixed-income, and directional. The list of strategies/streams is ordered by the 2013 strategy size with the smallest percentage at the top and the largest percentage at the bottom. Aside from creating a stream for the school of Chernoff Fish to swim in, the streams insinuate rivers that are widening or closing up to indicate its corresponding percentage. Dark blue color fill shows you how to highlight a particular strategy stream, whereas the other shades of blue alternate to simply distinguish one stream from another.

Known as *survivorship bias*, it is often the case that only the successful strategies are reported. Although it is true that the data is meant to report the top-performing funds, the Stacked Area chart also tracks the trends of declining strategies. The Stacked Area chart neutralizes survivorship bias for strategies and shows either growing success or failure within the top 100 list. As a stream of fund strategies either gaining or losing traction in the top 100, the Stacked Area chart shows you the strategy progress across the post-2007 financial crisis. It shows which strategies are increasingly making the top 100 and which ones are appearing or disappearing from the list.

Mathematically, more can be done to show you a relative ranking of the categories. The Stacked Area – Relative Rank chart shown in Figure 10.17 uses a new calculation to slightly adjust the results.

The Stacked Area – Relative Rank chart introduces the concept of ranking points. To accurately represent the strength of a strategy's presence, each of the 100 funds are assigned points based on the corresponding rank within the 100 list. The rank points are calculated using the formula

$$P = 100 - Rank$$

where P = Points and Rank = Corresponding rank within the 100 list. The yearly value for each strategy represents the sum of the assigned fund points. The y-axis total points reaches 4,950, which is based on 100 funds with ranking points ranging from 0 to 99.

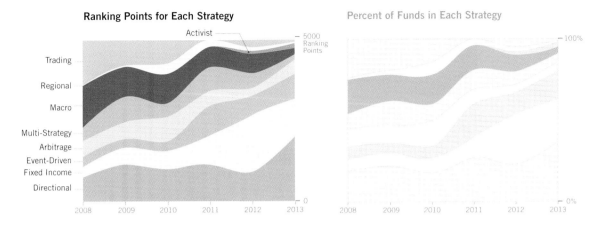

Figure 10.17 **Stacked Area – Relative Rank**

Although the changes are minor in this relative rank version, the nature of the chart's curves and flowing stacked sections makes it difficult for you to detect the difference in accuracy. Regardless, knowing that the chart represents an accurate description of the strategies provides confidence and trust in the visual. Understanding the calculation used to rank the funds is just one part of trusting the visualization. The reliability of a data visualization is dependent on managing:

▶ **How the data is gathered**—Is the data source credible? Are the definitions and approach well-thought-out?

▶ **How the data is calculated**—Are the values absolute or relative? Which formula best represents the data? Which formula best represents the question?

▶ **How the data is depicted**—How does structure, scale, orientation, order, alignment, color, and use of visual marks impact your interpretation of the data?

The listed order by descending rank points may cause confusion. At first glance, the upward trend of the streams subconsciously communicates an increase and even perhaps an improvement. After reviewing the chart, it is clear the opposite is occurring. In more than one-half of the strategies, 5 of the 9 are actually decreasing in performance rank. The next example reviews how slight changes to the chart's visual arrangement can impact your perception of the data. Figure 10.18 reorders the streams of strategies to experiment with your initial impressions.

Categories Ranking Points

Figure 10.18 **Reordered Stacked Area – Relative Rank**

Because the stream direction can change your initial perception of the data, the decision to select the right order of the strategies becomes an important part of presenting rank. The alphabetical order somewhat removes the automatic trend line of flowing up or down, whereas the other two inherently show the stream direction. Your job is to select the best default order to avoid a misinterpretation of the data.

Strategy Rank and Ranges

Aside from ranking strategies, you can explore other aspects of the ranking strategy data set regarding strategy average returns and range of least-effective to most-effective fund performance. The post-financial crisis period is an interesting time span to analyze these attributes of averages and ranges. During this period of uncertainty, an unbiased review of the attributes helps you to track the trends of top strategies and analyze when and how the returns responded to the market conditions.

As shown in Figure 10.19, the strategy attributes display in a series of bidirectional, equitable charts. *Which strategy did well across the years? Which years showed strong returns? How well did a strategy perform and how consistent was that performance within the strategy?* The Dot Matrix collection answers these questions with a flexible display that does not provide preference to one question over another. It also gradually incorporates additional attributes into each chart in the collection:

▶ Figure 10.19 A provides an overview of category average returns for the 3-year annualized returns.

▶ Figure 10.19 B shows each category's average returns as a dark blue center and most-effective fund performance in light blue outer circles.

▶ Figure 10.19 C adds the category's least-effective fund performance in the center one-half ring.

Strategy Performance

A. Average 3Y Returns

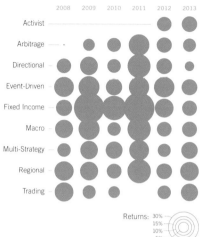

B. Average 3Y Returns, Most Effective Fund Returns

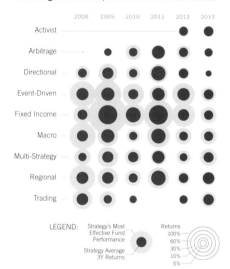

C. Average 3Y Returns, Most and Least Effective Funds Returns

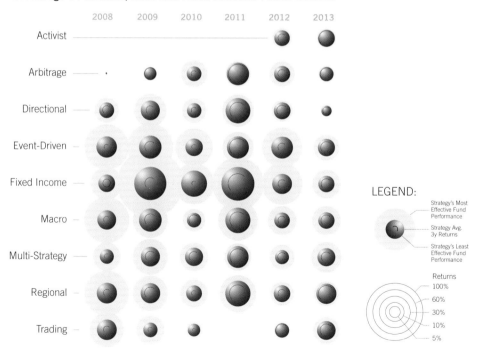

Figure 10.19 Dot Matrix

Because the dot shapes are directionally neutral, the data display can reveal strategy attributes. The sheer size of the dots lures your attention to the top performing strategies, whereas the range of attributes provides details and more context for further examination. The Dot Matrix approach can be used in other cases in which you need to review the data from two perspectives (of columns and rows) and do not want to emphasize one perspective over another.

Key Take-Aways

Accurate and neutral views of the data remove bias and allow the numbers to tell the story. How the data is gathered, calculated, and depicted can influence the understanding of the data. The Stacked Area is an example of recalculating the data to accurately represent rank, while the Dot Matrix neutralizes the data display by fairly representing all the attributes in an egalitarian way.

Strategy Analysis

It's a common practice to step back and look at the overall returns of a strategy category over a span of time. The following visualizations introduce a method to interact with 100 funds over a 6-year period. In his task analysis paper, "The Eyes Have It: Task by Data Type Taxonomy for Information Visualization," Ben Shneiderman outlines the series of steps to navigate and visually interact with large data. Shneiderman's *Visual Information Seeking Mantra* includes overview, zoom, filter, and details on-demand. The overview presents all the strategy averages per year and across the years. Next, the zoom view examines a single strategy and then zooms in further to examine the strategy at the fund level. Third, the filters are applied to focus on one year over another. Fourth, data display panels list the specific values regarding a fund.

The illustrations in the next section show an interactive system that follows these four steps and introduces a fifth task of comparison to the list.

NOTE Ben Shneiderman is a professor of Computer Science at the University of Maryland Human-Computer Interaction Lab. The paper referenced in this section was published in *Proceedings: IEEE Symposium on Visual Languages*. 3–6 Sep 1996. ISBN: 0-8186-7508-X. It's available online at http://www.interactiondesign.us/courses/2011_AD690/PDFs/Shneiderman_1996.pdf.

All Strategy Averages

The first step of providing an overview includes performance averages across all the strategies and years. A great candidate to show averages of performance, fund, and firm size of AUM with the capability to zoom and reveal details on-demand is a bubble plot.

The bubble plot is known to effectively reveal clusters and outliers. Later in this chapter you see how it can also show temporal data. Interactive bubble plots can be used to directly label items in dense regions of overlapping circles. Figure 10.20 illustrates how the interactive display can work to label and display supporting details such as: performance averages for the 2008–2013 period, averages in the 1-year returns, averages in the 3-year returns, averages in the strategy size of the fund assets, as well as averages in the strategy size of the firm assets.

The interactive display works by selecting the bubbles within the chart or selecting the strategy within the legend. Selecting a strategy in the legend highlights the strategy in the chart and displays the numeric values of both the average fund and firm assets. As you interact with the display, you can also decide to view the range and make-up of these averages for the 2008–2013 period. The presentation of averages consolidates the data and can be your entry point to zoom into the details of the data. Figure 10.21 zooms in to show you how the strategies perform across the years.

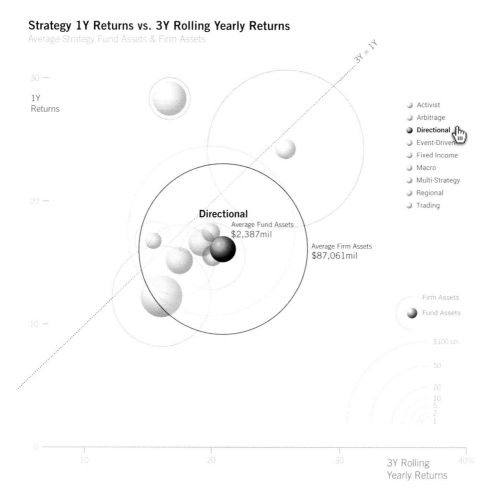

Strategy 1Y Returns vs. 3Y Rolling Yearly Returns
Average Strategy Fund Assets & Firm Assets

3Y = 1Y

30 —

1Y
Returns

Activist
Arbitrage
Directional
Event-Driven
Fixed Income
Macro
Multi-Strategy
Regional
Trading

20 —

Directional
Average Fund Assets
$2,387mil

Average Firm Assets
$87,061mil

Firm Assets
Fund Assets

10 —

$100 bln

50

20
10
5
2
1

0

10   20   30   3Y Rolling   40%
                                    Yearly Returns

Figure 10.20 **Radius Bubble Plot - Interactive**

The yearly returns shown in the Bubble Plot: 2008–2013 Returns chart (Figure 10.21) expand the scale beyond the 30% mark into the 40% mark and then dip into negative returns on the y-axis as they expand into each category's yearly returns. The 54 category bubbles in the chart show the distribution, concentration, and size of the fund assets. Size, color, and rendering style with slight transparency of the bubbles enable you to see more of the layered bubbles. Despite this richer picture of performance that expands the view, the overwhelming amount of information makes the display too dense to be useful.

Strategy 1Y Returns vs. 3Y Rolling Yearly Returns
Average Strategy Fund Assets & Firm Assets, 2008-2013 Yearly Data

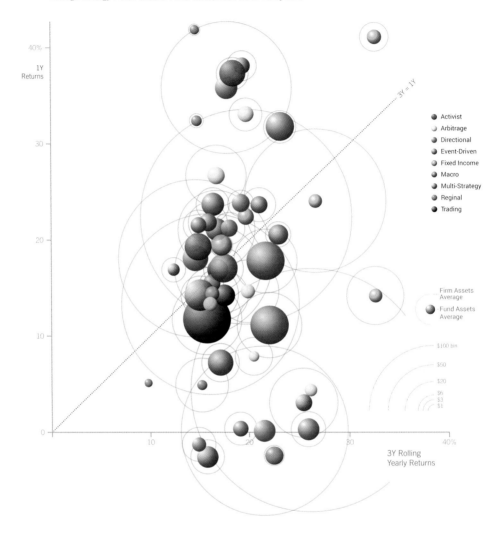

Figure 10.21 Bubble Plot—2008–2013 Returns

Single Strategy Averages

To show you both the strategy yearly returns in context of the previous views of averages, Figure 10.22 filters the display to show the yearly averages of a single strategy. Here, the interactive display reduces the visual overload and focuses on the Arbitrage strategy.

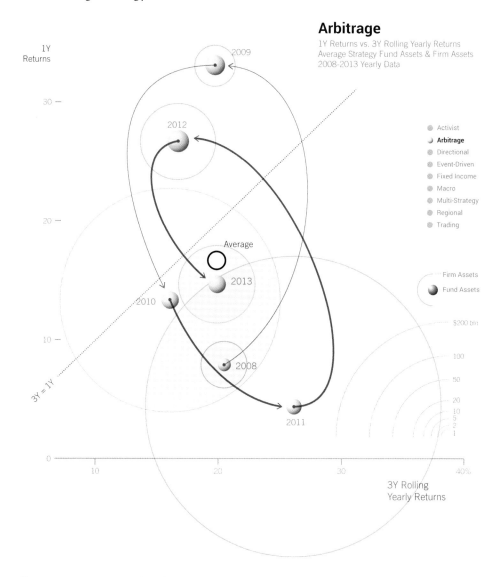

Figure 10.22 **Temporal Path - Arbitrage**

The selected display of one strategy view at a time produces the results in the Temporal Path – Arbitrage chart. The isolation produces a clearer image of a strategy's 6-year path. You can make the following observations of the strategy's past performance history:

▶ Large swings in performance gains and losses from year to year

▶ Somewhat consistent size of each fund's assets

▶ Inconsistent size of the corresponding firm's assets

The Temporal Path adds perspective to the relative average marker, shown in white fill, and enables you to discover more about the strategy's performance returns. Now that the system of filtering is established, you can further explore how other strategies have performed over the same period. Figure 10.23 and 10.24 display a filtered view of two other strategy categories in the list.

The Temporal Path – Directional chart shown in Figure 10.23 exposes the truth behind an average profile similar to the previous category of Arbitrage. Yet as is evident from the path, the movement across the years includes some extreme ranges of negative returns in 2008 to mid-30% returns in 2013. In the earlier years, the strategy represented a significant portion of firms AUM and was popular with firms with relatively small AUM, whereas in the latter years the strategy gained popularity with firms with large AUM. You may have made the same observations. The strategy shown in Figure 10.24, the Temporal Path – Event-Driven chart, provides you with yet another set of interesting observations.

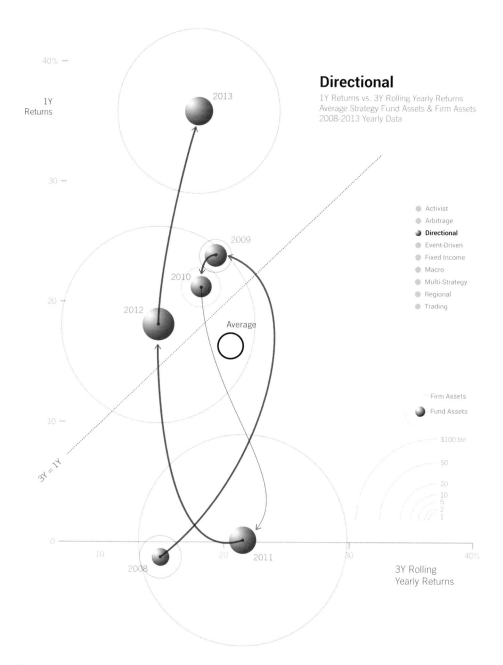

Directional

1Y Returns vs. 3Y Rolling Yearly Returns
Average Strategy Fund Assets & Firm Assets
2008-2013 Yearly Data

Activist
Arbitrage
Directional
Event-Driven
Fixed Income
Macro
Multi-Strategy
Regional
Trading

Firm Assets
Fund Assets

$100 bln
50
20
10
5
2
1

1Y
Returns

40%

30

20

10

0

3Y = 1Y

Average

2013

2009

2010

2012

2008

2011

10   20   30   40%

3Y Rolling
Yearly Returns

Figure 10.23 Temporal Path - Directional

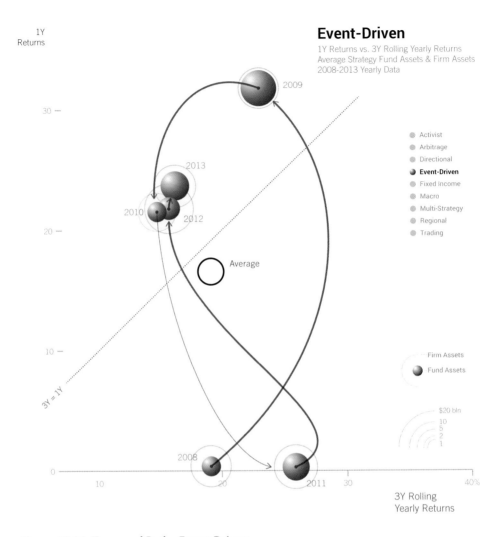

Figure 10.24 Temporal Path - Event-Driven

The Temporal Path – Event Driven chart reveals a few distinct qualities; 3 of the 6 years cluster around consistent performance returns, and the firm and fund assets are closely aligned to each other. After reviewing the three Temporal Paths of Arbitrage, Directional, and Event Driven, it is clear that the averages represent some shared behaviors. All three have low-performance years in 2008 and 2011 and exactly one superb performance year in the 30% range. You can compare and learn from Figure 10.25, which illustrates a collection of temporal category paths that reveal similarities, nuances, and divergence of performance.

Strategy 1Y Returns vs. 3Y Rolling Yearly Returns
Average Strategy Fund Assets & Firm Assets, 2008-2013 Yearly Data

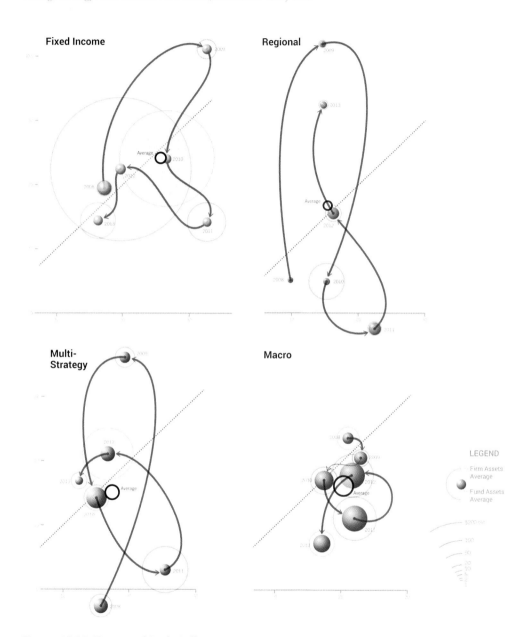

Figure 10.25 **Temporal Path Collection**

The benefits of the Temporal Path Collection are many. In addition to providing you with five data points (1-year returns, 3-year returns, fund size, firm size, and category average), the arrowed line paths tell a story about the strategy's sequential movements in returns and average assets under management. You can compare the consistency or inconsistency of each strategy's returns across the years. You can extend the years beyond this relatively small time span to show 10, 15, or more years of top performing funds. The paths take on their own descriptors, and you can even ponder labels such as the open lasso shown in the fixed-income, the infinity loop shown in regional, the pretzel shown in multi-strategy, and the single loop shown in macro strategy.

The next step shows you numeric details on-demand by providing the metadata to a selected bubble in the form of text-value pairs. Figure 10.26 illustrates how to provide specific metadata information to describe the strategy category.

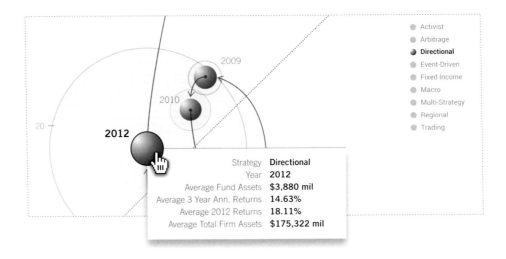

Figure 10.26 **Temporal Path – Interactive Year Display**

Beyond the the text display panel shown on mouse-over, you can also select the strategy year to see the underlying funds and ask more questions regarding the funds present in each year.

Fund Level Returns

If you select the Directional bubble, you can zoom in to see the underlying funds that comprise the strategy year bubble within the context of other yearly averages. Figure 10.27 illustrates how the funds performed in 2012 and identifies which funds make up the strategy with a fund level display panel.

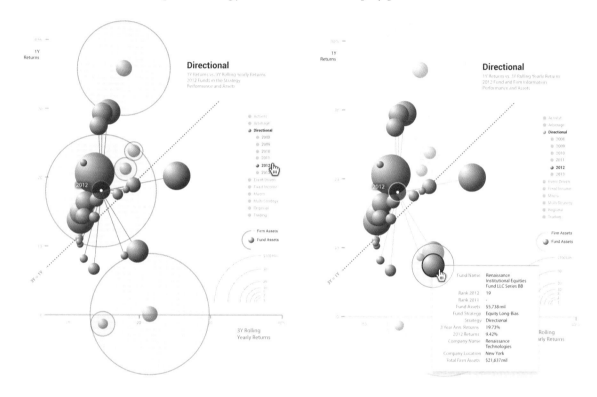

Figure 10.27   **Fund Bubbles– Interactive Fund Display**

You may have noticed that the display continues the pattern of zoom, filter, details on demand, and compare for better consistency across those tasks. Fund Bubbles – Interactive Fund Display (Figure 10.27) uses the following visual elements to provide a consistent experience:

▶ **Average marker**—The average marker shown in a transparent black circle is the weighted average anchor to all the underlying funds.

- ▶ **Bubble rendering**—The quantity of funds, large fund assets, and cluster placements make it a challenge to clearly see all the funds. You can mitigate this obstructed view with the use of transparency to see through the firm assets, three-dimensional sphere rendering to reinforce the layers, and rule-based layering of the bubbles to place the smallest fund on top.

- ▶ **Yearly context**—The five lighter bubbles shown in the background are present as context to the other 5-year averages. The legend shows you the strategy and year selected with the use of bold text.

- ▶ **Text display panel**—The name and descriptors help you to identify and learn additional details of the fund with a list of 11 data points.

With this perspective, you can explore and see which fund performed the best in the 3-year returns versus the 1-year returns, which fund had the most assets versus the smallest, and so on. The display can both zoom in to a specific strategy to uncover the underlying funds for 1 year as well as zoom out to see all the underlying funds across all years. Figure 10.28 illustrates the display as a view into all the funds across all the years for one strategy.

The overall effect of the All Years Directional Strategy chart is a big picture view of how the funds have performed over the years. The concentrations of performance returns, ranges, and size of the fund comprises this big picture view. To do so, this display uses the same visual elements of average marker, bubble rendering, and text display panel as well as a few others:

- ▶ **Historical context**—All funds are present and represent the years with a slight fade out to the earlier years; the effect pushes the earlier years to the background while highlighting the most current years to the foreground.

- ▶ **Negative returns**—The negative returns, shown with a gray fill background, emphasizes the underwater funds that still managed to make it on the top 100 funds.

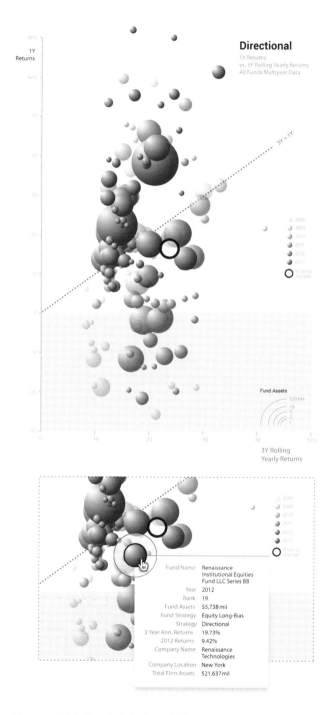

Figure 10.28 **Fund Bubbles– All Years One Strategy**

Similar to the Temporal Path Collection, Figure 10.29, Fund Bubbles – All Years Collection chart enables you to structure side-by-side views of each strategy.

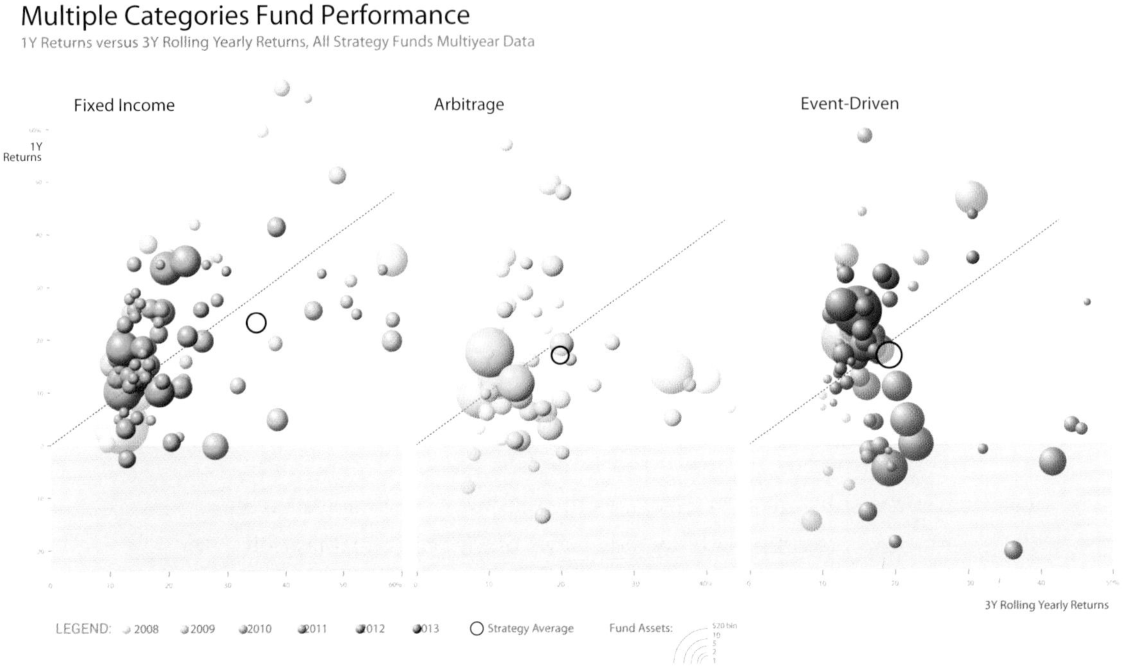

Multiple Categories Fund Performance
1Y Returns versus 3Y Rolling Yearly Returns, All Strategy Funds Multiyear Data
Fixed Income
Arbitrage
Event-Driven
1Y Returns
3Y Rolling Yearly Returns
LEGEND: 2008 2009 2010 2011 2012 2013
Strategy Average
Fund Assets:

Figure 10.29 **Fund Bubbles– All Years Collection**

These three sequentially placed views enable you to analyze the results for each strategy. For example, you can see the differences in behaviors and track the recently ranked activity to answer: *Which fund group observed the most 1Y negative returns? Which fund group shows the most promising 3Y returns track record?* The collection enables you to be in a position to review the set and formulate your own commentary to the observations.

The full set of bubble charts provides flexibility and enables you to explore the collections of temporal bubbles within the context of the strategy averages. The interactive system promotes your understanding of the data by applying the following design methods:

- **Grouping**—The top 100 hedge funds across 6 years results in 600 funds that are grouped into 9 strategies. You can isolate your observations by showing the group averages and providing views that are exclusive to one strategy or 1 year. Grouping enables you to detect and articulate specific behaviors that become characteristic of the group. Side-by-side views of the groups enable you to contrast these behaviors and create a detailed description of the group as you search for and point out similarities and differences.

▶ **Drill-down**—The ability to navigate through various levels, explore each level, and view details on demand all embody the drill-down method. The method provides a navigation structure to show where you are, where you were, and where you may go next. The transparent bubbles, navigation links, and display panel all support the drill-down design method.

▶ **Temporal Path**—Temporal paths are a series of points connected in sequential order of time. As a design method, the path makes good on the phrase "The journey is more important than the destination" and accentuates the storyline that describes the temporal movements. Again, the technique of providing side-by-side views of the paths enables rich commentary to develop.

Key Take-Aways

The interactive system showcases bubble plots as a conduit for exploring data and discovering hidden behaviors, trends, and outliers that may go unnoticed. Grouping data with averages and ranges, navigating through different levels, and seeing the linked temporal path are design methods to help you take notice and uncover how a strategy has performed over time, which funds make up those strategies, and how they compare to their peers. This section reviews the top 100 hedge funds at three levels: all strategies, individual strategies, and funds per strategy. The bubble plot system of interaction can be applied to other fund sets where the interest lies in understanding the rank of strategy category, percentage returns, size of fund, and firm AUM. Or you could also map different data to each axis and, for example, show the changes in risk versus reward the fund provides.

Summary

This chapter introduces new ways of interacting with data to rank, compare, and extract patterns across both small and large fund data sets. The chapter starts with the analysis of a single fund's short and long exposures to display multivariate data and ends with an interactive display you can use to analyze top-performing strategies with hundreds of funds in one view. In both cases, the previously conceived methods of Chernoff Faces and Schneider's *Visual Information Seeking Mantra* were referenced to show how you can apply those methods to create new visualizations. The visualization solutions include the following:

VISUALIZATION	DESCRIPTION	FIGURE
Butterfly Bar	Quantity represented with a continuous bar of opposing scales connected with a shared starting point.	10.1–10.3
Glyph	A symbol that uses marks to represent a specific meaning.	10.4–10.10
Encoded Glyph	A familiar object that uses the object's characteristics to represent a specific meaning.	10.11–10.15
Stacked Area	Layers of color fill that each represent a change in quantity for a variable.	10.16–10.18
Dot Matrix	Filled-in circles organized in a grid in which size indicates quantity.	10.19
Bubble Plot	Circles mapped to Cartesian coordinates in the form of bubbles that use color, size, transparency, outer rings, averages, temporal paths, and text display panels to layer in data points.	10.20–10.31

Each of the six visualizations serves a unique purpose and teach you key lessons along the way. The glyphs provide an identification system and prove to be an efficient method to communicate, decode, and see patterns emerge from the fund attributes. The stacked area shows you the changes in rank strategies and is a lesson in how you can recalculate and sort the data for better accuracy and perception. The dot matrix combines the category averages with minimum and maximum ranges to provide you with better context of rank and strategy attributes. From dots to bubbles, the full data set of top hedge funds in the industry provide an interactive display with a lot of aggregate and detail data points for you to explore. The key take-away from the bubble display is the flexibility to see an overview of averages, to zoom into a year or strategy, to filter the display results, to see details of the meta-data on demand, and to select a number of views to compare. Just as the examples show you how to apply Chernoff Faces and Shneiderman's patterns of use, you can apply specific methods, and consider the lessons learned for your own data sets.

PART 4

Next Steps

▶ **Chapter 11:** Data Visualization Principles

▶ **Chapter 12:** Implementing the Visuals

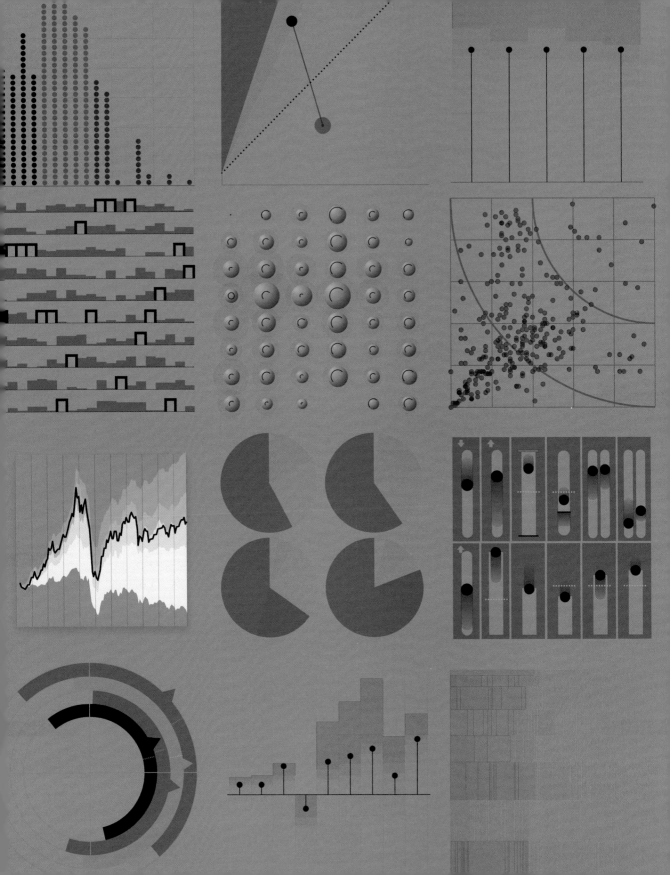

11

Data Visualization Principles

What makes a data visualization successful? What principles should we adhere to? If we could establish guidelines to direct good visualization for representing financial data, what would be included in the list? To start, data visualizations should answer key questions from the perspective of the intended audience. Like a story, a visualization should provide a rich and unfolding perspective on the data that provides multiple answers to its audience members. It tells a factual story, fully embedded in the data: It should be clear and efficient—qualities that may at times be difficult to achieve. This chapter discusses three major data visualization principles in greater detail and grounds each principle with a list of guidelines and examples from previous chapters. The overarching recommendations we discuss include:

- ▶ **Cater to your audience**—Focus on the audience, the purpose, and the storyline for each visualization. Know your audience well enough that you can anticipate the series of questions they will have of the data.

- ▶ **Provide clarity**—Present the data with the utmost accuracy, transparency, and clarity. Be straightforward so that each visualization properly represents the data.

- ▶ **Be efficient**—Strive to create effortless experiences for your audience. The visualization should work so that your audience doesn't have to.

These data visualization principles expand on a traditional set of best practices for good visual design. Such best practices provide a foundation of a good composition using design elements such as a point, line, shape, value, texture, and color. Within a composition, design elements build on our cognitive and aesthetic sensibilities. The visualizations need to do that, too, but go beyond basic design practices to deal with the complexity of data. This chapter focuses on data visualization principles and references good design practices as needed. We incorporate design practices as they relate to these three basic rules. In this way the principles are comprehensive and incorporate the relevant design practices.

As we review the principles, we review a list of guidelines to achieve each principle. Adhering to the guidelines can help you to produce quality visualizations. The list of guidelines is illustrated with charts sourced from the other chapters in the book. You can go to the original presentation of the figure to refresh and gather more details about the chart. Together each principle, set of guidelines, and design practices provides you with a more specific multi-prong approach to producing a successful visualization.

Cater to Your Audience

Visualizations reveal information contained in raw data. The job of the visualization is to show what otherwise might be missed if the raw data alone were reviewed. Visualizations should be informative and show robust views of the data. They should pique your audience's curiosity and ability to learn as much as possible. We create data visualizations to answer questions for others and ourselves. An engaging presentation of the data is vital to not only answer questions, but also to drive curiosity about what else the data can reveal. You can use specific guidelines to ensure you spur interest and meet your audience's needs.

To start, you need to identify the audience and the main storyline. First, ask yourself what is the main purpose of the visualization and what questions need to be answered by the visual. You also need to identify possible follow-up questions. Next, identify how you can direct a storyline to reach both the stated objective and unasked questions that might arise. Following is a list of guidelines that can be adopted depending on the intentions and needs of the audience:

▶ **Relevance**—Consider the fact that different audiences will have different priorities and perspectives that matter to them. Provide flexible views of the data to adjust and satisfy various interests. For example, incorporate interactive custom weights that you can set to reflect the interests or expectations of your audience. The closer you can come to creating a display that shows their preferences, the more your audience will relate to the visualization. You can create relevance using other techniques such as incorporating your audience's location, similar profile, or adjacent profiles, or any other data points that are timely and important now or in the near future. (Figure 11.1; reference: Figure 3.3 Results Framework) Figure 3.3 adjusts the referenced chart by rotating it 90 degrees to the left. This adjustment shows how adaptable the chart is to a different layout.

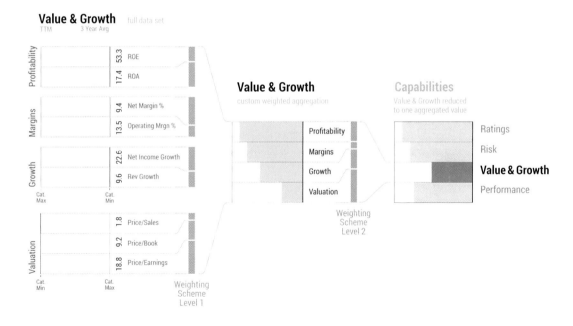

Figure 11.1 **Results Framework**

▶ **Context**—Provide context to compare and relate the primary data against. Context examples include time series, peer group or category average, category quartiles, benchmark, and more. Layering in the benchmark is a standard practice of adding a reference point. It allows better comparison with a variation from the benchmark to be shown. However, incorporating more information like the three-color bands that serve as ratings adds even more reference points that both the fund and the benchmark can be compared to. In this way your audience can gain a better appreciation for what is good, very good, or excellent and where a fund is in comparison to the benchmark. A design best practice is to render the context points in the background with more subdued colors. The fund is represented in dark blue, whereas the reference benchmark is shown in the background in gray. (Figure 11.2; reference: Figure 9.40 Sharpe Ratio Arc Bands)

Sharpe Ratio

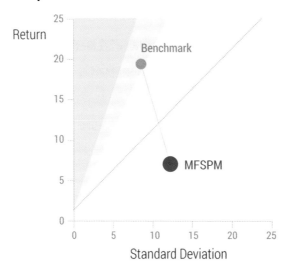

Figure 11.2 **Sharpe Ratio Arc Bands**

- ▶ **Focus tilts**—Be flexible with different possible perspectives of the data. Provide the same data with multiple views and emphasize different aspects of the data. Showing different aspects of the same data could involve a tilt toward short-term, long-term, historical, rank, cumulative, average, or variance performance results. As the views change, highlight where you want to draw your audience's attention to provide a guided and focused experience. A good design practice is to create focus with the use of a bold color or thicker line weight. Entice your audience into examining different aspects of the data. In one case, you can provide cumulative ranking, and in another you might provide period average returns and compare those to the benchmark. Make sure each tilt is important to your audience. (Figures 11.3 and 11.4; reference: Figure 4.7 Bar Track Chart – Row and Figure 4.8 Bar Track Chart – Row with Pivot Summary)

Figure 11.3 **Bar Track Chart - Row**

Calendar Year Returns: Sector Returns

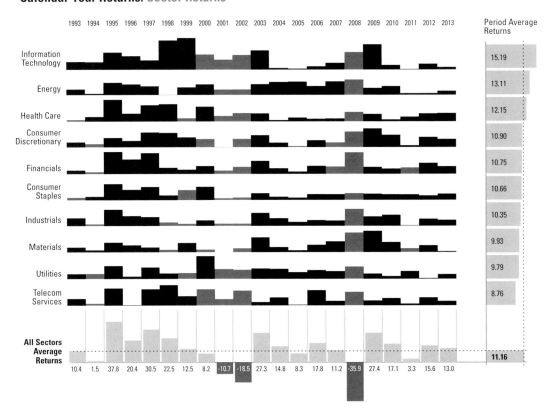

Figure 11.4 **Bar Track Chart – Row with Pivot Summary**

▶ **Relative and absolute values**—For example, relative and absolute value pairings can be used across data sets to show the actual value and a value based on comparable ratios. Figure 11.5 pairs relative and absolute values into side-by-side views to provide better comparison. Your audience can see that the expense ratio was stable across the years in absolute terms, but then contrast the observation with a relative view that shows there was also a significant trend heading toward the top quartile. (Figure 11.5 reference: Figure 9.22 Absolute and Relative Pairing)

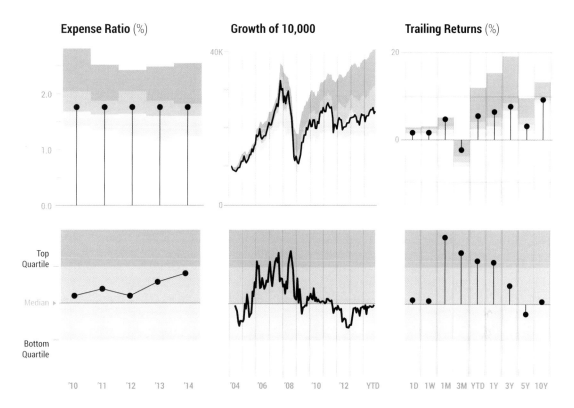

Figure 11.5 **Absolute and Relative Pairing**

▶ **Summary/detail**—Show summary and detail information so that the reader can make connections between cause and effect. Allow your audience to drill in multiple levels to investigate and understand the underpinnings of a total value. Provide a way to zoom into more detailed views and review the information up close for inspection. Summary level views can include aggregated totals, metadata, or averages. Detail views can include specific numeric values, provide historical context, or offer a higher resolution of detail. A good design practice is to layer the details so that your audience can see the specifics within the context of the summary view. (Figure 11.6; reference: Figure 7.16 Integrated Waterfall)

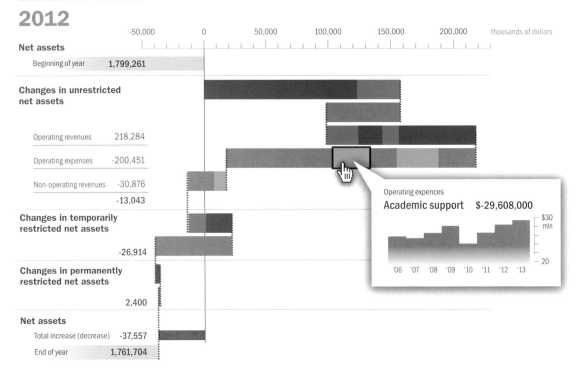

Statement of Activities

2012

	-50,000	0	50,000	100,000	150,000	200,000	thousands of dollars

Net assets

Beginning of year   1,799,261

Changes in unrestricted
net assets

Operating revenues   218,284

Operating expenses   -200,451

Non-operating revenues   -30,876

-13,043

Changes in temporarily
restricted net assets

-26,914

Changes in permanently
restricted net assets

2,400

Net assets

Total increase (decrease)   -37,557

End of year   1,761,704

Operating expences
Academic support $-29,608,000

$30 mln

20

'06 '07 '08 '09 '10 '11 '12 '13

Figure 11.6 **Integrated Waterfall**

▶ **Recalculation**—Review the data for opportunities to reveal a new story
through different calculations. Consider how you might recalculate
the data to clarify the story. The overlap of holdings typically shows
the relationship between two funds' underlying assets as fund A is xx%
of fund B and vice versa. The data is typically shown as a table matrix.
The purpose of the table is to show which fund pairings have the most
overlap of holdings. To best answer the overlap question, the data can be
recalculated. The new calculation we have provided is the square root of
the multiplication of those two relationships which are then organized
into a histogram to see the distribution of overlapping investments
across a firm. This allows your audience to quickly assess the range and
concentrations of overlap at the multi-fund firm level. The interactive
layer provides information about specific fund pairs. In addition, we have
used color to further distinguish the funds with significant overlaps and

those with low overlaps. This example of recalculations shows how to point out the underlying story of the data with the use of recalculation. (Figure 11.7; reference: Figure 4.24 Tiered Histogram)

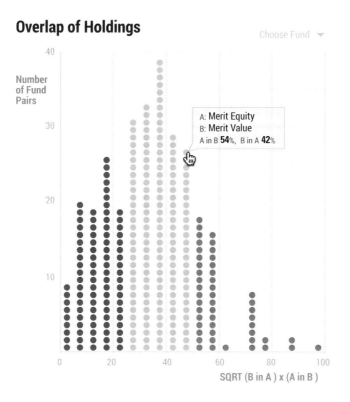

Overlap of Holdings

Choose Fund ▼

A: Merit Equity
B: Merit Value
A in B **54**%, B in A **42**%

Figure 11.7 **Tiered Histogram**

▶ **Categories**—Help make discoveries by creating categories and grouping similar objects. Removing details and aggregating group data allows the main themes to surface. This enables you to see the big picture and not get lost in the details. A certain level of abstraction anchors the data and makes it more manageable to comprehend. Grouping can help to see results that might otherwise be missed in large and complex data sets. Grouping objects can start with a simple sort to order the data in a logical order of sequential incremental values, time, or type. (Figure 11.8; reference: Figure 4.12, 4.13, 4.16 Heatmap Groups)

S&P 1500 Return: MTD Percent Change

	Beta	Volatility	B/P	S/P	ST Momentum	FY2 E/P	FY1 E/P	Liquidity	FCF/P	Short Interest/Share	Leverage	Days to Cover	14d RSI	E/P	LT Growth	90d Slope	3 Yr Sales Growth	3 Yr EPS Growth	Size	ROE	ROA	LT Momentum
F1-FN Spread	3.58	3.57	2.71	2.44	1.67	1.44	1.31	1.00	1.00	0.33	0.74	0.63	0.14	-0.10	-0.26	-0.41	-0.55	-1.13	-1.31	-1.83	-2.32	-4.24
Energy	3.68	-0.20	-2.69	-0.89	0.11	5.36	3.94	-0.83	5.34	-1.83	-0.95	-2.49	-0.34	2.15	5.22	4.90	-0.76	2.05	2.23	2.34	1.87	0.18
Materials	7.80	9.25	6.19	7.42	1.49	2.64	1.30	4.85	-1.70	3.22	0.73	-0.26	-0.84	-0.49	2.25	2.07	-2.89	-4.45	-2.38	-4.07	-5.29	-6.59
Consumer Staples	3.84	2.52	2.66	1.98	-0.66	2.62	1.12	6.81	-1.43	4.42	-1.53	1.44	-1.05	-0.21	1.20	-1.62	2.93	1.10	-1.59	-0.17	-2.52	-3.31
Information Technology	2.66	1.59	1.44	1.47	3.24	1.63	2.72	0.79	0.73	-0.18	-0.35	1.86	2.38	1.84	-3.82	1.25	1.44	-0.84	0.23	-0.44	-0.56	-2.34
Financials	3.02	5.04	2.72	1.56	2.24	1.86	2.05	2.57	1.37	0.33	2.14	-0.30	-1.21	0.74	1.60	-0.56	-1.34	-2.39	0.54	-1.70	-0.47	-5.11
Health Care	2.06	4.37	2.38	4.27	-0.94	2.12	1.60	1.11	1.97	1.66	1.46	0.63	0.31	0.60	-0.46	-3.14	-0.92	2.14	-3.50	0.30	-1.11	-3.50
Industrials	4.18	4.21	6.33	5.54	0.70	1.60	0.64	0.19	0.66	0.00	0.34	0.29	0.45	-2.02	-0.31	-3.77	2.29	-1.12	-3.35	-4.52	-5.96	-4.94
Consumer Discretionary	4.05	3.61	2.23	0.75	3.07	-0.87	-0.35	0.27	1.32	2.19	2.75	1.48	-0.51	-2.06	-0.70	-0.34	-0.51	-0.96	-2.17	-3.15	-3.97	-6.95
Utilities	1.33	-0.30	2.39	-0.38	0.23	0.09	-0.81	-0.10	-1.34	0.01	-0.19	-0.21	0.62	0.10	0.05	0.17	1.16	-0.44	-0.51	-1.90	-1.45	-1.36
Telecom Services	8.77	3.05	-5.82	2.68	8.79	-4.91	-4.91	-5.66	3.03	1.57	-3.64	5.04	3.03	-3.58	1.35	1.55	0.43	0.54	-7.74	-2.28	-3.38	-1.75

CATEGORIZATION

	Risk — Beta	Risk — Volatility	Risk — Liquidity	Risk — Days to Cover	Risk — Leverage	Tech Trends — ST Momentum	Tech Trends — Short Interest/Share	Tech Trends — 14d RSI	Tech Trends — 90d Slope	Value — S/P	Value — B/P	Value — FCF/P	Value — ROE	Value — ROA	Growth — LT Growth	Growth — 3 Yr Sales Growth	Growth — 3 Yr EPS Growth	Growth — LT Momentum	Per Share — FY2 E/P	Per Share — FY1 E/P	Per Share — E/P	Per Share — Size
Energy	3.68	-0.20	-0.83	-2.49	-0.95	0.11	-1.83	-0.34	4.90	-0.89	-2.69	5.34	2.34	1.87	5.22	-0.76	2.05	0.18	5.36	3.94	2.15	2.23
Materials	7.80	9.25	4.85	-0.26	0.73	1.49	3.22	-0.84	2.07	7.42	6.19	-1.70	-4.07	-5.29	2.25	-2.89	-4.45	-6.59	2.64	1.30	-0.49	-2.38
Consumer Staples	3.84	2.52	6.81	1.44	-1.53	-0.66	4.42	-1.05	-1.62	1.98	2.66	-1.43	-0.17	-2.52	1.20	2.93	1.10	-3.31	2.62	1.12	-0.21	-1.59
Information Technology	2.66	1.59	0.79	1.86	-0.35	3.24	-0.18	2.38	1.44	1.47	1.44	0.73	-0.44	-0.56	-3.82	1.25	-0.84	-2.34	1.63	2.72	1.84	0.23
Financials	3.02	5.04	2.57	-0.30	2.14	2.24	0.33	-1.21	-0.56	1.56	2.72	1.37	-1.70	-0.47	1.60	-1.34	-2.39	-5.11	1.86	2.05	0.74	0.54
Health Care	2.06	4.37	1.11	0.63	1.46	-0.94	1.66	0.31	-3.14	4.27	2.38	1.97	0.30	-1.11	-0.46	-0.92	2.14	-3.50	2.12	1.60	0.60	-3.50
Industrials	4.18	4.21	0.19	0.29	0.34	0.70	0.00	0.45	-3.77	5.54	6.33	0.66	-4.52	-5.96	-0.31	2.29	-1.12	-4.94	1.60	0.64	-2.02	-3.35
Consumer Discretionary	4.05	3.61	0.27	1.48	2.75	3.07	2.19	-0.51	-0.34	0.75	2.23	1.32	-3.15	-3.97	-0.70	-0.51	-0.96	-6.95	-0.87	-0.35	-2.06	-2.17
Utilities	1.33	-0.30	-0.10	-0.21	-0.19	0.23	0.01	0.62	0.17	-0.38	2.39	-1.34	-1.90	-1.45	0.05	1.16	-0.44	-1.36	0.09	-0.81	0.10	-0.51
Telecom Services	8.77	3.05	-5.66	5.04	-3.64	8.79	1.57	3.03	1.55	2.68	-5.82	3.03	-2.28	-3.38	1.35	0.43	0.54	-1.75	-4.91	-4.91	-3.58	-7.74
Average	4.14	3.31	1.00	0.75	0.08	1.83	1.14	0.28	0.07	2.44	1.78	1.00	-1.56	-2.28	0.64	0.16	-0.44	-3.57	1.21	0.73	-0.29	-1.82

AGGREGATION

	Risk Average	Tech Trends Average	Value Average	Growth Average	Per Share Average
Energy	-0.16	0.71	1.19	1.67	3.42
Materials	4.47	1.49	0.51	-2.92	0.27
Consumer Staples	2.62	0.27	0.10	0.48	0.49
Information Technology	1.31	1.72	0.53	-1.44	1.61
Financials	2.49	0.20	0.70	-1.81	1.30
Health Care	1.93	-0.53	1.56	-0.69	0.21
Industrials	1.84	-0.66	0.41	-1.02	-0.78
Consumer Discretionary	2.43	1.10	-0.56	-2.28	-1.36
Utilities	0.11	0.26	-0.54	-0.15	-0.28
Telecom Services	1.51	3.74	-1.15	0.14	-5.29
Average	1.86	0.83	0.28	-0.80	-0.04

Figure 11.8 Heatmap Groups

- ▶ **Outliers**—Distinguish and point out the outliers, the points that stand out. Make it simple to see what is different from the rest and set up a visual representation that shows those exceptions. Make it easy to see additional details to identify those outliers. Be vigilant with averages and aggregate values that strip data of underlying detail and hide the outliers. Provide information that shows just how much of an outlier the data point is. Distance, color, and bold outlines are all visual design practices you can use to highlight outliers in the visualization. (Figure 11.9; reference Figure 4.27 Weighted Bubble Cluster. Figure 11.9 adjusts the referenced chart by rotating it 90 degrees to the right. This adjustment shows how adaptable the chart is and highlights outliers located on the right and left extremes.)

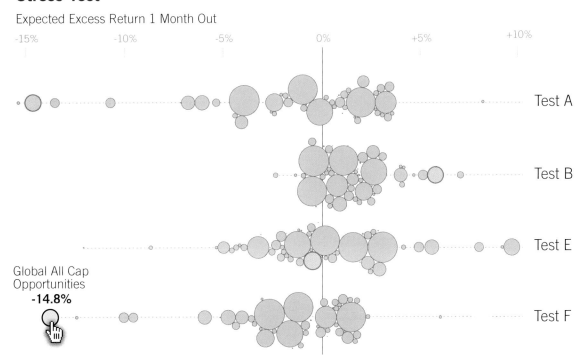

Stress Test

Figure 11.9 **Weighted Bubble Clusters**

Highly informative visualizations create the knowledge needed to let you see what is actually happening with the data. The more you can proactively provide and anticipate your audience needs with the right information, the more you can expand their understanding of the data. Using these guidelines will improve the richness and quality of the visualization. As you think about catering to your audience, consider incorporating these guidelines:

- Show **relevance** to your audience.

- Introduce **context** for better comparison.

- Provide **focus tilts** for more perspectives.

- Pair **relative and absolute values** for contrast.

- Connect the **summary and detail** data views.

- Reveal and simplify with a **recalculation** of the data.

- Create **categories** to bubble up themes.

- Highlight **outliers** so that they are not missed.

The guidelines are a list of considerations that you can apply and use according to your situation. Each item in the list can create better insights from the data to help you understand what the data means.

Provide Clarity

Accuracy, transparency, and accountability are all part of what it takes to visually present data in a clear, straightforward way. Creating a lucid visualization embraces accuracy and truth at all levels. From the start, how the data is gathered needs to be accurate. In the end, the presentation of the data needs to be true to the data. Many visualizations are accurate but not as many are true to the data and present the data with clarity.

It can be easy to misrepresent data and inadvertently create confusion. Complicated lists of labels, lack of details, and poor use of color are just a few attributes in an unclear chart. Clarity means we need to remove the struggle of trying to understand a chart and make it easy to get the right information from the chart. For example, a Pie chart is a commonly used chart that can accurately represent percentage weights. Most are comfortable with reading this type of chart because it is so familiar. However, it is not always easy to get the right information from a Pie chart. As soon as the number of slices increases to more than five, it becomes ineffective. The list of labels becomes harder to decode, details like the actual percentages are harder to see, and the colors needed to differentiate each slice are harder to select. Tracking percentages across slices within a Pie chart or as a side-by-side comparison of more than one Pie chart is difficult to do. It is difficult for your audience to decode labels and compare results in a straightforward way. Yet, it is commonly used to communicate sector allocations and their variations. This is an example of a chart that is accurate but not always clear.

Introducing transparency and accountability improves confidence in the chart. Transparency provides full disclosure and unveils the underlying calculations, definitions, and breakdown of an aggregated total. The more open a data visualization is to showing how a total was derived, the relationship and linking between data sets and such, the more your audience will rely and trust the communication. If there is a question, the full disclosure provides your reader with the source that is accountable. A clear accountable visual representation of the data requires you to consider various aspects of the display. *How is the data defined and calculated? How is the data depicted?* All visualizations should:

- ▶ **Use standard conventions in an organized display**—Strong rationale should be present to deviate from well-known conventions to organize the data display. Unconventional/unexpected layouts should be highlighted for the reader's awareness. Examples include reversing the direction of the x-axis or y-axis.

- ▶ **Provide accurate and proportional scale**—If there is a variation of the scale, make sure to explicitly point out any modifications.

- ▶ **Cite data source(s)**—Include the source of the data on all visuals. It communicates credibility to the reader.

- ▶ **Provide clear labels**—Data sets and markers should have labels to orient the reader and identify the subject matter and all involved data dimensions. However, the use of labels should reflect your readers' needs and their level of knowledge. For example, a novice user may need all data sets to be labeled and defined, while an expert may only need and want a few labels to orient themselves.

- ▶ **Provide definitions and formulas**—Not all labels will be inherently known; provide definitions with formulas when applicable.

- ▶ **Display details and the breakdown of calculations**—Provide a mechanism to show supporting details to the primary display. If aggregated totals are shown, show the breakdown of the totals.

- ▶ **Consistently use visual elements**—Each marker and visual element in a data visualization has a defined meaning. The use of each marker should consistently indicate the same meaning across the display system.

- ▶ **Ensure different elements are distinguishable**—Avoid confusion between elements and make sure to distinguish one element from another. For example, consider using markers that are different enough so that one marker is not easily confused with another. As another example, differentiate data representation, such as a line in a chart, from objects used for grouping or as callouts.

The guidelines provided here are a start to ensuring the data is presented in a forthright manner. Although the list is tactical, it focuses on a baseline set of items that are recommended to follow and can be checked off as compliant. This next list is more directional. Depending on the type of inferences and overall message that needs to be conveyed with the data, different visual practices can be used. Part of being honest with the data is aligning the data and message with the right visual practices. The following are a few guidelines to consider:

- ▶ **Edges**—Precise versus estimate, static versus dynamic, and stable versus unpredictable are sample connotations that straight versus curved edges can communicate. Straight edges are typically used to communicate precision, static, and stable data. And round edges are used to communicate estimate, dynamic, and constantly changing unpredictable data. Make sure to select the edge with the type of data and the main message you would like to communicate with the data. (Figure 11.10; reference: Figures 9.1 and 9.2 Pie Chart and Stacked Bar w/Table)

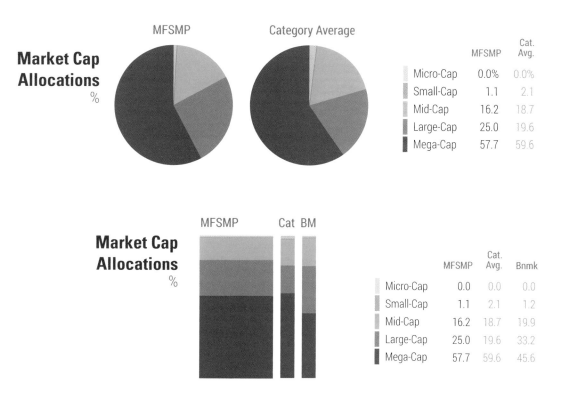

	MFSMP	Cat. Avg.
Micro-Cap	0.0%	0.0%
Small-Cap	1.1	2.1
Mid-Cap	16.2	18.7
Large-Cap	25.0	19.6
Mega-Cap	57.7	59.6

	MFSMP	Cat. Avg.	Bnmk
Micro-Cap	0.0	0.0	0.0
Small-Cap	1.1	2.1	1.2
Mid-Cap	16.2	18.7	19.9
Large-Cap	25.0	19.6	33.2
Mega-Cap	57.7	59.6	45.6

Figure 11.10 **Pie Chart and Stacked Bar with Table**

▶ **Markers**—Triangle, line, dot, and the square are commonly used markers to point and identify certain items on a chart. Selecting which marker and how many markers to use impacts your audience's understanding of the visualization. A large number of different markers can quickly overwhelm the visual. Limit markers and carefully select each. The triangle is a great marker for literally pointing out a precise spot or location. The line as a marker can show continuation, alignment, levels, and connections with exactness. The dot can be used to show an endpoint, and because it is inherently rounded, it brings along the associations of dynamic and unstable, as stated previously. Last, the square is an endpoint that communicates static and stable. (Figure 11.11; reference: Figure 9.29 Temporal Dial 1-10YRS)

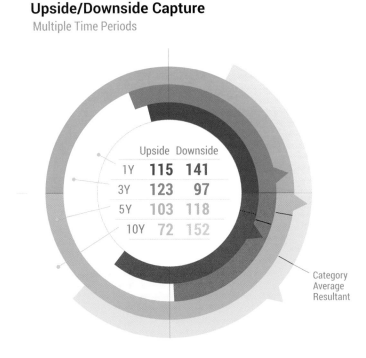

Upside/Downside Capture
Multiple Time Periods

	Upside	Downside
1Y	**115**	**141**
3Y	**123**	**97**
5Y	103	118
10Y	72	152

Category
Average
Resultant

Figure 11.11 **Temporal Dial 1-10YRS**

▶ **Color should be used carefully and sparingly.** Too many colors make the display confusing and hard to decode. The fewer colors, the more successful they are as a communication instrument. Three is better than five and five is better than seven, and so on. More than seven colors in a display makes the visual harder to understand. George Miller's cognitive load theory suggests our brain's working memory can handle seven plus or minus two. The rule of thumb of maintaining seven or fewer items to track and decode also reduces our mental effort. Within a gradient, there can be a significant range of transitional colors. In this case, you can limit the major color blocks to three to five. The major colors can transition from one color to the next by blending the colors. The transition from one color to the next can help to identify ranges with more precision and minimize how many color blocks are required. (Figure 11.12; reference: Figure 4.2: 3-D Surface Plot)

Asset Allocation Coordinates

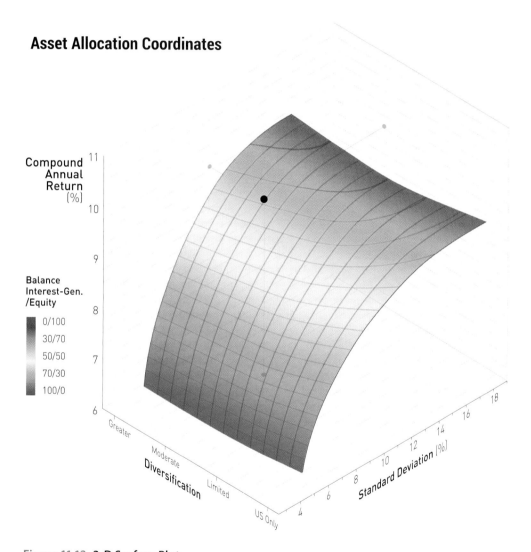

Figure 11.12 **3-D Surface Plot**

- **Color provides meaning.** Green means go, red means stop, and yellow means warning are each conventional uses of color. This use of color has been extended into our charts and dashboards as status of green for good, red for bad, and yellow for warning. Maintaining conventional color use makes the chart more familiar and understandable. If these three colors are used, we recommend to adjust to blue and red (instead of green and red) with orange (instead of yellow) for improved readability and greater accessibility across populations with color deficiencies. (Figure 11.13; reference: Figure 6.8 Segmented Butterfly)

NOTE Studies have shown that 8% of the male population and 0.5% of the female population worldwide cannot distinguish between green and red colors. In isolation green can still be used to highlight something good and red can indicate something bad.

Portfolio Gain/Loss Summary

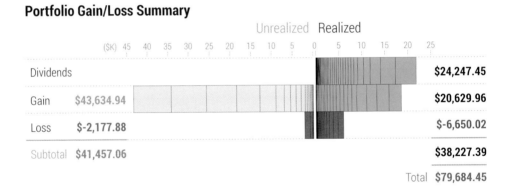

Figure 11.13 **Segmented Butterfly**

- **Color attracts our attention.** Saturated color can be used to highlight or emphasize certain points. This technique is especially successful if the rest of the visual is constructed of grayscale or subdued, monochromatic elements. In Figure 11.14, color is used to point out results that passed a certain threshold. (Figure 11.14; reference: Figure 9.51 Bar and Pin Chart)

Returns - Historical Span

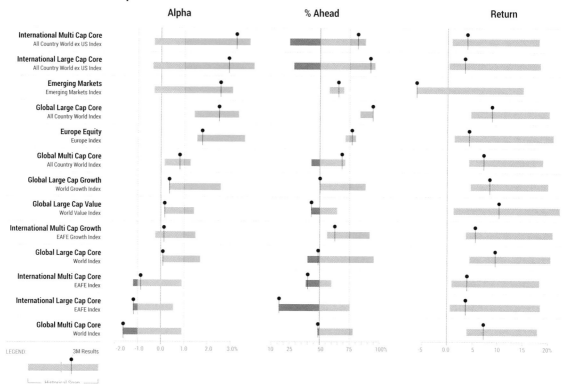

Figure 11.14 **Bar and Pin Chart**

▶ **Color Gradients**—Shades of a single color can show a stepped graduated scale. The technique can represent a continuous scale of values in one or two directions. *When should a monochromatic scale be used instead of a grayscale and how?* Because color conveys meaning as discussed in the previous point, you should match the color to communicate a specific meaning. *Is the graduated scale positive or negative?* Assign the color that best represents the data accordingly. The list of options include

   ▶ Achromatic gradients are created with black, white and shades of gray. Grayscale gradients from black to white can be used to show neutral or unknown representation of the data.

- Monochromatic gradients are based on a color scale that progressively changes from light to dark shades of a single color. You can use this gradient to convey a message with color and emphasize the values mapped to the darker shades of the color.

- Polychromatic gradients are based on a color scale that progressively blends two or more colors. Heatmaps are common applications of polychromatic gradients because they associate values to shades of two colors. Multiple color values of three or more associates groups of values, like percentage change in a scale, with color bands.

(Figure 11.15; reference Figure 6.2: Marimekko Chart – Monochromatic Gradient. Figure 11.15 adjusts the orientation of the chart. This adjustment shows how adaptable the chart is and prominently places the dark color values of the gradient.)

Market Sector Performance

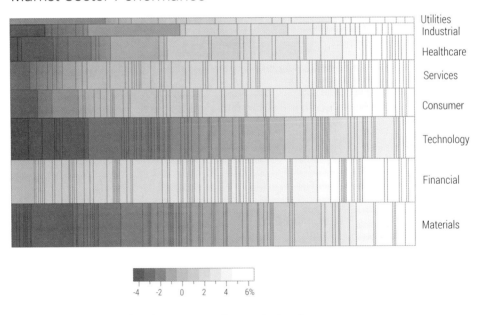

Figure 11.15 **Marimekko Chart – Monochromatic Gradient**

Truthful communications start with factual data and end with presenting the data as clearly as possible. The craft of creating clarity in a visualization is part

art and part science. The science part of the craft is the list of guidelines that are tactical and can be checked off as being completed. Adding the source, including the right label, and providing definitions are simple checklist items that are easy to incorporate. The art part involves judgment. Deliberate decisions define what and how you should apply lines/edges, markers, color, and gradients. The design practices listed in the chapter introduction provide guidance to each of these elements. Within the areas of subjectivity, the guidelines can be used to help direct the message that needs to be conveyed with the data.

Be Efficient

Data visualizations should make the experience as effortless as possible. The chart should do the majority of the hard work so that your reader does not have to. At the start, the main premise to creating a visual representation of the data is to maximize understanding and make the data more accessible. To make this point clear, consider the efficiency gains of a small data set, a data set that easily fits on one page or one screen (without scrolling). A table with 10 columns and 10 rows of data represents 100 data points. To compare and extract meaning from the possible relations between all these points can become close to impossible. The calculation requires having to go through 4,950 possible permutations of the data pairs. Maximized outputs with minimal effort as an input are both qualities that point to efficiency. A visual representation may show the important connections and comparisons between these 100 data points and relieve the user of the impossible cognitive task of numerical analysis of 4,950 connections. Therefore at the start, designing visual communications translates into less work and effort for the readers.

Transforming text into visuals can require more than a straight translation from one to the other. More can and should be done to create an efficient experience. In this respect, you should always look to see what can be added to create a more complete picture of the data as well as what can be pushed to the background or removed completely to simplify and provide your audience with more focus. The following are guidelines to this additive and subtractive process of making the visualization more efficient.

Additive Guidelines

▶ **Create structure and hierarchy**—Make sense of the data for your reader by organizing the structure and hierarchy. Figure 11.16 shows a grid structure that organizes the chart to be read horizontally and vertically; the dots make the order ambivalent. A design practice to achieve hierarchy is to use the position, order, color, line weight, and size of a mark to assign levels of importance. For example, provide primary information in the foreground of the chart and secondary information in the background. In this way, the information is communicated and read in sequential order to prioritize importance of certain data sets over others. Hedge Funds Return by Category shows attention is first commanded by the dark blue circles and then second by the detailed contextual information contained within the light blue background circles and foreground arches. (Figure 11.16; reference: Figure 10.19 Dot Matrix)

Hedge Funds Returns by Category

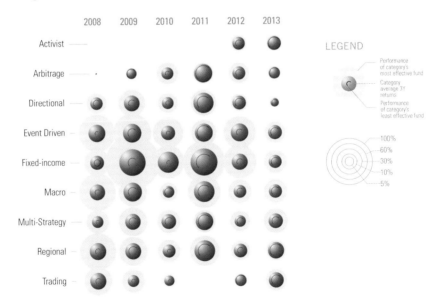

Figure 11.16 **Dot Matrix**

▶ **Provide reusable design elements**—Create core visual elements and use them across a set of charts to reduce the audience's need to learn additional meanings for those elements. A visual element can have specific meaning that requires some initial training to understand. When learned, the visual element can be reused and benefit from greater familiarity. Be consistent in how the element is applied but not necessarily uniform in how it is rendered. The element should have the same meaning but can be rendered differently if placed within a different tool. The visual element can be reused and be a part of a larger family set of elements. In the quote example shown in Figure 11.17, the moving ball bounces to show value change. This element is applied in successive charts to show the same meaning but is not uniformly rendered. The element does not need to be identical to be consistent and yet eliminate relearning. (Figure 11.17; reference: Figure 5.25 Visual System)

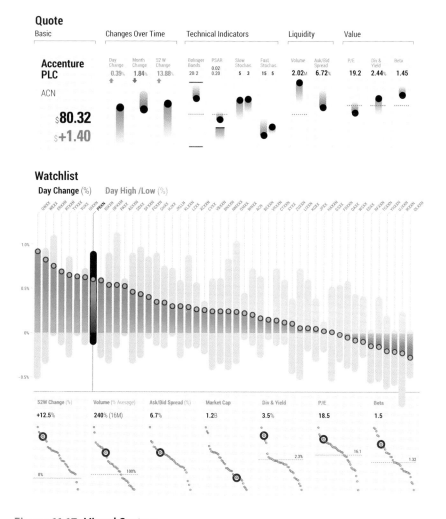

Figure 11.17 Visual System

▶ **Leverage our ability to see patterns**—The way our eyes see allows us to recognize faces and detect patterns. You can leverage this fact to create visualizations that connect data sets to recognizable objects. After you have encoded the object with a schematic diagram, the learned characteristics can be quickly decoded. As the Chernoff Fish example in Figure 11.18 shows, the legend identifies attributes of a fish with attributes of the data. This creates a system that makes it possible to classify a school of fish into categories. (Figure 11.18; reference: Figure 10.11 Chernoff Fish)

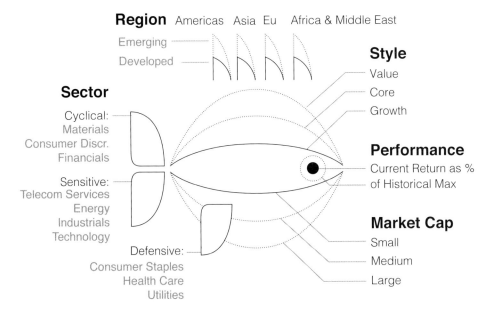

Figure 11.18 **Chernoff Fish**

▶ **Make everything legible**—Ensure the information is easy to read and legible. The font, image size, contrast, line weight, and color all contribute to ensuring readable results. Legibility can also be dependent on the audience and environment. For example, a white background is best in a well-lit environment; a black background is best in a darker, low-light environment. That way, the background matches the environment, removing the need for your eyes to adjust. The delivery channel should also be considered; paper, screen, projections, and so on all have different legibility considerations. For screen display, all marks should have enough contrast with a sufficient line weight and differentiating use of color. The white and black background displays shown in the figure affect the color selection of the dots. In the white display, the middle band uses teal dots, whereas in the black display they are replaced with yellow dots. Using yellow in the white version would not provide enough contrast to be as legible as the other color dots. (Figure 11.18; reference Figure 4.22 Tiered Scatter Plot; Figure 4.23 Tiered Scatter Plot (Black)

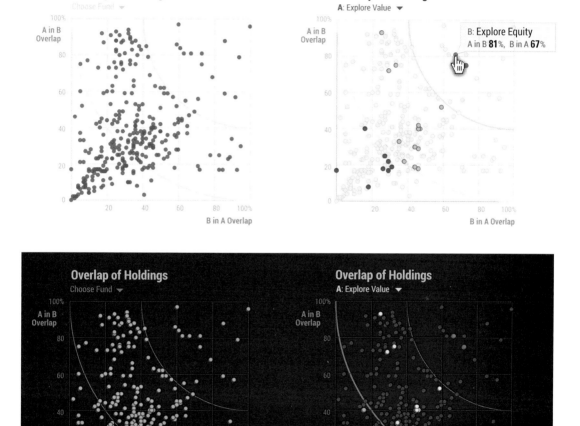

Figure 11.19 **Tiered Scatter Plot**

▶ **Add supporting details**—Incorporate details into the visual as an aid to
support and help see the representation with greater ease and less confusion. One example includes adding bar grid lines as units to track and tie
back to the numeric scale. Another example includes a light gray shade
fill where the % is present. These two details make the chart efficient
in tracking the percentages and comparing dollar totals. A third detail
in the chart is the notch that shows difference between gross and net
returns. And a forth includes the dotted line for benchmark. Although
you could use three bar charts to show the two returns and the benchmark, Figure 11.20 instead shows one consolidated yet detailed bar per
year. (Figure 11.20; reference: Figure 6.6 Interlocking Blocks)

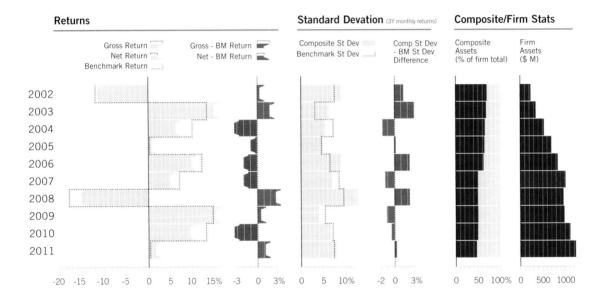

Figure 11.20 **Interlocking Blocks**

Subtractive Guidelines

▶ **Don't overload**—Do not burden your audience with too much stimula-
tion at once; instead provide filters and/or additional data displays on
demand. One way to minimize overload is to remove information from

the display. Figure 11.21 provides filters by both strategy type and year to help create focus. It also layers in the precise numeric values on demand and as supporting evidence. Progressively disclose detail views or additional views as needed. However, as comparisons are needed, ensure that additional detail includes the comparison data in the same view. Although you don't want to overload the display, you also don't want to limit the display for detail comparison. The figure shows one layer of details. Also, allow your audience to compare more than one layer of details so that you provide the ability to see multiple fund performances and read the details all in one view. (Reference the display panel view of: Figure 10.27 Fund Bubbles– Interactive Fund Display)

| 2008 |
| 2009 |
| 2010 |
| 2011 |
| 2012 |
| 2013 |

Fund Name	Renaissance Institutional Equities Fund LLC Series BB
Year	2012
Rank	19
Fund Assets	$5,738 mil
Fund Strategy	Equity Long-Bias
Category	Directional
3 Year Ann. Returns	19.73%
2012 Returns	9.42%
Company Name	Renaissance Technologies
Company Location	New York
Total Firm Assets	$21,637 mil

Figure 11.21 **Fund Bubbles– Interactive Fund Display**

- **Remove mental mapping**—Efforts to make connections or decode encoded labels should be removed or minimized. If you point to one data set to then compare it against another and jot those two points down on paper, then the visualization is not doing its job. The visualization should be designed to bring those two points together so that the comparison can be done in a side-by-side mode. (Figure 11.22; reference: Figure 4.19 Butterfly Chart - Opened)

Overlap of Holdings

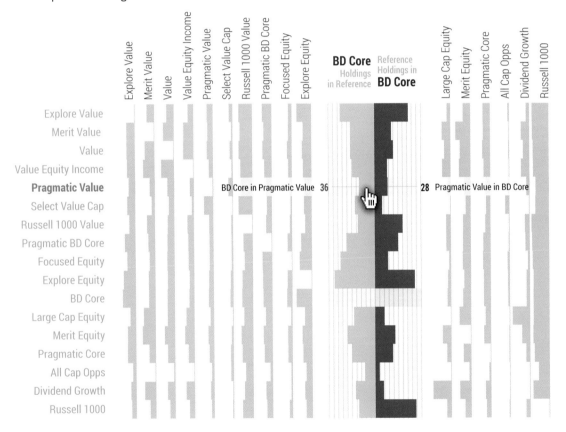

Figure 11.22 **Butterfly Chart - Opened**

- **Consolidate labels**—Consolidate, concatenate, and abbreviate labels as much as possible without introducing confusion. Data needs to be labeled to orient and explain any data visualization. However, smartly and elegantly labeling the data sets can improve the representation. For example, instead of making a legend, directly label items in context of the display. If legends are required, place the legend in close proximity to the data headers so that the labels work for both the headers and the legend. (Figure 11.23; reference: Figure 9.48 Label Consolidation)

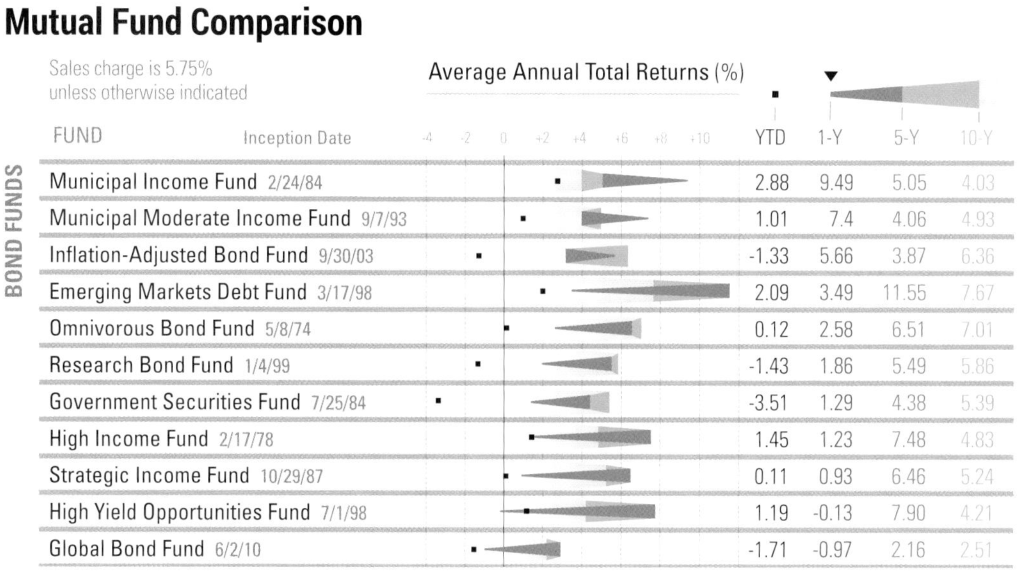
Mutual Fund Comparison
Sales charge is 5.75% unless otherwise indicated
Average Annual Total Returns (%)
FUND Inception Date
YTD 1-Y 5-Y 10-Y
BOND FUNDS
Municipal Income Fund 2/24/84 2.88 9.49 5.05 4.03
Municipal Moderate Income Fund 9/7/93 1.01 7.4 4.06 4.93
Inflation-Adjusted Bond Fund 9/30/03 -1.33 5.66 3.87 6.36
Emerging Markets Debt Fund 3/17/98 2.09 3.49 11.55 7.67
Omnivorous Bond Fund 5/8/74 0.12 2.58 6.51 7.01
Research Bond Fund 1/4/99 -1.43 1.86 5.49 5.86
Government Securities Fund 7/25/84 -3.51 1.29 4.38 5.39
High Income Fund 2/17/78 1.45 1.23 7.48 4.83
Strategic Income Fund 10/29/87 0.11 0.93 6.46 5.24
High Yield Opportunities Fund 7/1/98 1.19 -0.13 7.90 4.21
Global Bond Fund 6/2/10 -1.71 -0.97 2.16 2.51

Figure 11.23 **Label Consolidation**

- **Combine related charts**—This guideline minimizes the number of charts that need to be reviewed. Our example consolidates six charts into one and makes direct connections across all data sets. Instead of having to review multiple charts, your audience now has to review only one. If the data sets allow, as in Figure 11.24 and Figure 11.25, apply this approach to reduce the display size required. (Reference: Figure 8.26 Bar Charts, Figure 8.27 Fold-Over Stack Chart)

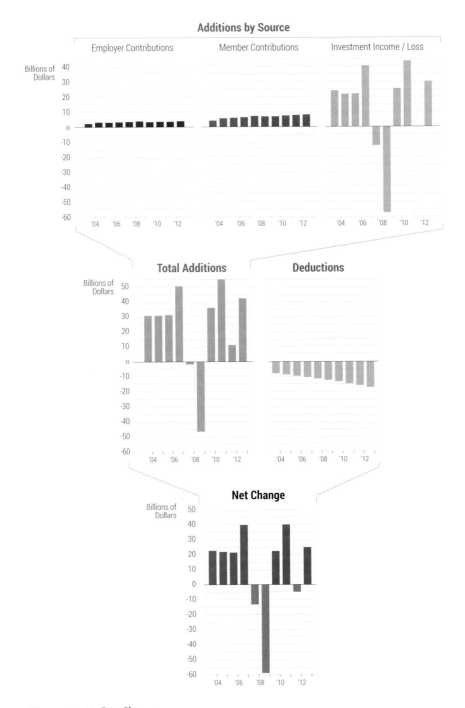

Figure 11.24 **Bar Charts**

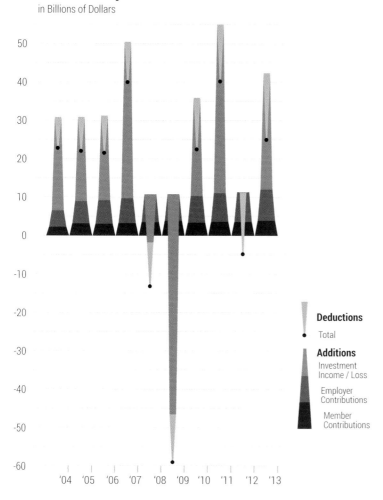

Additions by Source and Deductions
in Billions of Dollars

Figure 11.25 **Fold-Over Stack**

Sometimes, displaying less information is more effective, and other times more in a display is helpful. Our list rationalizes the two and shows what can be done to display the data more efficiently. All these guidelines can be applied to make an efficient visualization. The set of guidelines below encompass how to add more to a display or how to reduce, remove, and consolidate:

▶ Create hierarchy and structure.

- ▶ Provide reusable elements.

- ▶ Leverage our ability to see patterns.

- ▶ Make everything legible.

- ▶ Add supporting details.

- ▶ Don't overload the chart.

- ▶ Remove mental mapping.

- ▶ Consolidate labels.

- ▶ Combine related charts.

There are levels to efficiency you can strive to achieve. Being efficient requires you to replace complex charts that are hard to comprehend with simple ones that require less effort. Your focus to do so will result in benefits of speed and accuracy: quicker action taken based on confident understanding of the data and better decisions based on clearer insights.

Summary

The principles outlined in this chapter can direct the design of your visualization to ensure it caters to your audience to anticipate and answer their questions in a clear and efficient way. The goal of these combined principles is to create a reliable display of the data so that your audiences feel confident in their understanding of it. To recap, each principle has a set of guidelines and integrated visual design practices that show you how to follow each principle. (See the following table.)

The result of following these principles creates a solution that is reliable and actively sought after to present data. Beyond a solution, the visual representation starts to create a shared understanding of the data. Visually articulating a data set can create instant knowledge share for you and your audience. As your visual representations become more sophisticated, your fluency in data conversations will, too.

CATER TO YOUR AUDIENCE	PROVIDE CLARITY	BE EFFICIENT
Focus on the audience, the purpose, and the storyline for each visualization. Know your audience well enough so that you can anticipate the series of questions they will have of the data.	Present the data with the utmost accuracy, transparency, and clarity. Be straightforward so that each visualization properly represents the data.	Strive to create effortless experiences for your audience. The visualization should work so that your audience doesn't have to.

CATER TO YOUR AUDIENCE

- Show **relevance** to your audience.
- Introduce **context** for better comparison.
- Provide **focus tilts** for more perspectives.
- Pair **relative and absolute values** for contrast.
- Connect the **summary and detail** data views.
- Reveal and simplify with a **recalculation** of the data.
- Create **categories** to bubble up themes.
- Highlight **outliers** so that they are not missed.

PROVIDE CLARITY

- Use standard conventions and an organized display.
- Provide an accurate and proportional scale.
- Cite data source(s).
- Provide clear labels.
- Provide definitions and formulas.
- Display details and breakdown of calculations.
- Consistently use visual elements.
- Ensure different elements are distinguishable.
- Express associated meaning through the use of edges, markers, color, and gradients.

BE EFFICIENT

- Create hierarchy and structure.
- Provide reusable elements.
- Leverage the ability to see patterns.
- Make everything legible.
- Add supporting details.
- Don't overload the chart.
- Remove mental mapping.
- Consolidate labels.
- Combine related charts.

Common   Partial   Unique
Print   Print & Digital   Print, Digital, & Spatial
None   One   Role-Based   Fully Cofigurable
1 Language   2 Languages   Multiple Localizations
None   Singular Internal/External   Multiple
None   Single Layer   Multiple Paths & Layers
One Release   Several Releases   Multiple Year Release
Batch Schedule   On Demand   Streaming
Mega   Giga   Tera

Common   Partial   Unique
Print   Print & Digital   Print, Digital, & Spatial
None   One   Role-Based   Fully Cofigurable
1 Language   2 Languages   Multiple Localizations
None   Singular Internal/External   Multiple
None   Single Layer   Multiple Paths & Layers
One Release   Several Releases   Multiple Year Release
Batch Schedule   On Demand   Streaming
Mega   Giga   Tera

Common   Partial
Print   Print & Digital
None   One   Rol
1 Language   2 Lan
None   Singular Internal/Ext
None   Single Layer   Mult
One Release   Several Releases   Multiple Year Release
Batch Schedule   On Demand   Streaming
Mega   Giga   Tera

Project 2: **Statement of Cashflows**
Project 1: **New Ticker for Lobby**
Project 3: **Performance Attribution**

12

Implementing the Visuals

This chapter offers a structured approach for determining how and when to implement the visualization ideas presented in this book. As we will show, there are many facets to deciding how to select an implementation method: The uniqueness, complexity, and interactivity of the visuals are just a few. Depending on the situation, implementation may entail building a custom solution with available charting packages, using an open source programming language, or using visualization software. Although growing rapidly, the methods for implementing visuals are still in the early stages. Simply knowing what methods are available will help you determine how to proceed. However, rather than advocating the use of specific tools, we provide a framework to help you assess what *type* of tools and resources will work best in your own case.

To provide a better sense of how to apply the framework, we present three project examples that showcase a range of requirements and implementation possibilities. From a small project to a large one, this chapter clarifies what elements you must consider in order to implement a visualization solution.

Job one for selecting an implementation method requires evaluating the business value of the visualization against your resources and capabilities. Perhaps the visualization is simple to implement and you do not need additional resources—or perhaps not. Regardless, ask yourself: *Do you have the skill-set needed to implement the visualization? Which implementation approach best suits your needs? How do you prioritize among a list of projects? What new resources are required?* A spectrum of business criteria, including the importance of the visualization and the frequency of its use, and whether it's intended internally for staff members or externally for clients, can also be taken into account.

The second part of the selection process outlined in our framework focuses closely on assessing the effort required to implement the visualization based on their level of complexity. As part of that, we show that audience needs and organizational requirements are two of the most important variables to consider.

Finally, we offer a way to compare possible visualization projects and score their viability based on a side-by-side assessment.

Business Value Assessment

Well-designed data visualizations can provide significant business value. They can improve efficiency and reduce costs by saving time, provide effective decision-making displays, and produce quality communications. As we assess the business value of each project, assume each of the visual solutions have been thoughtfully crafted and executed to satisfy the audience. The decision, then, comes down to selecting the data visualization(s) that will provide the most business value.

The Business Value Assessment (BVA) outlined below calculates how impactful a new visualization solution will be and provides guidance about whether you should proceed to implement it. It also helps answer the critical follow-up question: *How should I implement the solution?* A well-thought-out BVA connects the visualization solution to business drivers, purposes, and goals. Essentially, it provides a mini-business case into the value of the project. With the information in hand, the BVA can help to assess not just one project, but many. Perhaps the question is not just whether you should take on this project, but which project(s) should you take on this year? The BVA framework can prioritize projects and provide a straightforward method for project comparison.

The BVA is based on five core factors that each connect to a five-point scale. The higher the ranking, the more appropriate the effort. However, each firm needs to assess the relative associations of high or low efforts. A higher level of effort for one firm may be small to another. Consider and rank the following criteria to assess overall business value:

▶ **Business critical**—How important or core to your business is the implementation solution? Will the solution greatly impact how your business runs by improving efficiency? Can it help improve communications, increase understanding, reduce risk, improve accuracy, raise standards, and enable you to be more competitive? Will the project enable you to increase your revenue? Does the solution impact downstream or upstream processes? Can the solution be reused across different applications?

▶ **External facing**—Will the solution be used for prospects, clients, and at private events or public conferences to display thought leadership? Will the solution improve how your clients perceive you?

▶ **Internal facing**—Will the solution be used internally for staff members? Will the solution be used in one organizational group or across multiple groups/functions at the firm?

▶ **Frequency of use**—How often will the visualization be used—quarterly, monthly, weekly, daily, or hourly?

▶ **Number of users**—How many people will interact in some capacity with the solution—dozens, hundreds, or thousands? Although you may release the project to hundreds of users, you may find that it applies or is adopted only by a few dozen. Consider how many users will benefit from the project and include all user types, ranging from the occasional user to the target user.

Criteria within the core functions, target audience, and frequency of use assess the overall impact. If the implementation will be used frequently and by a high number of users, improved visual tools can quickly show a return on the effort. If the BVA score is low, consideration may still be taken to implement some level of an improved visual that provides the user with a better communication.

As you review each ranking, consider the overall business impact to make the right decision faster.

The BVA lists each criterion with equal weights as a simple starting point. However, proprietary weights for each criterion can also be included. Out of the five individual BVA criteria, some firms may put more emphasis on client communications and would assign the external facing criterion a higher percentage weight. Other firms may focus on operational improvements and would therefore provide higher weights to the internal facing metric. Once weights are assigned, they can be used as the standard for prioritizing work. This can create a more objective method for selecting project work. As illustrated in Figure 12.1, the categorical relative weights stack the BVA score into an aggregated value scale of high, medium, and low.

Business Value Assessment

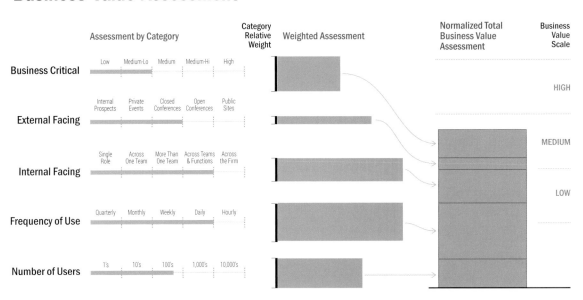

Figure 12.1 **BVA Criteria**

A formulaic approach that assigns varying numeric values to each criterion provides a precise measurement as well. The BVA formula is $B = \sum (B1 \times W1)$, $(B2 \times W2)$, $(B3 \times W3)$, $(B4 \times W4)$, $(B5 \times W5)$, in which B represents the business score, B1-B5 represents the business criteria, and W1–W5 represent the weights, such that the sum of all the weights (W1–W5) equals to 1.

You may have noticed that the formula does not include resources like time and budget. It would be a mistake to include available time and budget in the BVA model as *inputs*. Instead, time and budget need to be provided and established as *outputs* of the assessment. When the BVA is completed, the results should demonstrate the impact of the visual solution and how it could replace the legacy system, improving cost and time efficiency. As outputs, time and budget should be connected to the business value and complexity of the solution for full alignment and support of business goals. Using this orientation, the statement "We don't have the budget for that" goes away and instead becomes "We can't afford not to create a better solution." The concern that "We just don't have the time to focus on that solution" is replaced with "We will save time if we focus on a better solution."

Often times, deciding between multiple projects that you believe will improve the business as usual model may be a challenge. If you cannot take on multiple projects at once, deciding how to select the project that will be the most impactful to the business can be difficult. Figure 12.2 provides a sample of three projects that have applied the BVA approach. The projects show different criteria rankings that result in different aggregate totals for the normalized business value.

You may have noticed that each of these projects was introduced in a previous chapter. Each of these projects have the same firm weights, varying criteria levels that are specific to the project. Yet, two of the three produce similar results within the medium total business value band. But the total business value is not the final criteria for your project selection. There is more to the framework. The next part of the framework includes the implementation effort based on the complexity of the visual solution.

Business Value Assessment

Figure 12.2 BVA Score Projects 1, 2, 3

Implementation Effort

The implementation effort should take into account your audience needs, the firm's requirements for the solution, as well as the complexity of the solution.

With that in mind, the points listed below are sample considerations that can be adjusted or extended based on your situation. In addition, consideration of the implementation effort extends beyond the visual solution, also requiring an analysis of the appropriate delivery channel. The first question to ask is what delivery channels need to be supported by the effort. You should make sure that these channels are tightly aligned to where, when, and how your audience will access the visual solution. Delivery channels range from print to interactive installation. They include but are not limited to the following:

▶ **Print**—Paper presentation materials for a meeting or event

▶ **Large screen**—Screen presentation for group use

▶ **Desktop/laptop**—Screen display for individual desk use

▶ **Mobile**—Phone or tablet access

▶ **Wearable**—Embedded displays in wearable devices, including smart-watches, optical and projected displays, sensory and connected devices within the Internet of Things (IoT).

▶ **Interactive installation**—Gesture or sound activation in a physical space

The visual solution should be 1) optimized for the selected delivery channels, 2) consistent across the selected channels, and 3) seamlessly integrated between the digital channels. If more than one delivery channel is required, you need to consider how the visual communication manifests itself across those channels and how to take advantage of the strengths of each.

Understanding your audience's needs also extends into assessing how simple or complex the solution needs to be. More features are not always better whereas simple solutions can leave your audience asking for more rigor. The visual solution needs to address the correct level of needs and map those back to the task at hand. Provided the task needs are well defined and identified, the following are a few considerations of complexity to help define the scope:

▶ **Uniqueness**—How conventional is the visual solution? Is it a commonly used bar chart or is the visual more unusual or even unique? Does it require creating a new chart type or can it utilize existing chart elements?

▶ **Delivery channels**—As discussed above, the delivery channels can vary dramatically. Does the solution need to support just physical presentations, or do more varying digital aspects of a digital experience need to be considered? Or, would a spatial physical experience be more effective?

▶ **Entitlements**—How many user profiles need to be configured? One user may be entitled to full access while another is granted limited access.

▶ **Language/localization translation**—Are there different language or localization needs based on a regional population? How many languages does the solution need to support? Does the solution need to support the metric and/or the imperial (U.S.) system of measurement?

▶ **Integration**—How many applications need to be integrated into the visual solution? Are these applications internal or external? Are the data feeds open and available?

▶ **Interactivity**—How many layers of data displays are there to navigate? How extensive is the data manipulation required to recalculate or filter sets of results? How many screens need to be designed and implemented?

▶ **Multiple releases**—Do you foresee a phased approach to the implementation with multiple releases? Will there be future implementations or improvements to the visual solution? Do the dependencies between each phase increase the number of releases?

▶ **Data refresh**—Is the data static or streaming, and what are the refresh rates to the display?

▶ **Data volume**—How large is your data set? How large do you expect your data set to be in 6 months to 1 year and beyond?

This criteria list can use the same framework as the BVA to visualize and estimate a score and indicate complexity. The resulting Complexity Score, as shown in Figure 12.3, illustrates a scalable framework that is designed to incorporate additional criteria. The flexibility of the Complexity Score framework enables you to customize your criteria list and make it as comprehensive as you need.

Complexity Assessment

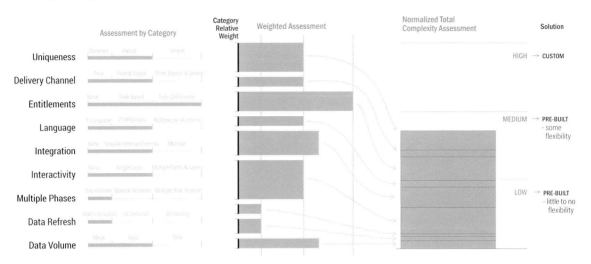

Figure 12.3 **Complexity Criteria**

Similar to Figures 12.1 and 12.2, a basic formula can represent the same visual. The formula that represents Figure 12.3 is C = ∑ (C1×R1), (C2×R2), (C3×R3), (C4×R4)… (C9×R9), in which C represents the complexity score, C1–C9 represent the complexity criteria, and R1–R9 represent the weights, such that the sum of all the weights (R1–R9) is equal to 1. This formulaic approach answers the question "Should I use a tool with prebuilt solutions or design a custom solution?" The more complex the solution, the more custom changes typically occur. In addition, the more demand for control and flexibility to modify, the more likely a custom solution is required.

Another possibility is that you may need to compare a list of projects that you would like to implement. Figure 12.4 displays three hypothetical projects. These are the same projects from the previous BVA list. The complexity assessment results combine the inputs and outputs into one view so that you can see how the influential factors add up.

Complexity Assessment

Figure 12.4 Complexity Score—Projects 1, 2, 3

The same framework produces a cumulative weighted bar chart that informs the level of effort required to implement projects from prebuilt to custom endeavors.

After completing this assessment, and examining the bar chart, you will be more prepared to discuss your implementation needs and the extent of effort. This method is meant to guide you through the main points and provide guidance toward a better assessment. It is a precursor to a project plan that a program or project manager might create. The variable criteria within the complexity assessment reflect the assumptions that drive the project scope and ultimately the implementation plan. What it does not provide is an assessment of the ongoing maintenance and support of the solution.

The next section reviews various options for implementing visuals to further address the question of whether to use a prebuilt package/framework or to build a custom solution and what those options require.

Available Methods

The current available methods for implementing interactive visualizations include statistical software packages, technical computing languages, visualization software packages, online tools, open source programming languages, close-ended web-based libraries, open web-based libraries, and, of course, custom code in a proprietary programming language. These solutions range in programing skills required, design flexibility, and interoperability. Although they are changing and expanding continuously, they can be organized into three categories:

- **Prebuilt solutions that require no programming**—These include visualization software packages and online tools. Prebuilt solutions are the least flexible, provide canned solutions, and require little-to-no design skills.

    There are a mix of prebuilt examples. Some, with more robust features and greater flexibility, require licensing, whereas the least flexible set of options are free to the public.

- ▶ **Prebuilt solutions that require some programming**—Examples include statistical software packages, technical computing languages, and close-ended web-based libraries. Adjustments to the visuals are minimal and, as such, required design skills are minimal. Although some of these are free, a few, such as the technical computing languages, require a license.

- ▶ **Custom solutions**—These solutions are open canvasses and allow for the most flexibility. Examples include open source programming languages and open web-based libraries. There is no charge to use these solutions. However, programming and design skills are required to create thoughtfully implemented or customized solutions.

The options in the custom solutions bracket require a combination of skillset and implementation resources. For example, the right mix of analytics, design, and programming capabilities need to be acquired. Programming skills will depend on the technical stack used for implementation and will need to mirror the implementation language. For example, if D3 is used, then having someone with strong HTML5 and Java scripting skills is key. Design skill requirements include a user research/data analyst who understands the task and data sets, and analytical visual designers who can structure the visual aspects of the visualization and ensure they are well composed. In more robust solutions, a mix of all these skills is needed to define the overall experience of the visualizations.

Solution Score

The final comprehensive assessment considers business value and complexity to deliver a solid metric. Outputs from the Business Value Assessment and Complexity Assessment become inputs for the Solution Score grid by layering in the coordinates as project scores. A simple rank view across projects is produced with Figure 12.5, Solution Score. The final Solution Score is produced by 1) placing the project scores onto the grid; 2) mapping them back to the consideration line; and finally 3) delineating an exact rank within a high-to-low consideration scale.

Total Score

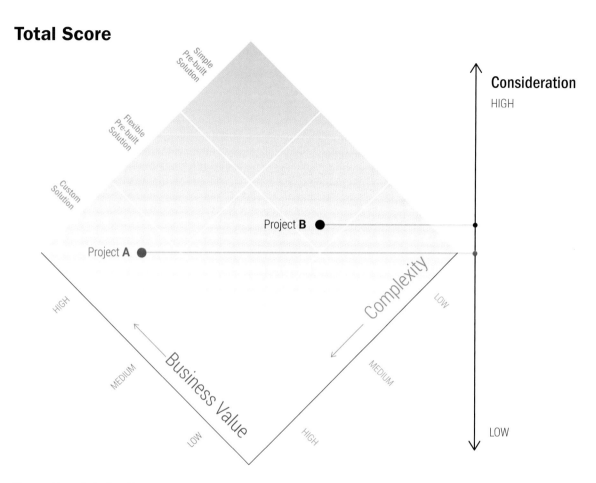

Figure 12.5 **Solution Score**

As illustrated in Figure 12.5, the formula for the final project solution is S = B + C, such that B is the business score, C is the complexity score, and S is the solution score. The culmination of assessing business value and complexity assigns a ranked score to each project. Each score lands within one of the nine squares. Rotating the grid automatically lists each project in prioritized order from top to bottom. As an estimation tool, the project rank listing and overall Solution Score formula guides the project direction to assign the right resources, effort, and level of review to the project.

The Solution Score combines the business value and complexity scores and enables multiple projects to be plotted and compared at once. Next, Figure 12.6 plots our three projects: 1) Ticker in the Lobby 2), Statement of Cashflows, and 3) Performance Attribution. The resulting rank shows Statement of Cashflows at the top rank for consideration, New Ticker as the second, and Performance Attribution as the third.

Total Score

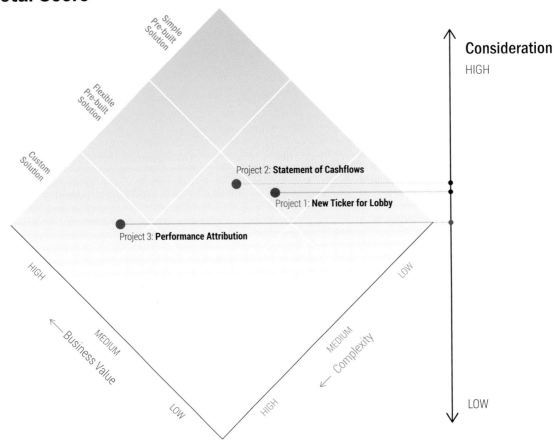

Figure 12.6 **Solution Score Project 1, 2, 3**

The Solution Score provides both a visual and formulaic approach to assessing project value and complexity. The visuals and formula serve different purposes and benefits and can be used together or independent of each other. The formula provides a simple ranked list of each project with a corresponding BVA and complexity score. The formulaic approach may be all you need to decide upon subsequent actions to take. You don't have to create a visual to assess a visualization project. However, if you would like to see how the results are derived, then a visual is useful. Figures 12.2, 12.4, and 12.6 provide a visual explanation of the formula. The visuals show you how the weights for each criterion impact each score and how the combined score is plotted and ranked. The visual highlights which criteria contribute the most to the final score.

Similar to our weighted criteria list, you can also add weights (as shown in Figure 12.7) to the business value or complexity. This is an optional step that might apply if you also have to consider a department's additional input as a final step in the process. Or, it can reflect a firm's quarterly sentiment towards project selection. For example, the pull toward business value preference can provide flexibility and tugs against the pull toward complexity preference, which can provide immediacy. The former typically connects to longer-term solutions, whereas the latter is a usually connected with shorter-term solutions.

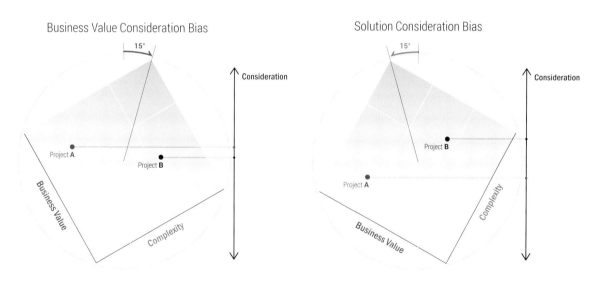

Figure 12.7 **Pivot Bias**

Pivoting the 3×3 grid to the right or left to change the balanced 45-degree angle view introduces a macro-level weighted system. A business value bias (left grid in Figure 12.7) reinforces and supports a longer-term (strategic placement) investment into the solution by ranking a project tied to a custom solution at a more elevated level of consideration. In contrast, a push toward a solution consideration bias (right grid in Figure 12.7) places the emphasis on the near-term (speed to market) solution. The solution consideration bias elevates and increases the rank status of a likely prebuilt solution. The 15-degree tilt in Figure 12.7 represents a macro weight adjustment of an additional 1/3 toward business value or complexity. As a comparison, a 45-degree tilt toward the right would represent a complete 100% business value bias. The formula that represents a business bias is $S = 1/45(45-D) C + 1/45(45+D) B$ such that S is the Solution Score, D is the degree of bias, C is the Complexity Score, and B is the Business Score. The formula that represents a complexity bias is $S = 1/45(45+D) C + 1/45(45-D) B$ such that S is the Solution Score, D is the degree of bias, C is the Complexity Score, and B is the Business Score. The pivot can significantly change the rank order of the listed projects.

As stated above, the bias formulas are optional but can be useful to apply under certain conditions. For example, in the event your firm was to license a certain implementation package, then you may want to apply the complexity bias formula to re-evaluate the project list. If you need to differentiate yourself in the market place then the business bias formula directly applies to your needs.

Summary

A well-constructed data visualization capability provides significant value for your firm. It improves how your firm is perceived—as one with advanced methods of displaying, communicating, and analyzing data. It also enhances your own ability to make meaning from the data and "see" what may otherwise go unnoticed. All told, data visualizations can give you the extra edge you need to make decisions with a higher level of confidence.

If you currently use spreadsheets and tables to evaluate and present data, you may likely want and need to convert those data tables into data visualizations.

Therefore, if you have limited time and resources, selecting which projects to transform to data visualizations becomes an important step. As shown in this chapter, an informed assessment can be done to delineate the business value and project complexity.

Using the system described herein provides a framework to determine the value of projects and decide which implementation method you should consider and why. Used as a visual and formulaic assessment tool, each part of the framework can derive an output. The framework removes the guesswork and creates a standard for project assessment and comparisons. With the mini-business case and directional ideas of the complexity in hand, you are now that much closer to implementing your data visualization projects.

Index

3D charts, diversification, 63–66
3D surface plot
    asset allocation, 64
    square binning, 64

A

Absolute and Relative Pairing Chart,
    mutual fund performance, 292–293
accounting data, 6, 10
allocation profile (mutual
    funds), 271
    historical allocations, stacked bar
        chart, 273
    market cap
        pie chart, 269–270
        surface area variations
            chart, 276
    region allocation
        Geometric Map, 272
        stacked bar chart w/table, 271

surface area variations chart, 276
    sector allocation
        stacked bar chart w/ table, 271
        stacked bar groups chart, 274
        surface area variations
            chart, 276
alpha factors
    groups, 81
    sectors and, 78–79
Arc Bands Collection, Sharpe Ratio,
    mutual funds, 310
Arch Collection, Sharpe Ratio, mutual
    funds, 309–310
Arch Construction, Sharpe Ratio,
    mutual funds, 308–309
Arch Schematic Chart, Sharpe Ratio,
    mutual funds, 307–308
area bar charts
    area and bar combo chart,
        CalPERS, members, 222–223
    gradient, 210

highlight, 208–209

offset, 211

area charts

    area and line charts, CalPERS, funding, 260–261

    and bar combo, 222–223, 226

    CalPERS, funding, 255–256

    comparison, 221, 225

    stacked, 222, 225

area comparison chart

    CalPERS, retirement program, 236–237

area comparison chart, CalPERS funding, 258

    member salary history, 254–255

    members, 221

    retirees, 252–253

Asset Allocation, 62–66

    3-D Hexagonal Surface Plot, 65

    3D surface plot, 64

    efficiency frontier, 65

attributes, comparisons, 18

attribution

    Return Attribution, 161–162

        BHB and, 162

        coordinate system diagram, 166

        quadrant overlap, 167

        security selection hyperbolic plane, 170

        security selection hyperbolic quadrants, 170

        security selection quadrant table, 169

        space conversion, 166

        weighting effects hyperbolic plane, 168

        weighting effects hyperbolic quadrants, 164

        weighting effects hyperbolic quadrants with gradient, 165

        weighting effects quadrant table, 162–163

        weighting effects weighted bubbles, 163

    Risk Attribution, 161

        Bar Delta, 174

        Bar Delta Columns, 176–177

        Bar Delta Stacks, 175

        Risk Data Table, 172–174

AUM (assets under management), 336

B

Ball and Hash Marks, Ticker Comparison, 113

Bar and Pin Chart, mutual fund benchmarks, 327

Bar Bracket chart, mutual fund benchmarks, 328–329

bar charts

    area

        gradient area bar chart, 210

        highlight, 208–209

        offset area bar chart, 211

    average returns, 77

    CalPERS, 243

    consistence, 77

    core chart, 77

Marimekko charts, 146–148
  segmented, linked, 160
Bar Delta, Risk Attribution, 174
Bar Delta Columns, Risk
    Attribution, 176–177
Bar Delta Stacks, Risk Attribution, 175
bar track chart
  Bar Track Chart-Column w/
      Pivot Summary, Sector
      Analysis, 74, 76
  Bar Track Chart-Row, Sector
      Analysis, 71
  Bar Track Chart-Row w/Pivot
      Summary, Sector Analysis, 73
  columns, with pivot
      summaries, 73, 76
  rows, 71
benchmarks, hedge funds, 344
BI (Business Intelligence), 8
binning, 64
Bond ETF Tiles, 50–55
Bond Tiles (Tile Framework), 42–44
Bubble Plot, hedge funds, 366
Bubble Trace, mutual fund
    benchmark, 330–331
Butterfly charts
  Butterfly Bar Glyph, hedge
      funds, 339–340
  Butterfly Net Bar, hedge
      funds, 337–338
  closed, 90–91
    Holdings Overlap, 90–91
  hedge funds, 336–337
  opened, 91–92
    Holdings Overlap, 91–92

  opened and sorted, 92–93
    Holdings Overlap, 92–93
BVA (Business Value Assessment), 418
  criteria, 419–422
    complexity, 425
  inputs, 421
  outputs, 421
  score, 422

C

Calendar Year Returns chart, 67–69
  bar track chart
    columns, 74
    rows, 71
  heat map, 69
    grayscale heatmap, 70
  Sector Rank & Average
      Returns, 74–75
  Sector Ranking, 71–72
  Sector Returns chart, 72–74
  Variation From All Sectors
      Average, 76–77
CalPERS (California Public Employees'
    Retirement System), 217
  Additions by Source, 241–242
    bar charts, 243
    deductions and, 244
    End of Year Net Position bar
        connectors chart, 247
    End of Year Net Position
        directional waterfall
        chart, 248–249

End of Year Net Position folded
bar chart, 249
fold-over stack chart, 244–245
Net Change bar shadow
chart, 246–247
Changes in Net Position, 242
funding
area and line charts, 260–261
area charts, 255–256
area comparison chart, 258
Progress chart, 257
Ratio Zoom chart, 261
stacked area charts, 259–260
member salary history, 253–254
area comparison
chart, 254–255
salary table, 254
Members in Valuation
area and bar combo
chart, 222–223, 226
area comparison chart, 221, 225
line chart, color
coded, 220–221, 224
stacked area chart, 222, 225
Valuation Table, 219
plan members, 218–241
post retirement mortality, 227–228
post retirement survival rate
color-coded line chart, 229
dual line chart, 230
paired area and line chart, 231
paired line chart, 231
Retirees & Beneficiaries, 250–251
area comparison chart, 252–253
Fold-over chart, 251

retirement programs, 232–233
area comparisons
chart, 236–237
ratio area chart, 237
ratio zoom chart, 240
stacked area charts, 234–236
zoom chart, 238–239
zoom collection chart, 239–240
Cascade charts
Comparison, 200–201
Multi-Year Cascade,
for-profits, 194–195
Multi-Year Interactive Cascade,
for-profits, 196–197
Summary, 200
cash flow statements
for-profits, 191–201
nonprofits, 184–191
categories, 23
Category Returns *vs.* Benchmark
Table, mutual fund
benchmarks, 325–326
Characteristics Tile (Tile
Framework), 37
mutual fund application, 44–50
charts. *See also* specific charts
3D, diversification, 63–66
aesthetically pleasing, 28
area
and bar combo, 222–223, 226
comparison, 221, 225
stacked, 222, 225
bar track chart
columns, 74, 76
rows, 71

comparisons, 17–19

conciseness, 27

conclusions, 22–24

immediacy, 26–27

leveraging, 25–30

line, 220–221, 224

Marimekko charts, 146–148

memorability, 28–29

open source charting languages, 9

periodic tables, 67–68

purpose, 16

quilt charts, 67–68

relationships, 19–22

reusability, 30

revealing, 29

sector charts, 67–68

time, 19

universality, 26

versatility, 30

Chernoff Fish, 349–351

Detailed, 354

Directional, 353–354

childhood illustration, 28–29

Classic Ticker, 111–112

cluster charts, revealing, 29

color scale, 151

color-blind readers, text and, 80–81

color-coded line chart, CalPERS, post retirement, 229

Comparison Cascade, Statements of Cash Flows, 200–201

Comparison Dial Chart, mutual fund upside/downside capture, 297–298

Comparison Dial Collection, mutual fund upside/downside capture, 299

comparisons

attributes, 18

charts, 17–19

rank, 17–18

time, 19

complexity criteria, 425

complexity score, 426

conclusions

pattern recognition, 22–23

themes/categories, 23

visual calculations, 24

conflicts, 7, 10

connections, relationships, 19–20

correlations, 21–22

drill down visualizations, 20

networks, 20–21

Context Bar Charts (mutual funds), 303

Quartile Background, 281

quartile background, 290

quartile bands, 291

stepped averages, 280–281

Trailing Returns, 289

Context Line Charts (mutual funds), 285–286

highlight spread, 287

quartile background, 288

quartile bands, 289

coordinate system diagram, Return Attribution, 166

corporate actions, 7

correlations, 21–22

cultures, 7, 10

currencies, 7, 10
custodian bank data, 6, 10

D

data sources, 6
    accounting data, 10
    custodian bank data, 10
    fund data, 10
    investor data, 10
    market data, 10
    news data, 10
    portfolio data, 10
    securities data, 10
    transactional data, 10
Data Table, Stress Test data, 100
data visualization
    audience and, 383, 384–385
        absolute values, 388–389
        categories, 391–392
        context, 386
        detail, 389–390
        focus, 387
        outliers, 393–394
        recalculation, 390–391
        relative values, 388–389
        relevance, 385
        summary, 389–390
    clarity, 383, 394–395
        color, 398–403
        consistency, 396
        conventions, 395
        definitions, 396
        details, 396

edges, 396
formulas, 396
labels, 396
markers, 397–398
scale, 395
sources, 395
    efficiency, 383, 403
        additive guidelines, 404–408
        subtractive guidelines, 408–414
    software, 8
delivery channels, 423, 424
desktop, 10
desktop/laptop presentation, 423
Detail Waterfall
    for-profits, 192
    nonprofits, 187–188
    Statement of Financial
        Activity, 204
    Statements of Cash
        Flows, 187–188, 192
Detailed Chernoff Fish, 354
Dial Gauge chart, mutual fund upside/
    downside capture, 297–298
Directional Chernoff Fish, 353–354
display, high resolution, 10
diversification
    3D charts, 63–66
    efficiency frontier and, 62–63
Dodd-Frank Act, 7
Dot Link Quadrant Chart,
    mutual fund upside/downside
    capture, 301–302
Dot Link Quadrant Tilt Chart,
    mutual fund upside/downside
    capture, 302–303

Dot Link Temporal Collection, Sharpe Ratio, mutual funds, 307
Dot Plot chart, Sharpe Ratio, mutual funds, 306
drill-down visualizations, 20
    Stock Mutual Fund Tile, 47–48
dual line chart, CalPERS, post retirement, 230

E

economic commentary, 6
efficiency frontier, 62–63
    asset allocation adjustments, 65
    hexagonal binning, 66
embedded sources, 10
ETFs (exchange-traded funds), 50–55
external communications, 11

F

financial statements, 183–184
    cash flow
        for-profits, 191–201
        nonprofits, 184–191
        Statement of Financial Activity, 202–206
    operating budget, 206–207
        gradient area bar chart, 210
        highlight area bar chart, 208–209
        offset area bar chart, 211
Firm Performance chart, 148–149
FLCSX, 296

Fold-over chart, CalPERS, retirees, 251
frameworks, 35
    Tile Framework, 36–39
frequency matrix, Holdings Overlap, 88–89
fund data, 6, 10

G

GAAP (generally accepted accounting principles), 183
GIPS (Global Investment Performance Standards), 144, 151–153
    Benchmark 36 Month St Dev, 152
    Composite 36 Month St Dev, 152
    Composite Gross Return, 152
    Composite Net Return, 152
    composites, 152
        Firm Composite data table, 153
        Firm Composite Interlocking Blocks, 153–155
    Custom Benchmark Return, 152
    Internal Dispersion, 152
    Number of Portfolios in the Composite, 152
    standard deviation, 155–156
G/L Data Table, Portfolio Gain/ Loss, 158
globalization demands, 7, 10
Glyph Collection, hedge funds, 342–343
Glyphs
    Mini Tricolor Glyph, 345–346
    Tricolor Glyph, 344–345
    Tricolor Glyph Collection, 347–348

gradient area bar chart, financial statements, 210
grayscale heat map, Calendar Year Returns chart, 70–71
Grouped Butterfly Bars, hedge funds, 338–339
groups
    alpha factors, 81
    Detail Waterfall, 187–188
    Heatmap Groups, 81–85

H

hardware, 8–9
    desktop, 10
    embedded sources, 10
    mobile, 10
    processing power, 10
    storage, 10
    wearables, 10
heatmaps
    Blue and Orange, sectors, 79
    Calendar Year Returns chart, 69
    grayscale heat map, Calendar Year Returns chart, 70–71
    Green and Red, sectors, 79
    Heatmap Groups, 81
        consolidated, 83
        Consolidated, sectors, 83
        Expand and Collapse, sectors, 84
        expand/collapse, 84–85
        numeric values and, 82

sectors, 81
    w/ and w/o numeric values, sectors, 82
Prior Day Factor dashboard, 79–85
Sector Analysis, 69–70
    grayscale, 70–71
tree maps and, 144–145
hedge funds, 335–336, 364
    benchmarks, 344
        Glyph Benchmarks, 348–349
    Chernoff Fish, 349–351
        Detailed, 354
        Directional, 353–354
    fund level returns, 373–377
    long positions
        Mini Tricolor Glyph, 345–346
        Tricolor Glyph, 344–345
        Tricolor Glyph Collection, 347–348
    long/short positions
        Butterfly Bar Glyph, 339–340
        Butterfly chart, 336–337
        Butterfly Net Bar, 337–338
        Glyph Collection, 342–343
        Grouped Butterfly Bars, 338–339
        Mini Glyphs, 341
    ranges, 361–362
        Dot Matrix, 362–363
    School of Funds, 351–352
        Detailed, 355–356
    strategy analysis, 363–364
    strategy averages, 364
        Bubble Plot, 366

Radius Bubble Plot, 365
  single, 367–372
  Temporal Path
    Collection, 371–372
  Temporal
    Path-Arbitrage, 367–368
  Temporal Path-Directional, 369
  Temporal
    Path-Event-Driven, 370
  strategy rank, 356–357
    Reordered Stacked Area
      chart, 360–361
    Stacked Area chart, 357–360
hexagonal binning, 64
  efficiency frontier, 66
high resolution display, 10
highlight area bar chart, financial
  statements, 208–209
histograms
  Tiered, 97–98
  tiered, 97–98
holdings, overlap, risk management
  and, 87–98
Holdings Overlap chart
  Butterfly Chart - closed, 90–91
  Butterfly Chart - opened, 91–92
  Butterfly Chart - opened and
    sorted, 92–93
  frequency matrix, 88–89
  instructional directions, 94
  Tiered Histogram, 97–98
  Tiered Scatter Plot, 94
  tracking, manual, 93
  visual noise, 94

I

implementation, 422
  complexity, 425
  delivery channels, 423, 424
  desktop/laptop presentation, 423
  integration and, 424
  interactive installation, 423
  interactivity, 424
  large screen presentation, 423
  methods, 427–428
  mobile presentation, 423
  print delivery channel, 423
  Solution Score, 428–432
  wearable presentation, 423
individual displays, 11
industry demands, 6–7
information delivery, 5–6
instructional directions, 94
Integrated Waterfall, Statement of
  Financial Activity, 205–206
interactive installation, 423
internal presentations, 11
investor data, 6, 10
investor mandates, 7

J

JIT (just in time), delivery, 159

L

languages, 7, 10
large screen presentation, 423

line and bar chart, CalPERS, 255–256

line charts

area and line charts, CalPERS, funding, 260–261

color-coded, 220–221, 224

colored, CalPERS members, 220–221

Linked Segmented Bar Chart, 160

Portfolio Gain/Loss, 160

M

Map of the Market, 145–146

Marimekko chart, 146, 179

color scale, 151

monochromatic gradient centered, 148

monochromatic gradient unidirectional, 147

polychromatic Gradient, 149, 150

market, 6

market data, 10

market performance, Map of the Market, 145–146

MiFID II, 7

Mini Glyphs, hedge funds, 341

Mini Tricolor Glyph, 345–346

mobile hardware, 10

mobile presentation, 423

MPT (Modern Portfolio Theory), 62–63

Multi-Cascade charts, Statements of Cash Flows, 193–194

Multi-Year Detail charts, Statements of Cash Flows, 198–199

Multi-Year Detail Waterfall

nonprofits, 188–189

Statements of Cash Flows, 188–189

Multi-Year Interactive Cascade, Statements of Cash Flows, 196–197

Multi-Year Summary Waterfall

nonprofits, 190–191

Statements of Cash Flows, 190–191

mutual funds, 267–268

allocation profile, 269–277

Alpha, Beta, Sharpe Ratio

Context Bar Chart, 303

Context Bar Chart-Highlight Spread, 304

downside capture ratio, 294

benchmarks, 324

Bar and Pin Chart, 327

Bar Bracket chart, 328–329

Bubble Trace, 330–331

Category Returns *vs.* Benchmark Table, 325–326

Stem/Bubble Steps, 329–330

Characteristics Tile, 44–50

comparisons, 318–319

Label Consolidation, 321–322

Ribbon, 321

Ribbon comparison, 323–324

total returns, 319–324

expense ratio

Context Bar Chart - Quartile Background, 281

Context Bar Chart w/stepped averages, 280–281

Context Levels Chart - Quartile
 Background, 282–283
Context Levels Chart -
 Quartile Bands, 283
Context Line Chart, 283–284
fees, 277
Fund Fact sheets, 312–318
fund operating expenses, 277
 Net Bar Chart, 278
 Net Bar Chart w/ table, 278
 Net Bar Chart with Data
  Labels, 279
performance
 Absolute and Relative Pairing
  Chart, 292–293
 Context Bar Chart-quartile
  background, 290
 Context Bar Chart-Trailing
  Returns, 289
 Context Level Chart-quartile
  bands, 291
 Context Line Chart, 285–286
 Context Line Chart-highlight
  spread, 287
 Context Line Chart-quartile
  background, 288
 Context Line Chart-quartile
  bands, 289
 trailing returns, 289–291
R^2 levels, 305
risk, 293–294
 components, 310–312
Sharpe Ratio, 305–306
 Arc Bands Collection, 310
 Arch Collection, 309–310

Arch Construction, 308–309
Arch Schematic
 Chart, 307–308
Dot Link Temporal
 Collection, 307
Dot Plot chart, 306
Stock Mutual Fund Tile, 44–45
Stock Mutual Fund Tiles
 Schematic, 45–46
Tile Bands, 46–47
 Level 1, 47
 Level 2, 48–49
upside capture ratio, 294
upside/downside capture
 Comparison Dial
  Chart, 297–298
 Comparison Dial
  Collection, 299
 Dial Gauge chart, 297–298
 Dot Link Quadrant
  Chart, 301–302
 Dot Link Quadrant Tilt
  Chart, 302–303
 FLCSX, 296
 Pointer Chart-zoom, 295
 Pointer Collection, 296
 Temporal Dial Chart, 300

N

Net Bar Charts (mutual funds)
 with Data Labels, 279
 operating expenses, 278
  w/ table, 278

networks, 20–21
news data, 6, 10

O

offset area bar chart, financial
    statements, 211
online visualization tools, 9, 10
open source charting languages, 9–10
overlap of holdings, risk management
    and, 87–98

P

paired area and line chart, CalPERS,
    post retirement, 231
paired line chart, CalPERS, post
    retirement, 231
pattern recognition, 22–23
pension funds, 217. *See also* CalPERS
    (California Public Employees'
    Retirement System)
PERF (Public Employees' Retirement
    Fund), 218
Performance Analysis, 143
    attribution
        Return Attribution, 161–171
        Risk Attribution, 161
    Portfolio Gain/Loss, 157–161
Performance Measurement, 143
    Firm Performance chart, 148–149
    GIPS (Global Investment
        Performance
        Standards), 144, 151–153
    market performance, 144

periodic tables, 67–68
    Sector Analysis, 67–68
Pictorial Superiority Effect, 28
pie chart, market cap, 269–270
Pointer Chart-zoom, mutual fund
    upside/downside capture, 295
Pointer Collection, mutual fund
    upside/downside capture, 296
Portfolio Construction, 61–62
    Asset Allocation, 62–66
    diversification, efficiency frontier
        and, 62–63
    MPT (Modern Portfolio
        Theory), 62–63
    Sector Analysis, leadership, 67–78
portfolio data, 6, 10
Portfolio Gain/Loss, 157
    G/L Data Table, 158
    Linked Segmented Bar Chart, 160
    Segmented Butterfly, 159
print delivery channel, 423
Prior Day Factor dashboard, 78–84
Profile Tiles (Tile Framework), 36–37
programming languages, 9, 10
Progress chart, funding, CalPERS, 257

Q

quadrant overlap, Return
    Attribution, 167
quilt chart, Sector Analysis, 67–68
quilt charts, 67–68
quotes (trading), 117, 118
    18 Data Points, 118
    30 Data Points, 120

data points, 117–121

Discrete Time Bars, 123

discrete time bars, 123

Five Data Points, 117

Horizontal Contrail, 124–125

horizontal contrail, 124–125

Nested Time Bars, 122

nested time bars, 122–123

relative performance, 119–120

single row layout, 124–125

vertical contrail, 126

R

Radius Bubble Plot, hedge funds, 365

rank, comparisons and, 17–18

ratio area chart, CalPERS, retirement programs, 237

Ratio Zoom Chart (CalPERS)

    funding, 261

    retirement, 240

regions, 7, 10

regulations, 7

relationships, 19–20

    correlations, 21–22

    drill down visualizations, 20

    networks, 20–21

research labs, 9

Results Tile (Tile Framework), 37–39

revealing cluster chart, 29

risk, 7

    mutual funds, 293–294

Risk Attribution, 161

Risk Data Table, Risk Attribution, 172–174

Risk Management

    Butterfly Chart-Closed, 90

    Butterfly Chart-Opened and Sorted, 92, 93

    ex ante, 85–86

    ex post, 85–86

    Frequency Matrix, 88

    overlap of holdings and, 87–98

    Tiered Histogram, 97–98

    Tiered Scatter Plot, 94–96

rule demands, 7

    corporate actions, 10

    investor mandates, 10

    regulations, 10

    risk, 10

S

scatter plots

    tiered, 94–95

Schneiderman, Ben, 363–364

Sector Analysis

    Bar Track Chart

        Column w/Pivot Summary, 74, 76

        Row, 71

        Row w/Pivot Summary, 73

    heatmap, 69–70

        grayscale, 70–71

    leadership, 67

        periodic table, 67–68

        quilt chart, 67–68

        sector chart, 67–68

sector charts, 67–68

Sector Ranking Cumulative charts, 72

Sector Returns chart, 72–74
sectors
    alpha factors and, 78–79
    Heatmap Groups, 81
        Consolidated, 83
        Expand and Collapse, 84
        w/ and w/o numeric values, 82
    Heatmaps
        Blue and Orange, 79
        Green and Red, 79
securities data, 6, 10
security selection (Return Attribute)
    hyperbolic plane, 170
    hyperbolic quadrants, 170
    quadrant table, 169
segmented bar charts, linked, 160
Segmented Butterfly, 159
series, time series, 19
Sharpe Ratio, 305–306
    Arc Bands Collection, 310
    Arch Collection, 309–310
    Arch Construction, 308–309
    Arch Schematic Chart, 307–308
    Dot Link Temporal Collection, 307
    Dot Plot chart, 306
Simplified Ticker, 112
single, hedge funds, 367–372
software, 9
    data visualization, 8
    online visualization tools, 10
    open source charting languages, 10
    programming languages, 10
    technical computing, 9, 10
    visualization research labs, 10

Solution Score, 428–432
space conversion, Return
    Attribution, 166
sparklines, 118
stacked area charts
    CalPERS
        funding, 259–260
        members, 222
        retirement programs, 234–236
stacked bar charts
    allocation profile (mutual
        funds), 273
    Marimekko charts, 146–148
    region allocation, 271
    sector allocation, 271
stacked bar groups, sector
    allocation, 274
Starting Mark, 115
Statement of Financial
    Activity, 202–203
    Detail Waterfall, 204
    Integrated Waterfall, 205
Statements of Cash Flows, 185
    for-profits
        Comparison Cascade, 200–201
        Detail Waterfall, 192
        Multi-Cascade charts, 193–194
        Multi-Year Detail
            charts, 198–199
        Multi-Year Interactive
            Cascade, 196–197
        Summary Cascade, 200
    nonprofits, 185
        Detail Waterfall, 187–188

Multi-Year Detail
   Waterfall, 188–189
Multi-Year Summary
   Waterfall, 190–191
Summary Waterfall, 186–187
Stem/Bubble Steps, mutual fund
   benchmarks, 329–330
Stock ETF Tile Schematic, 50–55
Stock Mutual Fund Tile, 45–50
Stock Tile, 39–41
storage, 10
Stress Test data, 99–100
   Data Table, 100
   Weighted Bubble Chart, 101–102
   Weighted Bubble
      Clusters, 103–104
   Weighted Bubble Clusters -
      Selected Fund, 105
Summary Cascade, Statements of
   Cash Flows, 200
Summary Waterfall, Statements of
   Cash Flows, 186–187
surface area variations chart
   market cap, 276
   region allocation, 276
   sector allocation, 276

T

tapestry bar charts, 71, 73, 74, 76
technical computing, 10
   software, 9
Temporal Dial Chart, mutual fund
   upside/downside capture, 300

Temporal Path Collection, hedge
   funds, 371–372
Temporal Path-Arbitrage, hedge
   funds, 367–368
Temporal Path-Directional, hedge
   funds, 369
Temporal Path-Event-Driven, hedge
   funds, 370
text, color-blind readers and, 80–81
themes, 23
Ticker Comparison, 112–113
   Ball and Hash Marks, 113
   Trailing Ball and Goal Mark, 115
   Trailing Ball and Starting
      Mark, 115
tickers, 110–111
   Classic Ticker, 111–112
   Simplified Ticker, 112
   Starting Mark, 115
   Ticker Comparison, 112–113
   Trailing Ball, 113–115
   Trailing Price Story, 114
Tiered Histogram, 97–98
   Holdings Overlap, 97–98
Tiered Scatter Plot, 94
   Holdings Overlap, 94
Tile Collection, 55–58
Tile Framework
   Bond Tiles, 42–44
   Characteristics Tile, 37
   Profile Tiles, 36–37
   Results Tile, 37–39
time
   comparisons, 19

series, 19

top-level aggregates, Detail
  Waterfall, 187–188

tracking, manual, 94

trading

  quotes, 117

  tickers, 110–111

    Classic Ticker, 111–112

    Simplified Ticker, 112

    Starting Mark, 115

    Ticker Comparison, 112–113

    Trailing Ball, 113–115

    Trailing Price Story, 114

  watchlists, 127

    contrail - day change
      alignment, 128–129

    contrail with spread, 128–130

    detail contrail *versus* summary
      dot plot, 137

    dot plot and horizontal
      contrail, 132–133

    dot plot column
      summary, 131–132

    period changes, 128–130

    vertical contrail with dot plot
      summary, 134, 136

Trailing Ball (Tickers), 113–115

  and Goal Mark, 115

  and Starting Mark, 115

Trailing Price Story, 114

trailing returns, 289–291

transactional data, 6, 10

treemaps, 144

  heatmaps and, 144–145

Tricolor Glyph, 344–345

Tricolor Glyph Collection, 347–348

V

visual calculations, 24

visual communications

  enabling factors, 8–11

  industry and, 6–7

  information delivery, 5–6

  overview, 3–4

visual noise, 94

visualization research labs, 9, 10

W

watchlists

  Contrail with Spread, 128

  Contrail-Day Change
    Alignment, 128

  Data Table, 127

  Detail Contrail *versus* Summary
    Dot Plot, 137

  Dot Plot and Horizontal
    Contrail, 132–133

  Dot Plot Column Summary, 131

  vertical contrail with dot plot
    summary, 134, 136

waterfalls

  Detail Waterfall, Statements of
    Cash Flows, 187–188, 192

  Integrated Waterfall, Statement of
    Financial Activity, 205

Multi-Year Detail Waterfall,
    Statements of Cash
    Flows, 188–189
Multi-Year Summary Waterfall,
    Statements of Cash
    Flows, 190–191
Statements of Cash Flows,
    nonprofits, 186–191
Summary Waterfall, Statements of
    Cash Flows, 186–187
wearables, 10
    presentation, 423
Weighted Bubble Chart, Stress Test
    data, 101–102
Weighted Bubble Clusters, Stress Test
    data, 103–104
Weighted Bubble Clusters - Selected
    Fund, Stress Test data, 105

weighting effects hyperbolic plane,
    Return Attribution, 168
weighting effects hyperbolic
    quadrants, Return Attribution, 164
weighting effects hyperbolic
    quadrants with gradient, Return
    Attribution, 165
weighting effects quadrant table,
    Return Attribution, 162–163
weighting effects weighted bubbles,
    Return Attribution, 163

Z

zoom chart, CalPERS, retirement
    programs, 238–239
zoom collection chart, CalPERS,
    retirement programs, 239–240